ISAK DINESEN
and the
Engendering of
Narrative

Women in Culture and Society

A series edited by Catharine R. Stimpson

ISAK DINESEN

and the Engendering of Narrative

SUSAN HARDY AIKEN

94-52

The University of Chicago Press · Chicago and London

The University of Chicago Press, Chicago 60637
The University of Chicago Press, Ltd., London

Library of Congress Cataloging-in-Publication Data

Aiken, Susan Hardy, 1943–
    Isak Dinesen and the engendering of narrative / Susan Hardy Aiken.
        p.   cm. — (Women in culture and society)
    ISBN 0-226-01112-7 (alk. paper). — ISBN 0-226-01113-5 (pbk. :
alk. paper)
    1. Dinesen, Isak, 1885–1962—Criticism and interpretation.
2. Women in literature.   3. Women and literature.   4. Sex role in
literature.   I. Title.   II. Series.
PT8175.B545Z54   1990
839.8'1372—dc20   89-20482
                                                                   CIP

SUSAN HARDY AIKEN
is associate professor in the
department of English at the University
of Arizona. She is coeditor of *Changing
Our Minds: Feminist Transformations
of Knowledge*.

For my family

Contents

Foreword

In 1982, Judith Thurman published *Isak Dinesen: The Life of A Storyteller.*
It was to become the standard biography of the Danish writer, who was
born Karen Dinesen in 1885, six years after the first major production of
A Doll's House. Her rebellions were even greater than those of Ibsen's
Nora. For Karen Dinesen studied art in European capitals. She published
under pseudonyms. She did not marry until she was twenty-eight. Then,
as Karen Blixen, a baroness, she moved to Africa. In 1931, she reluctantly returned to Denmark and became Isak Dinesen, a legend, a literary
lion. "Dinesen" reclaimed her maiden name. She took "Isak," a male
name, from the Old Testament and the Hebrew word for laughter.

Now Susan Hardy Aiken has written *Isak Dinesen and The Engendering of Narrative.* For Aiken's generation, it will be the most original, force-
ful, provocative, and elegant critical reading of this Danish writer. Two
contemporary ways of regarding literature have influenced Aiken: post-
structuralism, a method of reading that doubts certainties, unities, cogen-
cies; and feminism, a method of reading and acting that first doubts
women's relationships to society, culture, and textuality. Chivalry, Blixen
wrote in a letter, is a system in which a man "first binds fast the legs of
the object of one's homage in order to serve her." Feminism then becomes the architect and carpenter of new relationships.

Both post-structuralism and feminism oppose the epistemological
and moral tradition that structures the world as a set of binary oppositions: subject/object, self/other, mind/body, reason/imagination, no-
bility/commoner, white/black, or, that well-choreographed two-step,
male/female. Only one term can be top dog: white over black, for
example, or male over female. To replace that tradition, both post-
structuralism and one powerful brand of feminism offer narratives about
the self, language, and the world that tell of hidden meanings rather than
transparent meaning, flux rather than stability, fragmentation rather
than coherence, marginality rather than centrality, heterogeneities rather
than homogeneities, excess rather than control, multiple differences
rather than those dreary old dualities.

In particular, some French feminist theoreticians (Cixous, Clément, Iragaray, Kristeva) have speculated that women's writing (écriture féminine) will embody this story. One of several theoretical tensions is whether such writing expresses "women themselves" or "woman herself" (both tricky terms), because women are the world of flux and fragmentation; or whether such writing textualizes "women as metaphor" (another tricky term), because women best represent such a world. Women also best exude its poetics.

Writing with sweep and sureness, Aiken shows Blixen/Dinesen as a prophet—in detail—of post-structuralism and feminism. She is defiantly unplaceable, comic and capricious, ironic and demonic. Her pages reveal a woman unbinding her legs in order to mount and to ride the broom of the witch exuberantly. Her work dislodges the belief that the genealogy of texts must run down through a paternal, not a maternal, line. She mocks, mimics, and parodies the fathers' books, their master narratives and muses, their Genesis and infernos. She authorizes an alternative lineage in the polymorphous wildness and savagery of the Gothic. Did not Blixen/Dinesen invent "Isak Dinesen" in *Seven Gothic Tales* in 1934?

When Blixen returned to Denmark from Africa, she felt as if she had left home and gone into exile. This "heretical" reviser accepted the atavistic equation of women with nature and nature with a language beyond and below civilization. The landscape of Africa became a mother's body, that body an origin of a different speech, a different writing. Fused, land and mother promised "nurturance and openness, security and liberation. . . ." To be out of Africa was to have been expelled from the womb of an earthly paradise. Compelled by things at once similar and split apart, Dinesen would write first in English, the tongue imposed on Africa, and then write the same text again in Danish, originally her "mother tongue," but the language of a country that she could but partially describe as home.

The most popular picture of Dinesen today is that of a stylish white woman who lived on an African farm, was moved by the natives, was madly in love with a cultivated white hunter, Denys Finch Hatton, and wrote about it all in the autobiographical *Out of Africa* (1937). *Isak Dinesen and The Engendering of Narrative* easily refutes that pastel pastoral of a reputation. At the beginning and end of her book, Aiken accepts a far harder task, mapping the degree of Blixen's real complicity with European colonialism and its imperial metaphor of Africa as the dark continent that could serve as the restless European's submissive Eden. Compare her intricacies to the passionate lucidities of a contemporary South African woman writer, Nise Malange, born near Cape Town in 1960:

I'm here
Living under a black cloud
Here, living in a thinning light
Here
Freedom is nailed to a tree
To die.
Here I am living: in a matchbox[1]

At the same time, however, Aiken shows a Blixen who resisted colonialism. Other Europeans thought her "pro-native." If most white writers exemplify the Orientalism that Edward Said has anatomized, Blixen often "disorients" us.

In brief, Aiken writes that Blixen "simultaneously participated in, benefited from, despised, and repeatedly sought to subvert" the colonialist project. These and similar contradictions have haunted the lives of many wellborn women who have been both inside and outside of the mess of their birthright. Part of Aiken's accomplishment is her subtle but forthright interweaving of this psychological and social doubleness with Dinesen's sinuous art.

Blixen died in 1962. In that year Tanganyika became a republic. Kenya was to gain independence the next year. In 1962, Doris Lessing also published *The Golden Notebook*. Although less fantastical than much of Dinesen, it is nevertheless a narrative, from the next generation of women writers, about history, sexuality and sexual difference, white women in colonized Africa, art and language, and the tension between the trajectories of narrative and the swirls of experience. Deliberately, my allusions juxtapose history and literature, juxtapositions that Blixen/Dinesen demonstrates, contorts, and conceals. Far more richly, Aiken's readings ask about women's writing and history. Aiken places Blixen/Dinesen in history, in space and time. Yet, Aiken also suggests that Blixen/Dinesen is a matrix of a woman's literature that implodes and springs from space. So exercising, it can rushingly escape from too rigid and mechanical an ordering of the march of time. How contemptible, Aiken would agree, if women's writing also failed to uproot the nails that history hammers into a tree of freedom.

Catharine R. Stimpson

1. "I, the Unemployed," *From South Africa: New Writing, Photographs, and Art,* edited by David Bunn and Jane Taylor, with Reginald Gibbons and Sterling Plumpp (Chicago: University of Chicago Press, 1988), p. 294.

Acknowledgments

Perhaps the greatest pleasure of completing a project like this is having the opportunity to tell of all those who helped to make it possible. I owe a special debt to the women at the University of Arizona, friends and students, who in 1982 asked me to conduct an independent studies graduate seminar on feminist theory and criticism. That seminar, and the informal discussion group that grew out of it, provided an early forum for the development of my ideas on Dinesen. I thank all those who participated in our discussions—especially Nancy Mairs, Karen Brennan, Cynthia Hogue, Laura Hinton, Janice Dewey, Nancy Sternbach, and Julia Balén—as well as the many undergraduate students who, in subsequent seminars, read Dinesen with me—particularly Linette Davis, Lynn Gerou, Rachel Beck, Blaine Paradise, and Parsifal Smith.

My research was assisted by a grant from the Women's Studies Advisory Council of the Women's Studies Program at the University of Arizona, and by a University of Arizona Humanities Travel Grant. Funds provided by a University of Arizona Foundation Creative Teaching Award and a Burlington Northern Foundation Award freed my summers for writing. Parts of chapter 10 were presented in the Phi Beta Kappa Address and the Faculty-Community Lecture Series at the University of Arizona in 1986 and in the A. J. Head Memorial Humanities Lecture at Furman University in 1987. Other parts of the book were originally given as papers, and I wish to thank Michael Riffaterre, Myra Dinnerstein, Poul Houe, Susan Horton, Nils Hasselmo, Claire Kolins, William Christie, John H. Crabtree, Douglas Canfield, and Shirley Geok-lin Lim for invitations to speak about Dinesen on various occasions. I also acknowledge permission to reprint several parts of the manuscript that have appeared in different form in *Contemporary Literature, Scandinavian Studies, Exposure,* and *Women's Writing in Exile,* edited Mary Lynn Broe and Angela Ingram, © 1989 The University of North Carolina Press.

I am indebted to the Rungstedlund Foundation for permission to use and quote from the Karen Blixen Archives; to Florence Feiler for providing helpful information about Dinesen's publications; to the staff of the Royal Library in Copenhagen for assisting my research; and to P. M.

Mitchell for amiably introducing me to the procedures of the reading room there. Above all I wish to thank Clara Selborn, who gave graciously of her time and hospitality during my trip to Denmark in 1984 and has continued to provide generous assistance and advice to me over the years. I am deeply grateful for her kindness.

I am indebted as well to several Danish colleagues. Else Cederborg supplied much useful information, especially about the Danish background of Dinesen's texts. Aage Henriksen offered encouraging support of my early work. Poul Houe's invitation to participate in the first international conference on Karen Blixen/Isak Dinesen at the University of Minnesota in 1985 provided an invaluable opportunity to meet and confer with other scholars from Denmark and America.

My research trip to Denmark was made not only possible but festive by a group of wonderful people: Tom and Jytte Bradstrup-Holm, whose house became our abode; Merete and Peter Hjørne, who, at the instigation of our mutual friend Bill Christie, made all the arrangements; Joan Sandin and Sigfrid Leijonhufvud, who provided generous hospitality in Sweden; and especially Kirsten, Bjørn, Anne, and Rune Myrthue, whose encouragement, love, and confidence in me have buoyed my spirits through the years. Anne also patiently tutored me in Danish while living with us in Arizona and has continued to help me from afar by answering endless questions and tracking down diverse Danish publications. To them all, *mange tak*.

Thanks also to the colleagues in this country who have assisted my work in various ways: Nancy Miller, Hillis Miller, Morris Philipson, Diane Middlebrook, Carol Clover, Judith Lee, Jane Marcus, Mary Lynn Broe, Angela Ingram, and Annette Kolodny. I am particularly indebted to Catharine Stimpson and Robert Langbaum, whose wise counsel and encouragement since the earliest stages of the project have been invaluable, and to Robert Con Davis for his helpful reading of the finished manuscript.

It is one of the paradoxes of gratitude that in the very process of expressing it, one becomes most acutely aware of the inadequacy of words. But those who have been closest to me as this project developed, whose faith in its worth has sustained me, know what a great debt I owe them. Jerrold Hogle, Lynda Zwinger, Barbara Babcock, and James Kilgo all read large portions or entire drafts of the manuscript at various stages and provided illuminating comments and unfailing support. Dialogue with them was crucial to my work, as were my ongoing discussions with Patrick O'Donnell, Jan Swearingen, and David Jacobs. Scott Momaday offered generous help and good counsel. Herbert Schneidau, Barbara Schneidau, Ed Dryden, Larry Evers, Barbara Grygutis, Susan White, Tenney Nathanson, Charles Scruggs, Adele Barker, and Sandra Flowers gave me vital encouragement. My colleagues and friends in Women's Studies, especially Myra Dinnerstein, Karen Anderson, Judy Lensink, Pat MacCorquodale, Jan Monk, Ruth Dickstein, and Eliana Rivero, consoled and cheered me on.

Finally, I am deeply grateful to my family, whose nurturing presence in my life has made it all possible: my late father Sutton Hardy, who inspired my love for language; my mother Mae Eppinger Hardy, who has sustained me in more ways than I could ever enumerate or repay; my sisters Kathie Smith and Jan Miller, who have supported me loyally during every phase of a project that must have seemed interminable; and members of my family by marriage—particularly Gladys Carroll, Mary Rose Duffield, Mardy Stotsky, and my stepsons Joshua and Zachary Carroll—who have had faith in me. My son James and my daughter Alden have had faith in me too, though they must sometimes have regarded this book as a kind of rival sibling. Nevertheless, they have tolerated its vicissitudes with more patience and good will than I could possibly have expected and have forgiven me my distraction, my late hours, my frequent unavailability. And they have given me abundant joy and solace.

To my husband, colleague, and friend Christopher Carroll, my gratitude exceeds all measure. For many years he has nourished my mind and spirit, discussed Dinesen with me, accompanied me on research expeditions, read and commented on successive manuscript drafts, provided his considerable expertise on the mysteries of computers, and made me laugh. He has also put up with my preoccupation, endured being awakened in the middle of many nights by my flashlight and scratching pen, and helped to print, collate, and xerox more pages than he cares to remember. But I remember—I remember it all, and am forever in his debt.

Susan Hardy Aiken
Tucson, Arizona
June 27, 1989

Abbreviations

In citing Isak Dinesen's major texts throughout this study, I have used the following editions and abbreviations:

SGT   *Seven Gothic Tales* (New York: Random House, 1934).
OA   *Out of Africa* (1937; New York: Vintage-Random House, 1972).
WT   *Winter's Tales* (New York: Random House, 1942).
AA   *The Angelic Avengers* (New York: Random House, 1946).
LT   *Last Tales* (New York: Random House, 1957).
AD   *Anecdotes of Destiny* (New York: Random House, 1958).
SG   *Shadows on the Grass* (New York: Random House, 1961).
C   *Carnival: Entertainments and Posthumous Tales* (Chicago: University of Chicago Press, 1977).
Essays *Daguerreotypes and Other Essays,* trans. P. M. Mitchell and W. D. Paden (Chicago: University of Chicago Press, 1979).
E   *Ehrengard* (New York: Random House, 1963).
LA   *Letters from Africa, 1914–1931,* trans. Anne Born, ed. Frans Lasson (Chicago: University of Chicago Press, 1981).
MM   *On Modern Marriage and Other Observations,* trans. Anne Born (New York: St. Martin's Press, 1986).

Dinesen's unpublished manuscripts are housed in the Karen Blixen Archives in the Royal Library, Copenhagen, cited as KB Archives, followed by the appropriate file number.

Introduction

She is neither one nor two. . . . She renders any definition inadequate. . . . she has no "proper" name.

Luce Irigaray, This Sex Which Is Not One

I

To say that this book is about "Isak Dinesen" is to identify a subject neither so obvious nor so unambiguous as might at first appear, for that authorial signature—the most famous and persistent of Karen Blixen's many pseudonyms—covers unsettling forms of discontinuity.[1] We might begin, for example, with the discrepancies in the name itself. Only half-pseudonymous (the surname Dinesen was hers by birth), it reveals even as it conceals authorial identity. Yet as a public fiction of masculine authority, the counterfeit designation of a putative "father" for literary offspring that were in fact fatherless, such a name by its very *mis*naming hints at an illegitimacy, a duplicity in both senses, within the texts.

Dinesen's enactment of difference-from-herself reappeared in her remarkable double textual system. In a gesture unprecedented even in the case of other bilingual writers like Conrad or Nabokov, she wrote virtually every fiction twice—first in English, then in her native Danish—to be published in different countries, often simultaneously, under different signatures.[2] Making English her primary literary language, she displaced herself from her native tongue; recomposing the texts in Danish, she displaced them from their own ostensible origins. This dual inscription opens a rift in our reading of her work that goes beyond the distance between national borders and literary canons: just as the sexual doubleness of her signature mystifies the "true" nature of the author's body, so the textual doubleness of her literary production calls into question the "true" nature of her narrative corpus—the body of her fiction. In both cases, writing marks a process of dislocation; the position of the author becomes indeterminate, neither inside nor yet wholly outside the codes "s/he" constructs and is constructed by. Mary Douglas has observed that

for many cultures the birth of twins constitutes "a great ritual crisis" because their existence explicitly challenges unitary classification schemes
based on discrete identity boundaries.[3] Similarly, twin personae and
narratives might be said to generate a kind of textual crisis, for such
doubling, like punning, creates an interpretive gap, each fiction at once
affirming and annulling its counterpart. Karen Blixen both is and is not
"Isak Dinesen." Thus to read Isak Dinesen is always necessarily to read
across borders, engaging certain concepts of intertextuality with extraordinary immediacy. Her writing practice disrupts monological discourse
in the most fundamental sense, forever deferring the possibility of a
single, "real," official work and thwarting the readerly desire for some
final "authentic" authorial inscription—or author.[4] She is also neither
here nor *there* in received canonical structures. As the author of parables,
"Gothic" narratives, short stories, novellas, one "illegitimate" novel,[5]
and a series of seemingly fragmentary, unclassifiable memoirs—all generic stepchildren in the house of "high" literature—she violates not only
the normative categories by which Western cultural traditions have ordinarily placed persons, but the standardizing categories by which the
Euro-American academy has placed authors and literary works.

These perplexities of text and signature become figures of other ambiguities. Consider only the most obvious: fictions that Dinesen called
tales and often delivered as performative utterances, evoking an orality
which their inscription manifestly denies;[6] the formal, faintly archaic style
that belies their modernist effects and strategies; the proliferations of their
interior narratives—plurally framed, infinitely regressive structures like
The Thousand and One Nights, which she claimed as one of her preeminent models; the thematics of duality and difference elaborated through
figures of masking, puppetry, theatrics, mirrors, mimes, transvestism,
and other forms of reflection and inversion that pervade her work; and her
frequent use of symbolic doubles, like the twins Atanasio and Dionysio
of "The Cardinal's First Tale."[7] Further, as that title implies, the texts
themselves often divide and multiply. There is also a "Cardinal's Third
Tale"—though, provocatively, no "second." "New Gothic Tales" and
"New Winter's Tales" in *Last Tales* gesture toward their titular antecedents in earlier volumes. And like the eponymous protagonist of the two
Cardinal's tales, characters frequently recur in subsequent, ostensibly unrelated fictions, setting up metatextual reverberations that complicate our
prior readings. In all these cases, as with every instance of repetition, each
reiteration constitutes an implicit commentary on its predecessors, compelling a reinterpretation of what had seemed fixed and final. Evoking
the possibility of an endless dialogical chain, Dinesen's writing practice,
like the Scheherazadean narrations to which she compared it, perpetually
postpones the sense of an ending.[8]

Yet despite the disjunctions and contradictions suggested by even these most obvious complexities, a prevailing view holds that Dinesen tended, as Judith Thurman puts it, to "unify and simplify" what is "in fact ambiguous"—to create, in Eric Johannesson's phrase, "a neat and orderly structure."[9] In assuming a divergent perspective, I would invoke one of Dinesen's own witty observations about the epistemological estrangement inherent in reading from an alternative position: "Viewed from different sides of the globe, things look different. Seen from my own farm, the Big Dipper was upside down."[10] Similarly, if one views Dinesen's writing from a "different side," a ground outside that established by critical tradition, what seems most striking is not its simplicity and orderliness but its vertiginous plurality, its refusal or subversion of univocal categories, and its concomitant resistance to stable categorization. Like Ariel, to whom she compares the female artist in "Tempests," Dinesen seems always, textually, in flight.[11] Neither truly English nor simply Danish, neither "oral" nor yet fully written, neither "man" nor "woman," she dissolves both self and texts into a continual play of transformations that resembles the dizzying effects of the "mirror-room of the Panoptikon" she describes in "The Roads Round Pisa," "where you see . . . a hundred glasses each of which distorts . . . in a different way" (*SGT*, 166). Pellegrina Leoni's declaration of independence from fixed meaning in "The Dreamers" aptly describes the practice of the author who wrote Pellegrina as her own double: "I will not be one person again, . . . I will always be many. . . . Give up the game of being one" (*SGT*, 345).[12] Wherever one seeks to place Dinesen, she is always also elsewhere.

Crucial to all these issues is the problematic of sexual difference. To raise questions of placement and boundaries is to evoke the logic of opposition by which Western culture has organized and maintained itself—whether in its constructions of the body (me versus not me, inside versus outside, same versus different), of the thinking/speaking subject (self versus other, conscious versus unconscious), of the familial, tribal, or national group (us versus them), or of language and textuality (speech versus writing). As Hélène Cixous observes, such organizing modes are inseparable from the hierarchical construction of gender, that opposition of "male" to "female" that pervades and subtends all other oppositions in Occidental metaphysics.[13] Significantly, Dinesen represents Pellegrina's meditation on multiplicity within the frame of a larger speculation on woman as sign and signifier, at odds with a world that would assign her a fixed place—a site designated by the proper name. Pellegrina equates this positioning with being "bound up" and buried, literally turned to stone and monumentalized beneath "a marble plate, [with] a short inscription upon it"—with becoming, in sum, a permanently fixed text (*SGT*, 344).

I shall return to this passage, but suffice it to say here that if we would understand the implications of Dinesen's resistance to fixation, we need to attend not only to the manifold complexities of her dual textual production, her ambiguous positioning within and between authorial signatures, and her problematic situation as a "foreigner" to both the Danish and the Anglo-American literary scenes, but also to her status as an outsider in another and more profound sense than the geographical: that of every woman writing and reading within a language and a literary tradition historically dominated by men. This book takes up an inquiry into the intricate relations of gender, sexuality, and representation in Dinesen's writing, asking how its form and meaning are affected by her engendered "foreignness" within androcentric culture and how this alterity intersects with other forms of displacement in her texts. I hope not only to show the relevance of contemporary theories of sexual difference and signification for reading Isak Dinesen, but to demonstrate that Dinesen also provides a major anticipatory "reading" of those theories—indeed, that her texts blur the boundaries traditionally assumed to divide "fiction" from "theory." As a figure situated on the margins of discourse in several senses, traversing the intersections of diverse languages, cultures, canons, genders, and genres, she offers a unique perspective on a concern posed acutely by various feminist theories: the possibilities of what is culturally construed as "peripheral" to put the "center" into question.[14]

According to the evaluative criteria currently in force in the Anglo-American academy, Dinesen is often regarded as a marginal, "minor" author. But as Gilles Deleuze and Felix Guattari observe, it is precisely so-called "minor literature" which may offer the most radical challenge and revitalizing possibilities to the dominant culture within and outside of which it is simultaneously situated. Being "on the margins . . . allows the writer all the more the possibility to express another possible community and to forge the means for another consciousness and another sensibility," thus generating "the revolutionary conditions for every literature within the heart of what is called great (or established) literature": "There is nothing that is major or revolutionary except the minor. To hate all languages of the masters."[15] Although Deleuze and Guattari themselves adopt a problematic stance on questions of gender,[16] their paradigm is peculiarly applicable to the situation of women writing within a hegemonic patriarchal culture—those for whom the "language of the masters" carries a particularly poignant resonance. It is from the perspective of these margins that I propose a rereading of Isak Dinesen.[17]

Here are some of the crucial questions with which we might begin. In a cultural and literary lineage in which women have been written primarily as mediatory objects, what becomes of their narrations? Where, given their historical exclusion from public discourse, are the sites from which they may speak? And what, if any, unique forms do their discourses develop in response to this positioning? How do women engender narrative, in the sense of both "giving birth" to it in male-oriented language and simultaneously opening up the question of gender that a masculinist symbolic order would naturalize and neutralize? Dinesen would take up these questions repeatedly throughout her life. Her letters, fictions, and essays constitute a series of astute, passionate speculations on the problematics of sexuality, desire, and discourse within this larger cultural context. In seeking to unfold some of the implications of that concern, I want to show that Dinesen's texts persistently assert the inseparability of gender and the engenderings of narrative. Read from this perspective, her work may be seen as a far-reaching inquiry into how sexual difference informs the ways we constitute culture, subjectivity, and the language that is their medium—or, to use her own preferred terms, the ways we tell ourselves (as) "stories."

2

Any new study of Isak Dinesen is constrained by the relatively limited familiarity with her writing among Anglo-American readers. While she currently enjoys, for better or worse, something of a mythic status in the popular imagination, the fact remains that many who know a great deal about her life have read surprisingly little of her work.[18] Despite recent signs of a revival of scholarly interest, even specialists in modern literature often lack close or extensive acquaintance with her texts—a problem at once epitomized and compounded by her exclusion from Anglo-American canons and the relative scarcity of Anglo-American criticism of her fiction. And even those who have read her often know only *Out of Africa,* consequently assuming—erroneously—that she is primarily a colonialist author.[19]

In seeking to work within some of these lacunae, I have not attempted to provide exhaustive, panoramic coverage, though I do make certain generalizable claims about Dinesen's practice. Rather, I want to reverse the critical optic, engaging certain important texts through a series of readings, discrete at first but, following Dinesen's own procedure, progressively intertwined. As one of the several implications of my title suggests, I concentrate on the great narratives written during the early years of her career, *Seven Gothic Tales* and *Out of Africa,* books on which, as Robert Langbaum notes, "her reputation still rests,"[20] though I also consider a number of later fictions, including certain crucial narratives commonly regarded as marginal or inconsequential. By focusing on the distinctive intricacies of these texts, I implicitly suggest ways of reading Dinesen that are applicable to all her work.

Such an approach reveals not only the continuities, but the rifts and ambiguities which are among the most vital qualities of Dinesen's writing but which a more distanced perspective too easily overlooks. The teleological imperative that sustains the comprehensive overview does not necessarily lead to the most illuminating assessment of Dinesen's work, for there is, strictly speaking, no *telos* or closure toward which her writing moves. Though it can be divided into chronological phases, after the first decade it did not "develop" in any conventionally progressive, evolutionary fashion.[21] Indeed, as we shall see, the teleological model itself, with its focus on linear temporality and its assumption of beginnings, middles, and endings, is profoundly antithetical to Dinesen's fictive world. Rather, her work might better be conceptualized as spiral: her later texts bear traces of their predecessors, like palimpsests to which she returned over the years in a process of elaboration, intensification, and transformation comparable to the method she employed in composing each individual text.[22] Many of her late fictions are most interesting precisely as instances of the revisionist hermeneutic by which she in effect reread, via a process of rewriting, her earlier texts. Her observation about her early Gothic tales might be extended to her entire oeuvre as it folds back upon itself: "They must be rewritten time and again!"[23] It is characteristic that the remarkable "Carnival," one of the last fictions she reworked before her death (it was published as the title story of the posthumous collection), was also one of her first compositions. Begun as "La Valse Mauve" before she went to Africa, rewritten there, and initially included among the tales that she intended to publish in her first collection, "Carnival" became at last the finale that returns the scene of her writing to its opening act.

A few further qualifications. Though I make references throughout this study to Karen Blixen's Danish oeuvre, my analysis is grounded on the premise that we should read "Karen Blixen" and "Isak Dinesen" as different though intricately intertextual authors—both children of a single but by no means single-minded literary mother. The parallel Danish and English texts are not unlike the discourses of twins: often mutually illuminating, even intertwined, but certainly not identical.[24] "Isak Dinesen" diverges from Karen Blixen in another sense as well. Traditionally, one of the most prominent critical responses to her work has been the effort to locate the author behind the texts, reading them through the lenses of the life or, conversely, using the texts as unmediated evidence of their author's presumed ideas or intentions. I assume on the contrary that the primary way we come to "know" Isak Dinesen is as a textually embodied figure, the product of diverse representations—written, oral, or iconographic—constructed by her or by others who took her as their subject. Though I consider Karen Blixen's life as it relates to the production of her narratives, my interest lies primarily in the biography as another form of inscription, inseparable from her textual corpus and comparably subject to diverse readings—in Isak Dinesen as what she herself called, with rueful irony, "a piece of printed matter." [25] As she remarked more than once, because we live "in a world of symbols," even "the spoken word does not have the rights of a firstborn." [26] Biographical "facts" are also textual products, subject to the mediations and interpretive discontinuities inherent in any relation of reader or listener to writing or telling. [27] In dealing with the historical contingencies of her work, then, I would reiterate her observation that "history" is itself a cultural construct.

As an entry into these questions and a way of situating my later readings, I want first to take a closer look at Dinesen's relation to certain contemporary reconceptions of literature, focused through an analysis of a fiction generally acknowledged as a touchstone of her work: "The Cardinal's First Tale." Published near the end of her career, it provides an exemplary vantage point from which to begin a review of her engendering of narrative. Like all her greatest texts, the story sets in motion what in the unpublished essay "On Feminism and Womanhood" she called "the infinite possibilities" of "interplay" between "heterogeneous" elements, inviting thereby a reconception of the categories *man* and *woman, author* and *text*. [28] In staging a confrontation between "father" and "mother," the narrative reveals them not as stable oppositional entities but as shifting, mutually inflecting modes operative in culture, in subjectivity, and in the discursive systems through which both are constituted. Chapters 2 and 3 approach that interplay from another perspective, considering the significance of sexual difference in the formation of Dinesen's own "story" and the intersections of that (auto)biographical text with the poetics of displacement she evolved in response to certain crucial events and relationships in her life. Chapters 4 through 9, while devoted primarily to *Seven Gothic Tales,* also reach beyond the borders of those fictions to later texts in order to demonstrate both the persistence of Dinesen's concern with the engendering of narrative and the nature and implications of her self-revisions. Chapter 10 continues that project with *Out of Africa,* attempting both to show its distinctiveness as a colonialist text and to situate it, together with *Shadows on the Grass,* within Dinesen's larger oeuvre by charting the connections it draws between the politics and poetics of colonialist discourse, the politics and poetics of gender, and the production and interpretation of narrative. Finally, as an epilogue, I take up another version of Dinesen's self-revision, her fabrication of her own image as a kind of performative artifact: the theatrical, exquisite iconography through which she would merge the fiction of her body with the body of her fiction.

Late in life, reviewing a newly published Danish novel, Dinesen remarked that "in all books where the really decisive events precede the first page, much must remain . . . in a *clair-obscur*, so that the reader can make his way through the narrative only step by step. The proper reader is more captivated than wearied by the exertions such meandering requires" (*Essays*, 162). In writing this book, I have often recalled those words, for Dinesen's own narratives both demand and reward such attentive scrutiny. If my decision to work "step by step" through a few important texts necessarily leaves much "in a *clair-obscur*," I hope that the meanderings that follow will be sufficiently suggestive to lead others to reread the texts I have not been able to include, and to rethink the entirety of Dinesen's engenderings.

PART ONE

OPENINGS

The book must be read more than once. Many
things in it mean more—mean sometimes something
different—than they appear to do at first.

ISAK DINESEN
Daguerreotypes

1

"Caprice de femme enceinte":
Reconceiving Isak Dinesen

"She" is indefinitely other in herself. This is doubtless why she is said to be whimsical, incomprehensible, agitated, capricious. . . . Hers are contradictory words. . . . One must listen to her differently in order to hear an *"other meaning" which is constantly in the process of weaving itself, at the same time ceaselessly embracing words and yet casting them off to avoid becoming fixed, immobilized.*

Luce Irigaray, *This Sex Which Is Not One*

I. WRITING MOTHERS

We are not going to refuse ourselves the delights of pregnancy, which . . . is always dramatized or evaded or cursed in classical texts. For if there is a specific thing repressed, that is where it is found: the taboo of the pregnant woman (which says a lot about the power that seems invested in her). . . . How could woman, who has experienced the not-me within me, not have a particular relationship to the written?

Hélène Cixous, *The Newly Born Woman*

In a pivotal scene in "The Cardinal's First Tale," an autocratic Italian nobleman has just discovered that his wife has been pregnant for some time without his knowledge: "'*Caprice de femme enceinte*,' the Prince exclaimed, not a little piqued at an order of nature which would confide a momentous family matter to a lady, before informing her lord" (*LT*, 9). His defensive, condescending jest marks a critical moment in an ongoing confrontation between the father's authority and the elusive, capricious figure of the mother. It also captures with remarkable precision a certain conception of "woman" as she has been written within the confinements of an androcentric symbolic economy. To situate Dinesen's own reconceptions of these subjects, let us briefly consider that larger cultural text and some of its implications for the writing of woman.

3

During the past two decades the figure of the *femme enceinte* has become the locus of diverse, often contradictory discourses on the significations of maternity and maternity as signification.[1] Kristeva's representation of pregnancy in "Motherhood according to Giovanni Bellini" might well serve as a trope for the expanding corpus of criticism the mother has engendered: "Cells fuse, split, and proliferate; volumes grow, tissues stretch, and body fluids change rhythm. . . . Within the body, growing as a graft, there is an other."[2] Kristeva's reading of gestation as a "proliferation" of internal difference, a "strange form of split symbolization," and a negation of "the social symbolic bond" suggests that the figure of the *femme enceinte* potentially threatens not only traditional Western notions of the single, sovereign self but also traditional views of language (and the "volumes" that "grow" out of it) as unitary, monological, and transparent.[3]

The anxieties generated by "motherhood's impossible syllogism" find exemplary expression in two renowned earlier texts on gestation and birth. Widely recognized as primal inscriptions of the prevailing gender dynamics of the Western world, both turn on an attempted inversion of the maternal and paternal roles in reproduction. I refer to what Kenneth Burke has wittily termed the "unnatural obstetrics" of Genesis 2— woman's "birth" from man's body—and to the equally perverse biology represented by Athena, Daddy's girl *par excellence,* in the debate over mother-right versus father-right that closes Aeschylus's *Oresteia:* "the mother is no parent to that which is called her child."[4] Leaving aside their important differences, one might argue that whatever else these texts represent, both register the intensity of a masculine need to *contain* the dangerous feminine excess Kristeva evokes, to recuperate a potentially destabilizing energy into a phallocentric order through a symbolic usurpation of woman's generative power. Both reveal man's desire to incorporate that which originally incorporated him, to write woman's scandalous plenitude in safer terms by making *himself* her *enceinte*—literally and figuratively her "confinement."[5]

And no wonder. For since, as Freud famously remarked, "maternity is proved by the evidence of the senses while paternity is a hypothesis, based on an inference," the mastery of the mother's generative mystery, the colonization of her desire, has served not only to alleviate certain fundamental masculine anxieties but to found the official structures of Western civilization.[6] In a system that equates female propriety with male appropriation, any woman who refuses to relinquish her parental priority—refuses, as they say, *to name the father*—risks being read and written as an *improper figure,* an illicit sign of the ultimate capriciousness. It is no accident that in major Western discourses of aesthetics and moral philosophy, as Barbara Herrnstein Smith has shown, the term "capricious" is a recurrent antonym to regulatory (what Smith calls "standard-izing") terms like "law," "rationality," "wholeness," or "soundness"—terms employed by dominant groups that seek to control those who threaten the status quo by labeling them marginal, eccentric, deviant, or pathological.[7] Smith does not mention women in this context, but they are of course the largest of all such marginalized groups in Western history.

Significantly, the depictions of unnatural gestation in both Genesis and the *Oresteia* conflate biology with language: the new-made man confirms his authority over the newly born woman by twice assuming the right to name her (Gen. 2:23; 3:20), and Athena speaks her founding word, warranty of future civilization, in the name of the all-Father, who had, we recall, originally devoured her pregnant mother.[8] These mythographies find literary replication in the widespread conventional trope of writing as pregnancy or childbirth—that conceit of conception which assigns to male authors the maternal power of generation in the (re)production of textual progeny.[9] Such figures are reinforced by oedipal/patrilineal models of authorship that envision both narrative structure and literary history as forms of male succession, governed, like Western culture historically, by forms of (masculine) oedipal desire and by figurative homologies with the system of patrilineage.[10] In arguing that the "unity or integrity" of Occidental narrative, grounded in both classical and Judeo-Christian traditions, depends on "a series of genealogical connections: author-text, father-son, beginning-middle-end," beneath which lies "the imagery of succession, of paternity, of hierarchy," Edward Said expresses a characteristic preoccupation of much recent narratology with problems of fatherhood, authority, legitimacy, and the textual consequences of their disruption.[11] Such genealogical imperatives lead not only to the schematization of traditional narrative as a patrilineal syntax but also to Harold Bloom's well-known psychomachic paradigms of literary history as an ongoing oedipal struggle between fathers and sons, or to Roland Barthes's reading of the text as the maternal body with which the (male) child/author "plays."[12] When Barthes explicitly identifies the image of the father with the drive of narrative itself, he reveals the enabling assumptions of the metaphoric system that grounds these discourses: "Death of the father would deprive literature of many of its pleasures. If there is no longer a father, why tell stories? Doesn't every narrative lead back to Oedipus? Isn't story telling always a way of searching for one's origin. . . . ?"[13] As Barthes's rhetorical questions make clear, such metaphors, like the cultural system of patrilineage itself, tend to suppress the female role in generation by evoking, like the trope of the male author's "labor," a sort of biological miracle: an unbroken series of fathers begetting sons, apparently without maternal assistance.

Within these schemata, writing is further authorized by biblical analogy, which represents the founding Father as the One who worded the world as a great text and textualized the Son as a great Word, inspiring later scribes to repeat—both to tell and to reenact—the originary divine *poesis*. Beginnings, middles, and ends in Western cultural discourses appear to reinscribe not only an androcentric oedipal or Aristotelian logic but also the teleological thrust of history envisioned within scriptural paradigms.[14] As Said puts it, "in the patrimony of texts there is a first text, a sacred prototype, a scripture, which the reader is always approaching through the text before him as petitioning suppliant or as an initiate among many in a sacred chorus supporting the central patriarchal text. . . . [T]he displacing power of all texts derives finally from the displacing power of the Bible, whose centrality, potency, and anteriority inform all Western literature."[15] As with the supplanting of midwives by male obstetricians in seventeenth century Europe, a politically charged phenomenon wherein, as Ann Oakley notes, "the defining characteristic of the corpus of 'knowledge' which constitutes obstetrics" was "its claim to superiority over the expertise possessed by the reproducers themselves," so the erasure of woman effected by such masculine claims to textual reproduction suggests an appropriation of massive historic proportions.

Crucial connections exist between the figure of male authorship as pregnancy or of literature as patrilineage and the anomalous position female authors have occupied historically in male-dominated canonical traditions. As the concept of canonicity suggests, these traditions, despite their demonstrable contingency, repeatedly drive toward consolidation and stasis based on the exclusion or recuperation of extreme difference, the deflection of potential challenges to official categories or interpretative authorities.[17] Indeed the very term *canon* is rooted in regulatory phallic imagery (Greek *kanon,* rod or rule, akin to Greek *kanna,* reed = a long, straight, firm object useful as a standard of measure). Not surprisingly, in view of the overwhelmingly masculine character of academic discourse, those few women traditionally admitted into the canonical lineage have too often been read *as if they were men*—that is, as if their sexual difference were a matter of in-difference, an historical accident worth passing remark, but fundamentally irrelevant to the meaning of their writing. Such a move, coupled with that of excluding most women writers altogether from the canonical tradition, has until recently sustained with surprising effectiveness the fiction that, in effect, only "men" give birth to significant texts.[18]

These conceptions of sameness, of course, have been radically unsettled over the past two decades by diverse feminist theories. It is a critical commonplace that certain historical turning points can occur in the official academic reputation of any writer when, most often posthumously, s/he is reconceived through some critic's compelling rereading, which by challenging traditional formulations determines how the author will "live" for future generations of readers, heirs of the critic's labor. Such authorial rebirths are especially striking when they also signal moments of crisis in the institution of criticism: periods of epistemological stress and buckling that produce not merely new conceptions of individual writers but new paradigms of reading, possibilities previously obscured or repressed by the tacit ontological assumptions that constrain all interpretation. Feminist critics have shown us that with women writers such a revisionary hermeneutics is complicated by women's anomalous place within the history of Western culture, their subsumption under the "human" norm that, as the unmarked term "man" suggests, has traditionally been male, and their consequent sense of self-estrangement, of existing as split subjects, at once within and outside the dominant symbolic order. As Xavière Gauthier remarks, "Women are . . . caught in a very real contradiction. . . . As long as [they] remain silent, they will be outside the historical process. But, if they begin to speak and write *as men do,* they will enter history subdued and alienated."[19] Because woman's writing represents a peculiarly divided subjectivity, a doubled positioning that embodies both subordinate and dominant cultures, reading the text(s) of woman demands more than ordinary attention to a certain engendered polylogue—what some feminist critics have called "double-voiced discourse" but what might well be called multivoiced discourse—if one would decipher the inscriptions of feminine difference that remain all but invisible within androcentric critical frames.[20] As Elaine Showalter puts it, "We must keep two alternative oscillating texts simultaneously in view"; as the "orthodox plot recedes, . . . another plot, hitherto submerged in the anonymity of the background, stands out in bold relief."[21]

In this context, Dinesen provides a striking case in point. For despite her increasing inclusion in feminist analyses, she has been overwhelmingly represented as a type of Athena, quintessentially her father's daughter, devoted in her work as in her life to a constellation of values supremely androcentric—a psychological and textual as well as a sociohistorical ancien régime.[22] Hence two remarkably different, mutually exclusive "Isak Dinesens" stand before us, as in a double exposure—a divided figure poised between ex-centric feminist reconceptions and the perdurable law of the Same. Thus "reading Isak Dinesen" might serve as a synecdoche for the kinds of epistemological crisis the question of gender provokes for contemporary criticism.

Yet even Dinesen's feminist critics tend to overlook what I take to be the most salient and revolutionary quality of her writing: the radical discursive practices that undermine what appears to be, in Eric Johannesson's phrase, "a neat and orderly structure." Dinesen's complex, self-reflexive texts brilliantly anticipate not only feminist concerns with women's historical experience in androcentric societies, but also conceptions of language and subjectivity more recently articulated by continental writers like Cixous, Kristeva, and Irigaray, who focus primarily on semiotic systems, reading "woman" as a both a psychosexual being and a discursive category.[23] Implicit in my rereading of Dinesen is an attempt to negotiate the gap between these two discourses on woman, often characterized as mutually exclusive. Yet I use these dual designations only provisionally and heuristically, as general indices of the theoretical positions I would traverse, for whatever their divergences, both perspectives pose fundamental questions about the cultural construction of gender and the gendered construction of culture, questions that compel a massive revision of received notions of subjectivity, authorship, and representation. Thus rather than reject either approach, I prefer to draw on their different strengths, allowing each to open up textual implications that might otherwise remain obscured—and indicating, by the way, the degree to which each presupposes and inflects the other. A writer as playful as Dinesen (who attributed inconsistency not only to femininity and divinity but to inspired authorship) demands flexible, eclectic reading practices capable of dwelling in apparent contradictions, setting theoretical differences in dialogue, and suggesting the ways such oppositions may themselves be called into question.[24]

While the traditional view of Dinesen holds that "the writer begins where the woman ends,"[25] I want to suggest that where the writer begins, the "woman" goes underground, constituting a dynamic of disruption and recreation that undermines the surface structures of the text. In one of her lectures on the status of women in Western culture, Dinesen herself addressed the question of woman's "double-voiced discourse," maintaining that women in a patriarchal society might best subvert the "ancient citadels of males, the strongholds of the church, science, and law," by *acting*—"as in their time the Achaeans did in Troy, by going within the walls in a wooden horse. That is, [by making] their entry in disguise, in a costume which intellectually or psychologically represent[s] a male." In this context she proposes a revisionist reading of Shakespeare's Portia that implicitly recapitulates her own strategy as a woman in male disguise:

> In the performances of *The Merchant of Venice* which I have seen, Portia has . . . been played incorrectly. In the court scene she has been all too solemn and doctrinaire. . . . Just as she sparkles in the entire comedy, . . . quick to laughter, she should also, I think, sparkle in the closed, severely masculine world of the court. She has been called in to clarify an orthodox matter. . . . And her magic lies

precisely in her duplicity, the pretended deep respect for the paragraphs of the law which overlies her . . . quite fearless heresy. (*Essays*, 80, 82–83)

As Dinesen rereads Portia (whose "laughter" echoes the Hebrew meaning of "Isak"), so we might reread Dinesen.[26] "She always liked a surplus, an excess, the feeling that more power was hidden than was visible on the surface," remarked the Danish critic Bent Mohn, one of her longtime friends.[27] That surplus, I would argue, concentrates itself in the operations of the feminine in her texts. Like her name, her narratives stage a dialogical interaction between overt, apparently androcentric content and the "excess" it cannot contain. Earlier in the same lecture she had spoken of her "belief in the significance of interaction and conviction regarding the . . . unlimited possibilities" in the "interplay" of two dissimilar entities (*Essays*, 69). Just such an interplay occurs in her texts. Without continual attention to its "possibilities," we miss the most distinctive quality of her fiction. To seek to read what, in "Sorrow-acre," she calls "the story of the woman" (*WT*, 69) is to discover that far from upholding paternal primacy, her stories persistently enact its undoing.[28]

"Rules," Foucault has remarked, "are empty in themselves and unfinalized; they are impersonal and can be bent to any purpose. The successes of history belong to those who are capable of seizing the rules, to replace those who had initially imposed them; controlling this complex mechanism, they will make it function so as to overcome the rulers through their own rules."[29] Dinesen expressed keen sympathy with such an enterprise, for that which breaks the rules by moving, as she put it, "away from the conventional" to liberate "the free play of impulses" (*LA*, 234–35; cf. 246). Yet as the analogy of Portia suggests, she did not conceive this iconoclastic project in terms of direct attack. Consider how she managed her anger at the insensitivity of the British to the African peoples they had colonized (an anger complicated by her paradoxical awareness of her own complicity in the colonialist enterprise she deplored): "I dare not talk to any of the English, I think my influence here as a woman and a foreigner must be strictly confined to being an example; if I start to preach I shall lose my power, which must be won through being a hostess and friend" (even though, as she continues, "the 'example,' takes effect so slowly, [that] sometimes one feels like firing off a broadside right in their silly faces . . . !") (*LA*, 240–41). Her literary situation involved comparable alienations: not only "a foreigner" writing for an English-speaking audience, she was also, as a woman, a member of that group itself most thoroughly colonized by patriarchal "civilization."[30] It was a condition implicit in her persistent sense of living in "exile," a state of existential "loneliness" by which she felt herself "as-

sailed" all her life (*LA,* 286). Given her extensive speculations on the
complex relations of masters and servants, her choice of a subversive
strategy for coping with this displacement may have arisen in part from
her recognition of the Hegelian master-slave paradox: that in mounting
direct opposition against the oppressor's power, one implicitly acknowledges and risks reconstituting it. In her texts Dinesen maintains her own
"power" precisely by a refusal to "preach," working instead through an
elegant, playful irony so refined that it can, if viewed through an androcentric optic, be overlooked. Beda Allemann's remark that "the conditio
sine qua non of the highest reaches of irony" is "the lack of cues" becomes especially pertinent here.[31] As Geoffrey Hartman notes in commenting on Allemann's text, irony forces us to "imagine the possibility of
speaking *through* the face (per-sona) without distorting it into mask or
grimace. . . . Irony limits *being known*—being defined or betrayed by
words, or by the very assumption that there is a nuclear and intuitable
essence to our being, a naming that coincides with an 'I am.'"[32]

The specificity of this sort of irony for women within a phallocentric
discursive economy has been brilliantly analyzed by Irigaray, whose concept of *mimétisme* recalls Dinesen's preference for "duplicity" and "play"
over direct assault. To "solve the problem of the articulation of the female
sex in discourse," writes Irigaray, one must use not "direct . . . challenge"
but a "play with mimesis" by which woman may "recover the place of
her exploitation by discourse, without allowing herself to be simply reduced to it." Thus she can "resubmit herself . . . to ideas about herself,
that are elaborated in/by a masculine logic, but so as to make 'visible,' by
the effect of playful repetition, what was supposed to remain invisible:
the cover-up of a possible operation of the feminine in language"—

> if women are such good mimics, it is because they are not simply re-
> absorbed in that function. *They also remain elsewhere.* . . . [T]he issue
> is not one of elaborating a new theory . . . but of jamming the theo-
> retical machinery itself, of suspending its pretension to the produc-
> tion of a truth and of a meaning that are excessively univocal. Which
> presupposes that women . . . do not claim to be rivaling men in con-
> structing a logic of the feminine that would take onto-theo-logic as
> its model, but that they are rather attempting to wrest this question
> away from the economy of the logos . . . [by signifying] that with
> respect to this logic a *disruptive excess* is possible on the feminine side.[33]

Dinesen's lifelong preoccupation with masquerade and miming suggests that what has been traditionally interpreted as her conservatism
might better be read as a "capricious" poetics of appropriation and revision whereby that which is ostensibly asserted is simultaneously distanced, disturbed, rendered problematic. Like Irigaray, Dinesen uses the

mask to open a certain space of free play, for the expression of an alternative subjectivity. Her texts seldom simply oppose the order of the father. Rather she embraces—that is, envelopes—the paternal *logos,* undermining even while incorporating its key terms. Not the mastery of the master, but the mystery of the "mistress" who can *play* "the hostess and friend" in order to engender gradual transformations that a more direct onslaught might preclude—this is her characteristic mode.

For a paradigmatic instance of this sort of unsettling feminine *mimétisme,* let us return now to "The Cardinal's First Tale." One of the last fictions she published before her death, it is generally regarded not only as one of her greatest narratives but also as "an open confession of her creed as a writer."[34] As a narrative of identical twins, one claimed and named by the father, the other by the mother, it constitutes a culminating instance of Dinesen's self-referential reflections on her own subversive duplicity, explicitly figured through the "caprice" of the *femme enceinte.* The critical tradition construes the tale as a parable of authorship, and so it is, but not merely—or even primarily—for the reasons usually suggested by those who cite the Cardinal's closing critical pronouncements about "the story" as a direct, unmediated transcription of Karen Blixen's own aesthetic tenets. I would redirect attention to moments literally more central to the narrative structure, but generally seen as peripheral, moments that unsettle not only the critical categories and oppositions the Cardinal expounds in the tale's conclusion but indeed all categorical notions of boundaries, frames, and oppositions—ideas grounded in the fundamental division of male/female through which conceptions of reading, writing, and subjectivity have been traditionally organized and maintained.[35]

2. THE USES OF DUPLICITY

> Seen from the outside, the "Vièrge Ouvrante" is the familiar and unassuming mother with child. But when opened she reveals the heretical secret inside her. God the Father and God the Son, usually represented as heavenly Lords who in an act of pure grace raise up the humble, earth-bound mother to abide with them, prove to be contained in her; prove to be "contents" of her all-sheltering body.
>
> Erich Neumann, *The Great Mother*

"Who are you?" A calculated ambiguity informs the question that opens "The Cardinal's First Tale." Represented as a hermeneutic "riddle" (*LT,* 4), the words invite us with startling directness to consider *what "Isak*

Dinesen" means—in both senses of that phrase. Situated on the outer limit of the narrative, the question constitutes a frame for the tale's frame story; and since frames are quite literally liminal, paradoxical constructions, at once participating in the meaning of the objects they demarcate and occupying a place in the world beyond, we might read the query not only within the bounds of the fiction but also as an implicit interrogation of the identity of the reader, of the "self" in Western discourse, of the "author" in literary history, or of "Isak Dinesen" as a woman writing under a male pseudonym.

As with Dinesen's other texts, that pseudonym complicates all the questions of difference and identity she raises here. If, as Showalter has suggested, nineteenth-century novelists like George Eliot or Charlotte Brontë adopted male *noms de plume* to conceal "'deviant' aspects of the author's personality," [36] then Dinesen, who adopted such a signature long after the era when sociocultural pressures made it necessary, might be said to have enacted a kind of double deviance. Through the sheer artifice, even flamboyance, of the masculine name, she implicitly posed, by inversion, a question much debated of late: what does it mean to write "as a woman"?—or, in this case, what (for a woman) does it mean to write *as a man?* [37] These questions are further complicated in "The Cardinal's First Tale" by a peculiar historical circumstance—what might be called a literary *misconception*—that attended its composition and inflects its questioning of self and signature. While Dinesen was at work on the manuscript, there appeared in Denmark a novel entitled *En Aften i Kolera-Aaret* (*An Evening in the Cholera-Year*) by one "Alexis Hareng," written in so close an imitation of Karen Blixen's style that many readers—and even some of her friends—believed it to be hers. Indeed, the actual author of the book, Kelvin Lindemann, one of her acquaintances and proclaimed admirers, had planned the novel's publication precisely to magnify such speculations. Despite her wry recognition of its comic dimension, the Lindemann/"Hareng" hoax precipitated for her a momentary crisis of both authorship and identity: "When I devote myself to writing 'The Cardinal's First Tale,'" she remarked, "I see a caricature of myself. If I come into a gathering and meet a person who is dressed up and masquerading as me, how can I, myself, be there?" [38] The episode reversed the usual genealogical question, mystifying the identity not of the father of the newborn text, but of its proper mother. What was at stake as a paradoxical marker of "self"-possession and textual authority was the authenticity not of the signature, but of the *pseudo*-signature. Lindemann was that rarest of literary transvestites: a man disguised as a woman who disguised herself as a man. [39] It is within this context, as well as the others I have mentioned, that the inaugural question of "The Cardinal's First Tale" reverberates, opening an inquiry into the problematic conceptions of "woman" and "author" in Western patriarchal discourses.

Like the text itself, the question originates with a woman, a "lady in black" who remains significantly unnamed but whose confession to the Cardinal, a speech outside the confines of the frame, precipitates all subsequent utterances. Thus, in more than one sense, the lost pretext for the Cardinal's tale, the untold story behind *this* story, is a feminine narrative—a haunting, generative absence that Dinesen represents as a "contradictory" "multitude of fragments" uttered by one psychologically situated in the "wild," "at the edge of an abyss" (4). Significantly, Dinesen recurrently employed this same image as a reflexive figure for her own situation as woman and writer.[40]

The implications of the counterconfession the lady proposes anticipate Foucault's observation that the confessional reverses the usual links between discourse and power, since "the agency of domination does not reside in the one who speaks . . . but in the one who listens and says nothing, not in the one who knows and answers, but in the one who questions."[41] Karen Blixen's earlier observations in one of her lectures are pertinent in this context: to "ask the question 'Who am I?'," she asserted, is to precipitate "a revelation" tantamount to a kind of stripping, "divesting" oneself of all those external, culturally authorized symbols that ordinarily guarantee one's "identity."[42] Since *divest* means not only "disrobe" but also "dispossess or deprive of possessions, qualities, rights" (and since, as the Cardinal begins speaking, the lady "pulls on her long gloves," *recovering* herself both literally and psychologically), we see that to answer her question the Cardinal must abandon his ordinary position of power and rhetorically *dis-mantle* himself, figuratively shedding both priestly vestments and patriarchal *in*vestments, putting off the habits of the father in both senses. On another level, however, this self-exposure is only a further concealment, for what he offers is not some naked "truth" about the "self," but a punning discourse of deferral: "'Who am I? . . . Madame, you are the first of my penitents who . . . has ever [presumed] that I might have an identity of my own to confess to. . . . I am not in the habit of talking about myself. . . . Allow me, then, in order to save my modesty, to answer you in the classic manner, and to tell you a story" (3,5).

Thus the story of the frame and the framing of the story work inseparably, standing like the priest and the woman, face to face, reflecting on each other. And as with the specular operations of two facing mirrors, what their reflections produce is not a direct, simple mimesis of "reality" but a kind of infinite regress, stories that engender further stories, like the rows of books in the library where, the narrator puns, "the two found themselves." Insofar as a frame should contain or circumscribe, should establish an *enceinte,* this narrative frame conspicuously fails its ostensible purpose—a fact that puts in question the various paternal claims to frame, so to speak, that follow.

The Cardinal's tale of origins is the story of a woman's transformation from passive object, exchanged within a patrilineal economy, to disruptive agent who through the unfolding—literally the *explication*—of her own desire, rewrites both herself and the cultural text that would reduce her to a mere sign within its borders.[43] Princess Benedetta is "given away" at fifteen to a "brusque and bigoted nobleman three times her age," who "took a wife to have his name live on." At first she passively reproduces her society's gender codes, reading her own gestating body as "a fragile, precious vessel within which a rare seed had been laid down to germinate," so that at last it seems "her husband's old name to which she had given birth." And indeed, the newborn son pointedly literalizes this phallocentric script, for "the child was delicate and had but one eye" (5–6)—a figural replication of both traditional iconographies of the ritual *phallos* and what Jacques Lacan terms the "Name-of-the-Father" as phallic signifier.[44]

Persuaded that the mother's youth has caused this grotesque embodiment of his genealogical hopes, Prince Pompilio—his own name a resounding parody of patriarchal pretensions—imposes a three-year term of sexual abstinence on his wife. This claustration comically turns the paternal dream of "woman's place" into a nightmare, for in confinement Benedetta liberates her own desire and voice through a series of impassioned encounters with inscriptions—words and musical notations—which the text figures as symbolic adulteries. Amid the "tall tomes" in the villa's library, repository of Western patriarchal culture, Benedetta discovers less legitimate books, poetic "volumes of longing and levity"—literary bastards, as it were, that "had happened to leap in among" their more "ponderous" counterparts.[45] Here, "when her husband [is] away," she enacts a subversive *plaisir du texte* that Dinesen represents as a kind of immaculate (self) conception: her "rich tresses, as she was reading, tumbled forward and caressed the parchment," and "she seemed lifted from her chair by her own deep sighs of. . . delight." The library "fell in love with her; it became a bower above the fountain nymph, shaking down on its own the sweet fruits her heart demanded" (6). Through the act of reading she reconceives both the texts and herself, discovering a feminine hermeneutic which, within the paternal literary *enceinte,* imports both *im*purity and danger.[46]

Properly alarmed, Pompilio pronounces such "excessive reading . . . harmful to his wife's health and mind" and attempts to divert her with singing lessons. Diversion indeed, for Benedetta's new practice exceeds the seductions it displaces: "She gave herself up to music, as she had . . . to books; her nature had at first listened, now it sang" (7). Her preference for "the deceptive cadenza, the *cadenza d'inganno,*" reveals the disruptiveness of this devotion, for *inganno* suggests not only cadenzas, but cuckoldry; both maritally and musically, the mode "makes every preparation for a perfect finish and then suddenly breaks off and sounds an unexpected, strange, and alarming close." But in this feminine version of false play it is no male lover but Benedetta herself who generates her own creative ecstasy. And like her erotics of reading, this blissful creation has semantic as well as sexual implications, for music here is associated with the child's prelinguistic attachment to the maternal body, with the womb as *matrix* or *chora*—and with that signifying process Kristeva calls the "semiotic": "feeling, displacement, rhythm, sound."[47] "Here, [Benedetta] felt, was a . . . human language within which things could be truthfully expressed. . . . Here, the girl's heart told her, was the infallible rule of the irregular" (7). Here, in other words, is the polyphonic "song" of woman, construed repeatedly by male theorists from Aristotle to Lacan as "irregular," aberrant, deviant, anomalous, a *diversion* from the masculine norm—*inphallible* indeed.[48]

This mounting female desire-in-language reaches a grand comic climax in an encounter that both exploits and explodes psychoanalytic figures of woman's supposed castration. Removed from her dangerous music-making to a social season in Venice, Benedetta is further "transported" by the singing of the opera star Giovanni Ferrar, who, as Dinesen's humorous puns indicate, is in several senses a *man made woman:* "a *soprano,* formed and prepared in the Conservatorio of Sant 'Onofrio, and once and for all cut off . . . from real life" (8).[49] Having reconceived herself within a phallocentric order that would write her desire only as elision, Benedetta now conceives of—and then symbolically conceives *with*—a "lover" like herself:

> How describe the beatitude into which . . . her whole being was transported. It was a birth, the pangs of which were sweet beyond words, a mighty process which needed, and made use of, every particle of her nature, and in which, undergoing a total change, she triumphantly became her whole self. . . . At the seventh recall, before the last drop of the curtain, . . . a pair of blue and a pair of black eyes met across the pit in a long deep silent glance, the first and the last. (7–8)

In this orgasmic conjunction of absences, gaps are bridged, lacks assume invisible substance, and "wounds" are annealed by being *doubled* as the "two pairs of eyes" meet "across the pit," and ruptures give way to raptures. This "Seraphic love affair" also remakes Giovanni in another register: "Might there not . . . be young inamoratas with such genius for devotion that their glance will bestow upon its object the manhood of a demigod? . . . Their eyes met! Was, then, the unfortunate young singer, in the same way as the lady, wounded in the heart? All authorities agree that that year . . . something happened" to the castrato: his "world-famous treble" voice "was changed." Thus Benedetta's overflowing bliss creates "manhood" out of *nothing*.[50]

The adulterous erotic "wound" that engenders the "birth" in this parodic immaculate conception is also a silent word between the "inamorata" and "her only true lover"—a word soon afterward made flesh when the long-deferred Pompilio takes his wife again "into [his] arms." But what he provides is at best an anticlimax. Though "the Princess became with child," her husband serves as little more than a *stand-in*. In depicting Benedetta's duplicitous impregnation, Dinesen plays semantic havoc with patrilineal kinship systems, exploiting the etymological affiliations of *castration, chastity,* and *caste.* That the latter two words possess a common root in *castus*—"spotless, innocent"—implies the dependence of genealogical purity on maternal impeccability; but all three terms are also akin to *carēre,* "to be without," related to Greek and Sanskrit words meaning "to split," "to cut to pieces" (*keazein, sásati*). The *chaste* mother, then, necessary guarantor of patrilineal *caste,* must also exist as a kind of eunuch, symbolically dismembered by a phallic culture, severed from her own desire. But Dinesen playfully undoes these implications: technically chaste, having literally committed adultery with "no man" (9)—Benedetta nonetheless *cuts the father off* from his own lineage by effecting a symbolic substitution: if her first conception embodied "her husband's name," her second is decisively signed by her own.

As the narrative implies by having the Cardinal identify himself with his story, this drama of conception is also a scene of writing, figuratively parallel to that of Dinesen herself as the textual mother who uses the male signature to subvert the paternal name. She tacitly suggests here that her own unfathered texts, like the twins born of Benedetta's double, symbolically self-engendered pregnancy, are conceived in a "feminine" space, a confluence of body, music, and language—that aesthetic "free play of impulses" that she celebrated as inseparable from all great art (*LA,* 235).

Having authored and authorized her own pregnancy, Benedetta refuses to submit it to paternal editing, keeping "the happy state of things to herself" as "long as possible" (9)—a decision that provokes the paternal outburst with which this chapter began. "*Caprice de femme enceinte*": in several senses, the phrase arrests us. The flow of English falters at its French, a linguistic flagging given a further turn by the fiction that the English itself is a "translation" from the Cardinal's native Italian. By its sheer linguistic excess, then, the moment conspicuously invites its own explication. Since *enceinte* denotes not only "pregnant" but also "an enclosure or surrounding wall," and *caprice* names that which disrupts or transgresses confinement, we can read in Pompilio's exclamation a pointed, paradoxical expression of masculine anxiety about *un*bounded female desire, an anxiety repeatedly inscribed in revered Western texts from antiquity to the present—what Vico called the "infamous promiscuity" and Rousseau "the disorder of women," prime emblem of anarchy in a culture that defines itself through official androcentric boundary systems, those "lines" and "signs"—whether geographical, genealogical, or linguistic—that guarantee paternal sovereignty by restraining female sexuality and generativity.[51]

The caprice that so provokes Pompilio culminates in Benedetta's subsequent "shocking" contest with him over the right to name. In a comic anticipation of Irigaray's concept of woman's subversive "mimicry," Dinesen has the Princess stake her claim through a parodic repetition of Pompilio's own pronouncement. Significantly, this exchange transpires in a feminine space replete with images of fertility, Benedetta's "green boudoir, which overlooked the valley and the lake."

> He made her a little solemn speech. . . . If his patience was to be rewarded with the birth of a son, the infant should become a pillar of the Church. In order to find the right name for this future light of the family—*for a name is a reality, and a child is made known to himself by his name*—he had made his librarian go through the whole of the *Vitae Sanctorum,* and had settled upon the great Father of the Church St. Athanasius, who is known as "the Father of Orthodoxy." . . . The Princess . . . very quietly informed her husband that she too had been pondering the future and the name of her son, and had made up her mind. She had borne the house of her husband one son; now she was free. The child to come was to be the son of his mother. . . . His name should be Dionysio, in reminiscence of the God of inspired ecstasy, *for a name is a reality, and a child is made known to himself by his name.* (10–11; my emphasis)

Rendered significantly "speechless" "to hear his wife, to his face, defy Heaven and him," the Prince welcomes the subsequent birth of twins as a blessed resolution (12), but the doubling only restages the parental contest: Pompilio's "Atanasio" honors not only the life of "the father of Orthodoxy" but also his doctrine that the Son shares the Father's substance; Benedetta's "Dionysio" invokes not only "the god of inspired ecstasy"— a reiteration of her own at his symbolic conception—but also the feminine affiliations and androgynous, indeterminate sexuality of that god, reinforcing her claim that this son is "one of mind and body with her."[52] Despite the opposition their names proclaim, however, the boys are

"alike as two peas," distinguishable only by an external marker of difference, the blue silk ribbon tied round Dionysio's neck (13).[53]

"Once back with the mother," writes Geoffrey Hartman, "are we
not also with Dionysus and . . . Christ? There may not be a great distance, after all, between . . . Christ and Dionysus."[54] Dinesen evokes
precisely this convergence, not only recalling Nietzsche's representation
of the Dionysian mother's child but also anticipating more recent speculations on the maternal associations of both Christ and Dionysus. After
the twins are christened, an event that ritually splits father-text from
mother-text, Benedetta's passionate suckling of Dionysio—"like kisses,"
with "reciprocal givings and takings of vigor and bliss" (13–14)—enacts
an *imitatio virgo* that revives all the suppressed scandal of the Madonna as
Great Mother Goddess, the "Queen of Heaven" who, like Benedetta,
also conceived a "fatherless" son in a moment of divine in-spiration and
who, in countless iconographies, fondles her "infant . . . lover," as
Dinesen puts it, "in the manner of a grande amoreuse" (14). Such encounters constitute a "divine jest" indeed (14), but at the father's expense.[55] And like Benedetta's other maternal moments, these too become
inseparable from issues of signification, for as Walter Ong points out,
"The infant's contact with its mother is a distinctly oral and lingual one in
more ways than one. Tongues are used early for both suckling and speaking, and language is usually . . . learned while a child is still at the
breast. . . . First languages especially are associated with feeding, as all
languages are to some extent."[56] Thus it seems inevitable that the "exalted, flaming love" between mother and son—an explicit incarnation of
the *lingua materna*—should be literalized when a fire breaks out in the
patristically dominated library, and that the flames should consume the
paternal name and word—"old missives from the Holy See to a worthy
ancestor of the Prince"—before killing one of the twins (14–15).

Over the small person of the survivor, unidentifiable because the silk
ribbon has also been destroyed in the conflagration, the deferred parental
confrontation resumes in new form. Ostensibly the name of the father
prevails: the child grows up as "Atanasio," while "Dionysio" is supposedly buried both literally and figuratively—reduced to a cryptic inscription on "a marble tablet in the family mausoleum" (16). Yet while
outwardly "submissive" to this paternal rewriting, the mother covertly
renews her power. For though the silk ribbon has vanished, a "long
burn" etched on the child's left cheek leaves a "scar" that she reads as a
sign that this child is hers. As confirmation, she gives him the secret
name "Pyrrha," simultaneously recalling the feminine name given to the
transvestite Achilles by his mother in *Achilles at Scyros,* the opera through
which Benedetta had symbolically conceived Dionysio; the fiery redness
of dionysian spirits and blissful fires of dionysiac maternal jouissance;

and, finally, what might be termed a *maternalingually* induced resurrection—both son's and mother's—from the ashes of their "flaming love."

The difference *between* becomes the difference *within*. "[A]dopting
and perfecting . . . the doubleness of his elders," the boy grows up forever of two minds, a contested text whom his parents read "in totally
different lights" (18–19).[57] Ineluctably self-divided, he baffles interpretation: "you may meet one of the two, speak to him and listen to him . . .
and at the hour of parting be unable to decide with which of them you
have spent the day" (20). Publically a father of the church and later "sole
heir to the great name and wealth of the family," he appears to uphold the
paternal order at every level, especially after Benedetta dies. Yet even
after death, the mother lives on, inhabiting her son, speaking her story
through his voice. He finds her haunting presence-in-absence in the
"faint fragrance" still emanating from her empty "flask of perfume," a
relic evoking her elusive, "multitudinous" maternal *essence* (20).[58] It is his
prayer to her—not to the father—that he recounts (17), fulfilling the literal meaning of her name as "Blessed" one and suggesting that the
priest's official benediction may be subversively transposed as the concealed artist's true prayer, "*In nomine Matris.*"

Finally, however, the order of the father appears to reassert its domination. Dinesen shows that even the Cardinal, for all his disclosures,
would at last repress the unsettling discourse of the mother. We have seen
how, as a condition for telling the tale at all, he has symbolically dismantled his identity, revealing the maternal power veiled behind "His
Eminence." Toward the end of his narrative, however, he begins to reverse this divestiture, symbolically *redressing* himself through—and in—
the habits of the father, by attempting, in effect, to deny what he has just
uncovered—to displace, disclaim, and distance the mother.

Two pivotal moments mark this conversion. The first occurs immediately after his narrative of Atanasio's dual accession to the order(s) of
the father—as priest and heir to the paternal name and estate. Now
he seeks to reverse his former filial relation to his mother—to become,
both ritually and rhetorically, *her* father—by subjecting her to symbolic
diminution: "Even that fair lady the Princess Benedetta, like to a child at
eventide, yawned and let go of her dolls. Her son, by then a bishop, had
the happiness of administering extreme unction to her"—a "happiness"
with ominously dual implications. The second moment forecloses the
evocative passage about the reliquary flask. Here an actual syntactic rupture—a dash—marks the splitting of consciousness precipitated by the
moment of denial: "a multitude of things were in [the flask], all in one.
Smiles . . . and tears, dauntlessness and fears, unconquerable hope and
certainty of failure—*in short: what will, I suppose, be found in the belongings
of most deceased ladies*" (20; my emphasis). Dinesen underscores this tonal

shift into dismissive condescension by locating it shortly after the Cardinal's reverent celebration of the mother as a woman who, out of the most extreme confinement, against odds that "would have perplexed and bewildered" any "man," has "dethroned," "overpowered and laid low" both this Father's father and his prideful paternal erections—all those *enceintes* that would keep her *in place* (17–18).

In exposing the Cardinal's defensiveness against the mother, Dinesen ironizes his subsequent foray into literary criticism, those dicta generally cited as Karen Blixen's own naked, unmediated credo. The Cardinal begins with an undeniably Blixenesque claim: "the divine art is the story. In the beginning was the story. At the end we shall . . . view, and review it" (24). This vision of the world-as-text, generated as in Genesis and the Fourth Gospel out of the divine *Logos,* seems at first incontestably congruent with the patriarchal Judeo-Christian tradition that the priest, as "artist," represents.[59] But we cannot read these claims neutrally, in isolation from the Cardinal's preceding narrative. And that "story," as the term "review" implies, exerts a strong *revisionary* pressure on them, calling their fundamental categories into question. For "The Cardinal's First Tale" has shown that neither "story" nor generative *Logos* originate with the father (whether Yahweh, Pompilio, the Cardinal, or "Isak" Dinesen). Their real "source" is the mother (whether Great Goddess, Benedetta, or Karen Blixen)—she who "willed the world" into existence as she wished it, like a fiction (17).[60] This reading is reinforced by the Cardinal's figure of "the story" as the "evaporated bouquet" of an uncorked "bottle of noble wine" (24), a trope homologous to his earlier image of the mother's presence-in-absence in the evanescent "fragrance" of her empty perfume flask. Even as he attempts to deny the mother's continuing power, then, his very language reinscribes it, equating it symbolically with the power of "the story" itself.

This ironic discrepancy invites a rather more skeptical reading of the Cardinal's narratology than critics have usually favored. It is surely no accident that this tale conflating genre with gender, text with sex, should close with a generic meditation that makes the difference between "hero" and "heroine," "masculine" and "feminine," a figure for the dynamics of "the story." But it is precisely *because* the narrative has repeatedly interrogated such rigid oppositions—has revealed difference to be as much an internal as an external dynamic—that the Cardinal's sex-typed categories seem inadequate to the more complex and radical conception of "self" and "story" to which his very being—and his text—bear eloquent witness. His own tale has already discredited that symbolic economy wherein "a young woman . . . by the sole virtue of being [female] becomes a prize of the hero and the reward of his every exploit." Indeed, the story of Pompilio and Benedetta undermines this system, and the narrative of Atanasio/Dionysio ruptures it entirely, revealing the "hero" so pervasively inhabited by the "heroine" that neither he nor we know *who* says "I" when the Cardinal—who is also the "story"—speaks. Dinesen suggests that every speech act, every text, every self-enunciating subject operates in doubleness and difference; and that the incarnation of this disconcerting, destabilizing process is the capricious, duplicitous *femme enceinte,* that moving figure whose "story" inflects the Cardinal's at every level.

To return, then, to the question of the frame: to answer it, the Cardinal has told a story—a phrase which, in the colloquial lexicons of both English and Danish, nicely associates artistry with lying. Its end, in both senses, is the death of the mother. Through storytelling, the priestly father appears to contain—incorporate and encrypt—the mother who made him. But even as he enfolds her in his discourse, seeking thereby a hermeneutically grounded mastery over her (and thus himself), he ineluctably discloses her continuing power as a mobile, uncontainable force, eloquent and compelling as the fragrance of her womblike flask or "the divine art of the story." Dinesen suggests that to bury the mother as immediate presence is only to allow her a more expansive imaginative freedom; repressed, her power intensifies. Like the mother of the text itself, if she seems to be erased, it is only to reinvent herself from a different ground. In "The Cardinal's First Tale," her dis-covery is the Story of the story.

In this sense, the mother's effacement becomes symbolically equivalent to the loss of the silk ribbon. The external marker of maternal power disappears, but the duplicity it signified remains as a scar, branded into the very flesh of the priestly father who, like the Father of Genesis or the Fourth Gospel, speaks the story we read into existence. As a graphic trace of a loss and an absence, this stigma hieroglyphically signs the "father" as the mother's text even as it marks the site of her erasure. Thus it becomes figuratively equivalent to the signature "Isak Dinesen" on Karen Blixen's literary *corpus,* a sign wherein the mother, with ultimate capriciousness, is always simultaneously present and absent, named and unnamed.

The conclusion reasserts this connection. For here Dinesen rewrites the inaugural question of identity explicitly as a question of the "authority" behind the "story": not only "who speaks?" but "in whose name?"

> "The lady in black stood still, sunk in thought. . . . 'My friend,' she said, 'I see and understand, by now, that . . . the Master whom you serve is very great. . . . Yet . . . are you sure . . . that it is God . . . ?' . . . 'That,' he said, '. . . is a risk which the artists and the priests of the world have to run.'" (26)

If not God, then who? The answer is perhaps less obvious than might at first appear. Indeed, in keeping with the ambiguity that inhabits this story at every level, the unspoken Other here—so deeply dangerous that s/he cannot even be named—may well be not one, but two (or more): mother or devil, demonic mother or maternal demon, a figure multiply transgressive of the law of the father. The root sense of *diabolic* is, after all, doubleness.[61] This possibility finds support in Karen Blixen's earlier speculations, in her letters, on her own "calling" as a kind of "priest" and on her artistic conceptions as the products of an alliance with "my angel Lucifer" (*LA,* 281–82, 246–49). As we shall see, throughout her life she would represent herself in these terms, envisioning her work as demonic and revolutionary, a craft like that of the witch, whose rites and writings parodically invert and subvert the orthodoxies of the patristic order.

These implications further illuminate Dinesen's choice of authorial signature. Langbaum rightly observes that "in taking the pseudonym Isak—which means laughter—she must have remembered Sarah, who laughed when she bore Isaac because she thought it a fine jest of the Lord's to give her, after a lifetime of barrenness, a child in her old age. 'And Sarah said, God hath made me laugh, so that all that hear will laugh with me' (Gen. 21:6)."[62] But we might go further. As "the one who laughs" Dinesen announces her own eruptive, ironic voice beneath the vatic patriarchal mask of the narrator and reminds us that Isaac was, after all, as much the embodiment of his mother's laughter—originally a challenge to masculine authority—as of the Father's "word" (Gen. 18:10–12). By claiming *Isaac* as the name of the mother Dinesen implicitly destabilizes the formulaic triad that epitomizes Western patriarchal genealogy— "Abraham, Isaac, and Jacob"—by appropriating and feminizing its central term. Moreover, in a text which focuses like Genesis 2 on names and naming as signifiers of authority, Dinesen's self-nomination, especially her appropriation of a patriarchal name, is tantamount to claiming in yet another sense her own oblique access to both language and subjectivity.[63] In "The Cardinal's First Tale," which as much as any text she ever wrote concerns itself with patrilineal succession, filiation, and patriarchal authority, the irony of the pseudonym is particularly acute. For as the fatherless "son" of an authoring mother, *Isak* represents the quintessence of textual illegitimacy.

3. Reconceiving Writing

A feminine text cannot fail to be more than subversive. It is volcanic; as it is written it brings about an upheaval of the old property crust, carrier of masculine investments. . . , in order to . . . shatter the framework of institutions, to blow up the law, to break up the truth with laughter.

Hélène Cixous, "The Laugh of the Medusa"

This reading of the conclusion retrospectively illuminates certain crucial connections between the diverse meanings of *caprice,* connections that take us beyond the story at hand to the larger questions engendered by the juxtapositions of Isak Dinesen and theories of sexual difference. So far, I have focused only on the term's more familiar denotations of deviation, eccentricity, playfulness—meanings that recall the long misogynist tradition of woman as the capricious term, the *barbarism* in phallic discourse, the "disorder" that must be cured or curbed, kept in line within a paternalized *enceinte.* But etymologically, *caprice* also means "a head with the hair standing on end" (*capo* + *riccio*), hence shivering, horror (cf. Italian *capricciarre,* "to shudder"). Indeed, the confrontation with the absent mother is precisely what Freud identified as the deepest mechanism at work in the experience of the uncanny, the *unheimlich*—that anxiety generated by an encounter with something simultaneously alien and intimate, strange yet hauntingly "familiar": "old-established in the mind [but] alienated from it . . . by the process of repression."[64] As Freud observed in explaining his male patients' feelings that "there is something uncanny [*unheimliche*] about the female genitals," the ultimate "*heimliche*"—hence *unheimliche*—place is the entrance to the womb; "the former *Heim* (home) of all human beings, . . . the mother's body" (245). Similarly, Freud elsewhere suggested analogies between the sight of the mother's genitals, chilling the male child with castration terrors, and the Medusa's head.[65] And of course that uncanny head, with its serpentine "hairs" standing on end, is, quite literally, a *caprice.* Thus it is to this *unheimlich heim,* this *caprice,* to which, all unexpectedly, shockingly, fearfully, the uncanny moment transports the male subject again, in a hair-raising *frisson* of recognition.

Reading *caprice* as *uncanny* in this light opens up new interpretive possibilities to explain the Prince's dismissive ridicule of his pregnant wife's covertness. For as Freud observes, *heimlich* means not only that which is "familiar and congenial"—literally homey (cf. Danish *hyggelic*)—but also "that which is concealed," secret (225–56). "The Cardinal's First Tale" suggests, as we have seen, that the *hidden* mother(hood) is precisely that unacknowledged source of power the father most deeply fears and defends against. Read in this context, the prince's apparently casual ridicule of Benedetta's concealment (like the Cardinal's apparently casual dismissal of her life) in fact discloses the father's terror of precisely that about which he makes light: the *caprice* of the mother, in its several senses, carrying as it does the covert possibility of a willful, potentially castrating power that if released might uproot and overwhelm not only these fathers and their sacred genealogical successions, but the phallocentric symbolic order that genealogy represents and erects itself upon.

Freud himself, of course, speaks from a phallocentric position. The primary patients to whom he refers in his analysis of the uncanny were male. But if, as recent feminist psychoanalytic theories suggest, a woman's relation to the mother is strikingly different from a man's, then what Freud claims operates for men as the deepest source of ambivalence and fear may perhaps evoke for a woman more positive responses, responses more closely allied with the implications of playful freedom and revelry inherent in the alternative definitions of *caprice*.[66] Margaret Homans offers an acute summary:

> Our recent mythographers, from Freud to Lacan's current explicators, view [the girl's] continued preoedipal attachment to the mother as the daughter's tragedy because it means she is deprived of the experience they value most highly. Freud argues that a girl's superego is relatively weak because she is wounded from birth and cannot be castrated a second time; because women are thus not susceptible to the threats of the father's law, they lack the well-developed moral and ethical sense of men. . . . And yet from the daughter's point of view, there might be another and more positive way of viewing [her] continued attachment to the mother. Only in an androcentric culture would it be considered tragic for a girl not to experience pain, if that pain is preeminently a masculine experience.[67]

Comparably, "The Cardinal's First Tale" suggests that for a woman *caprice* is not horror, but pleasure, not repression but liberation, not castration but *jouissance,* the laughing gesture toward an *elsewhere* from which the mother, though deprived of voice, name, and authority, may yet speak, writing her creative difference in the gaps—or, to borrow Dinesen's words, the "open spaces"—of language.[68] The text of her pleasure is a distinctively feminine *capriccio,* for that term also signifies a rare, playful, and paradoxical art like the "deceptive cadenza," a "language" of the "irregular" at which Benedetta—and Isak Dinesen—are expert.[69]

If, as critical tradition holds, " 'The Cardinal's First Tale' sums up . . . the essence of Isak Dinesen's work,"[70] then what it suggests about the engendering of narrative invites a rereading of Dinesen's entire oeuvre. "God loves a jest": so runs her famous phrase. Since "God" within her literary lexicon signifies the ultimate artist, the assertion intimates that the finest jest of all might well issue from the mother of the texts, whose duplicity defies the limits of those representational frames within which androcentric criticism would place her. It is no accident that one who repeatedly analogized her own writing to the "divine jest" of the Madonna as "grande amoreuse" would recall through her pseudonym the "laughter" that originated in a woman's concealed mockery of a paternally conceived conception. As her choice of signature suggests, the texts' ultimate jester—ludic inverter and capricious contradiction of the father's law—was the author herself.

In a passage from "Tales of Two Old Gentlemen" that echoes "The

Cardinal's First Tale," she makes these connections explicit. The two elderly interlocutors are speculating on the unfathomable contradictions of life. "I arrived at the conviction," remarks one, "that we should . . . understand the nature and the laws of the Cosmos if we would from the beginning recognize its originator and upholder as being of the female sex . . . Divine Mother of the Universe" (*LT,* 64, 67), for only "ladies" can "move with such perfect freedom in such severely regulated figures," maintaining a thorough "understanding" of "Paradox" (66,68). The passage reflexively illuminates Dinesen's own position as "originator" of her textual cosmos. In creating the illusion, literally the playful mockery (Lat. *illudo*), of a masculine stance, perspective, and voice—"perfectly regulated figures"—but rendering it ironically her own, she at once defuses and infuses it with the "freedom" of woman's paradoxical Word, the playful poly-logos that animates her texts.

Reconceiving "Isak Dinesen," then—to return to our point of departure—offers a model of a certain "feminine" critical practice: a capricious art that would elude paternally conceived *enceintes,* rereading woman's much-deplored marginality as a powerful positive position, both for the perspective it offers for a critique of the center—and the centrisms—of the fathers, and as an ever-moving site of vision, horizon rather than limit. And if, from a patriarchal perspective, such capriciousness makes women Medusas, Dinesen would seem to share Cixous's view that the Medusa is terrible only to those immured within phallocentric confinements: women who look beyond those walls may rediscover her as a figure of joyous liberation—a reflection of themselves reread. I refer, of course, to "The Laugh of the Medusa." As an entry into the following readings of one who named herself "laughter," I could hardly do better than to quote it more fully:

> They riveted us between two horrifying myths: between the Medusa and the abyss . . . anchored in the dogma of castration. . . . But . . . isn't the worst, in truth, that women aren't castrated, that they have only to stop listening to the . . . men . . . for history to change its meaning? You have only to look at the Medusa straight on to see her. And she's not deadly. She's beautiful, and she's laughing.

2

Becoming "Isak Dinesen": The Fiction of the Author

> She had a great variety of selves to call upon, far more than we have been able to find room for.
>
> Virginia Woolf, *Orlando*

The laughter that reverberates in Dinesen's pseudonym did not come easily. Before turning to her other fictions, I want to consider the events that led to their inscription. Those events, of course, are now themselves inscriptions: the letters, memoirs, essays, iconographies, records of oral narratives, and diverse other documents that make up the stuff of biography, that life-writing that intersects with an author's texts.[1] With that condition in mind, I propose what follows as a kind of reading—one of many possible explications of Dinesen's life scripts and the narratives they engendered.

I

The outlines of the story are well known. Born in Denmark in 1885 to a family of country gentry, Karen Christentze Dinesen—called Tanne, later Tania, by those who knew her best—felt her difference acutely from her earliest years. Her mother Ingeborg Westenholz Dinesen had had her own more daring impulses stifled by the rigorous social conditioning to which girls of her class and era were routinely subjected, "merely," as Karen Blixen would later write bitterly of her own situation, "because they belong[ed] to the female sex" (*LA*, 250). But Ingeborg's apparently docile capitulation to domesticity was deceptive; for in her marriage, as her daughter later observed, she obliquely asserted herself anew, selecting as husband a man who was already a legendary black sheep, neither "good" nor "secure" by Westenholz standards (*LA*, 380).[2] Wilhelm Dinesen was an author, adventurer, and sometime soldier of fortune whose allure is at least partially attributable to the passionate conviction with which he adopted these essentially literary roles. Having been disappointed in various quixotic military ventures, he enacted the nineteenth-century American dream—another masculine topos—more fully than most Americans, "lighting out for the territories" early in life to spend two years among the Chippewa in the North American wilderness.[3] Returning at last to a more staid existence as *pater familias,* he would turn his adventures to text in *Jagtbreve* (*Letters from the Hunt*), a Thoreauvian memoir that became a minor classic in Danish literature and a major paternal precursor to *Out of Africa.* Wilhelm nurtured both the imagination and the unconventionality of his daughter, whose talents as an artist and a writer became apparent in early childhood. He nurtured, too, her longing for escape from the confines of a bourgeois Danish existence, which, as Isak Dinesen would ruefully remark, offered women few outlets beyond "*Kirche, Kinder,* [and] *Küche*" (*Essays,* 68). The relation of father and daughter, beginning with her own representations of it from childhood onward and perpetuated by biographers and critics alike, would assume mythic proportions, appearing to reiterate in its individual contours the law of the Father as a construct and constructor of the daughter's text.[4]

In reading the lineaments of Isak Dinesen's life and work, the critical tradition has construed this familial romance as the chief impetus of her creativity, establishing an opposition between "father" and "mother" that privileges the former term while implicitly or explicitly denigrating the latter. Judith Thurman's dichotomy, in a chapter significantly bearing the Kierkegaardian title "Either/Or," is paradigmatic: "Isak Dinesen was born to two people who embodied very different attitudes to life. . . . From her childhood [she] saw the two families as antitheses, one infinitely alluring, the other infinitely problematic. . . . In [her] revolt [against her mother's family], her father was an ally and an inspiration. . . . Indeed, when Isak Dinesen uses the word 'life' it is often synonymous with the word 'father.'" And later: "There is in Dinesen's work and thinking a frontier—more of a fixed circle . . .—that separates the wild from the domestic. Within it there is firelight and women's voices . . . , the clockwork of women's lives. Beyond it there are passions, spaces, grandeurs; there lie the wildernesses and battlefields. Wilhelm led his daughter out of the domestic limbo into the 'wild.' . . . He gave her a taste of a man's life, uninhibited and sensual, which was an alternative to the limited world of the women. . . . For all the women in the household—before her sisters and even before her mother—Wilhelm had chosen her. This was the decisive privilege of her life."[5]

Such a model yields a Karen Blixen who was intensely, even obsessively, androcentric—a common characterization which has had important formative effects on the interpretive tradition surrounding her work. In spite of the labyrinthine structures and multiple ambiguities that make Dinesen's fictions so difficult to categorize, most studies, whatever their diversities, have asserted her single-minded devotion to values associated with a reactionary, masculinist ideology, centered on the concept of a single, sovereign (and paradigmatically male) "self" and grounded in a strongly hierarchized, patricentric worldview. Extrapolating from a bipolar reading of the life that stresses her lifelong attachment to the aristocratic value system her father represented, critics find in the work a consistent defense of the ancien régime which assumes the privileges of class and property, exalts chivalric codes, authorizes the paternal name, and sanctifies patrilineal genealogy.[6]

Now there is no doubt that Karen Blixen chafed against the social mores and gender codes represented and enforced by her maternal relatives—especially her mother's mother (known to all as "Mama")—and associated her father with liberation from those constrictions (see, e.g., *LA*, 245, 250). Nor is there any question that she idealized and idolized her father, the more so after his suicide in 1895 left her with the mixed grief, guilt, and desolate sense of abandonment classic in children who suffer such losses.[7] The *horror vacui* of which she frequently wrote as an adult bears traces of the abyssal quality of this, the first of the many devastating bereavements she would suffer en route to becoming "Isak Dinesen." Her feelings about Wilhelm were classic in another sense as well, for in traditional patriarchal societies many of the most creative, independent, and unconventional women are the daughters of strong, supportive—and often also seductive—fathers. Such connections are hardly surprising, given the power the figure of the father exerts in the psychological formation of the subject in Western culture. But in accepting the androcentric, dichotomous model on which such oppositions rest, one risks occluding the differences between (and within) daughters and sons—the consequence of differently acculturated relations to both mother and father. They are differences which, as we have seen, a gynocritical analysis may read otherwise than phallocentric psychoanalytic paradigms appear to allow.[8]

One risks, as well, taking at face value the apparently patriarchal discourse of aristocracy that emerges in Dinesen's life and work. I leave aside the most obvious difficulty of ascribing to a woman an unproblematic nostalgia for a feudal system within which, as Nancy Miller astutely remarks, "the only destabilizing difference is sexual."[9] Given its predication on male agency, female objectification, and the legal subordination of women, such a system could hardly mean the same thing for a female author—even one who may appear, like Karen Blixen, to have internalized its worldview to a high degree—that it might for a man. Even a woman who consciously seeks to ratify its claims must at very least position herself differently than a man, must engage in a more complicated process of rationalization and self-construction in order to identify with its dominant ideologies. From this perspective, its function in both Karen Blixen's life and Isak Dinesen's texts needs to be read as problematic rather than self-evident. An analysis might well begin with Karen Blixen's own substantial critique of the gender politics of the ancien régime.[10] But even if we grant that the received traditionalist views represent accurate accounts of one aspect of her life text and fictional world, we must nevertheless observe that they arise from and perpetuate a highly circumscribed conception of her writing that responds primarily to manifest content while eliding structural, syntactic, and symbolic elements that disturb, contradict, and complicate that surface. Finally, we also risk overlooking the disruptive feminine text that may be deciphered from the same biographical materials, the equally significant rage and fear the figure of the father may inspire in his seemingly dutiful daughter, and the literary consequences thereof.[11]

Even if the arguable assumption that fiction reinscribes biography be granted, for example, we can observe that for every condemnation Karen Blixen registered of "woman's sphere," there are equally powerful letters castigating "the old laws and ideals" that constituted that sphere and celebrating women's emancipation as the most powerful force for cultural transformation in the modern world.[12] One of the crucial sites for a reading of her responses to these interactive issues is the text of her letters to her mother's sister Bess Westenholz, one of Denmark's leading feminist activists. Despite Karen Blixen's impatience with her aunt's tendencies toward rigidity and increasing conservatism, their correspondence provided her both the theoretical apparatus and the major forum for the radical discourse on woman she would articulate during her years in Africa, passionate speculations on feminism and women's subjection that thread like a leitmotiv throughout the letters, interwoven with her reflections on her own developing vocation as a writer.[13] As pre-texts for the fiction itself, epistolary commentaries composed in some cases while she was crafting her early tales, these letters offer a compelling interpretive perspective on the relation of gender to the engendering of her narratives.

Further, and perhaps more important, for every ambivalent or negative statement she made about her mother, there are at least as many equally intense declarations of love, devotion, and gratitude—passages that prompt a careful rereading of the mother-daughter text in both the *Letters* and the fiction. Prefiguring an image connected in her later texts with woman's subversive writing, she represents her mother as "*word of God made flesh,*" a redemptive feminine Christ figure whom the daughter would address repeatedly and ardently as "beloved snow-white Lamb."[14] Her persistent associations of Ingeborg with the imagery of music, "the sound of waves from the Sound," burgeoning wild nature, and paradisial blessedness—images to which I shall return—recall the aptly named Benedetta's blissful immersion in the semiotic.[15] It is tempting to speculate that if Karen Dinesen left Denmark in part to avoid becoming (like) her mother, the very distance she put between them enabled her to begin to read both herself and her mother *otherwise*. Even when expressing most strongly her differences from Ingeborg—in every sense a crucial project for the daughter who, in traditional Western culture, is at risk of developing inadequate ego boundaries between self and (m)other— Karen Blixen also moved increasingly toward a new conception of her.[16] The letters evolve a reconfiguration of the mother-daughter bonds—in both the positive and the negative senses of that term—whereby the daughter eludes a feared engulfment in the very process of *writing (to) the mother*, redefining both her mother and herself as separate, yet intensely interactive, subjects.[17] Certainly, a powerful thematics of secrecy runs throughout the correspondence, the covert injunction not to "tell Mother" becoming a recurrent code whereby the daughter seeks to claim an unsanctioned space for her own transgressive impulses.[18] Yet one also finds an insistent counterthematics to this injunction of silence and separation. For each time the mother learns what her daughter has feared to tell, she responds not as censoring voice of the law but as transgressive subject in her own right, a willing co-conspirator and advocate of the daughter's freedom and separateness.[19] She becomes, that is, *another* mother than the law allowed or than the daughter had feared (for).

Indeed, one stunning effect of the editorial arrangement of *Letters from Africa* is that it permits, quite literally, the voice of the mother *as subject* to emerge at last from her daughter's text: one of the final letters in the collection, the only one not authored by Karen Blixen, was written by Ingeborg Dinesen on the eve of her daughter's departure from Africa. And what it records is not the suppression but the celebration of the daughter's difference:

> The sole consideration for me is that she should live according to her nature. . . . She has often caused me anxiety, probably more than any other of my children, but she has filled my life with so much love, so much festivity, I have been,—and am—so proud of her, that whatever she may come to do I will always love and bless her. I would rather never see her again than that she should feel herself 'incarcerated.' . . . I think the worst possible thing that could happen would be to lure or push her into a situation that oppressed her. . . .[20]

In the light of such reflections, it is not surprising that as their relationship matured, what Karen Blixen came to perceive as quintessentially maternal was the "mobility of spirit" that she herself celebrated as the prerequisite and product of creative freedom.[21] The most frequent of her

recurrent figures for her mother is the image of fertile natural landscape—that ancient maternal topos which Isak Dinesen would invest
with radically subversive implications in later texts like "The Poet,"
"The Caryatids," "Sorrow-acre," or "A Country Tale." [22] Mapping a
blissful mother–daughter erotics before or beyond the imposition of the
father's law, it is a trope at once of nurturance and openness, security and
liberation: "To return to one's mother and feel her arms around one is the
same eternal, natural miracle as when the trees break into leaf every year;
the bleak and open fields where one is buffeted by all the winds of the
world suddenly arch over into a shelter, a hiding place, yet so free and
alive and fresh, everything bows down over one as if to bless one, and
when one goes on again, that blessing remains with one always" (*LA,* 53;
cf. 311.) And increasingly, this topos becomes metaphorically interchangeable with the daughter's mythic figurations of the "wild world" of
Africa with which she herself identified: "I want to thank you once
more,—thousands and thousands of times,—for coming out here; . . .
Everything here has acquired significance, a kind of gleam like that the
evening sun gives to the Ngong Hills; you have tuned all the various
strings here and in my life with your light beloved hand so that they play
together in harmony." [23]

Correlatively, as Anders Westenholz has persuasively demonstrated,
Karen Blixen's insistent idealization of her father concealed a surplus of
repressed anger. [24] Among the most telling instances of her intense, interlocking ambivalences toward a father she simultaneously idolized and re-
sented and a mother she both distanced and adored is a letter to Ingeborg
Dinesen in 1921. First distinguishing between her mother's family and
the mother herself ("For after all it is *you* who represent 'home' to me and
that I love best in Denmark"), she continues:

> I think my greatest misfortune was Father's death. Father under-
> stood me as I was, although I was so young, and loved me for my-
> self. . . . [I]f I can . . . make something of myself again, . . . then it
> is Father who has done it for me. It is his blood and his mind that will
> bring me through it. . . .
>
> No doubt each one of your children thinks that he or she loves
> you most, and so do I. . . . I think that there is something in the way
> I love you that resembles the way Father loved you. For me you are
> the most beautiful and wonderful person in the world; merely the
> fact that you are alive makes the whole world different; where you
> are there is peace and harmony, shade and flowing springs, birds
> singing; to come to where you are is like entering 'heaven.'
>
> And so you must allow me to write to you as you would have
> allowed Father to write. Without showing it to anyone. . . . Don't
> let them make you see it in their way; understand me, as only *you*

can. And imagine that Father is sitting beside you perhaps talking anxiously too about this child of yours out here. . . . Yes, talk about me to Father. It is really he who is responsible, for he deserted me and must have seen that things were not going to be easy for me. (*LA,* 110–11)

As the dizzying positional and emotional shifts in this passage suggest, even as Karen Blixen's writing figures as an extension of a practice associated with "Father," it also operates as a displacement of him, a process whereby she would in effect *take his place* through an appropriative move that allowed her (as one of several readings of her male pseudonym would suggest) to "father" herself—and to "husband," in both senses of the word, her mother as an endless source of generativity. While appearing to be thoroughly androcentric, a wholehearted embrace of the Name-of-the-Father at every level, such a gesture is complicated by Dinesen's ambiguous position(s) as daughter. In taking the place of the father, a woman may undo, rather than simply reinscribe, the masculine oedipal paradigm, for within a patrilineal symbolic order predicated on men's right to exchange women, a daughter who construes herself as subject is doubly disruptive: her sexual difference effects not only the murder, via displacement, of the father, but a dismantling, via rewriting, of the paradigm whereby woman serves only as mother/object for the masculine subject.[25] Notably, in Karen Blixen's later critique of the "old world order" in which "women . . . were excluded" from all but domesticity, reduced to the status of ciphers that "somehow . . . did not exist until the men came home," it is her father whom she cites as a prime negative example (*LA,* 263). Simultaneously, as so often throughout her correspondence, she assumes in the same letter a tone at once maternal, sororal, and passional toward Ingeborg (frequently addressed, diminutively, as "My own . . . little Mother," or figured through imagery that recalls the tropes of courtly love poetry) even while continuing to operate as a daughter for whom mother is *the* subject, in both senses. In moving thus fluidly across and outside traditional subject positions, Karen Blixen questions the regulatory boundaries whereby identities are signified and fixed within a masculinist psychosexual economy.

The very need on the part of readers to construct "father" and "mother" as oppositional terms, to privilege the former and denigrate the latter, points to the larger theoretical context within which Dinesen's discourse on gender evolved. Throughout her writings she would condemn what she called the "disease . . . of dualism."[26] As the texts we have examined illustrate, a careful reading of the letters suggests that what Dinesen rejected was neither her mother nor her own femaleness, but the confining place and idea of "woman" for which "mother" serves as synecdoche within the traditional gender codes of Western culture, which insure, as Karen Blixen wittily observed, that "a mother is a martyr." [27] In such a system, she would angrily declare, woman was debarred from "all the glories and possibilities of the world": "No work, no talent, no form of productivity could pay women anything nearly so much as pleasing, or making themselves necessary to a man" (*LA,* 261). As she wrote to her brother,

> it may . . . be that because you are so much younger than I am and a man as well you find it easier than I to avoid a feeling of bitterness where the old laws and ideals are concerned. It is easy to judge a defeated opponent with impartiality and appreciation, one can even come to have some fondness for him and see his regime as something poetic or idyllic; but while he held the power he was still just as unbearable for all that. [W]here the case of the emancipation of women is concerned, I myself feel, despite my affection for much that was beautiful and graceful in the old ideals, despite my gratitude toward those old women who struck the first blow for our freedom and independence, that the accounts have not been quite settled with a world, a system . . . that with a perfectly clear conscience allowed practically all my abilities to lie fallow and passed me on to charity or prostitution. . . . I find it intolerable to "be an object." [28]

Anticipating recent feminist speculations, she developed an astute critique of a symbolic order in which "humanity" is equated with maleness and "'womanliness' signifies those qualities in a woman . . . that [are] pleasing to men, or that they have need of." [29] She deplores social systems that "make . . . women solely sexual beings, . . . real prisoners": "To me the protective role played by men has something . . . unbalanced about it. . . . All my life I have cared more for Diana than for Venus . . . however many rose gardens and dove-drawn coaches she may have." [30] As she would observe in a passage from *Modern Marriage* that echoes both Wollstonecraft's *Vindication of the Rights of Woman* and Mill's *Subjection of Women,* the "inequality" engendered by such a system—in which a woman "knew that the whole life, welfare and property of herself and her children were utterly dependent on" man—was tantamount to "slavery," warping both "the slaveowner" and the "slave" with its "tyranny." [31] It is especially destructive for women who would be artists, depriving them of that sense of "play" or "bliss"—Dinesen's version of *jouissance*—necessary to both loving and creating: "'The best side of my nature reveals itself in play, and play is sacred.'" "But there has been some inequality here, and women were not in a position where they could play, even when they had a predisposition to do so" (*MM,* 80, 84). In a passage from the letters crucial to her own authorial project, she observes that a social regime that would circumscribe female creativity within the limits of male desire enforces a strategy of accommodation in women who seek at once artistic expression and professional success:

> Men had no particular need for or pleasure from, and therefore no need to encourage, women painters, sculptors, composers,—but they did for dancers, actresses, singers, and it was . . . sensible . . . for artistically gifted women to adopt such careers. A man might well be attracted to and admire a woman who took a passionate interest in the stars, or who cultivated flowers with which to beautify his home; but she would be sinning against the idea of womanliness if she sought to establish a direct relationship with nature in these branches by taking up astronomy or botany,—for how could such ambitions have anything to do with him and his happiness?[32]

As we shall see, one of Dinesen's most persistent tropes for the liberation of woman's desire, power, and creativity was the metaphor of flight, a figure later used by theorists like Cixous and Claudine Herrmann.[33] In the letters she began to elaborate its implications:

> I once read an article on feminism written by a man, . . . which . . . criticized women for their foolish efforts to acquire the glories of life on their own initiative when they could get them so much more easily through a man who loved them. In his argument he used the fable of a flying competition held among all the birds of the world in which . . . the eagle mounted to a great height by means of a great effort and then the little goldcrest,—which had hidden itself in the eagle's feathers . . . [and thus] flew a very little bit higher still—won the first prize. He felt that this illustrated how a woman could gain everything in the world for herself by allowing herself to be supported by a man . . . instead of in sheer foolishness attempting to take an independent part in life's flying competition. . . . The only way to reply to all this is: but what if we *want* to fly ourselves!? . . . And if we show that we can do it,—then why shouldn't we? (*LA*, 261–62).

She would argue that given the predication of Western culture on the sort of sexual hierarchy she here contests, the most important revolution of the modern world was that inaugurated by a feminist critique that would not only modify the sociopolitical system but begin to dismantle the psychosymbolic order by which androcentrism operates:

> In its present-day form [feminism] has come to mean something very different from what was signified by the term when it was first evolved three-quarters of a century ago. I think that one can see now that those who were at that time filled with horror at the thought of women being made eligible to take the student examination and

thought that that would bring about the collapse of the whole existing state of things . . . were right, it did collapse, and took very
much more with it than they had thought possible; and that is what
always happens whenever the very possibility of criticism and radical
change in an area previously considered to be raised above it, or
immune from it, enters the consciousness. . . . I consider that "feminism" . . . on the whole . . . should be regarded as the most significant movement of the nineteenth century, and that the upheavals it
has caused are far from "*done with*" at the present moment; for it has
not reached its goals by having made it possible for women to become lawyers, doctors, priests, etc., by a new marriage law and
equal right of inheritance for women and for men; all these things are
only manifestations of the far deeper rooted movement. If I were
asked what this movement does consist of, I would reply that . . .
women now,—in direct contrast to what was previously the case,—
desire and are striving to be human beings with a direct relationship
to life in the same way as men have done and do this. (*LA*, 258–59;
cf. *MM*, 82–83)

Judith Thurman, expressing a common view, asserts that Dinesen
ultimately rejected "feminism."[34] But we might well ask, "which feminism?" The suffrage movement to which Bess Westenholz subscribed
was indeed problematic for her niece; it emerged, like a comparable
major strain of nineteenth-century American feminism, from Protestant,
quasi-Puritanical traditions, grounded in a (possibly strategic) suspicion
of sexuality that Karen Blixen rejected even as she celebrated the ad-
vancement of women's liberation effected by feminist reformers.[35] But
given the current fluidity and heterogeneity of the term "feminism" and
the broader range of meanings it now signifies, the insistence on woman's
desire and eroticism which Thurman associates with Dinesen's rejection
of the women's movement seems less clearly "antifeminist"—seems,
indeed, extraordinarily contemporary, a major anticipation of recent
theoretical speculations on the revolutionary possibilities of woman's
jouissance as related to a different, "feminine," writing.

Those few commentators to address this question have generally assumed, like Thurman, that despite the "feminist" sympathies voiced in
the letters, Dinesen ultimately disavowed such affinities. The text commonly cited as proof is "Oration at a Bonfire, Fourteen Years Late," especially the line (often quoted out of context) "I am not a feminist." But
the implications of this remark appear far denser and less determinate
when it is restored to its sociocultural and literary context and read in the
light of Karen Blixen's letters and *Modern Marriage*.[36] First, the lecture was
directed at a particular, historically specific Danish feminism—a largely
empiricist, pragmatic sociopolitical movement rooted in the nineteenth-
century suffragism toward which she remained intensely ambivalent.

Even so, her lecture, rather than simply rejecting "feminism," complicates the term in precisely the ways certain feminist theories have recently
done. Though generally taken at face value, her remarks are actually
worded with such deliberate ambiguity that they openly invite an ironic
reading. She begins with a tongue-in-cheek account of having been asked
"in the summer of 1939" to address "a large international women's congress in Copenhagen," and claims to have responded, "'I cannot accept
this assignment, for I am not a feminist.' 'Are you against feminism?'
asked Mrs. Hein. 'No,' I said, 'I can't say that I'm that, either.' 'How do
you stand upon feminism?' asked Mrs. Hein again." Blixen's response indicates the complexity of her position:

> If those women who thirteen years ago asked me to give their oration
> had been present today . . . , they would perhaps . . . say, "Yes,
> thank you, we need hear no more. We understand that, despite all
> your assurances . . . , you are in reality *against* feminism. . . ."
>
> I would have to protest immediately and say, "I know in what
> debt I stand to the older women of the women's movement now in
> their graves. When I myself have been able to study what I wished
> and where I wished, when I have been able to travel around the
> world alone, when I have been able to put my ideas freely into print,
> yea, when I today can stand here at the lectern, it is because of these
> women. . . . I know that in order to achieve such advantages for un
> born generations of women, in their lives they had to go through
> much and sacrifice more, that they had to endure scandal and ridicule,
> and that without cessation they had to struggle against prejudice and
> suspicion." (*Essays*, 65–66, 78–80)

In this context she goes on to elaborate the theories of woman's heretical
"duplicity" and subversive mimetic play which, as we have seen, so vividly configure her own discursive strategies.

If Dinesen appears "apolitical," then, it is only in the more obvious
sense of that term, according to a definition of the political that signifies
only official institutions and the organized movements that seek change
in the public arena.[37] According to an alternative, complementary definition, which takes into account the power dynamics of discourse, the radical possibilities of Dinesen's attitude become more readily apparent.[38]
Thus, for example, her stress on feminine difference and multiplicity (*Essays*, 69–78, 80–86), often viewed as simply reactionary, appears prophetic of the directions taken by diverse feminist theorists during the last
decade; and her rereading of feminine duplicity, as we have seen, anticipates Irigaray's notion of mimicry which, within a patriarchal order, may
be a crucial provisional strategy for resistance and transformation. That
transformation, Karen Blixen had written in a letter to her sister, "will
bring many glorious revelations. For there is hardly any other sphere in

which prejudice and superstition of the most horrific kind have been retained so long as in that of women, and just as it must have been an inexpressible relief for humanity when it shook off the burden of religious prejudice and superstition, I think it will be truly glorious when women become real people and have the whole world open before them" (*LA,* 163).

2

The speculations on woman recorded in the letters and *Modern Marriage* evolved in response to a crucial geographical transposition. If for Karen Blixen "Denmark" was the site and sign of repression, a "fatherland" evadable only by flight (*LA,* 55), Africa became for her the locus of liberation, a space where she might elude the gender codes that would install her within "woman's place": the "narrow circle" of domesticity (*LA,* 250). Driven by the dream of a life outside the bounds of European society, she made plans in 1913 to marry her distant Swedish cousin Baron Bror von Blixen-Finecke.[39] For all its unconventionality by bourgeois standards, the couple's decision to immigrate to British East Africa in 1913 was itself, of course, the reenactment of a well-worn convention: the European topos of Africa's "terra incognita" as a fertile, alluring El Dorado.[40] As Bror would recall, "between us we built up in our imagination a future in which everything but the impossible had a place. The promised land which hovered before our eyes was called Africa."[41]

But neither Africa nor the promised land of marriage conformed to this idyllic vision. Bror Blixen shared with Wilhelm Dinesen the ambiguous ability to become a legend in his own time—celebrated, in Beryl Markham's words, as "the toughest, most durable White Hunter ever . . . to shoot a charging buffalo between the eyes while debating whether his sundown drink would be gin or whiskey."[42] Hemingway used him as the model for the safari leader in "The Short, Happy Life of Francis Macomber," and indeed the two friends had much in common by both predilection and philosophy.[43] But as with other legendary masculine wanderers, fidelity and industry were not among Blixen's virtues. A compulsive womanizer, within a year of Karen Blixen's arrival in East Africa in early 1914, he had infected her with syphilis.[44] By a fluke of fortune, he remained asymptomatic, dying in 1946 not of disease but of injuries from an automobile accident. But Karen Blixen, despite the remission of symptoms that masqueraded as a cure in 1915, would suffer from syphilis for the rest of her life, dying at age seventy-seven, after years of pain and progressive debilitation, of the malnutrition produced by the disease's attack on the spinal nerves controlling digestion. As we shall see, however, she would turn even this, like other losses, to imaginative account: the figures of infection, sickness, and dismemberment that pervade her texts write her body as/in a fictional corpus, at once displaying and displacing the perpetual struggle with her own infirmity enforced by her male-authored illness, which she archly claimed to be the price she had paid the devil for the gift of storytelling.

The health of both the marriage and the farm deteriorated as well: the couple separated for good shortly after the end of World War I, and Karen Blixen ran the six thousand-acre coffee plantation—already a failing enterprise—on her own. What did not change for her was her mythic perception of Africa as a locus of both nurturance and freedom, "a wild world outside" the bounds (*LA*, 224)—the place for which she had felt "homesick" all her life (*OA*, 238): "Up in this high air you breathed easily, drawing in a vital assurance and lightness of heart. In the highlands you woke up in the morning and thought: Here I am, where I ought to be" (*OA*, 2). Years later, looking backward over time, she would rewrite it thus: "I sailed into the heart of Africa and into a *Vita Nuova*, into what became to me my real life. Africa received me and made me her own" (*Essays*, 6). As the Dantean allusion suggests, it was in Africa that she found her real vocation as an artist, found the place—psychological and symbolic as well as geographical—where she could at last "speak freely and without restraint." [45] And it was through the metaphors of maternity that she would represent this generativity. Even as she identified her mother with both the landscape of Africa and the forces of creation, so she figured the African landscape as both mother and poetic inspiration:

> Of all the idiots I have met in my life . . . I think that I have been the biggest. But a certain love of greatness, which could not be quelled, has kept a hold on me, has been 'my daimon.' And I have had so infinitely much that was wonderful. She may be more gentle to others, but I hold to the belief that I am one of Africa's *favourite children*. A great world of poetry has revealed itself to me and taken me to itself here, and I have loved it. I have looked into the eyes of lions and slept under the Southern Cross, I have seen the grass of the great plains ablaze and covered with delicate green after the rains, I have been the friend of Somali, Kikuyu, and Masai, I have flown over the Ngong Hills,—"I plucked the best rose of life, and Freja be praised." (*LA*, 416)

Obviously, such mythologizations might be dismissed as mere rescriptions of imperialist formulae that figured Africa as both virgin territory and paradisial maternal land, made to bear fruit to colonists replicating Adam's role in the Eden narrative. [46] But as such sexualized tropes imply, this discourse makes "colonist" synonymous with "man." [47] If, as

Christopher Miller remarks, colonialist discourses construed "Africa" as "a blank slate on which the name of the firstcomer would be forever inscribed,"[48] the same is of course true of "woman" construed within the patriarchal symbolic order, as Dinesen would suggest in "The Blank Page." The question arises, then, whether a European woman's responses to the figure of Africa might not potentially be as different from a European man's as would her relation to the maternal/feminine figure(s) in her psychosexual history. I shall return to the intricacies of Karen Blixen's ambivalence toward colonialism and the political, moral, and literary implications of her ineluctable complicity with it, but the import of her doubled positioning—at once subject and object within the imperialist frame of reference—requires remark. For despite her affiliations with the colonialist project, which implicitly predicated her "freedom" to "speak" on the silencing of Africans, as a woman she was also among the colonized. The definitions of woman evolved throughout Western cultural history are strikingly similar to the definitions of Africans evolved by colonialism, both groups having been construed as naturally secondary, properly subordinate, and acceptable only when kept "in their places" for the sake of (masculine) "civilization."[49] In her letters she recognized these affiliations, developing extended critiques of the racial as well as the gender structures of her culture—of all those institutions that shut people in "cages" (LA, 278)—and calling for the transformations in "consciousness" that would enable "radical change in [areas] previously considered to be raised above it, or immune from it" (LA, 258).

This context illuminates the powerful, if problematic, sense of kinship she expressed with African peoples, an attitude that set her strikingly apart from other colonists. It is undeniable, of course, that in many ways she reflected the presuppositions and prejudices of her age, class, and race, or that she was deeply implicated in the colonialist enterprise. Even her assertion that coming to know Africans "was to me a magnificent enlargement of all my world" (OA, 17) is disquietingly double, figuring transformation of consciousness in terms that also recall imperialist expansionism. Yet it is equally undeniable that she remained remarkably free, given her historical circumstances, from the smug ethnocentrism typical of most white settlers. As Abdul JanMohamed observes in his study of the politics of literature in colonial Africa, Dinesen is "a major exception to the . . . pattern of conquest and irresponsible exploitation" characteristic of many colonialists and colonialist authors.[50] Despite her connections with the British establishment, which had wrested the land she farmed, like all the other land in Africa, from the native populations, her relationship with the Africans was also distinctively different from that of most other colonists. "One loses," she writes to her brother, "a good deal of racial superiority out here; it seems obvious to me that the

natives surpass us in many ways" (*LA*, 8). Even as she participated in
the colonialist project, she also sought repeatedly to subvert it: "where
the natives are concerned the English are remarkably narrow minded; it
never occurs to them to regard [Africans] as human beings, and when I
talk to [them] on racial differences . . . they laugh patronizingly, touched
by my eccentricity" (*LA*, 4). Her refusal to cultivate more than a fraction
of her farm's six thousand acres—a financially ruinous decision—arose
from her reluctance to displace further any of the African families who
lived there. Remy Martin, the developer who purchased the farm from
Karen Coffee Company, explicitly attributed her failure as farm manager
to her "stubborn devotion to the Africans":

> "No one . . . made a success of coffee in Karen at six thousand
> feet. . . . [I]t was hopeless. But it would have made an ideal mixed
> farm . . . ; it was ideal for cattle. But to do that profitably she would
> have had to take back her squatters' land, and she wouldn't touch it.
> Her servants had the run of her place . . . and she couldn't bear to
> interfere with them. Instead, she ran the coffee at a dead loss, and the
> Africans made the profit. There were three thousand head of squatter
> cattle on the farm when I took it over."[51]

Many of the severest tensions between her and the British settlers in
Kenya grew up around this difference of perspective. For if, judged by
contemporary standards, Dinesen's attitudes toward Africans and colonialist issues appear condemnably conservative or reactionary, we do well
to remember that among her own contemporaries she was widely regarded as suspiciously radical. As JanMohamed notes, she is virtually
unique in "criticizing in a substantial manner the economic, religious,
and ethnocentric motives at the heart of the colonial endeavor."[52] Her admiration for African tribal peoples is a major theme of both her letters
and the African texts, reaching an apex in her close relationships with
individual Africans like Farah Aden and Kamante Gatura, and in her unprecedented determination, before she left Africa, to find land for those
who had lived on her farm so that their community could remain intact—a feat that she achieved against all odds and in defiance of the
strenuous disapproval and discouragement of the colonial officials. "These
attitudes," remarks JanMohamed, "earned Dinesen the rare respect of
later African nationalist leaders, and the displeasure of her colonial contemporaries—she was labeled 'pro-native' . . . by the settlers." Further,
"Dinesen's concern for the welfare" of the Africans, "her respect for their
dignity, and her general, but genuine interest in their cultures led the Africans to accept, respect, and even venerate her."[53] Long after her death,
those who had known her recalled affectionately what she described (not
unproblematically) as that "understanding between us [that] lay deeper

than all reason" (*OA*, 332). Kamante Gatura, whose life she had saved when as a child he had nearly died from an infected sore, remembered her thus: "we found this woman was kind and merciful to everybody. We called her our mother."[54]

Dinesen affirmed a particular connection with African women: "They were the people who called me Jerie"—"the one who pays attention," literally, the one who simultaneously *listens* and (as the economic metaphor in the phrase implies) *renders what is due,* thus reversing momentarily the symbolic economy within which the colonized, for the sake of survival, learn to pay both attention and financial tribute to the colonizers.[55] Recognizing this kinship and acclaiming the African women's subversive strategies for dealing with their public subordination, she also found a model for her own authorship. We have seen that in her disagreements with the British over colonialism, she had eschewed as futile all direct assaults ("As a woman and a foreigner, . . . if I argue I shall lose my power"), choosing instead to play "the hostess and friend" who seeks, despite her anger, to persuade through indirection. In analogous ways, she saw in the Somali women's storytelling a figure of the duplicitous discourse of women authors who used narrative to contest a male-dominated symbolic order—outwardly conforming to its conventions, but communicating, to those who have ears to hear, an Other message:

> Sometimes, to entertain me, they would relate fairy tales in the style of the Arabian Nights. . . . It was a trait common to all these tales that the heroine . . . would get the better of the male characters and come out of the tale triumphant. The mother sat and listened with a little smile on her face.
>
> Within this enclosed women's world, so to say, behind the walls and fortifications of it, I felt the presence of a great Ideal, without which the garrison would not have carried on so gallantly; the idea of a Millenium when women were to reign supreme in the world. The old mother at such times would take on a new shape, and sit enthroned as a massive dark symbol of that mighty female deity who had existed in old ages, before the time of the Prophet's God. Of her they never lost sight. (*OA*, 179–80)[56]

In view of the fact that one of the major "walls and fortifications" she herself would construct when she published her first book was the signature *Isak*, it is significant that what she recalls most frequently about the African women is precisely their playful or mocking laughter—"like a chime," overflowing constraints with "ripples and cascades of mirth."[57] Sarah's explanation of her choice of Isaac as the name for her newborn child—"God has made me to laugh, so that all who hear will laugh with me" (Gen. 21:6)—is echoed in *Shadows on the Grass* in Dinesen's recollection of an exchange with Kikuyu women who have just made a fool of her: "After a minute or two I could not help laughing. And . . . they joined me. One after another all faces round me lightened up and broke into laughter. In the faces of toothless old women a hundred delicate wrinkles screwed up cheeks and chin into a baroque, beaming mask— and they were no longer scars left by the warfare of life, but the traces of many laughters" (*SG,* 102).

3

The pangs of love become a condition of writing.

Julia Kristeva, *Tales of Love*

Finally, it was in Africa that Karen Blixen found Denys Finch Hatton. "There are some," she wrote, "who have the gift of 'making myths'; their personalities remain alive in people's consciousness . . . and the particular kind of poetry they represented . . . goes on gathering or maturing around them; people continue to add to it" (*LA,* 394). She was referring, significantly, to her father. So it was also with Finch Hatton. The second son of the thirteenth earl of Winchelsea, he had come to British East Africa for many of the same reasons that lured Karen Dinesen and Bror Blixen two years later: the need for space, both topographical and psychological, and for freedom from the conventional obligations imposed by class and family. Trader and safari leader, Finch Hatton would later share with Bror Blixen the reputation as one of the most skillful white hunters of his day. When the then Prince of Wales—soon to become though not long to remain Edward VIII of England—came to Africa on safari, they were the two whom he sought to accompany him. Legendary for stunning good looks, erudition, wit, charismatic charm, eccentricity, and near-compulsive independence, Finch Hatton was praised, by many who knew him, in hyperbolic terms. "He suffered all his life," as his biographer nicely remarks, "from adulation."[58]

Karen Blixen became acquainted with Denys Finch Hatton at a dinner party in Nairobi in 1918, and soon writes to her brother: "If you should get to France as a pilot it is just possible that you will meet someone called Denys Finch-Hatton, who is also a pilot on the French front, and that would make me very happy. For I have been so fortunate in my old age to meet my ideal realized in him" (*LA,* 89). And later: "That such a person as Denys exists—something I have indeed guessed at before, but hardly dared to believe—and that I have been lucky enough to meet him . . . compensates for everything else in the world" (*LA,* 171). In her oblique representations of their love affair, which began soon after their first meeting and endured for over a decade, she reenacted her love for the land: "Denys had watched and followed all the ways of the African High-lands, and better than any other white man, he had known their soil and seasons, the vegetation and the wild animals, the winds and smells. . . . Here in the hills, . . . gazing out over the land . . . , he had taken in the country, and in his eyes and his mind it had been changed, marked by his own individuality, and made part of him" (*OA, 356*). The passage per-forms the very appropriative gesture it describes, turning both land and lover into mythologized figures within Dinesen's larger dream of "Af-rica," their material reality "changed" by the shaping "eyes" and "mind" of the woman who, "marking" them with her "own individuality," re-makes them both as story.

In this mythos Finch Hatton becomes a catalyst for her imagination. First an intellectual companion and (significantly) paternalistic mentor ("Denys taught me Latin, and to read the Bible, and the Greek poets . . ." [*OA, 226*]), he later serves as the primary audience for her narratives:

> Denys Finch Hatton had no other home in Africa than the farm, he lived in my house between his Safaris, and kept his books and his gramophone there. When he came back to the farm, it gave out what was in it; it spoke,—as the coffee-plantations speak, when with the first showers of the rainy season they flower, dripping wet, a cloud of chalk. . . .
> Denys had a trait of character which to me was very precious, he liked to hear a story told. . . . Fashions have changed, and the art of listening to a narrative has been lost in Europe. . . . Denys, who lived much by the ear, preferred hearing a tale told, to reading it; when he came to the farm he would ask: "Have you got a story?" I had been making up many while he was away. In the evenings he made himself comfortable, spreading cushions like a couch in front of the fire, and with me sitting on the floor, cross-legged like Scheherazade herself, he would listen, clear-eyed, to a long tale, from when it be-gan until it ended. (*OA, 225–26*)

These "stories" were the beginnings of her mature narratives. On one level, then, Dinesen's fictions might be seen as forms of seduction or apotropaic rituals—designed, like Scheherazade's tales, to keep at bay the little "death" Karen Blixen underwent each time her lover departed (*LA, 224*). Thurman suggests that she used "the erotic power of narrative . . . to test her power to enchant, to hold in thrall—and thereby to sur-vive"[59]—making storytelling a kind of love potion. Taken alone, this in-terpretive paradigm—itself a seductive reading of Karen Blixen's African years—seems to reinforce Hannah Arendt's assertion that had this life continued, Blixen would never have become a writer, remaining instead merely "the mistress" of Denys Finch Hatton.[60]

But leaving aside the potential reductiveness and overdetermined romanticism of Arendt's view, which elides both the complexity of Karen Blixen's life in Kenya and the existence of her earlier writings,[61] I would rather venture that had Denys Finch Hatton not existed, Dinesen would have invented him. In some sense she *did* invent him, not only as the beloved of heart's desire, the "outcast" hero wandering the wild spaces of a similarly mythologized "Africa," but also as a necessary artistic fabrication, the figure of an ideal listener whose active attentiveness, like a silent answer, assisted her fulfillment of her own genius. "The family of Finch Hatton," she would write in "Mottoes of My Life," "have on their crest the device '*Je responderay*,' 'I will answer.' The device was meaningful and dear to me . . . for an answer is a rarer thing than is generally imagined. There are many highly intelligent people who have no answer in them . . . And how, then, can you yourself go on speaking?" (*Essays*, 6–7)

Arendt's assertion also obscures the fact that Karen Blixen's stories were not simply seductions, enchanting tokens told to entice the errant lover home again, but rather an increasingly important, and importantly separate, activity of her own devising. Though her writing may have begun in the "dry season" when "the long rains" with which she recurrently associates Denys had "failed" (her oblique shorthand for both the decline of the farm and her unpredictable lover's lengthy absences, both physical and psychological[62]), it continued, after awhile, out of its own accumulated energies:

> I was young, and by instinct of self-preservation, I had to collect my energy on something, if I were not to be whirled away with the dust on the farm roads, or the smoke on the plain. I began in the evenings to write stories . . . that would take my mind a long way off, to other countries and times. . . . At first I wrote in the evenings only, but later on I often sat down to write in the mornings as well, when I ought to have been out on the farm. (*OA*, 44–45).[63]

In any case, the life Arendt describes did not continue. Though Karen Blixen had desired "to live and die in Africa" (*OA*, 352), she was forced, after years of unremitting struggle, to confront the bankruptcy of both the farm and the dream it had represented for her. What she called the "impossible"—the source of her most "terrible nightmares" (*LA*, 417)—became reality. But the worst was yet to come: on May 14, 1931, Denys Finch Hatton's Gipsy Moth crashed and burned. The earliest text of this event, from her one-sentence telegram to her brother Thomas on May 15—"DENYS KILLED FLYING . . ."—is poignantly elaborated in *Out of Africa*:

> I looked out for Denys on Thursday. . . . But when he did not come . . . I drove in to town. . . . There was, somehow, a deep sad-

ness over the town . . . and in the midst of it everybody was turning away from me. . . . I drove up to the lovely old Nairobi house of Chiromo . . . and found a luncheon party there. But it was the same thing at Chiromo as in the streets of Nairobi. Everybody seemed mortally sad, and as I came in the talk stopped. . . . I thought: These people are no good to me, I will go back to the farm. Denys will be there by now. We will talk and behave sensibly, and I shall be sane again and know and understand everything. But when we had finished luncheon, Lady McMillan asked me to come with her into a small sitting room, and there told me that there had been an accident at Voi. Denys had capsized with his machine, and had been killed in the fall. It was then as I had thought: at the sound of Denys's name even, truth was revealed, and I knew and understood everything. (*OA, 348–51*)

She buried him in the Ngong Hills, in the place they had once laughingly selected as their common gravesite: "There was an infinitely great view from there: in the light of the sunset we saw both Mount Kenya and Kilimanjaro. . . . Now Africa received him, and would change him, and make him one with herself" (*OA, 348–51*).

To compare oneself with Scheherazade is to make the act of narration inseparable from the idea of death.[64] Dinesen's implicit connection of Denys with Sultan Shahryar hints at the darker side of their relationship—elided in *Out of Africa* but clearly disclosed in her letters. For Denys, as his biographer notes, had "an instinctive fear of commitment." Though for a time he indeed "had no other home in Africa" than hers, he had also a "wanderlust of mind and soul, a physical inability to remain for any length of time in one place."[65] More often absent than present, he stayed away for months at a time on safari or on return visits to England, providing Karen Blixen increasingly limited emotional support.[66] Thus their few weeks together each year were charged for her with the poignancy of impending loss. Thurman writes that she "made a virtue" of Denys's refusal of commitment, "writing of their friendship as a 'love of parallels,' scorning those lovers . . . who took possession of each other's lives. . . . But . . . she also suppressed a neediness that she wanted to disown."[67] It might appear supremely ironic, then, that it was not the death of Scheherazade herself, but that of her "princely" auditor, which put an end to her oral narratives.[68] Yet for her that death, in its staggering coincidence with her loss of Africa, seemed at first but the inauguration of her own death-in-life. In the numbing months that followed her return to Denmark, it was life itself, the necessity of living in history, that appeared like death to her. And it was death, and those who had joined the world of the dead, who like the figures on Keats's urn, forever young, maintained to her a stubborn vitality (*SG, 112–14*).

What brought her back to life was more storytelling. For it was at this time that she shaped those fragmentary narratives begun in Africa into *Seven Gothic Tales*. And if in one sense she had been constituted as a mature artist by the combined force of her experiences in Africa, her relationship with Finch Hatton, and her own developing genius, she would now reverse that process, creating "Africa" as a mythic space (*Out of Africa* appeared three years after *Seven Gothic Tales*) and lover as attentive audience—one of the several figures for the listener/reader implicit, like the haunting voice of the storyteller, in her fictions. She had once remarked that she could not create "until I had heard my own voice, seen myself in that mirror that is the person to whom one is speaking" (*LA*, 288–89). In *Out of Africa* Denys figures as a crucial "mirror" through which she came to see—reflect on—herself as artist. Through writing, she re-membered the dead in both senses, recalling Denys as the fictive listener without whose silent "answer" no storyteller can "go on speaking."

This reading, of course, raises with particular acuteness the problematics of gender. For insofar as Dinesen constructed Denys as a kind of ideal listener, she appears to have confirmed Adrienne Rich's wry observation that within a patriarchal symbolic order "every woman writer has written for men."[69] Yet on another level, by figuring Denys as silent auditor or muse, Dinesen also undermines the phallic script that casts *woman* in those roles: the inspiring Other who brings man's text to bear or the fetishized audience—absent, mute, or dead—whom the male lover-speaker apostrophizes as the screen for the masculine readers he actually addresses.[70] Remaking Denys in her own image and in the service of her own authorial project—that new life that replaced the mythologized "Vita Nuova" she lost in Africa—Dinesen turns him into a figure not unlike the Beatrice prototypically constructed by Dante in his own *Vita Nuova* as the emblem of his poetic inspiration. Like the "Africa" personified in Dinesen's recollection of Denys's death, she too "changes" him, molding him into a fictive figure in her own autobiographical text, and thereby making him "one with herself." In so doing she dismantles the traditional construction of man as the subject who writes, woman as the object who is written—or, as Dinesen would later put it, "the blank page" for masculine inscriptions.

Ironically, of course, these transformative exchanges committed her to another kind of "death": by turning herself into "printed matter" (*Essays*, 196), "she" too necessarily became, long before her physical death, a kind of fictive artifact—an effect heightened by the iconographies in which she represented "herself" as a kind of elegant corpse, the "inspiring figure" of "a memento mori," or an elegantly fabricated mask.[71] Yet it was also through the engendering of these fictions that she would give birth to herself as "Isak Dinesen," offspring of a woman who brought forth textual children in the waning years of her life, obtaining thereby a kind of immortality. In her narratives, as we shall see, she would elaborate these paradoxes, reviving herself again and again as the uncanny "story-teller" who, in Walter Benjamin's stunning phrase, "has borrowed . . . authority from death."[72]

3

Writing (in) Exile: Reverie, Recollection, and the Poetics of Displacement

[T]heir history, their stories, constitute the locus of our displacement. It's not that we have a territory of our own; but their fatherland, family, home, discourse, imprison us in enclosed spaces where we cannot keep on moving, living, as ourselves. Their properties are our exile.

Luce Irigaray, This Sex Which Is Not One

I was constantly in flight, an exile everywhere.

Isak Dinesen, Shadows on the Grass

I

People who dream . . . know that the real glory of dreams lies in their atmosphere of unlimited freedom . . . the freedom of the artist.

Isak Dinesen, Out of Africa

Out of the story of her life Dinesen would construct the story of her stories. Let us return to one of its pivotal moments:

> Day is a space of time without meaning, and . . . it is with the coming of dusk, with the lighting of the first star and the first candle, that things will become what they really are, and will come forth to meet me. . . .
>
> During my first months after my return to Denmark from Africa, I had great trouble in seeing anything at all as reality. My African existence had sunk below the horizon, . . . then faded and disappeared. . . . The landscapes, the beasts and the human beings could not possibly mean more to my surroundings in Denmark than did the landscapes, beasts, and human beings of my dreams at night. Their names here were just words. . . . There they were, all of them, nine thousand feet up, safe in the mould of Africa, slowly being turned into mould themselves. And here was I, walking in the fair woods of Denmark, listening to the waves of Öresund. . . . What

business had I had ever to set my heart on Africa? . . . As I myself could not find the answer, a great master supplied it. He said, "What is Africa to you or you to Africa . . . ?"

Thus, in "Echoes from the Hills," Dinesen recalled her bereavement on losing the place she had called "my heart's land."[1] Paradoxically, going "home" to "the fair woods of Denmark" in 1931, after seventeen years in Kenya, seemed to her tantamount to entering a condition of permanent exile, a forced dwelling in a space—psychological as well as geographical—from which she had felt herself estranged since earliest childhood. Recording this event in *Out of Africa* and *Shadows on the Grass,* she would repeatedly write repatriation as *exmatriation:* within this mythography, "Africa" was more than a homeland of the spirit; it was also the place she saw as the matrix of her creativity, the place where she had begun to "speak freely and without restraint."[2] Thus to leave Africa was not only to become an orphan and outcast (the etymology of "Echoes" literally recalls the cries of a grieving child),[3] but potentially to lose that authorial voice as well.

Yet it was, after all, the voice alone that remained to her when she returned—ill, bankrupt, and bereft—to Denmark, and with it she would make her future as a writer. Her response to the revised Shakespearean query in the passage above was to take those "words" to which her African existence had been reduced and transform them into the body of writing that would bring her worldwide recognition. Inherent in her recollections, then, is a retrospective poetics of displacement, emerging from a reading of the author's diurnal, living "reality" as a form of death or dream, an exile wherein, like an unquiet spirit, she becomes a permanent wanderer. In this oneiric realm "words"—which seem at first ghastly remnants, the insubstantial traces of lost plenitude—paradoxically become the very stuff of resurrection, the material from which she would fabricate both a persona and a literary corpus. For Dinesen, writing was at once a sign of wounding, a form of mourning, and a way to regeneration: "words," even while bearing witness to her permanent loss of what she called "my real life," would also give rise to the life of her texts.[4] It is no accident that the figure of dreaming, with its connotations of discontinuity, displacement, and uncanniness, would become one of her recurrent tropes not only for exile but for narrative itself.[5]

Beginning in a literal, geographical alienation, displacement operates in Dinesen's fiction at many levels, most obviously in her extraordinary double textual system and her use of a masculine pseudonym that literally divided her from herself. Like her letters, that hybrid signature bespeaks her sense of woman's irrevocable status as a displaced person, a foreigner dispossessed by patriarchal culture and discourse. Writing "as a

man," Dinesen made a name for herself that was both the sign of alienation and an ironic instrument of resistance, inscribing her own distance
and difference from phallocentric tradition even as she appeared to enact
her erasure within it. It is notable that the narrative of Sarah and Isaac
directly conflates female generativity with nomadic exile. In every case,
writing marks a process of dislocation, rendering the place of the author,
like her sex, indeterminate—a *shuttling between* rather than a *location
within* specific positions. Significantly, the image of dreaming in "Echoes
from the Hills" is itself doubled and displaced by the figure of the author
as mime. Like the Shakespearean scene recalled in the passage above,
wherein the Hamlet who questions an actor's mimicry of Priam's grief is
"himself" the product of an actor's mimicry, the scene of Dinesen's writing became for her a stage of multiple masquerades, a theater for the play
of receding, echoing voices.

Like the dream, the figure of echo with which she named the text
(and which she repeated, echoing Echo, throughout her career) suggests
both the quality of undecidability she associated with her writing and the
distinctively gendered effects with which it reverberates. For Echo—
whose enunciations, like Dinesen's, are associated with too great a love
for a narcissist—is lost to the land of the living. The ultimate missing
person, "she" remains only in/as *remains:* a name that signifies no-thing,
the trace of an ever-shifting voice that is not a voice—elusive, disorienting, teasing the senses with lapses and dislocations.[6] Yet Dinesen would
also redeem the mournful meanings of that name with another kind of
echo: the self-reflexive language of stories suffused with what, describing
one of the many subversive female artists in her fiction, she called a
"laughter of liberation."[7]

This conflation of exile, sexual difference, voice, and writing is elaborated in many of her greatest works, most obviously, of course, in memoirs like *Out of Africa* and *Shadows on the Grass.* I shall return to those
texts in chapter 10, but here I want to consider the operations of displacement not in one of her fictionalized autobiographies, but in one of her
earliest autobiographical fictions: the novella entitled "The Dreamers."[8]
Just as Dinesen blurred the boundaries between names, nationalities,
and sexual identities, so she would put into question traditional generic boundaries separating fiction from "fact," story from theory. "The
Dreamers," as its linguistic link to the autobiographical meditations
quoted above suggests, is an intensely reflexive text, an explicit reflection
on the meaning of her own creative project. In its frame story she develops a poetics of displacement which, like "Echoes from the Hills," specifically equates dreaming, dis-ease, exile, and loss with the ecstatic
engenderings of narrative.[9]

The character who elaborates that figural conjunction in "The
Dreamers" is one of the many tale-tellers in Dinesen's oeuvre who be-

came fictive doubles of their author. Mira Jama, "the inventions of whose mind have been loved by a hundred tribes," is a permanent outcast from his native land, a wanderer who, having lost the ability to dream up new fictions, now dwells in and on the fictions made up in dreams:

> "In my dreams I . . . carry with me something infinitely dear and precious, such as . . . no real things be. . . . And it also seems to me that I shall be struck down and annihilated if I lose it. . . . The air in my dreams . . . is always very high, and I generally see myself as a very small figure in a great landscape. . . .
>
> "You know, . . . that if, in planting a coffee tree, you bend the taproot, that tree will start, after a little time, to put out a multitude of small delicate roots near the surface. That tree will never thrive, nor bear fruit, but it will flower more richly than the others.
>
> "Those fine roots are the dreams of the tree. As it puts them out, it need no longer think of its bent taproot. It keeps alive by them—a little, not very long. Or you can say that it dies by them, if you like. For really, dreaming is the well-mannered people's way of committing suicide." (*SGT*, 276–77)

These figures reappear in "Echoes from the Hills." In "my dreams," writes Dinesen,

> I move in a world deeply and sweetly familiar to me, a world which belongs to me and to which I myself belong more intensely than is ever the case in my waking existence. . . . The second characteristic of my dreams is their vastness, their quality of infinite space. I move in mighty landscapes, among tremendous heights, depths, and expanses and with unlimited views to all sides. . . . Dream trees are very much taller than day-time trees. . . . Long perspectives stretch before me, distance is the password of the scenery, at times I feel that the fourth dimension is within reach. I fly, in dream, to any altitude, I dive into bottomless, clear, bottle-green waters. It is a weightless world. Its very atmosphere is joy, its crowning happiness, unreasonably or against reason, is that of triumph.
>
> For we have in the dream forsaken our allegiance to the organizing, controlling, and rectifying forces of the world, the Universal Conscience. We have sworn fealty to the wild, incalculable, creative forces, the Imagination of the Universe. (*SG*, 108–10)

As its title suggests, this text, juxtaposed with "The Dreamers," sets up an echoic dialogue across the span of Dinesen's career, illuminating both the text of its author's life and the life of her texts. This discourse is extended in two further narratives. The first, in *Out of Africa*, celebrates the "tremendous views," "joy," and "glory" of flying, a "splendid liberation" for which "language is short of words": "In the air you are taken into the full freedom of the three dimensions; after long ages of exile and dreams the homesick heart throws itself into the arms of space" (*OA*,

238–39).[10] The second, a late companion story to "The Dreamers," treats the same protagonist at an earlier moment in her fictive wanderings. Its title, "Echoes," also connects it to *Out of Africa* and "Echoes from the Hills"—that reminder and remainder of *Out of Africa*—as elements in a kind of metatextual reflection on writing in—and as—exile. In the poetics inherent in these conjunctions, Dinesen not only associates dispersal, loss, and death with creative "triumph" but implicitly genders this symbolic nexus. Her description of dreaming/fiction-making as a radical subversion of "the organizing, controlling and rectifying forces of the world," a transgressive eruption of "wild, incalculable, creative forces," parallels psychoanalytic concepts of dreaming in relation to the repression of the feminine as the "unconscious" of culture and psyche and anticipates theoretical speculations on women as speaking subjects who inhabit a "wild space" beyond official discursive boundaries. It is from this "elsewhere," as Irigaray calls it, that the possibilities of an other, feminine discourse may be imagined.[11]

Peter Brooks has argued that "deviance is the very condition for life to be 'narratable': the state of normality is devoid of interest, energy, and the possibility for narration. In between a beginning prior to plot and an end beyond plot, the middle—the plotted text—has been in a state of *error:* wandering and misinterpretation."[12] Such a reading of narrativity (which recalls Dinesen's own cherished parable of the stork, reiterated in her letters and *Out of Africa* as a figure of both her life and her writing) raises acutely the question of woman, to whom traditional phallocentric cultures have allotted the most extreme status of the deviant.[13] In this context, an equivalence emerges between narrativity and femininity, each being construed, according to phallocentric law, as the principle of deviation, swerving—literally *extra-vagance*. And if the story of woman is the story of stories, then the greatest storyteller of all, potentially, would be "woman" herself, who both embodies and engenders the "narratable" by *telling her own tale.* Such an affirmation, of course, may appear hopelessly utopian in light of a totalizing psychoanalytic paradigm that would assert all narratives to be already, ineluctably, properties of the father. Can the narratable—can language itself—exist outside the phallogocentric symbolic order?[14] Dinesen was profoundly concerned with just such questions. In "The Dreamers," as in many of her other texts, she evokes the possibility of an affirmative answer, suggesting that even within the confines of patriarchal culture, those "wild, incalculable, creative forces" can find expression in/through "woman."

Consider first Mira Jama, whose monologue about his authorial impotence becomes an implicit speculation on Dinesen's own situation. Like "Isak Dinesen" Mira—as the pun on his name suggests—is a reflection of his author, a masculine mask that doubles Karen Blixen's pseudonymy—hence an implicit sign of her multiply alienated status as a woman speaking (through) a male discourse. A permanent exile, Mira is also a mutilated man—"the nose and ears of his dark head cut clear off" in a symbolic emasculation which, like Benedetta's encounter with the Marelli, suggests an oblique parody of the notion of woman's supposed "castration," undercutting even as it reinscribes the Freudian model. But his wounds figure Dinesen's in another sense as well: the dismemberment inherent in the breakup of the Ngong farm and the severance from Africa that precipitated her particular sense of exile as well as the transformative possibilities that attended it. Significantly, the events of the frame story transpire on a dhow sailing off the African coast, carrying the freight of incipient revolution. It is an image that becomes crucial to the poetics the tale unfolds.[15]

Mira's inability to tell stories becomes the precipitating condition for the story recounted by his companion Lincoln Forsner, the tale of a woman, who, "twenty years ago, taught . . . [him] to dream." Like the echoes to which Dinesen analogizes it, this "tale" is a proliferation of mutually displacing accounts wherein "woman" *is* the indecipherable, ever-elusive "story"—remembered in/as a kind of dream text, at once product and producer of multiple male-authored narratives. I shall return to the problematics of the tale's several male narrators, but first let us consider the narrative of the woman who knew the art of dreaming. It is through this tale that Dinesen obliquely tells not only her own story, but the story of her stories as well.[16]

2

In feminine speech, as in writing, that element which never stops resonating . . . is the song: first music from the first voice of love which is alive in every woman. The Voice sings from a time before law, before the Symbolic took one's breath away and reappropriated it into language under its authority of separation. The deepest, the oldest, the loveliest Visitation. Within each woman the first, nameless love is singing.

Hélène Cixous, The Newly Born Woman

A woman's (re)discovery of herself can only signify the possibility of not sacrificing any of her pleasures to another, of not identifying with anyone in particular, of never being simply one.

Luce Irigaray, This Sex Which Is Not One

Briefly summarized, Forsner's narrative concerns the wanderings of the renowned operatic diva Pellegrina Leoni, who loses her voice through injuries from a fire in the Milan opera house. This event precipitates her lifelong wandering, a self-imposed exile from former place and name, and her refusal to become "tied up" in a stable, permanent, unitary identity: "I will not be one person again. . . . I will be always many persons. . . . Give up this game of being one (*SGT,* 347, 339). First fabricating her own "death" by erecting a monument inscribed with her name—literally turning herself into a text—Pellegrina begins a lifelong play, assuming new names, new personae each time the old threaten to constrain her. Her serial staging of perpetual self-differentiation is aided by her loyal "friend" and "shadow" Marcus Cocoza—a wealthy Jew from Amsterdam whose ambiguous relation to Pellegrina becomes one of the story's principal interpretive conundrums. Insofar as her proper name persists at all, it remains only in his memory, a trace like Echo's receding voice, perpetual sign of its owner's absence. Even its etymology bespeaks drift, dispersal, and the danger of what is out of bounds: *peregrinus* signifies not only "wandering" but "foreign, strange, alien."

Forsner's tale emerges, like Pellegrina's shifting incarnations, as an exfoliating series of narratives. These flashbacks are generated from his own recollections and from the tales told to him by two other narrators, men he had met "one winter night" twenty years before in an inn situated in the divide between northern and southern Europe, "amongst mountains, with snow, storm, great clouds and wild moon outside" (279). Like Forsner himself, each of his companions has fallen in love with, and subsequently lost, an extraordinary, magnetic woman, so powerful a presence that she has become for each the ultimate object of desire. What enables them to read their "different" women as in fact the same is the mark imprinted on her body like a signature, "a long scar from a burn, which, like a little white snake, ran from her left ear to her collar bone" (285). Paradoxically, the stigma that certifies identity is also the hieroglyphic sign of its absence; emblematizing Pellegrina's lost voice, name, and selfhood, it is the memorializing trace of another story, as yet untold: the tale of how her wanderings began.[17]

At the very moment that their narratives are ending, a veiled woman enters the inn, as if called forth on cue from their discourse. Seeing the three companions, she hastily departs, but not before being recognized, belatedly, by her former lovers. Strangely desperate to elude them, she takes a coach upward toward an Alpine pass that leads through the otherwise impassable mountains—continuing afoot when her coach becomes immobilized in the snow. Pursuing her amid "this wildness of the elements," her lovers enter an unmarked terrain, borderland and liminal site of transition between opposites.[18] Here, as in a dream or "fairy tale" (318), time seems suspended and only hunter and hunted exist.

But here I would like to halt my own tracking of the story to raise a question: what do these men seek? What does this dream/woman mean? And what can we—in our uncomfortable positions as counterparts of her fictional pursuers—read in the linguistic traces that represent her even as they mark her disappearance?

Pellegrina's peregrinations may appear picaresque, but the roles she chooses are not random: she becomes, successively, whore, revolutionary, and saint, enacting thereby three of the most overdetermined versions of "woman" in Western patriarchal culture.[19] But with a difference. For by playing these roles to the full yet retaining the power to abandon them at will, she can remain at once inside and outside the semiotic systems that would codify "woman" according to masculinist logic, resisting even as she appears to fulfill traditional categorizations of the feminine. In traversing the whole continuum that would polarize woman as virgin or whore, domesticated object or revolutionary agent, Pellegrina demonstrates the essential interchangeability—and hence the invalidity—of these oppositions. Through her carnivalesque play with traditional "feminine" roles, she exposes the provisionality and instability of phallocentric conceptions of woman, thus implicitly threatening the foundations of a culture predicated on the control of women as both bodies and signs.[20] Significantly, in role after role, what she finally flees is involvement with a male lover whose desire would appropriate hers. Dinesen brilliantly anticipates Beauvoir's famous observation that "man dreams of an Other not only to possess her but also to be ratified by her."[21] If, like the audiences with whom Pellegrina had shared a "great passion" (333), each of her lovers offers her adulation, he also seeks to co-opt her power, claiming her permanently as "his" by writing her into his own finalizing script. She eludes these appropriations by flight, literally dropping out of (his) sight, fabricating another "self," another script to be enacted elsewhere. In suggesting that this flight is also a kind of theft of the very identity by which each man would construct himself, Dinesen prefigures Cixous's play on the double meaning of *voler* (fly/steal) for the woman who "doesn't hold still": "as long as the personal, the permanence of identity is not fetishized . . . , where woman is wandering, roaming . . . flying (thieving) . . . [the] power to be errant is strength. . . ."[22]

Entering perpetual exile, Pellegrina has cast herself as a moving signifier in liberating herself from the domination of masculine speculations even as she deliberately solicits them. It is notable that in attempting to represent her, her lovers can "only explain" her in terms of "metaphor" (305)—the creator of "miracles of art" (297). Forever in flight, like the peregrine falcon her name recalls, she makes exile and displacement the sources of creative energy. True to her name, she is simultaneously rover and devourer, a "winged lioness" (332) who consumes the men who would tame her and shut her "up in cages" (340) or, as Dinesen would express it in "Echoes," who seek "to hold her fast" as their object, putting her in her (their) "place."[23] As every man's ideal woman, she appears to be the ultimate embodiment of "*le sexe*" adored and feared by the masculine imagination that constructed it; but Dinesen, anticipating Irigaray's speculations (and investing with new meaning the operatic tradition of *la donna mobile*), subverts that conception by representing Pellegrina as the "*sexe qui n'en est pas un*"—a multiple, mobile figure who *cannot be read* by the appropriative gaze of the other, and who therefore evades androcentric interpretive control even while acting as its ever-elusive object. Like "the affirmative woman" in Sarah Kofman's revisionist reading of Freud and Nietzsche (whom Dinesen herself repeatedly revised), Pellegrina is both a "great criminal"—transgressor of masculine law—and a "great humorist" or artist who, like the criminal, "has succeeded in conquering . . . ego." Figured, like Pellegrina, as both "lioness" and "Raptor" (bird of prey), the "affirmative woman" is ever "enigmatic and ungraspable," an embodiment of "multiplicity." Because she "remains irreducible, diabolical," she undoes not only traditional Occidental conceptions of "masculine" and "feminine," but whatever depends on "a definitive and immovable position."[24]

If in this context Pellegrina seems to turn men into dreamers, the text suggests that they are victims not of a woman but of their own desire and its constituent fantasies, solipsistic mirror images that ultimately focus not on the woman, but on themselves.[25] But insofar as each of Pellegrina's male lovers becomes a type of author, seeking to inscribe and circumscribe Pellegrina within his own life text, her power as an artist is manifest precisely in the way her fictions, lionlike, swallow up—literally incorporate and thus transform—his.[26] Each male narrator purports to tell the "true" story of woman, to name and hence to claim "her," but each story is subverted by the others. For the woman who is the supposed center of them all remains a constantly moving, *self*-displacing, ec-centric and de-centering *figure*. In this sense she is like the narrative itself, a figural play that eludes our readerly quest for the critical mastery contingent on the discovery of some central truth.

Yet the text never lets us forget that *story* cannot ultimately elude *history:* that it is, finally, a man's world from which Pellegrina seeks liberation, and that given the historical realities of that world for women, the price of freedom may be mortally high. As Cixous observes, if the "power to be errant is strength, it is also what makes [woman] vulnerable to those who champion the Selfsame."[27] Caught on the border, at the "mountain pass" (319), Pellegrina faces an *impasse* of androcentric constructions. She is surrounded at last by former lovers whose echoic, relentlessly reiterated demand, "Tell me who you are," is in fact a question of *masculine* identity: "by being the woman I desire, tell me who *I* am; reflect me to myself."[28]

Overtaken—and nearly taken over—by those who would constrain her in this way, Pellegrina answers the question of identity not with words but with a gesture that severs her from the consuming gazes that would fix her forever as mere reflection. Having already constituted herself as a floating signifier, she now puts herself, quite literally, *en abîme,* condensing and re-enacting all her earlier flights/thefts: "The next moment she did what I had always feared that she might do: she spread out her wings and flew away. Below the round white moon she made one great movement, throwing herself away from us all. . . . For one second she seemed to lift herself up with the wind, then, running straight across the road, with all her might she threw herself from the earth clear into the abyss, and disappeared from our sight" (327).

What Forsner and his companions rescue from "the abyss" is no more than what they would have made her from the outset: the inert shell of woman, no longer resistant to their manipulations. Afterward Pellegrina, mortally injured and "immovable" on a stretcher at a nearby monastery, a totalizing male space whose very name conflates oneness with encarceration,[29] is also cloistered by the monological discourse of the men who wait, at last, "to get an answer . . . of her." Here, then, she would seem to die doubly—not only literally, but by becoming the object of a final male-authored narrative: the account of Marcus Cocoza, the wandering Jew who, having "shadowed" her throughout her exile, now proposes to tell her "true" story, to disclose "her real name." Its conclusion, however, is of her own engendering: a final fiction that returns her to the opera, reviving "Pellegrina Leoni" as creator and casting Marcus Cocoza (figured as "moon" to her "earth"), as a character in her script of desire. His words become her entrée into her own reclaimed "song"— paradoxically a scene from *Don Giovanni,* the quintessential figure of the phallic appropriation of woman:

> As she spoke [the] words of the old opera a wave of deep dark color . . . washed over her. . . .
> Suddenly her face broke, as the night-old ice on a pool was broken up when, as a boy, I threw a stone into it. It became like a constellation of stars, quivering in the universe. . . .
> "Oh," she cried, "look, look here! It is Pellegrina Leoni—it is she, it is she herself again,—she is back . . . on the stage again. . . ."
> Of a sudden he took up his little walking stick and struck three short strokes on the side of the stretcher.
> "Donna Pellegrina Leoni," he cried in a clear voice. "*En scène pour les deux.*"
> . . . she collected herself at his words. Within the next minute she became quiet in a gallant and deadly calm. . . . In one mighty movement, like that of a billow rising and sinking, she lifted the

middle of her body. A strange sound, like the distant roar of a great animal, came from her breast. Slowly the flames in her face sank, and an ashen gray covered it instead. Her body fell back, stretched itself out and lay quite still, and she was dead. (351–52)

Like the complex relations of Pellegrina and her male "shadow," or the letter on which the reenacted *scène* (like the scene of writing it figures) reflexively turns, this passage invites contradictory readings. According to one, it enacts a deceptive and destructive deathbed delusion which, born of hysteria and manipulated by the Mephistophelian character whose words direct the woman in her final moments, culminates in the incoherent and deadly "roar" that concludes her fantasy of return.[30] In this reading, she is indeed destroyed by the paternal order that beckons her *en scène* before the all-engulfing masculine gaze and voice.

But who, one wonders, controls whom? Who speaks through—and for—whom? In this discourse on the power of the name, whose name does Marcus Cocoza invoke? And what of Pellegrina's own voice? Her final "song" can be heard by the men who surround her only as incoherent noise, as uninterpretable as the inchoate sounds of the tongueless Philomela to which the text compares her (342). But Dinesen implies that for Pellegrina herself, that song has an altogether other meaning, an untameable, liberatory potential that she herself has created by ventriloquizing her desire through Marcus's words, making him a mimetic *means to her own end* in both senses of that phrase. One recalls that earlier, when she played out the fiction of her "death," she had commissioned Marcus to erect her tombstone. That vicarious inscription of her "self" as monumental text—a text that leaves her free to "rise again" (344) like a phoenix from the flames, to move on to other fabrications—becomes a figure of the whole narrative structure of "The Dreamers": textualized by male narrators throughout the tale, Pellegrina is also the generative force behind their narrations.[31] "If women are such good mimics it is because they are not simply reabsorbed in this function. *They also remain elsewhere*": through Pellegrina's paradoxical relation to her roles—in the opera and in "life"—Dinesen brilliantly prefigures Irigaray's ideas on the complex power of masquerade for women within a male-dominated social order.[32] Like the great nineteenth-century actresses who played (on) the feminine as a means to a power beyond what their cultural positioning would allow, Pellegrina uses her operatic roles, presumably constructed by/for the male gaze, to stage her own freedom, power, and essential difference from, or within, what she mimics—and at the same time to suggest to her female viewers a possibility for seeing themselves differently.[33] One might argue that in the final moments of Pellegrina's story, this subversive feminine mimicry is *doubled,* for just as in the opera Pellegrina used her roles at once to displace and display herself, so here she "speaks" through both Marcus's discourse and her own, giving voice to an "elsewhere" that is hers alone, unfathomable to the men who hear it. And that doubled discourse is in its turn redoubled, for behind all the voices in the text is the ventriloquizing voice of "Isak Dinesen," another masculine mask through which a woman speaks. The text suggests that even as Marcus's story would tie up the loose ends of Pellegrina's life, imposing his own final "truth" on her, she ultimately transforms those alien narrative structures with her creative energy, turning him into the instrument for regaining her voice and herself. In comparable ways, Dinesen's own narrative pervades and incorporates all the male-authored narratives in the text, using them at last to ventriloquize her own encompassing tale(s), her own "elsewhereness." Thus she at once erases and proclaims herself, kills and creates herself in the same moment, imaging creation as "song" born of violence, suffering, and death.[34]

But what does it mean to regain "oneself" in this context? The text suggests that *being oneself* is not the same as being *one self*. Paradoxically, Pellegrina Leoni is most herself when she is least herself. She "lives" most intensely as operatic actress, a plural *figure* or moving *character* who "sings" many roles in many voices, giving double meaning to the term *poly-phony*. For her, "real life" is fiction—and vice versa: the very interchangeability of those terms and the irresolvable ambiguity of their statement emblematizes the sorts of paradox Dinesen plays out through Pellegrina. The fundamental truth about the self which Pellegrina enacts is that there may be no fundamental truth about the self: whether as diva or deviant wanderer, in the theater as an imitation of life or in life as an imitation of theater, she performs "selfhood" as a dynamic of displacement, making literal the internal multiplicity that traditional conceptions of identity and self-presence would repress. In this sense she has never left the theater; hence her passionate affirmation of "return"—"it is she, she herself again, Pellegrina Leoni"—is inseparable from its qualifying conclusion: "on the stage again" (352).

Even in death, then, Pellegrina—like her author—resists reductive readings that would turn her into a sign "tied up" within another's finalizing discourse (347). Ultimately, the question of "who is speaking" in "The Dreamers" becomes as undecidable as Pellegrina's identity.[35] This elusiveness of both woman and narrative finds a metaphor in the opening scene of the text, in the floating world of the frame story. From the dhow moving on the midnight ocean, the ordinary, separable positionings of up and down, above and below, are rendered problematic, "bewildering," as sky and sea become indistinguishable, mirroring one another in an infinite series of reflections

> as if something had happened to the world; as if the soul of it had been, by some magic, turned upside down. . . . The brightness of

> the moon upon the water was so clear that it seemed as if all the light
> in the world were in reality radiating from the sea, to be reflected in
> the skies. The waves looked solid as if one might safely have walked
> upon them, while it was into the vertiginous sky that one might sink
> and fall, into the turbulent and unfathomable depths of silvery worlds,
> forever silver reflected within silver, moving and changing. . . . The
> heavy waters sang and murmured. . . . (271)

In comparable ways, Dinesen dislocates her readers, sets us afloat as wanderers in the "vertiginous" world of her texts, at once lured and unmoored by the story of woman which, like Pellegrina or the "heavy
waters" beneath the floating dhow, has depths that "sing and murmur"
in many voices—voices that from a phallocentric perspective may appear
indecipherable, "bewildering," even incoherent—"a distant roar"—but
that persistently invite another hearing, rewriting exile as exploration
outside the bounds, a form of creative ecstasy.

These waters reappear in "The Diver," a late narrative from *Anecdotes of
Destiny* that forms a bridge between "The Dreamers," "Echoes," and
"Echoes from the Hills," extending the poetics of displacement those
texts elaborate. Here, Dinesen returns to Mira Jama in a context that illuminates her other representations of writing in/as exile, wound, and
resurrection, and of her own immersion in the "wild incalculable forces"
of the imagination. Questing for material for new stories, Mira visits a
group of pearl fishermen "in order to hear [their] adventures, and make
them mine":

> For many things happen to those who dive to the bottom of the
> sea . . . ; if you follow the career of a single pearl it will give you
> material for a hundred tales. And pearls are like poets' tales: disease
> turned into loveliness, at the same time transparent and opaque, se-
> crets of the depths brought to light to please young women, who
> will recognize in them the deeper secrets of their own bosoms.
> (*AD*, 12)

He is directed at last to "the man who had become famous" because he
"would dive down into greater depths and stay down . . . longer than
any other fisherman." This diver's uncanny ability to discover "the finest
pearls" has given rise to the rumor that "he had got, in the deep water, a
friend—maybe . . . some demon of the sea—to guide him" (13). Finding
the happy man, and eager to prove his storyteller's skill, Mira begins to
recount the tale of a young man's disappointment, dispossession, and
flight with which "The Diver" began, only to realize near his story's
end, in one of those dizzying self-reflexive moments so characteristic of
Dinesen, that the subject of his tale is the very man to whom he speaking:
"It is to a poet a thing of awe to find that his story is true." Having heard

Mira's tale out, the diver completes it with his own narrative—a comic fable of the deep that becomes at once a parabolic account of woman's enmeshment within patriarchal culture and a playful self-portrait of Isak Dinesen, the aging author who has eluded those confinements:

> ". . . when I first went down to the bottom of the sea, in search of a certain rare pearl . . . an old cowfish with horn-rimmed spectacles took me in hand. As a very small fish she had been caught in the net of two old fishermen, and had spent a whole night there, in the bilge water of their boat, listening to [their] talk. . . . But in the morning . . . she slipped through the meshes and swam away. Since then she smiles at other fishes' distrust of men. For really, she explains, if a fish knows how to behave . . . , she can easily manage them. She has even come to take an interest in the nature and the customs of man, and often lectures upon these to an audience of fishes. . . ." (16–17)

The "philosophy" she "has imparted" is the doctrine of mobility—of that which escapes masculine "nets" by slipping through their interstices. Like her author, she links feminine jouissance, creativity, and that "blessed" condition common to flying, diving, and writing: the ability to move in multiple dimensions, so that—as Karen Blixen put it in a letter about flying over Africa—"there is actually no longer any up or down." "And this," she continues, "is . . . what I want to write about: the capacity of moving in three dimensions is a part of bliss . . . or transfiguration" (*LA,* 412–13). Looking forward to "Echoes from the Hills," which links dreaming not only to flight, but to swimming "in bottle-green waters" (*SG,* 110), "The Diver" also looks backward to the vertiginous floating world of "The Dreamers," symbolic analogue to Pellegrina's ever-shifting selves and voices and to Dinesen's own protean texts. As with Pellegrina's wanderings, but without their risks, the world of the fish is one of infinite motion and multiplicity. Like the Kristevan semiotic, it represents a fluid, rhythmical, maternal excess that "slips through the meshes" or overflows the linear constrictions of the symbolic order:

> "Man can move but in one plane, and is tied to the earth. . . . [H]e must bear his own weight and sigh beneath it. . . . We fish are upheld and supported on all sides. . . . We move in all dimensions, and whatever course we take, the mighty waters . . . change shape accordingly . . . and the pattern of the universe we read with ease, because we see it from below." (17–18)

From this position "below," the place of the repressed, the she-fish reads both history and its authoritative inscriptions differently:

> "We carry with us, in these our floatings about, an account of events excellently suited to prove to us our privileged position. . . .

It is known to man also and even takes up an important place in his history, but in accordance with his infantile conception of things in general, he has but a muddled understanding of it. . . . When God had created heaven and earth, the earth caused him sore disappointment. Man, capable of falling, fell almost immediately, and with him all that was in the dry land. . . . But the fish did not fall, and never will fall, for how or whereto would we fall? . . . So the Lord . . . resolved to reward the fish according to their merit." (18)

That "reward" appears in a revisionist interpretation of the Biblical narrative of the flood, figured here as an upsurge of that same feminine "deep" that Dinesen recurrently associated with the return of the repressed and figured through mythoi of the Great Mother Goddess on whose suppression patriarchal religion erected itself: "So all the fountains of the great deep were broken up, and the windows of heaven were opened, and the waters of the flood came upon the earth. And . . . all that was on dry land died" (18–19).[36] Yet after that period of blessed, free-floating feminine "abundance, . . . man, although fallen and corrupted, once more succeeded, by craft, in coming out on top." Nevertheless, his "triumph" may be only "apparent," as Dinesen suggests in a punning passage that connects phallic anxieties with the formation of cultural hierarchies: "How will real security be obtained by a creature ever anxious about the direction in which he moves, and attaching vital importance to rising or falling?" The feminine undersea world, operating outside the linear, hierarchical world of man, has no such perils: "For our changing of place in existence never creates, or leaves after it, what man calls a way, upon which . . . illusion . . . he will waste inexplicable passionate deliberation" (18–20). The world of the fish resembles the "fluid and free subjectivity" toward which Kristeva gestures in "Women's Time."[37] And like the new world tentatively imagined at the end of that essay, it is a space at once apocalyptic and utopian: beyond temporality, beyond gender, beyond ego, knowable if at all only evanescently, and then only to those who dive deep into the dangerous currents that a phallocratic social order would repress. As Dinesen has her deep-sea double remark, "The inhabitants of the liquid world have brought past and future together in the maxim: *Après nous le deluge*" (20).

In "The Immortal Story," among the last tales published before her death, Dinesen returned to these conjunctions, linking that oceanic mother tongue with the engendering of narrative through the figure of a "big, shining pink shell," emblem of a female sexuality and generativity that subverts the supposedly "omnipotent" plots of the lordly Mr. Clay (*AD*, 157, 173): "when you hold it to your ear, there is a sound in it, a song . . . a deep low surge . . . like the distant roar of great breakers." That sound is, of course, an illusion, the product of the body's own coursing blood; the "song" arises precisely from the hollowness of the instrument that seems to echo the resonances of its own place of origin. Yet for just these reasons the shell's "surge" recalls the semiotic sonorities of that other place of origin, the mother's long-lost body. The "story" repressed by the phallocentric symbolic order, it is utterly remote yet uncannily familiar: "he . . . lifted the shell to his ear. . . . He had a strange, gentle, profound shock, from the sound of a new voice . . . in the story. 'I have heard it before,' he thought, 'long ago. Long, long ago. But where?'" (231).

It is this semiotic "voice," this "deluge" of feminine "song," that Dinesen associates with Pellegrina. "Thus," we are told, "did she swim along within the depths and mysteries of the great world" (*SGT,* 332). As a mobile, endlessly inventive figure, she inspires, like "The Immortal Story," an ever-widening process of interpretation and creation. Even after death, she continues to engender narratives:

> "I have thought," said Lincoln, "what would have happened to this woman if she had not died then? She might have been with us here tonight. . . . Or she might have gone with us into the highlands . . . and have been honored . . . as a great witch. In the end . . . she might perhaps have decided to become a pretty little jackal, and have made herself a den on the plain. . . . I have imagined that so vividly that on a moonlight night I have believed that I heard her voice amongst the hills." . . . "Ah la la," said Mira. . . . "I have heard that little jackal too. . . . She barks: 'I am not one little jackal, not one; I am many. . . .' And pat! in a second she really is another, barking just behind you: 'I am not one little jackal. Now I am another.' Wait . . . till I have heard her once more. Then I shall make you a tale about her, to go with yours." (353–54)

Just so, Dinesen herself proves equally resistant to finalizing readings or writings. The story of woman as artist and exile both enacts and explicates its author's own transgressive, fluid art—a discourse of dis-closure that like dreams, or the echo-chambers of shells, or like pearls, "at the same time transparent and opaque" ("The Diver," 12), invites yet always surpasses interpretation. The name Leoni, we recall, was also Dinesen's; "Lioness" was one of her several appellations, the sheer profusion of which, like Pellegrina's many names, suggests her refusal to be fixed within any single *logos.*

The late tale "Echoes" reinforces these implications in reverse. There Pellegrina loses her power precisely when she seeks to recover a lost sameness and unity by treating the young singer Emanuele just as her lovers in "The Dreamers" treat her: as a mere operative of egocentric desire. Discovering in Emanuele what she thinks is her own rebirth—his singing exactly echoes "the voice of the young Pellegrina Leoni" (*LT*, 167)—she tries to use him as a means of vicarious return to the central, single self she had earlier repudiated: "from the beginning they had but one voice" (176). But in attempting to reclaim her "self" as a stable, monological, and in-different entity, she paradoxically loses both herself and the voice she would control as a sign of her own creation. At the outset of "Echoes," Dinesen represents Pellegrina as a "nameless" redemptive outcast who offers her body to the self-damned recluse Niccolo in a restorative maternalized Eucharist, enacting thereby an heretical "jest" that mimes "God's terrifying fancifulness" (158–65). But in attempting to reverse this process, to incorporate Emanuele as a sign of her own identity, she becomes instead a "vampire" who symbolically devours the child in a perverse imitation of the Mass (185, 187). Dinesen marks Pellegrina's recognition of the futility of this project through the figure of voice debased: "she stopped short, for her ear had caught her own voice. What should have been the roar of a lioness was the hissing of a gander and a pain in her throat and chest" (187). Only in renouncing her claims to oneness—symbolically dying, once more, to herself—does she at last experience a paradoxical restoration, figured through the regenerating "consummation of the Host" that reiterates her own willing commitment to imaginative self-sacrifice (189–90).

Late in life Dinesen would repeatedly speak of Pellegrina's lost voice as a figure for her own loss of her life in Africa. If, out of Africa, she imagined her existence as an exile, a living death, a "dream," by a great act of courage and imagination she also plunged into those depths, turning the space of that dream—the dislocations of that life—into the site of restorative creation. And if in that process she also died, figuratively, into "printed matter," it is paradoxically through the displacements of writing that she continues to live, marking the place of exile as the everreceding horizon of new readings.

PART TWO

SPINNING TALES

Real art must always involve some witchcraft.

KAREN BLIXEN,
Letters from Africa

4

Gothic Cryptographies

The Gothic spirit . . . broke through . . . law wherever it found
it in existence; it not only dared, but delighted in, the infringe-
ment of every servile principle; and invented a series of forms of
which the merit was, not merely that they were new, but they
were *capable of perpetual novelty* . . . , a great system of perpetual change.

John Ruskin, "The Nature of Gothic"

The real difference between God and human beings . . . [is] that
God cannot stand continuance. . . . And human beings cleave to
the existing state of things. . . . Their art itself is nothing but the
attempt to catch by all means the one particular moment, . . .
and make it everlasting. It is all wrong . . . to imagine paradise
as a never-changing state of bliss. It will probably, on the contrary, turn out to be, in the true spirit of God, an incessant whirlpool of change.

Isak Dinesen, "The Monkey," in Seven Gothic Tales

I

As the haunting figure of Pellegrina Leoni suggests, the capricious reconceptions of the uncanny that Dinesen would elaborate late in her career in
self-reflexive parables like "The Cardinal's First Tale" were already at
work in her earliest English texts. Paradoxical conjunctions of horror
with pleasure, monstrosity with laughter—and the sexual and textual
implications thereof—are inherent in her designation of her inaugural
collection as "Gothic."[1] It was a mode to which she would repeatedly
return, and one distinctively well suited, as we shall see, to exploring the
notions of writing and sexual difference that her letters unfold. In *Seven
Gothic Tales* Dinesen uses Gothicism self-consciously and parodically not
only as her narrative medium but as a metacritical device to comment
obliquely on her own engenderings of narrative.

To represent a fiction as "Gothic" is not only to declare its hair-raising potential but to make it virtually synonymous with multiplicity, excess, and transgressiveness. Consider first the referential indeterminacy of the term itself, a protean polysemy that records and recalls its historical and semantic permutations.[2] Its accretions might be traced, figuratively, in terms of a southerly sweep, beginning with the "barbarous" marauders of northern Europe from whose name the term arose, moving through certan dominant forms of art and architecture from the twelfth to the sixteenth centuries (what John Evelyn, in the seventeenth, would call "a fantastical and licentious manner of building"), and extending eventually to both the architectural revivals of those audacious structures and their literary appropriation as machinery for the "terrorist" romance of the late eighteenth and early nineteenth centuries, its prototypes set in Italy and Spain.[3] Hence to unearth the meaning of "Gothic" is to encounter a multitude of topographies, social histories, and interactive discourses.

Dinesen's choice of the term as the descriptive rubric for her first book evokes this entire cultural chronicle. As a Dane writing to capture an English audience, she playfully assumes the role of a latter-day northern "barbarian," translating writing into a kind of raiding. The title also recalls those late medieval structures which Ruskin, in perhaps the single most famous analysis of "The Nature of Gothic" (1853), had read as a powerful expression of psychological as well as social impulses, an exuberant manifestation of the spirit of "play . . . , but with small respect for law."[4] Yet for all its resonant recollections of earlier constructs, Dinesen would maintain that her own version of the genre was preeminently affiliated with that ersatz "Gothic" developed in English, American, and Continental literature from the mid-eighteenth century onward: "When I used the word 'Gothic' I didn't mean the real Gothic, but the imitation of the Gothic, the Romantic age of Byron, the age of that man—what was his name?—who built Strawberry Hill, the age of the Gothic revival."[5]

On its most obvious level, Dinesen's book announces the nature of its particular Gothic through its author's tongue-in-cheek deployment of conventions patent to the genre: the wild landscapes and seascapes, the haunted and haunting mansions, the decaying battlements and cryptic chambers, the skeletons and the specters, the doublings and metamorphoses, the stock characters—abbesses, apparitions, witches, madwomen, charlatan priests, bedeviled wanderers, sinister fathers, victimized daughters. "Ruins, ghosts, and lunatics" are, as she implies in the arch, self-reflexive description of Gothic romances that opens the "Deluge at Norderney," the very stuff of her fictive discourse (*SGT*, 1). But she invests these properties with multileveled significance, making them not merely geographical and architectural loci for sensationalist "Gothic" action and

stock types, or predictable occasions for the generation of synthetic terror, but iconographies of psychic, cultural, and literary dynamics—
hieroglyphics whose spelling and spells the reader, as the guest in her
haunted house of fiction, is invited to decipher.

Dinesen's stress on her Gothicism as doubly mimetic, the imitation
of an imitation, is underscored by her insistence on its duality in another
sense: by "Gothic," she would observe, she signified "something simultaneously elevated and capable of breaking into jest and mockery, into
devilry and mystery."[6] The formulation recalls both Walpole's prefatory
comment on the mixture of "fooleries" and "bufoonery" with serious-
ness in *The Castle of Otranto*[7] and Ruskin's famous declaration that "the
tendency to delight in fantastic and ludicrous, as well as in sublime, images, is a universal instinct of the Gothic imagination."[8] But Dinesen's
use of Gothic is not the reactionary reprise of an obsolete form that such
echoes might suggest. Indeed, what emerges most clearly from her comments is her distinctive perception of the peculiarly modern theoretical
potential of Gothicism.

Her emphasis on the Gothic instrumentation of "mockery," for
example, prefigures Bakhtin's analyses of the "parodic travestying 'mimicry'" that undermines, by *re-presenting,* traditional genres and the officially sanctioned cultural codes they underwrite: "It is as if such mimicry
rips the word away from its object, disunifies the two, shows that a given
straightforward generic word . . . is onesided, bounded, incapable of ex-
hausting the object; the process of parodying forces us to experience
those sides of the object that are not otherwise included in a given genre
[and] introduces the permanent corrective of laughter."[9] Bakhtin's association of laughter with creative disordering—a connection that recalls
the several implications of Dinesen's pseudonym—brings to mind that
other multiplicity inherent in Gothicism: its baroque collocation and irreverent play with fragments of past culture, the "traces of centuries and
generations," as Bakhtin describes the Gothic setting, that "are arranged
in it in visible form."[10] In choosing her inaugural genre, Dinesen clearly
recognized that for all its apparent anachronism, its elaborate evocations
of the ancien régime, the Gothic is potentially, in Michael Sadleir's well-
known formulation, "as much the expression of a deep subversive impulse" as "the French Revolution"—or, one might add, of modernist and
postmodernist projects.[11] Through its exploitation of its own generic affiliations, Dinesen's text anticipates more recent analyses of the radical
philosophical, political, and narratological potential of the genre to call
into question the sacredness and "truth" of those constructs formerly
held to be beyond question. Writing Gothic, she would suggest, provided an ideal means for dismantling traditional codes in the very process
of appropriating them: "with the past . . . I find myself before a finished

world, complete in all its elements, and thus I may the more easily re-shape it."[12] Like Strawberry Hill and later Gothic revival buildings—that concatenation of architectural discourses that one art historian has aptly termed a "babel of styles"—literary Gothic is quintessentially a decon-structive and redistributive form, designed to keep the reader *on edge* in more than one sense.[13] In the world of canonical literary genres it might be analogized to English representations of the peoples from whom it took its name: a "barbarous" marginal force that continually imperils the center. "All margins," writes Mary Douglas in a summation that nicely recalls Dinesen's treatment of the Gothic, "are dangerous. . . . Any structure of ideas is vulnerable at its margins."[14] As an anomalous fiction of extremities, a genre outside the bounds of "high" literature, Gothic perpetually threatens the borders of traditional social and textual struc-tures. Given its synthetic origins, its adulterous commingling of puta-tively discrete categories, and its consistent exclusion, throughout the nineteenth and early twentieth centuries, from "legitimate" canonical status, the Gothic becomes the ultimate literary bastard, perpetually dis-placed from—and displacing of—"proper" sources of authority and authorship.[15] In this context, it seems hardly fortuitous that, as Jan B. Gordon recently remarked, "almost every Gothic novel points to the cri-sis . . . involving language and succession."[16] As a narrative syntax, Gothic operates as an aberrant amalgamation of past tenses that import a present without the certainty of a presence. Dinesen's reference to "ruins, ghosts, and lunatics" may be read, then, not merely as an autoreferential inventory of her own Gothic properties, but as a symbolic indication of her radically subversive narratology. If Dinesen is difficult for many readers to grasp, it is at least in part because she employs what appears to be an antiquated, even reactionary, narrative form to achieve distinctively modernist effects. Despite their superficial traditionalism, her narratives deploy a deconstructive poetics that challenges conventional categories of writing and reading.[17]

Dinesen's texts likewise unsettle and dissolve their own apparent sta-bility. With their multiple narrators, labyrinthine story-within-a-story narrations, echoic redoublings and repetitions, and complex forms of self-referentiality, they repeatedly circumvent their own ostensibly or-derly plot progressions. Dinesen's multifoliate narrative effects recall the literal features of Gothic architectonics represented in eighteenth and nineteenth century romances: "unpredictably various, full of hidden as-cents and descents, sudden turnings, unexpected subspaces, alcoves, and inner rooms, above all, full of long, tortuous, imperfectly understood, half-visible *approaches* to the center of suspense."[18] *Approaches,* pre-cisely—for no *arrival* is possible: like the architectural structures that gave the genre its name, *Seven Gothic Tales* is a building without a center.[19] Hegel's description of the vertiginous proliferations of the Gothic cathedral is equally applicable to Dinesen's house of fiction: "No one thing completely exhausts a building like this. . . . It is . . . an infinity in itself. . . . The substance of the whole is dismembered and shattered into the endless divisions of a world of individual variegations."[20] As Linda Bayer-Berenbaum remarks of Gothic edifices, "just as the line in Gothic ornament does not circumscribe a space, so too in Gothic architecture lines indicate movement rather than encompass an area. . . . The internal volume is not defined by firm walls."[21] Just so, not only by its disruptions of linearity but by the sheer proliferation of narrative in each story, Dinesen's text challenges the very concept of the "firm walls," the authorized and authoritative discourses, of a "master narrative," with all that concept implies of legitimacy, power, and paternal priority.[22]

Yet this narrative de-centering does not, in *Seven Gothic Tales,* import the kind of nihilism some commentators have attributed, problematically, to earlier Gothic romance (or, for that matter, to post-structuralist critical theory). As with Gothic architecture, Dinesen's narratives use what Hegel called "incalculable multiplicity" to evoke not chaos, but "infinity."[23] Like a Gothic cathedral, that space marked, as Bayer-Berenbaum writes, by "progressive divisions" and an "open, boundless interior," by "tiny intricacies and divisions-within-divisions," Dinesen's textual structure also "challenges the mind to imagine the unimaginable."[24]

That "unimaginable" in *Seven Gothic Tales,* the unspeakable power encrypted within its labyrinthine passages, is repeatedly associated with the effects that Western culture has alloted to the feminine. Dinesen never lets us forget that Gothic is a genre marked by gender. Digression and transgression, proliferation and peripheralization, fragmentation and eroticization: these characteristic effects of Gothic are also precisely those of what Alice Jardine, analyzing the relations between modernism and contemporary conceptualizations of the feminine, has called *gynesis,* the "woman-in-effect."[25] Like E. T. A. Hoffmann, whom Dinesen, like Freud, recognized as a preeminent artist of the uncanny, and whom she claimed as one of those predecessors whose work her texts at once resembled and revised, she used Gothic to provide an archaeology not merely of aesthetic and cultural codes and forms, but of consciousness.[26] And for her the place of the unconscious—that "repository," as Peter Brooks puts it, "of the fragmentary and desacralized remnants of sacred myth"—is associated with what Freud, in an oft-quoted negative reformulation of Bachofen, called "those dim Minoan regions" of psyche and culture: the place for the play of the maternal.[27] Leslie Fiedler, writing of the eighteenth- and nineteenth-century romance, has argued that

> the guilt which underlies the gothic and motivates its plots is the
> guilt of the revolutionary haunted by the (paternal) past which he has

been striving to destroy; and the fear that possesses the gothic and
motivates its tone is the fear that in destroying the old ego-ideals of
Church and State, the West has opened a way for the inruption of
darkness; for insanity and the disintegration of the self. . . . Beneath
the haunted castle lies the dungeon keep: the womb from whose
darkness the ego first emerged, the tomb to which it knows it must
return at last. Beneath the crumbling shell of paternal authority, lies
the maternal blackness—imagined by the gothic writer as a prison, a
torture chamber.[28]

Such formulations, in suggesting the preeminent source of that "dread"
which most critics have maintained as the raison d'être of traditional
Gothic romance, also expose the peril for a feminist practice of the connection, currently deployed in a variety of critical lexicons, of the mater-
nal/feminine with the world of irrationality and non-sense.[29] But
Dinesen would exploit these figures by a crucial shift of emphasis, rereading what, within androcentric perspectives, would be named as a
locus of "insanity," "disintegration of the self," and "maternal blackness" not as deathly or inchoate, but as yet unmapped sites of creativity—a cause not for "guilt" and terror but celebration. Such a connection
gives fresh meaning to Judith Thurman's astute observation that Dinesen
"would often go to the edge of the abyss and even peer down into it,
but the exercise never failed to cheer her up."[30] We have seen that in
the oneiric spaces she explores—represented by the storyteller in "The
Dreamers" as a source of sustenance, "a deep well" from which "a spring
of water . . . runs out . . . like the rays of a star"—it is "woman" who
"teaches you how . . . to dream" (SGT, 277, 279). "Dreams," she would
remark of her own in the autobiographical reverie that begins "Echoes
from the Hills," "are not confined to spheres of the idyll . . . or to any
such sphere as in the life of day-time is considered safe or pleasant. Hor-
rible events take place in them, monsters appear, abysses open, wild tur-
bulent flights and pursuits are familiar features. . . . Only, on entering
their world, horror changes hue. Monstrosity and monsters, Hell itself,
turn to favor" (SG, 107–08). As we have seen, this conception of the
dream space, and its connection to the sources of her own writing, would
recur in various forms throughout her career. As "The Dreamers" and
"Echoes from the Hills" imply, Dinesen's version of Gothic resurrects,
through storytelling, the vanished, (re)generative "woman" whose
dreams materialize in/as narrative. If Seven Gothic Tales enacts an archae-
ological quest into those buried regions of consciousness and culture,
what Dinesen's excavations bring to "light"—to use her own termi-
nology—is no corpse or monster, but renewed "life," a buoyant "spirit"
of laughter and jouissance that allows a reconception of the very structures
on which traditional definitions of "femininity" are founded (LA, 247–

49). The "parodic travestying 'mimicry'" Bakhtin describes takes on particular significance, as Irigaray has noted, when it is performed by woman. Dinesen's pseudonymous identification of herself as "the one who laughs" assumes special resonance in this context. She anticipates the diverse but mutually illuminating speculations of recent theorists not only about the transgressive import of a distinctively feminine mimicry through which, in Irigaray's formulation, woman can "convert a form of subordination into an affirmation, and thus begin to thwart it," but also about the relation of that mimicry to parodic, bewitching laughter.[31] "Laughter breaks up, breaks out, splashes over," writes Catherine Clément in a rereading of witchcraft which, as we shall see, recalls Dinesen's figuration of her own relation to writing. "It is the moment at which the woman crosses a dangerous line, the cultural demarcation beyond which she will find herself excluded. . . . An entire fantastic world, made of bits and pieces, opens up beyond the limit, as soon as the line is crossed. For the witch . . . , breaking apart can be paradise."[32]

It is within this revisionist context that we may situate Dinesen's inaugural text. As Ellen Moers and others have rightly noted, Dinesen wrote within the tradition of "female Gothic," connecting herself with earlier novelists like Ann Radcliffe and Emily Brontë and with contemporaries like Djuna Barnes and Carson McCullers.[33] This is hardly surprising, for one of the major figures—arguably *the* major figure—in traditional Gothic romance is, as Judith Wilt observes, "the murdering father, whose power fills up every passage in the haunted castle" and whose phallic "dagger" seems inevitably aimed at "the heart of his daughter": "Some deep struggle for control of the springs of being itself seems to be the issue, some struggle by the parent to unmake or reabsorb the child and thus stop time, keep power, take back freedom and life." Within "this universe the old men hold fast to their wealth, their power, their obsessive purposes, their lives, with a monstrous passion that bids fair to suck the whole planet dry," seeking to deny "the sources of . . . being, especially the female sources," to which they counter "the desire to be [their] own source—and goal."[34] It is this omniphagous expression of phallocentrism, this voracious, power-hungry paternity, potentially deathly to its female progenitors and offspring, that Dinesen's Gothic undermines at every level. Preeminent among the "ruins" the texts depict are the decayed and decaying structures of patriarchy and patrilineage, what Bakhtin describes as the "dynastic primacy and . . . transfer of hereditary rights" embodied in conventions of Gothic romance: in "its architecture, in furnishings, . . . [in] the ancestral portrait gallery, [in] the family archives and in the particular human relationships" as well as in "legends and traditions [which] animate every corner of . . . its environs through their constant reminders of past events."[35] Among the ghosts that most insistently pervade Dinesen's labyrinthine passages, as we shall see, are just such "legends and traditions"—the intertexts of the androcentric literary canon and master myths that her tales simultaneously display and displace. It is no coincidence that in defining her own use of Gothic as related to "the age of that man—what was his name?—who built Strawberry Hill," the name Dinesen "forgets" is that of the "father" of Gothic romance. Her deliberate, tongue-in-cheek erasure, like her later acknowledgment, then rejection, of other male predecessors like Poe and Hoffmann, serves as a kind of synecdoche for the process of unfathering that unfolds in her distinctive vision of Gothic.[36]

2

> At the end of the sabbat, only the sorceress remains; Satan has disappeared, everyone has gone home. "But *she,* who made Satan, who made everything . . . what becomes of her? There she is, alone. . . ." And that is when she takes off—laughing. . . . Women-witches often laugh. . . . All laughter is allied with the monstrous.
>
> Catherine Clément, "The Guilty One"

The letters written concurrently with Dinesen's earliest sketches of the Gothic tales suggest the specific correlation of her notions of Gothic "mockery" and "jest" with her perception of her situation as a woman within patriarchal culture, relegated to the role of Angel in the House— that domestic "Paradise," as she ironically called it, that "paralyzed" female creativity in the name of propriety, bourgeois "femininity" and family duty (*LA,* 247; see 258–65). Here, as in the tales themselves, she repeatedly analogizes her craft to that of the witch, representing herself as the affiliate of "my angel Lucifer"—a "symbolic expression," as she glossed the phrase, by which she "conceive[d]" (in both senses of the word) "the search for truth, striving toward the light, a critical attitude— indeed, what one means by *spirit*. . . . And in addition to this . . . a *sense of humor* which is afraid of *nothing,* but has the *courage* . . . to make fun of everything":

> I am convinced that Lucifer is the angel whose wings should be hovering over me. And we know that the only solution for Lucifer was rebellion, and then the fall to his own kingdom. In Paradise,—if he had remained there,—he would have cut a poor figure. But Lucifer had greater stature than the undersigned, his humble servant who remained in Paradise and who cuts a poor figure there now, indeed, who has been annihilated in it. . . . The same is true of my

pathetic 'authorship.' I cannot, I cannot *possibly* write anything of the slightest interest without breaking away from the Paradise and hurtling down to my own kingdom. (*LA*, 246)

While this declaration bears obvious similarities to the Satanic and Faustian mythoi elaborated, in various guises, in European literature from Blake, Goethe, and Byron to Baudelaire, it is no simple recapitulation of Romantic or *fin de siècle* gestures.[37] As Dorothy Canfield observed in the Introduction to the first edition of *Seven Gothic Tales,* the text cannot be accounted for as "just some more Romantic School stuff": "Byron's moral atmosphere is that of a naive, kindly, immature youth compared to the tense, fierce, hard, controlled, over-civilized, savage something-or-other, for which I find no name, created in this book by its anonymous author" (vi). Even as Dinesen's Gothic looks backward to nineteenth-century predecessors, it extends their use of the form. Specifically, in writing self-consciously as a woman, Dinesen displaces the pervasive masculinist focus of the Satanic/Faustian myth and those cultural movements of which it became an emblem, rendering the myth at once more radical and more subversive than it could ever be in the hands of male authors who, whatever their extremities of alienation, nevertheless enjoyed the privilege of membership in the dominant order merely by virtue of their gender.[38] The "rebellion" Dinesen associates with the act of writing becomes inseparable from her depiction of her position as a woman seeking freedom from the "paradisial" social system which, grounded and synecdochized in the patriarchal institutions of marriage and family, restrained women's access to culture, vocation, and discourse "merely because they belong to the female sex."[39] It is Dinesen's connection of Gothicism with the disruptive force of repressed femininity—that energy "for which [one] can find no name"—that accounts for what Canfield called the "bizarre power" of the text and distinguishes it most notably from its more obvious masculine prototypes.[40]

The anticipatory poetics of rebellion articulated in the letters on Lucifer reappears as a retrospective hermeneutic in one of Dinesen's most important theoretical considerations of the politics of gender, the late essay "Daguerreotypes," which, together with the letters, brackets this discourse on the witch and her craft. Anticipating more recent femininist analyses, the text describes the three "official" categories within which "men of [the] older generation viewed women": "the guardian angel," the prostitute ("priestess of pleasure" playfully euphemized as "bayadère"), and the "housewife." Observing that in every case, woman is defined according to the logic of two interactive criteria, her relation to man and the level of her sexual repression, Dinesen insists on the fundamental equivalence of these conditions, each being subject to and enacted through the "taboo" against the exposure of the sexualized female body. In the socially mandated concealment of woman's anatomy "from the waist to the ground," the uncanny site and sight of transgressive eroticism becomes itself displaced and synecdochized as a fetishized obsession with female "legs," enacted through injunctions against their display.

Desexualized and idealized, "the guardian angel—unadulterated— shed a heavenly light at a man's side and protected him against the power of darkness. . . . [She] is surrounded by a mystical aura, and where she is envisaged in long white garments, hovering, it would certainly be profane . . . to direct attention to her legs" (*Essays*, 29–30). The housewife, while "more tangible," also "wears decent long garments," concealing that locus of engendering that is precisely the source of her power and thus, paradoxically, reifying it in displaced, idealized form: "to scoff at the mother or mistress of the househould was a sacrilege. . . . The housewife didn't have legs either" (30). While the bayadère, who "did have legs to be sure," seems a contradiction to the first two categories, in fact she merely confirms their grounding premises. Far from abolishing the sexual economy within which women are circulated, she "reinforces it: it is the same taboo expressed in a different mode." The punning reflection that follows situates these repressions within a male specular economy wherein women, money, and language are exchangeable in both senses of the term:

> Here the taboo may be defined in figures. . . . One might say that in this matter the true gentleman's loyalty vis-à-vis the dignity of woman found expression in the sums he was willing to pay to see the bayadère's legs. . . . The guardian angel and the housewife could not possibly sanction the existence of the bayadère. Nevertheless there must have been a certain satisfaction for them to have, in the bayadère, on paper and in definite figures, so to speak, a kind of proof of what their own womanly stake was worth. (31–32)

This entire meditation is itself an extension of a letter Karen Blixen had written in 1926, as she was beginning work on the Gothic tales. This document is crucial to an understanding of her developing conceptions of the sexual politics of cultural forms and formalities. Celebrating the progress of the feminist movement in effecting "radical change" that "would bring about the collapse of the whole existing state of things," she launches an acute critique of "the old world order" of male domination. Her synecdoche for this symbolic economy is a key paternal text:

> Father writes in . . . "Hunting Letters": "however enchanting a well-formed feminine leg may be when revealed by an incautiously lifted dress, there is nothing in the least alluring in being presented with the whole leg, right up to the knee"—no doubt presuming by this

pronouncement to have demonstrated to all decent sensible women the reprehensible foolishness of these skimpy skirts, as if it were unthinkable for us really to *want to run* and be free of clothes impeding our movements.

Her response to this assumption is scathing:

As if we could never want to have the whole of life—nature, art, science, open-air life, sport, and our own destiny—before our eyes without having to see all this through our relationship with men, *any more* than they should see all this through their relationships with us. It is often discussed how much influence the feminist movement exerts on women's morals, and these very discussions generally show to what a great extent women are regarded as sexual beings, to what a small extent as human beings. (*LA,* p. 263)

These remarks provide a more resonant context for the conclusion to Dinesen's remarks on women in "Daguerreotypes." There, over against the conscious, public economy of the angel, the housewife, or the bayadère, she invokes another female figure who eluded masculine control, both social and taxonomic:

I have said that . . . men . . . viewed their women from these points of view, or in three groups, officially. I use the word "officially" because in reality they had in their consciousness still another type of woman which for all of them was very much alive and present but was not mentioned or recognized by the light of day. The guardian angel, the housewife, and the bayadère—each had her calling, her justification, and her importance in relationship to man. . . . [I]t was for man's sake that woman existed. . . . But there was a woman who, long before the words 'emancipation of women' came into use, existed independently of a man and had her own center of gravity. She was the witch. . . . The witch had absolutely no scruples about showing her legs; she sat quite unconstrained astride her broomstick and took off. (*Essays,* 32–33)

To the obvious objection that the paramour of Satan is still enthralled by a male figure, Dinesen points out the degree to which witchcraft has functioned, symptomatically, as a category within an official, male-constructed discourse, amenable to the projections and defensive rationalizations of those who deploy it, and unimaginable outside those perimeters: "for most men the explanation is, that a woman who can exist without a man certainly also can exist without God, or that a woman who does not want to be possessed by a man necessarily must be possessed by the devil." But the witch may exist also in a wild space outside masculine imaginings, in "good relationship with her sister witches," constructing her own rules, her own feminine community, and her own discourse. Indeed it is precisely the anxiety about this possibility that accounts in part for the excess of both male fear of the witch and the violence it engendered on the part of "the judges at the witch trials who used every means to procure the witch's confession" (32–33).

Dinesen's reference here recalls an entire complex history that in the early decades of this century as well as in more recent years became (again) the subject of considerable critical debate. Among all the treatises on witchcraft produced at the height of the widespread witch panics in Europe between the fifteenth and seventeenth centuries, we might take as representative that classic Inquisitorial text, the *Malleus Maleficarum* ("Hammer of Witches"), one of the most influential and widely disseminated manuals for those who would *judge witchcraft* in any sense—whether in the diurnal recognitions deemed necessary to a man's own protection, in the patristic denunciations of the pulpit, or in the dark chambers of hall and mind where man's deepest psychosexual disturbances could literally be enacted under the cloak of religious and civic law. As Jeffrey Burton Russell notes, it was with the *Malleus* that "the witch phenomenon became thoroughly articulated."[41] According to the perverse logic of the pervasive discourse on witchcraft of which the *Malleus* became the exemplar, any form of violence and violation could be justified as necessary to *proper identification* in preparation for a kind of ritual sacrifice of the witch-scapegoat as representative of "the most abominable of all heresies."[42] Such a context brought to its monstrous logical conclusion man's traditional claim to the right to *name:* in a literal, historical realization of the pornographer's dream, sanctioned by both church and state, the suppression of woman was stamped in blood on thousands of humiliated and mutilated female bodies in a massive purge designed (like the old lord's sacrifice of Anne-Marie in Dinesen's great tale "Sorrow-acre") to restore the stability of the patriarchal social order by obliterating those it read as threat and pollution.[43]

As Dinesen observed, the terror the witch inspired was inseparable from questions of language. It is no coincidence that the *Malleus* associates witchcraft with an illicit claim to discourse. In identifying the witch's "slippery tongue" as one of her most fearful organs, the original Latin of the *Malleus* maintains the double meaning of *lingua* as both anatomical and linguistic signifier, explicitly conjoining the witch's speech with her terrifyingly unrestrained and unrestrainable sensuality.[44] In a revisionist reading of this conjunction that anticipates contemporary feminist representations of the witch as a powerful figure of feminine subversion, Dinesen suggests that the witch's craft—both power and artistry—lies not only in the soaring liberties of her body but in the flights of fancy that liberate her language: "She confirmed—in demonic fashion but with gravity—. . . that the secret of woman's power is suggestion."[45] The wise and worldly "French-born friend" whom Dinesen represents in the subsequent narrative as her ironic, maternal "teacher in the art of witch-craft" in Africa, elaborates on this semiotic power: "'That any female would lack reason to such a degree that she would start reasoning with a man—that is beyond my comprehension! She has lost the battle . . . before it began! No, if a woman will have her way with a man she must look him square in the eye and say something of which it is impossible for him to make any sense whatsoever and to which he is at a loss to reply. He is defeated at once" (35). The terms here prefigure Irigaray's notion of an "other language" that makes itself heard in a deliberately duplicitous feminine discourse—a provisional strategy for undermining the very order that would suppress woman's (double)talk. As Jane Gallop remarks in analyzing a passage from *Speculum,* "all clear statements are trapped in the same economy of values, in which clarity (oculocentrism) and univocity (the One) reign. Precision must be avoided, if the economy of the One is to be unsettled. Equivocations, allusions, etc. are all flirtatious; they induce the interlocutor to listen, to encounter, to interpret, but defer the moment of assimilation back into a familiar model. . . . [I]t is better for women to avoid stating things precisely."[46] This context makes new sense of the non-sense Dinesen describes in the passage above, and of her earlier, tongue-in-cheek definition of *Seven Gothic Tales* as "a nonsense book."[47]

Dinesen's own narrative strategy in "Daguerreotypes" partakes of this same bewitching double-talk. Ironically disclaiming responsibility for "the views . . . presented here" by displacing them onto her "old friend," she nevertheless carefully leaves the question open: "'It is of course up to you, *ma jolie,*'" she has the Frenchwoman remark, "'to make your own choice. I wish only in this connection to tell you a little story'":

> "As a young girl, my sister returned home from a trip to Italy and declared at a family gathering, 'I wouldn't give five francs for all the paintings in the Uffizi.' My half-grown brother cried out at once, 'For heaven's sakes, Marie-Louise, keep your opinion to yourself; you reveal a complete lack of business acumen.'" (36)

The two forms of obtuseness satirized here—the myopia that overlooks the value of great art and the literalism that miscalculates the symbolic economy of tropes—both turn on failures of reading. Likewise, if the reader who rejects the art of witchcraft resembles the girl who underrated the Uffizi, the reader who takes literally Dinesen's ironic disclaimer occupies the position of the fiscally minded brother—tone-deaf to linguistic play, oblivious to that "suggestion" that is the witch's secret power. As we shall see, throughout her career Dinesen would persistently return to the witch as a figure of subversive female potency and creativity whose craft was analogous to that of the woman writer. In both "Daguerreotypes" and *Out of Africa* she describes the hyena, reputedly the magically metamorphosed African witch, as a figure whose secret *jouissance* utterly obliterates the distinctions between masculine and feminine. Just so Dinesen herself, as a transgressive woman who like the hyena "takes the double part of male and female" (*OA*, 301) in her own writing and in whose pseudonym the hyena's haunting laughter echoes, challenges those sexual oppositions on which traditional notions of sexuality, order, and writing were founded. Indeed, on one level her work from beginning to end might be read as the elaboration of a revisionist discourse on witchcraft, a discourse that originated in her earliest Danish texts, recurred as one of the primary subtexts of *Seven Gothic Tales* and *Out of Africa*, and reappeared in later fictions like "The Sailor-Boy's Tale," "Echoes," "The Caryatids," and the posthumously published "Bjørnen og Kysset" ("The Bear and the Kiss").

Her conceptions of her writing as an "art of witchcraft" (*Essays*, 36) were abetted by Canfield's teasing Introduction to *Seven Gothic Tales*. "It feels," remarked Canfield on first looking into Dinesen's Gothic, "exactly like a spell" (v). A kind of anteroom through which we pass into the larger fictive structure, Canfield's essay makes a pretext of inviting the reader to seek the "father" of the fictions within while hinting that no such legitimating authority can be found: "I can't even tell you the first fact about it which everybody wants to know about a book—who is its author. In this case, all that we are told is that the author is a Continental European, writing in English although that is not native to his pen, who wishes his-or-her identity not to be known." Indeed "his-or-her" absence, uncertain gender, and cultural indeterminacy become figures for the peculiar, transgressive undefinability Canfield identifies as the distinguishing feature of the text, which she tropes as forbidden "fruit," bearer of unspeakable knowledge: "The person who has set his teeth into a kind of fruit new to him, is usually as eager as he is unable to tell you how it tastes. . . . He must twist his tongue trying to get its strange new flavor into words," only to produce, at last, a "nonsensical combination of impossibles."

Significantly, it was not only Dinesen's multifarious destabilization of traditional authority, conventions, and value systems but specifically the association of these ruptures with a reconception of woman that inspired one of the earliest and most vehement attacks on *Seven Gothic Tales*. Frederick Schyberg's notorious denunciation of the Danish edition pointedly locates what he labels its "perversity" in the text's unmooring of traditional gender categories: "*[T]here are no normal human beings in Seven Gothic Tales. The erotic life which unfolds in the tales is of the most* peculiar kind. Men love their sisters, aunts their nieces, various characters are enamoured of themselves, and young women *cannot* or *will not* bear children."[49] As Schyberg's attack makes clear, Dinesen's use of Gothic as a disruptive, "polluting," incestuous form that coupled those things that according to phallogocentric logic must be kept apart was inseparable from the inscription of the feminine force and generativity she would later embody in the figure of woman's *caprice*. It is precisely the profoundly conservative, masculinist perspective exemplified in Schyberg that Dinesen caricatured in figures like Pompilio and mocked in her tongue-in-cheek description of *Seven Gothic Tales* as "a nonsense book," an explicit and illicit challenge to traditional conceptions of law, order, and signification both cultural and narrative: "If we write like that . . . it must be disappointing for people who are expecting a book that has *meaning* in it."[50]

This definition, like her references to "mischief" and "devilry," returns us implicitly to where we began: the persistent synonymy of Gothic, throughout its history, with "barbarism," a term, as Dinesen's pun reminds us, that is the precise etymological equivalent to *non-sense*. Originating as a signifier for those whose speech was unintelligible to "civilized" (specifically Greek) peoples, *barbaros* simultaneously marks the language of the Other as the locus of alienation, disturbance, and meaninglessness and correlatively allows a definition of self as prior, unitary, transcendent, and normative. In this context, then, "Gothic" is quite literally the name of the unspeakable. And as Dinesen's remarks about witchcraft and her own particular Gothic imply, the "barbarians" without have not been the only threat to established social and discursive orders. The Western cultural tradition is pervaded by a discourse on woman as another kind of alien or barbarian, all the more fearsome because situated at the very core of culture—the "disorder," as Rousseau put it, that had to be regulated, controlled, colonized in order for "civilization" to continue.[51] As the history of discourses on witchcraft reveals, the unruly woman, unwilling to accept the "paradisial" inhibitions of the angel in the house, exposes the *hostility* to traditional symbolic orders that haunts the heart and hearth of the *hostess*.[52] As we have seen, Dinesen had already commented explicitly about the subversive possibilities of this notion of feminine hospitality in her remarks on "playing the hostess" in her disagreements with British colonialists over the question of their treatment of Africans; but her words also apply to the position she would assume in her writing (*LA*, 240–41). As she would suggest in "Babette's Feast," that late, great retrospective on her own authorial project, to accept the feast of fiction she proffers is to taste, as Canfield's analogies insist, "strange" and dangerous "fruit."[53] Edwin Ardener's theory of the discursive "wild zone" occupied by women as a "muted" and marginal group within phallocentric culture becomes especially illuminating in this context.[54] Since, as Showalter puts it, "dominant groups control the forms or structures in which consciousness can be articulated," that area of women's experience that does not coincide with the dominant androcentric sphere remains, from within that sphere, invisible and silent—literally non-sense and non-being: a "no-man's-land, a place forbidden to men. . . . [M]en do not know what is in the wild."[55] But as Dinesen herself would later suggest in "The Blank Page," "silence" is not "emptiness." Through the art of "story-telling women" the haunting, barbaric discourse of the wild space may find a voice, may become comprehensible or legible, so that finally, impossibly, scandalously, "silence will speak."[56]

Thus, if Dinesen constructed her Gothic texts as transgressive monuments to the improper, the marginal, and the deviant—the "feminine"—she also valorized the *outré* and outrageous as fundamental to the evocation of an alternative discourse, a "mystery" unfathomed and unfathomable by those who would remain secure within the dominant symbolic order. Her stress on Gothic as "*simultaneously* elevated" and "jest[ing]," on "mystery" as well as "mockery," calls attention to the paradoxical distinction of the genre as a form, like ritual, of *serious play,* the *ludic* in its strongest sense.[57] Her conception reminds us of the affiliation of literary Gothic from its inception with the Longinian "sublime," that conflation of beauty with terror that Edmund Burke codified in his *Enquiry into Our Ideas of the Sublime and the Beautiful* and associated with both "the multiplication of infinities" and, correlatively, with mysteries beyond ordinary comprehension, making sublimity and "irrationality" inseparable.[58] As the etymological links of *sublime* and *subliminal* suggest, the Gothic potentially impels us simultaneously toward the upper limits and beneath or beyond the ordinary thresholds of perception and representation.[59] It was an effect that Dinesen, again prefiguring Bakhtin, persistently associated with the eruptive "spirit of carnivalization," that "liberation from the prevailing truth and from the established order" that "marked the suspension of all hierarchical rank, privileges, norms, and prohibitions" in a festival of "becoming, change, and renewal."[60] Ultimately, the "nameless" and "bizarre power" that Canfield intuited at the heart of Dinesen's Gothic edifice is not death, but that "laughter of liberation" through which Dinesen figured woman's engenderings of an other text, an other way of being (*SGT,* 21). "This world," she would write in one of her many oblique commentaries on her own fictive cosmos, "is like [a] children's game . . . ; there is always something underneath—truth, deceit; truth, deceit! . . . The witty woman chooses for her carnival costume one which ingeniously reveals something in her spirit or heart which the conventions . . . conceal. . . . So speaketh the Arbiter of the masquerade:

'By thy mask I shall know thee.' . . . And [in] the hour in which Almighty God himself lets fall the mask . . . what a moment! . . . Heaven will ring and resound with laughter . . . !" (*SGT*, 26). Just so, while wearing the "mask" of masculinity and claiming the "conventions" of traditional Gothic, Dinesen carnivalizes her parent genre, parodistically subverting its subversions. Significantly, the passage above is introduced by a reflection on "womanly modesty" as a form of "deceit on principle" (25)—a strategy that takes mandated codes of feminine concealment and appropriates them to subvert the phallocentric order they appear to serve. Thus "God *himself*," the tale suggests, may be a *her*—sufficient occasion for the "laughter" that *re-sounds,* quite literally, in the pseudonym of the "Arbiter" of the text we read.[61]

In the late essay "On Orthography," in one of her many self-reflexive references to *The Thousand and One Nights*, Dinesen would write that "when Ali Baba's slave Morgana saw that the forty thieves had found her master's house and marked it with a cross in order to return and kill him, she took a piece of chalk and marked ninety-nine other houses in the neighborhood with the same sign, so that Ali Baba's house was undistinguishable among them. This was a stroke of genius and as a result Morgana has become . . . justly immortal, for she not only had energy and self-confidence, but she knew what she was doing: her purpose was to confuse" (*Essays,* 149). As we shall see, *Seven Gothic Tales* uses writing in comparable ways—as both protective device and sign of subversion. Like Morgana and her creator Scheherazade, Dinesen too, under the guise of submissive devotion to the father's law, would enact a ludic feminine duplicity in inscriptions that would ultimately make her, though apparently "slave" to the "master's house" of fiction, comically triumphant and "justly immortal."

5

"A world turned upside down"

Subordination of the feminine to the masculine order . . . appears to be the condition for the functioning of the machine. . . . What would become of logocentrism, of the great philosophical systems, of world order in general if the rock upon which they founded their church were to crumble? . . . Then all the stories would have to be told differently.

Hélène Cixous, "Sorties"

What extreme confusion would result if God were to perceive himself backward and the wrong way up. . . . If He had lost his grasp on those geometric landmarks that are indispensable in keeping the world moving along properly, in distinguishing and subordinating Same and Other.

Luce Irigaray, Speculum of the Other Woman

"Ah, but . . . [God] may like a world turned upside down."

Isak Dinesen, "The Deluge at Norderney"

As the inaugural narrative of an inaugural book, "The Deluge at Norderney" marks the genesis of "Isak Dinesen" and the symbolic threshold for the reader's entry into her fictional world. That this should be so is in part sheer historical accident: after many visions and revisions, Dinesen had begun *Seven Gothic Tales* with "The Roads Round Pisa," placing "The Deluge" at the center of the collection; but her American publisher Robert Haas reversed the two narratives, making "The Deluge" appear as a firstborn literary child.[1] In effect, then, it is a supplanter that begins Dinesen's textual lines. Yet that *Seven Gothic Tales* should commence with an unauthorized substitution and transference seems, in retrospect, curiously appropriate, ironically confirming Dinesen's claim that the "assaults of fate" might best be read imaginatively as cosmic jests, *figurae* both significant and beautiful (*OA*, 23, 250–53). For the book is preeminently concerned with unforeseen, often illicit substitutions, misplacements, reversals, and revisions. And "The Deluge"—with its vatic narrative voice, its eddying concentric circles of narrative, its play with disguise and duplicity, and its reflexive preoccupation with storytelling—functions brilliantly as an introductory paradigm of Dinesen's fiction. Finally, despite the death by water it ostensibly proclaims, "The Deluge" is also quintessentially a text of beginnings.

In "The Old Chevalier," the second tale in the collection, the eponymous protagonist makes the Judeo-Christian book of beginnings the foundation for his rueful reflection on " 'the emancipation of women' ":

> Most women, when they feel free to experiment with life, will go straight to the witches' Sabbath. . . . I have always thought it unfair to woman that she has never been alone in the world. Adam had a time . . . when he could wander about on a fresh and peaceful earth, among the beasts, in full possession of his soul, and most men are born with a memory of that period. But poor Eve found him there, with all his claims upon her, the moment she looked into the world. That is a grudge that woman has always had against the Creator: she feels that she is entitled to have that epoch of paradise back for herself. Only, worse luck, when chasing a time that has gone, one is bound to get hold of it by the tail, the wrong way around. Thus these young witches got everything they wanted as in a catoptric image. . . . All this they got from reading—in the orthodox witches' manner—the book of Genesis backward. (*SGT*, 87–88)

Following Dinesen's elaborate interlinking of the Gothic tales, which repeatedly echo one another in a reflexive colloquy on their own interactions, I would take this subsequent text as my own beginning, approaching "The Deluge" not prospectively but, "in the orthodox witches' manner," *preposterously*. As the passage reminds us, if the Genesis creation narratives be read "backward," woman precedes both man and the Lord's ordering logos. Though Dinesen exposes the chevalier's covert fear of such reversals (his uneasy, patronizing humor prefigures Pompilio's), she also uses his words to evoke the subversive potential of an alternative, illicit hermeneutic, a feminine rereading of Western cultural history which would radically interrogate the masculine priority his disquisition assumes. In her letters she had linked "biblical criticism" directly to "feminism" as harbingers of a "revolution" that "would bring about the collapse of the whole existing state of things" (*LA*, 259). Transposing the scriptural exegesis from "The Old Chevalier," I would suggest that "The Deluge" symbolically enacts that collapse, operating as the very catoptric Genesis the chevalier deplores. A counter-Creation that sweeps the reader both backward and (potentially) forward through the currents of history, psyche, and textuality, the narrative gestures beyond God the Father and the paternal word that founds his world to elaborate a renewed myth of origins that celebrates woman's Wording, anterior to the father's and yet its very ground, the polylogical undercurrent it must repress or silence in order to write its meanings firmly into law and literature. By playfully inverting and converting androcentric creation texts and master-myths—most prominently Genesis, but also the *Odyssey* and *Hamlet*—Dinesen poses her own fiction as an Other kind of beginning, a subversive comic scripture that simultaneously questions the canonical masculine authorities it incorporates and indirectly offers a way of interpreting her subsequent texts. It was a revisionist project that would absorb her throughout her career.[2]

I

"If the sea had asked people what they wanted her to be, they would have made but a muddle of her."

Isak Dinesen, "Peter and Rosa"

What's the meaning of these waves, these floods, these outbursts? Where is the ebullient, infinite woman . . . ? She, the outcast, has never ceased to hear the resonance of fore-language. She lets the other language speak—the language of 1,000 tongues which knows neither enclosure nor death. . . . Look, our seas are what we make of them . . . ; and we are ourselves seas, sand, coral, seaweed, beaches, tides, swimmers, children, waves. . . . We know how to speak them all.

Hélène Cixous, "The Laugh of the Medusa"

Literally outlined, "The Deluge" seems deceptively simple. Four characters—the elderly Cardinal Hamilcar von Sehestedt, the young Dane Jonathan Mærsk, the aging Danish aristocrat Malin Nat-og-Dag, and her sixteen-year-old ward Calypso von Platen Hallermund—are marooned in the loft of a barn during a flood at the northern European seaside resort of Norderney during "the late summer of 1835" (*SGT*, 2). Having relinquished their places in a rescue boat to a peasant family, they must wait until dawn for another boat's return, though the barn may collapse before that salvation. By way of diversion, they strike a Boccaccian agreement to pass the night by telling stories. As the allusion to *The Thousand and One Nights* which closes "The Deluge" suggests, their self-sacrificial gesture toward the peasants recalls Scheherazade, who also intervened in a deathly progression by putting herself in the others' place. In both texts narrative—engendered, like metaphor, out of the substitution of one body for another—keeps death at bay.

But before turning to the lofty scene of storytelling, the narrator lingers in the world it displaces. As a site where "ladies and gentlemen of fashion" move choreographically through the elaborate political, economic, social, and sexual rituals that signify and perpetuate traditional systems of masculine power and privilege, Norderney epitomizes the culture that has produced it. The text represents that culture as predicated on the principle of opposition, figured topographically as the division of the sea—which "had hitherto held the role of the devil, the cold and voracious hereditary foe of humanity"—and the land (1–2). Maintained intact by a system of dikes "made to resist a heavy pressure from seaward" (4), the land appears a locus of containment and solidity, the *terra firma* that grounds both androcentric social hierarchies and "the harmony of . . . philosophic system[s]" that reinforce them. Situated on one side of the divide between culture and nature, "civilization" and "wildness," the society seems unified, securely fixed by the laws of patriarchal primacy and patrilineal genealogy. Here titular and professional appellations—"Prince," "Duke," "General," "Professor," "physician," "the landed nobility," "the representatives of old . . . merchant houses"—encode a symbolic order wherein women—"young wives," "sisters," or "marriageable daughters"—are named only as circulating figures within the economy of sexual exchange that supports that order (1–2). According to the laws of this cultural grammar, "woman" can serve only as a signifier of "man," her very ability to *mean* predicated on her functioning as a subordinate term.

That this symbolic order resembles a narratology is suggested by the multiply reflexive analogues between its conventional scripts and those of certain nineteenth-century novels. At Norderney "life" perpetually mimics art: influenced by "the romantic spirit of the age," especially Gothic texts about "ruins, ghosts, [and] lunatics," the denizens of civilization come to the spa quite literally for *recreation*: their chief diversion is to stage themselves mimetically according to novelistic conventions. Regarding "a stormy night . . . and a deep conflict of the passions" as "a finer treat for the connoisseur than the ease of the salon," they self-consciously dabble with danger as they "walk upon the bleak shores and watch the untameable waves," courting the Gothic *frisson* of encountering—always at safe distance—the "eternal wildness" of both sea and psyche, and imagining "the terrible and faithless gray monster westward" as "some kind of *maître de plaisir*."

The possibility of this pleasure, like that of reading Gothic fictions, depends on the sense of security and control its practitioners enjoy in their "coquetry with the dangerous forces of existence" (2). The land, the social order it supports, and the concept of textuality they both embody appear alike invulnerable to any real perturbation. Yet just as the land is perpetually threatened by the very sea whose proximity permits pleasure to flourish, so on the borders of a seemingly stable social group, a rift opens. It is the women—the marginal, moveable figures within andro-centric culture—who most eagerly approach the periphery, that danger-ous, mobile line where the land meets the "wildness . . . of the open sea" (1). While "old gentlemen dug themselves down into political and dynas-tic discussions in the club . . . , their young wives walked to a lonely hol-low in the downs . . . to become one with nature, . . . and to gaze straight up at the full moon"; and the "rank briny smell" of the sea figures an "intoxicating" female sexuality (2). Verbal echoes reiterate this affiliation: inside the coaches returning them to civilization, "the young women pressed their faces to the window panes . . . , *wild* to catch a last glimpse of the *wild* scenery, . . . the one real place and hour of their lives" (3–4; my emphasis). "Woman" and "sea" thus become interchangeable, repre-senting both generative power and potential insurgency. In each case, what appears secured, tamed, or domesticated, a fixed sign within firmly established boundaries, implicitly threatens to rupture the systems that contain it.

This figurative equation resonates in the narrator's description of the "disaster" that befalls Norderney when, after a three-day storm, "the seas broke the dikes . . . and washed through," oblitering all intervening structures (2–3). Dinesen echoes Genesis 1, but in reverse: the deluge is a countercreation, a *devolution* that undoes the order of hierarchical opposi-tions—heaven and earth, sea and dry land, day and night (and implicitly "male and female")—established by divine fiat in the biblical myth of beginnings:

> It began with an evening of more than ordinarily heavenly calm . . . and a strange, luminous, sulphurous dimness. There was no distinguishable line of division between the sky and the sea. The sun went down in a confusion of light. . . . It was a highly inspiring evening. . . . That night people . . . woke up, terrified, by a new, swiftly approaching roar. Could their sea sing now in this voice? (3)

The deluge at Norderney is literally a *re-covery* of the land by "the deep," that primal source mastered and bound, in scripture, by the ordering, di-viding "spirit of God" (Gen. 1:1–2). On the psycholinguistic level, the sea's "voice" resembles the Kristevan semiotic or the maternal "fore-language" Cixous celebrates, a "resonance" of "1000 tongues" which from the site of the symbolic—like that system of hierarchical oppo-sitions erected by the word of the father in Genesis 1—can only be perceived as meaningless babble, "without form, and void." Yet in paro-dically inverting Genesis 1, creating the "world turned upside down" celebrated in the tale's later dialogue on divinity, Dinesen evokes not, as we might expect, the advent of chaos, but the murmurs of a prior narrative, the story of the mythic mother whose suppression by patrilogical *fiat* forms the unacknowledged subtext on which Hebrew myths of origin are founded: "that mighty female deity" (*OA,* 179–80) whose image Dinesen repeatedly associated with the empowering of a female narrative tradition. For "the deep" on which the order of the Father imposes itself is maternal: the cosmic "womb" of "the sea," as Job 38 puts it, which is "shut in," given "prescribed bounds," when "the Lord" lays "the foundation of the earth" and "stretches the line upon it."[3] It is this matrix, suppressed by the Father's order and yet its very ground, that rises again in the deluge at Norderney, erasing the "line[s]" that plot paternal domains and signifying systems. In this context, the Gnostic observations that inspire Malin's later comments on divinity assume new resonance: "There has been a fall, but I do not hold that it is man who has fallen. I believe that there has been a fall of the divinity. We are now serving an inferior dynasty of heaven" (56).

But even in effecting this apparent reversal Dinesen wryly acknowledges the tenacity of the patriarchal symbolic order: for the deep at Norderney, like that of Genesis 1, is itself subsequently recuperated, through *language,* by a paternal logos, stabilized and domesticated by being given, like woman, "a place and a name" (4) under the sign of the father:

> This flood lived long in the memory of the coast. . . . In the annals of the province, . . . it was called the flood of the Cardinal. This was because in the midst of their misery the terror-stricken people got support from one already half-mythical figure, and felt at their side the presence of a guardian angel. Many years after, . . . it seemed that his company in their dark despair had shed a great white light over the black waves. (4–5)

In identifying this priestly father—whose miraculous rescues analogize him to the divine Father he serves and reinforce the popular belief in his sanctity—as "The Cardinal Hamilcar von Sehestedt," Dinesen recalls that famous father of Hannibal whom Freud, among others, saw as the ultimate model of paternal heroism.[4] Significantly, the Cardinal's purpose at Norderney relates him explicitly to patriarchal textuality: he has come "to collect his writings of many years in a book upon the Holy Ghost. . . . [He] held that while the book of the Father is given in the Old Testament, and that of the Son, in the New, the testament of the Third Person of the Trinity still remained to be written. This he had made the task of his life" (5).

Following the narrator's lead, many critics, like the villagers, have assumed that "The Deluge at Norderney" is indeed "the Cardinal's flood"—a paternal inscription focused on the priest as chief spokesman for the textual father "Isak Dinesen."[5] And in fact, as author of a revisionist scripture, the Cardinal bears obvious resemblance to the narrator. Yet such an assumption becomes keenly problematic in the face of the unmasking that occurs near the end of the tale, when the legendary "Cardinal" declares himself an imposter, a professional *actor* who is also the valet and murderer of the real priest. In removing the authenticating sign of heroic identity, the blood-stained bandages that have bound his head throughout his rescue efforts, he takes the reader by surprise as well, exposing as deceivers both the "priest" and the narrator who has concealed his imposture.

In this context the bandage—whose bloody markings we, like the story's characters, have misread—becomes a figure of the tale itself. The moment of exposure is paradigmatic: from beginning to end, Dinesen poses her text as a series of such misrepresentations. Just as "nothing seemed to be firm" in the flood, which abolishes all ordinary signs, makes "moveable" all "foundation[s] and foothold[s]" (9), so in this text conventional narrative expectations—and the symbolic order that constructs and authorizes them—are repeatedly destabilized. All identities are rendered problematic, fluid, as the traditional narrative order—represented *par excellence* by "the book of the Father . . . in the Old Testament, and that of the Son, in the New" (5)—is progressively dismantled by a rising mother text, a "still . . . to be written" new New Testament that may engulf its paternal predecessors.

Such a formulation might appear paradoxical, for this flood, which unmoors all structures within the frame story of "The Deluge," also (temporarily) *confirms* the internal narrative by framing it, surrounding the space—like the barn itself—in which the interior fictions are constructed and performed by characters compared repeatedly to "marionettes" and "maskers" (13, 23–26). "'Nothing,'" Dinesen has the "Cardinal" remark in a pun that reflexively illuminates her own writing, "'is sanctified, except by the play of the Lord'" (14). The text, then, must be read not only as *deluge,* but also, like the barn, as a kind of theater, a place for *playing* in several senses: a scene for staging (its own) fiction-making processes. Significantly, Dinesen equates "game," "masquerade," and "illusion" with "poetry" (24–26). But just as the deluge of maternal "forelanguage" ruptures the apparent stability of paternal constructs, so in this theater what appears firm is in fact fluid: the "boards," quite literally, are shifting beneath the players' feet; the ground, frames, and "center" are equally unstable. In this disconnected space where "reality" is literally as well as figuratively *suspended,* nothing remains but talk and tale telling, the free "play" of language wherein all is permissible (14). When the ersatz Cardinal invites his companions to reveal their identities, then, it is in terms that make "self" inseparable from fabrication: "Tell

me who you are, and recount to me your stories without restraint" (27).
As an analogue to the larger book in which it appears, the barn is quintessentially a house of fiction.

It is a womblike space as well: Dinesen suggests multiple analogies
between the engendering of stories and the story of engendering. The
disjunctions and instabilities just sketched—and their narratological consequences—are directly related to the scandal of illicit birth. Parallel to
the flood's erasure of the signs and lines that establish the meaning of topography and the topoi of meaning—plots of ground, roads, narrative
structures[6]—is the effacement of *genealogical* lines: both women here are
orphans, both men bastards, cut off not only from land but from their
own origins. "Derelicts" (12) unmoored from that traditional ground of
reference, the name of the father, they resemble signifiers floating on the
currents of a semiotic flood. "Societies," remarks Catherine Clément,

> do not succeed in offering everyone the same way of fitting into the
> symbolic order; those who are . . . between symbolic systems, in the
> interstices, offside, are . . . afflicted with a dangerous symbolic mo-
> bility. Dangerous for them, because those are the people afflicted
> with what we call madness, anomaly, perversion, or whom we even
> label . . . "neurotics, ecstatics, outsiders, carnies, drifters, jugglers
> and acrobats." . . . But this mobility is also dangerous—or produc-
> tive—for the cultural order itself, since it affects the very structure
> whose lacunae it reflects. . . . And more than any others, women bi-
> zarrely embody this group of anomalies showing the cracks in an
> overall system.[7]

Dinesen sets just such motley characters adrift in "The Deluge." And in
the fluid space they occupy it is no accident that just as the Cardinal and
his Trinitarian writings are obliterated by the flood, so the patrilineal
symbolic order, which the Trinity reenacts and ratifies, is dissolved: fathers give way to mothers; sonship fades while daughters flourish.

2

> My mother says indeed I am his. I for my part do not know.
> Nobody really knows his own father.
>
> Telemachos, *Odyssey*

In a world to which legitimacy is the primary law and principle,
woman acquires a mystic value. She . . . alone . . . possesses
the power to transform the grapes of common earth into that
supreme fluid: the true blood. [She] was seal-keeper to the
name . . . and . . . according to the world of Rome she might

achieve without her lord and master what he could not achieve
without her.

Isak Dinesen, "Copenhagen Season"

Degenerate shadows of Truth, fakes, fantasies occur once man
meddles in the process of reproduction and representation. *The
offspring of Truth become bastards.* No one knows what origin,
what originating being to attribute them to.

Luce Irigaray, *Speculum of the Other Woman*

It is a critical commonplace that for patriarchal culture, as Tony Tanner
notes, bastards represent a "socially unstabilized energy that may threaten,
directly or implicitly, the organization of society, whether by the indeterminacy of their origin, the uncertainty of the direction in which they
will focus their unbounded energy, or their attitude to the ties that hold
society together and that they may choose to slight or break."[8] These
forms of social disruption find analogies in narrative disjunctions within
a system where textual genealogy, traditional narrative, and language itself operate, in Said's words, "dynastically," in "relationships linked together by family analogy: *father and son . . .* the process of *genesis, a
story.*"[9] As figures outside the bounds of legitimate culture, devoid of
"official" lineage or names, simultaneously antigenealogical and anti-
historical, bastards become persistently associated with the breakdown of
linear narrative.[10] Yet as Dinesen would repeatedly suggest, the figure of
the bastard conceals—even as it implicitly re-presents—a figure still
more scandalously anomalous: the bastard's mother, who by giving birth
outside the "legitimate" confines of what, in English, we so tellingly
name "wedlock," fractures the authorizing fiction of the father's creative priority.[11] Potentially more threatening to androcentric culture than
her child, it is she whose origins and origination that culture, in order to
maintain its authority, most insistently seeks to cancel or conceal. For
paradoxically, "legitimacy" itself depends on the mother's verbal guarantee: the necessary paternal affirmation—"this is my son"—is a leap
of faith across an unbridgeable gap in time and knowledge, an act of
interpretation hinged on *woman's word.*[12] The mother of the "illegitimate" child, paternity unknown, exposes the instability and finitude of
masculine authority by representing a subversive maternal lineage and
implicitly calls into question the symbolic order maintained in the Name-
of-the-Father. Thus woman's word becomes for the father *unspeakable*
in several senses, the ultimate scandal and potentially the most radical
source of disruption in a symbolic economy predicated on the control of
women's bodies, wills, and voices. In reserving the term "illegitimate"
for the fatherless child, so that to be "only" the child of a mother is to be

a sign cut off from any *proper* referent, the patriarchal system counters
that threat by doubly ratifying the erasure of the mother as origin and
name. Under these codes women's writings, those other fatherless offspring, become comparably illicit, disclosing the irreparable rifts in the
fabric(actions) of androcentric textuality.[13]

In making "identity" and "story" equivalent in "The Deluge,"
Dinesen underscores these interpretive issues. Through the male characters in the text, as in her male pseudonym, she reflexively enacts her own
"illegitimate" relation to a masculine literary lineage. By claiming linguistic authority, entering the domain of writing, she ruptures the lines
of male authorial genealogy and hence, implicitly, destabilizes the patriarchal order it supports. The responses her characters adopt toward illegitimacy may be read on one level, then, as her indirect theorizing of her
ambivalence concerning her own authorship. But she ultimately refuses a
genealogical model predicated on woman's erasure, for it is precisely
through the figure of woman that she interrogates the guilt-inducing
logic that conditions female authorial anxiety. Offering an alternative to
the essentially masculinist vision of law, history, and text perpetuated by
the figure of the bastard, she celebrates the mother's most flagrant gestures of "illegitimacy" as fertile sources of creativity and origin-ality. As
she has the "Cardinal" observe, it is only in the illicit that a new space
opens, and with it freedom to "play a fine game" (14) with signification itself, to make up new fictions with an imaginative "legitimacy" of
their own.

Let us turn now to the unfolding of these issues. If the "Cardinal"
initially proclaims his illegitimacy as radical liberation, Jonathan Mærsk
finds in his an intolerable *anomie* both literally and figuratively. He reads
his condition not as playful freedom but as a curse which, despite his
fierce would-be independence, dooms him to endless, unintentional repetition, making him no more than the figure of another (father) figure
entangled in a web of intertextuality. Significantly, the Danish pronun-
ciation of his name is virtually homophonous with the English "mask."
He first appears to us as a parodic Shakespearean text, his misanthropy,
coupled with the name of his native city, having earned him the comic
epithet "Timon of Assens." But as "a young Dane" suffering "from
a severe attack of melancholia" (10), he bears more obvious resemblance
to Hamlet. Officially "born [to] the skipper Clement Mærsk and his
wife Magdalena," Mærsk discovers, upon entering elite adult society,
that his "father" is—*not*.[14] Having "eaten of the tree of knowledge" he is
"closed . . . forever" out of "the garden" of innocence, permanently displaced from the paternal presence (35). Driven by helpless desire for the
symbolic restoration of the order that presence represents, and of his own
place as rightful heir within it, he longs only for pure "truth" of being, a

redemption from the status of threat, disruption, and falsehood that his bastardy represents (32).

Yet ironically, when this character in search of an author discovers one, his "authentic" father (about whose paternity, naturally, neither he nor we can ever be absolutely certain) seems only another figure of fabrication, a compendium of artifice: "He was a poet and musician, a diplomat, a seducer of women. . . . Still, all this was not what caught your mind about the man. But it was this: that he was a man of fashion. . . . [F]ashion itself was only, in Copenhagen at least, the footman of Baron Gersdorff" (30). The irony here is magnified by a further revelation: according to the homophobic standards of Mærsk's society, this "natural" father is supremely "unnatural"—a "seducer" not only "of women," but also of "pretty boys" (34), a gay connoisseur whose initial interest in Mærsk was purely sensual. Upon discovering the "truth" of Mærsk's identity, the baron joyfully relinquishes carnal knowledge for knowledge of his own reincarnation, proclaiming his paternity in an enraptured effusion that Dinesen writes as parodic Christian *credo:* "I believe this boy to be indeed the son of my body, and . . . as God liveth, I will legitimize him, and leave him all that I own. If it be not possible to have him made a Baron Gersdorff, I will at least have him . . . under the name of De Résurrection" (33).

"Filled with abhorrence" (35) at this version of patrilineal "legitimation," Mærsk attempts to flee, leaving in his place, significantly, a text— an explanatory letter to his father. But even in flight, he reflects both his biological progenitor and prior paternal master-plots. Upon reading his son's letter the Baron, "excited and delighted," launches into a rhapsody that recalls all the Shakespearian pre-texts Mærsk has disavowed: "'God, this misanthropy, this melancholy! How I know them. They are my own altogether! . . . It is young Joachim Gersdorff to a turn, but done all in black, an etching from the colored original. . . . Surely he shall be our heir, the glass of fashion, and the mold of form'" (36).

Desperate to escape this chain of textuality, Mærsk contemplates suicide; but even that gesture, the ultimate trope of melancholia, can only reinscribe the artifice he would elude (37–38). Finally, near despair, he seeks out his adoptive father, his very speech by now comically reduced to the echoic repetition he embodies: "'Father,' I said, . . . 'is Baron Gersdorff my father?'" But even this original figure of paternal authority becomes the agent not of firmness but of flux, his proposed remedy for his adoptive son simultaneously repudiating and unintentionally reifying the feminine: "'Little Jonathan, . . . you have fallen amongst women. . . . I know of a cure for everything: salt water. . . . Go and get well, . . . for you are looking very sick." As the site of a cure "by salt water," Norderney is, in several senses, Jonathan's last resort.

For this Hamlet, then, despite his title of "De Résurrection," the ghostly father can never be more than that: a tantalizing, ever-receding illusion. Even as Mærsk flees disorder, he also embodies it: he is forever, against his will, outside the bounds, cut off from the filiation he desires. As Dinesen implies, this specter of absence leads to speculation on the meaning of that other—Holy—Ghost. In the unstable Trinity in whose confines Mærsk/Hamlet seeks himself, the only certainty or "true" son-ship available to him is as the child of the mother whom he has repudi-ated and whose very name, Magdalena, signifies female disruption of the paternal project as surely as does the "salt water" to whose ministrations his "father" consigns him.[15]

If Mærsk constructs his autobiography as a life inseparable from fictions, the "Cardinal" explains his life by constructing a fiction inseparable from autobiography. His story, which narrates Simon Peter's post-Crucifixion encounter with a disguised and anguished Barabbas, in whose stead the Son has died, is a manifesto of filial guilt and retribution. As the text through which the "Cardinal" interprets his own fabrications, "The Wine of the Tetrarch" suggests that his boastful proclamations of the bas-tard's freedom conceal an anxiety as severe as Mærsk's about the patrilin-eal rupture he embodies. Both bastard and orphan, whose claims about his paternal roots neither we nor he can verify, "Kasparson" is also a self-proclaimed parricide, a false son who through murder becomes a false "father." Not only in his account of killing the Cardinal does he appear as outlaw like his double Barabbas—or, implicitly, like his classical ana-logue Oedipus; his personal illegitimacy also becomes the sign of a para-digmatic cultural rupture when he claims to be the illicit son of the Duke d'Orleans, "who . . . voted for the death of the King of France, and changed his name to that of Egalité. The bastard of Egalité! Can one be more bastard than that . . . ?" (73).[16]

In having the "Cardinal" call himself *Kasparson,* Dinesen works an-other complex play on the entanglements of "history" and "fiction": for Kasparson recalls that other outlaw, the wandering Swede Casparson who in 1928 sought Karen Blixen's assistance in escaping the British po-lice in Kenya. And far from being the heroic character that critics have construed in the "Cardinal," he appears in her letters as "a pathetic per-sonage," a "*hopeless case*"—a "wandering," childlike soul whom she, as indulgent hostess, maternally "adopts": "He was—an actor! . . . I like him very much; he is a really thorough 'sponger,' and they are always charming people,—pretty much of a toper too as befits the part, but what can you do with him?"[17] What, indeed, she might "do with" this questionable figure emerges not only in "The Deluge" but in *Out of Af-rica.* There, casting a significant hermeneutical glance at "The Deluge," she in effect claims and paradoxically "legitimizes" the criminal by a pro-cess of *re-naming:* re-calling him (as) "Emmanuelson"—literally, *the son of God with us* (*OA,* 196–204).[18] But Christ, as she would repeatedly suggest, was also the ultimate "illegitimate" child, his filial divinity utterly contingent on a woman's word.[19] Thus she makes Emmanuelson analogous not only to the Kasparson of "The Deluge," with his complex relations to the Father-Son dyad of the Trinity whose text the original Cardinal would have rewritten, but also to Jonathan Mærsk under his rubric "De Résurrection," and, most importantly, to "Isak Dinesen" as another "actor" whose mask conceals her true status as outlaw and outcast in the paternal textual lineage.

Dinesen's gesture of legitimation in *Out of Africa,* and the oblique commentary it implies on the mother's right to name, is replicated fictionally in "The Deluge." We have seen that even before the story begins, the father for whom the flood is named and about whom "the Annals" (and their analogue, the text itself) purport to tell has been *wiped out*— murdered and erased—by one whose identity remains perpetually open to question, who epitomizes displacement, substitution, and "charlatanry" (58). Despite the assertions of the official records, then, this is no fathered flood; the paternal authorship of the new New Testament it represents is spurious. Instead, like the flood that names it, "The Deluge" proclaims the rise of the maternal, a word that works, literally, as *contradiction* to all official records and conventional expectations. Dinesen obliquely signifies its ambiguous operations through the feminine dyad of Malin Nat-og-Dag and Calypso, whose names, relationship, and narratives ally them with the alternative maternal creation mythoi the flood evokes, prior to yet generative of the paternal fictions that would outlaw and appropriate them. It is significant that while both male characters exhibit tragic anxiety about their disruptive status as bastards, Malin and Calypso—both orphans and, as women, the ultimate "illegitimate" children of patriarchal culture—remain blithely free from such concerns. By liberating themselves from the categories of the symbolic order, they find a mobile, comic space of creativity and, as godmother and goddaughter, enact a feminine mythos older than the Trinity. It is this story that Dinesen recuperates as the condition for writing her own.

3

In the Name of the Father, the Son, and . . . the Woman?

Julia Kristeva, "Women's Time"

A young girl agrees with her mother, with her mother's mother, and with the common, divine Mother of the Universe.

Isak Dinesen, "Tales of Two Old Gentlemen"

"God and the Devil are one": the famous anti-Manichean declaration from *Out of Africa* (20) retrospectively illuminates Dinesen's representation of Malin Nat-og-Dag, the godmother whose penchant for French *bons mots* invites us to recall that in French *Malin* means "Devil"—a version of that "Lucifer" whose iconoclastic spirit Karen Blixen associated with her own writing. Underscoring the connection, Dinesen recurrently associates Nat-og-Dag with the demonic, suggesting her figurative identity with the sea, which has been cast as "devil" from the opening sentence of the text (*SGT,* 1; cf. 9,14,22). Malin's surname reinforces the association: in Danish "Nat-og-Dag," as the narrator notes, "mean[s], 'Night and Day'" (9), connecting Malin with cosmic cycles and suggesting that she, like the mother deities so feared and detested by the authors of Hebrew scripture, bears all oppositions within herself. Just as the paternal structures of the land gave way to the sea at the outset of the tale, so also the fraudulent "father" gives way, at the outset of their night of tale telling, to Malin, "as if handing . . . his leadership and responsibility over":

> "Madame, . . . I have been told of your salon, in which you make everybody feel . . . keen to be at his best. As we want to feel like this tonight, I pray that you will be our hostess, and transfer your talents to this loft. . . ." Miss Malin at once . . . took command of the place. During the night she performed her role, regaling her guests upon the rare luxuries of loneliness, darkness, and danger, while up her sleeve she had death itself . . . waiting outside the door to appear and create the sensation of the night. (15–16)

We have already considered some of the implications of Dinesen's own penchant for "playing the hostess." In "Daguerreotypes" she would apply this image directly to her writing, figuring her readers as "guests" in her house of fiction. In "The Deluge" it is to Malin, her own comic double, that she gives the most extreme expression of the free "play" that the flood enables in the floating "salon" of fiction which its hostess, like her author, "commands."[20] Given Malin's association with both divinity and the demonic, it is no accident that this play constitutes an uneasy dynamic, recalling the etymological conflation, in "hostess," of *hospitality* with *hostility*.[21] Dinesen implicitly reminds us that as "hostess" within the father's house, woman is simultaneously the crucial domesticated support for patriarchal culture and the potential source of its disruption.[22]

Sarah Kofman has demonstrated how obsessively and unsuccessfully Freud sought to "solve" the "riddle" of woman, to comprehend a power at once repellent and seductive to man, a fixation that he would struggle to control:

> Does he admit that woman is the only one who knows her own secret, knows the solution to the riddle and is determined not to share

it, since she is self-sufficient . . . ? This is . . . a painful path for man, who then complains of woman's inaccessibility, her coldness, her "enigmatic," indecipherable character. Or does Freud proceed, on the contrary, as if woman were completely ignorant of her own secret, . . . persuaded that she must be, that she is, "ill," that she cannot get along without man if she is to be "cured"? This path, reassuring for man's narcissisms, seems to be the one Freud chooses. . . . [T]he task assigned to thought in both cases seems in fact to be that of warding off some formidable danger. . . . Men wonder about [woman] because she worries them, frightens them, gives them the impression of a disturbing strangeness.[23]

Dinesen anticipates this critique of the masculine plight by representing Malin as the embodiment of woman at her most baffling, a "riddle" (19) who constitutes so extreme a contradiction that she can be accounted for only under the sign of "madness" (21): she is, by common report, "a little off her head" (16). In her youth this "madness" expressed itself in her irreverent play with a sexual economy that would predicate female "honor" solely on the preservation of chastity—a play that reduplicates Karen Blixen's own earlier critique of a system wherein "a woman's 'honor' always has to do purely with sex": "An 'honorable man' is in general thought to be a man who understands and follows such clear and simple, human concepts as honesty, reliability, loyalty, and fearlessness; an 'honest woman' is a woman who maintains certain traditions in her relationship with men."[24] Malin recognizes that because woman's body is her only "stock in trade" within this symbolic order, any reduction of the "sacred standard price" becomes "a deadly sin" (17–19). In a brilliant prefiguration of Irigarayan mimicry, Dinesen has Malin repudiate the traditional discourse on female "honor" through a parodically hyperbolic enactment of its central tenets: "Miss Malin . . . ran amuck a little in her relation to [this] doctrine. . . . Fantastical by nature, she saw no reason for temperance, and drove up her price fantastically high. In fact, in regard to the high valuation of her own body she became a victim of a kind of megalomania" (17–18). This (im)posture emerges as a form of deliberate feminine misinterpretation of "what [Malin's] governess had read her out of the Bible, that 'whoever looketh on a woman to lust after her hath already committed adultery with her in his heart'" (18). Taking "the words of Scripture *au pied de la lettre*," Malin liberates herself from (being) the currency of male desire by interpreting its signs as "a deadly impertinence, . . . as grave an offense as an attempted rape" (18). Since the "whole field of action" open to women "lay between the two ideas" of seduction and rape, the quickest way to "put . . . an end to their activity" was by "by amalgamating them"—that is, by reading these putative oppositions as, quite literally, the same.

Following one of the lines taken by Dinesen's intrusive narrator, critics have often interpreted Malin's "fanatical virginity" (18) negatively,
viewing her simply as a "pathetic figure" (18), the stereotypical "frigid"
spinster whose refusal of heterosexual union is a pathological sign of
"sexual deficiency."[25] Such a reading ignores both Dinesen's wry give-
away—"to the people who knew her well, it sometimes seemed open
to doubt whether she was not mad by her own choice" (16)—and the
implications of the extravagant comic exuberance with which Malin's
self-fabrications are represented. Anticipating Irigaray's interrogation of
"what the term 'frigid' means in masculine dicourse, and why women
adopt it only with a sense of guilt,"[26] Dinesen implies that Malin's strenuous refusal of the constraints imposed on her sex disrupts that paradigm
by means of which men control the circulation of women as of money
and language. By effectively removing herself as an object of exchange
within a masculine economy, by choosing, that is, to *own herself,* to set
her own "price" (17), she positions herself simultaneously as both "man"
and "woman." Thus she plays, as Kofman puts it, "*d'une manière double,*"
having it both ways at once, and becomes the very emblem of undecidability—a text unreadable by her culture's dominant interpretive
codes.[27] By operating outside the bounds of the oppositional representational models by which the symbolic order functions, she can only appear within those bounds as a locus of irrationality or non-sense. Yet it is
precisely this "caprice" (16)—like Benedetta's—that allows Malin an alternative play with cultural discourses, allows her to *write* as well as to
own herself. Abstinence, after all, does not quell but heightens and perpetuates desire by refusing its temporal (and inevitably less than totalizing) fulfillment. And like Scheherazade's stories, desire, by resisting
(en)closure, allows for the creation of further fictions.[28]

By driving "up her price fantastically high" (17), authoring her own
as opposed to her society's script for marriage, Malin ultimately sets all
the terms of that transaction, selecting as prospective husband "the idol
of his time . . . of the highest birth and enormously rich, . . . handsome
as an angel, a bel-espirit"—and, most significantly, a "young man [who]
had obtained everything in life—and women in particular—too cheaply"
(19). What attracts the aptly named Prince Ernest to Malin is precisely
what, in Kofman's analysis, obsessed Freud throughout his career: the
need to interpret, and thus to master, the "riddle" of woman—in Malin's
case the exhorbitant desires of a "woman about whom there was nothing
striking but the price": "Some people have an unconquerable love of
riddles. . . . Prince Ernest had this mentality, and, even from his childhood, would sit for days lost in riddles and puzzles. . . . When, therefore, he found this hard nut to crack, the more easily solved beauties
faded before his eyes" (19–20). Like Freud, however, Ernest dies before

achieving the solution or possessing the riddle, clasping at his demise "upon a battlefield of Jena" no more than a synecdochic trace of his elusive object: a "lock from an old maid's head" which, like "a wing feather of a Walkyrie, lift[ed] him from the ground" (20).

Characteristically resistant to the conventional denouement of such a plot, Malin refuses the nunnery, rejecting the literal role as "bride of the Lord" for another kind of life, fashioned with the aid of "a great fortune" into which, "at the age of fifty" she "came unexpectedly":

> There were people who understood her so little as to believe that it was this that went to her head and caused there the confounding of fact and fantasy. It was not so. . . . What changed her was what changes all women at fifty. . . . A weight fell away from her; she flew up to a higher perch and cackled a little. Her fortune helped her only in so far as it provided the puff of air under her wings that enabled her to fly a little higher and cackle a little louder. . . . In her laughter of liberation there was certainly a little madness. (20–21)

Money and menopause, which on the literal level remove her permanently from the phallic sexual economy she has so long eluded, on the figurative level become metaphors for her freedom *to represent herself,* in both senses—to speak for and to fashion herself anew.[29] Liberated from the patriarchal exchange system, she also liberates, through language, her long-preserved virginity, reveling in the currents of a transgressive *jouissance* that she, like her author, experiences not literally but as a function of *storytelling.* Just as she had earlier controlled the inscription of her own sexuality, so now she controls the erotics of discourse, which she appropriates and symbolically dispenses in excess:

> This madness took . . . the curious form of a firm faith in a past of colossal licentiousness. She believed herself to have been the grand courtesan of her time, if not the great whore of Revelation. She took her fortune, her house, and her jewels as the wages of sin, collected in her long career of falls, and because of this she was extremely generous with her money, considering that what had been frivolously gathered must be frivolously spent. She could not open her mouth without referring to her days of debauchery. (21)[30]

Significantly, despite its apparent reversal of her earlier "virginal" role, this one too stems from the parodic impulse that ruptures androcentric representational systems by taking them to "fantastical" extremes, elaborating a subversive feminine mode of signification that engulfs, via hyperbole, the authoritative text that would control its overflow:

> Faithful by nature, she stuck to the point of view of her youth with regard to the Gospel's words concerning adultery. She had the word

of the Bible for it that a multitude of young men had indeed committed it with her. But she resolutely turned them inside out, as a woman will a frock the colors of which have disappointed her by fading. She was the catoptric image of the great repenting sinner whose sins are made white as wool, and was here taking a genuine pleasure in dyeing the pretty lamb's wool of her life in sundry fierce dyes. . . . [A]ll the perversities of the human world of passion . . . were to her little sweetmeats which she would pick, one by one, out of the *bonbonnière* of her mind, and crunch with true *gourmandise*. In all her fantasies she was her own heroine. (22)

In his classic study of witchcraft, recalled repeatedly in *Seven Gothic Tales,* Jules Michelet had remarked that "the Witch does everything backward and upside down, in direct contradiction to the world of religion" and of the secular laws it upholds.[31] In analogizing Malin to legendary female transgressors who conflate horror and "ecstasy"—"the Mary Magdalene of the Gospel," "the Medusa," and the "witch," (22)— Dinesen reiterates her earlier depictions of her own craft. As a "riddle" to be interpreted, the source of a scandalous new narratology, "a catoptric image" of patriarchal representations of woman, Malin becomes a synecdoche of the tale she inhabits, another figure of a linguistic "deluge" that "breaks the dikes" upholding the security of a traditional symbolic order and turns the world "upside down" (60). And that tale, in turn, with its heretical free play with Scripture and its catoptric impulses, becomes a synecdoche of *Seven Gothic Tales*. As Dinesen suggests by exploiting the etymological connections of "riddle" and "reading" (OE *raedan,* "to read, to interpret"), to interpret Malin is to interpret her author's own fantastic fictions (19–20). Into this "abyss of corruption," this flood of "imaginary excesses," rhetorical *dépense,* and linguistic *jouissance,* the author, like her character, can "dive . . . with the grace of a crested grebe" (21–22).[32]

According to the word of the father, the Cardinal is the text's proper *alter deus:* "The Pope himself . . . said of him: 'If, after the destruction of our present world, I were to charge one human being with the construction of a new world, the only person whom I would trust with this work would be . . . Hamilcar'" (6). But with the character of Malin Dinesen shifts this paternal construct, proposing instead an *alter dea* whose illicit discourse, like the tale that articulates it, becomes a new, maternal scripture that in its sheer unrestrained prodigality shatters and overflows the boundaries of patrilogical authority. Thus the most profound "play of the Lord" appears as the play of her language, a spectacular ludic ritual which, as we have seen, Dinesen analogizes to "carnival" (26), that cultural "play" in which all official "identities" are put in question, all sexual categories ruptured.[33] As Malin remarks to the "Cardinal," the "divine" quality of woman is "deceit on principle": "I . . . have always held that the Lord has a penchant for masquerades. . . . And when I have, in my life, come nearest to playing the role of a goddess, the very last thing which I have wanted . . . has been the truth" (24–25). As Dinesen's self-referential pun on Malin's "laughter of liberation" suggests, the male pseudonym "Isak" becomes the insignia of that subversive carnivalization at work in her own fictions: " 'It is the sign of hidden power which gives courage'. . . . 'By thy mask I shall know thee'" (26).

4

The little girls and their 'ill-mannered' bodies immured, well-preserved, intact unto themselves, in the mirror.

Hélène Cixous, "Sorties"

Woman for women. . . . *In* her, matrix, cradler; herself giver as her mother and child; she is her own sister-daughter. . . . Everything will be changed once woman gives woman to the other woman. . . . It is necessary and sufficient that the best of herself be given to woman by another woman for her to be able to love herself and return in love the body that was 'born' to her.

Hélène Cixous, "The Laugh of the Medusa"

If, in re-making the text of her life, Malin symbolically becomes her own mother, analogous to the authorial mother whose fictive daughter/double she is, this maternal genealogy is replicated in her relation to her goddaughter. From her first appearance Calypso, "imagining herself as a great divinity of the sea," is figuratively equated with Malin, the deluge, and the text it names. Dinesen's metaphors situate this mother/daughter dyad, like the sea, on the margins of culture, as a perpetual threat: the women are "fierce devils" (14), "tigresses, one old and one young, the cub quite wild, the old one only the more dangerous for having the appearance of being tamed" (9; cf. 41). But if Calypso, like her godmother, embodies the feminine "deep" over which the paternal order seeks domination in Genesis, Malin's arch account of their affiliation appropriates Christological and Marian typologies as well, rewriting the New as well as the Old Testament. "You see this girl?" Malin asks Mærsk:

"She is not my own daughter, and still, by the Holy Ghost, I am making her, as much as . . . Baron Gersdorff ever made you. I have carried her in my heart and in my mind, and sighed under her weight. Now the days are accomplished when I shall be delivered, and here we have the stable and the manger. . . . There are more martyrdoms than yours, Misanthrope of Assens. . . . This girl has been fed on . . . salt plains and on brine and bitter herbs. Her little heart has had nothing else to eat. She is indeed, spiritually, an *agneau pré-salé,* my salted little ewe lamb." (40–41)

Beginning at the precise center of the tale (40), Malin's narrative of Calypso is also the symbolic core and the microcosmic analogue of the larger text as feminine scripture. Like the gospels it displaces, it unfolds a narrative of abjection, symbolic sacrificial death, and miraculous resurrection, with Calypso as "lamb" of god; but its operative logos is not paternal. Through Malin's narrative Dinesen gestures toward a new theology, joining god(the)mother and god(the)daughter in the beginnings of a feminine trinity. Significantly, in earlier, unpublished versions of the story, Calypso's name was *Caritas.*[34] Dinesen's decision to alter that name suggests that here, as in Mærsk's prominent resemblance to Telemachos and Kasparson's to Oedipus, her revisionist mythos would remake classical as well as Judeo-Christian master-plots. Calypso is a type not only of the Great Mother erased in Hebrew creation mythoi or of a feminine Christ, but most obviously of that goddess on whose island, in whose womblike "hollow cave," Odysseus was held prisoner.[35]

In his subtle etymological analysis of "The Name of Odysseus," George Dimock observes that in Odysseus's quest to establish his own "identity," Calypso's island represents "nonentity":

> Kalypso is oblivion. Her name suggests cover and concealment, or engulfing; she lives "in the midst of the sea"—the middle of nowhere . . .—and the whole struggle of the fifth book, indeed of the entire poem, is not to be engulfed by that sea. . . . Leaving Kalypso is like leaving the perfect security and satisfaction of the womb; but, as the Cyclops reminds us, the womb is after all a deadly place. In the womb one has no identity, no existence worthy of a name. Nonentity and identity are in fact the poles between which the actors in the poem move. . . . One must odysseus ["trouble"] and be odysseused, or else be kalypsoed.[36]

One might reverse the emphasis of this passage to observe that in a literary or critical discourse which assumes "identity" to be essentially masculine—inseparable, as Dimock notes,[37] from the establishment of the paternal name—Kalypso herself, and the womb with which she is associated, can only be ultimately *kalypsoed.* Dinesen's wry response to just this interpretive problematic appears in a brilliantly comic moment in *Out of Africa,* where she too engages in punning reflections on "the name of Odysseus." Dramatizing her ironic perception of her own writing within the weighty phallocentric traditions epitomized by Homer, she implicitly questions the interpretive stance that valorizes its masculinist perspectives:

> "Will your book be as heavy as this?" Kamante asked, weighing the Odyssey. . . .
> "No," I said, "it will not. . . ."

"And as hard?" he asked.

I said it was expensive to make a book so hard. . . .

. . . Still he did not go away, but stood by the table and waited, then asked me gravely: "Msabu, what is there in books?"

As an illustration, I told him the story from the *Odyssey* of . . . how Odysseus had called himself Noman. . . .

"How did he," he asked, "say the word, *Noman,* in his own language? Say it."

"He said *Outis,*" I told him. "He called himself Outis, which in his language means Noman."

Must you write about the same thing?" he asked me.

"No," I said, "people can write of anything they like." (*OA,* 48–49)

And yet, of course, in "The Deluge" she does "write about the same thing"—but seen through a "catoptric" feminine optic: it is no accident that Malin's narrative of Calypso turns on an encounter with a mirror, which Dinesen uses to reflect simultaneously on patriarchal representations of woman and on woman and representation. The episode, like Calypso's larger story, constitutes a dazzling speculation on the problematics of female authorship in an overwhelmingly masculinist textual lineage. In revising Homeric tradition, Malin's tale suggests what it means to be, quite literally, *no man*—to be, that is, *woman:* "annihilated" (45)— *calypsoed*—so thoroughly by a phallocentric order that she becomes precisely the "nonentity" that her own name signifies.[38]

According to Malin, Calypso is niece and ward of the misogynist homosexual poet August von Platen-Hallermund.[39] "Count Seraphina," as Malin wryly calls this foster father, has made his "huge castle" not only into an overwrought imitation of the Gothic (he "had a great predilection for the Middle Ages") but into a "heaven" of masculinity, a haven for one who "disliked and mistrusted everything female" (43). Dinesen underscores here not only the latent homosexual components of the Gothic novel but, more importantly, the extent to which male homosexuality might be read as the logical extension, the ultimate symbolic enactment, of the narcissistic premises of phallocentrism.[40] With its "tall towers aspir[ing] to heaven," "Angelshorn" is a phallic erection of hyperbolic proportions, "a highly exclusive monastery whereto only fair young monks . . . were admitted" (44) and where its owner could indulge himself in fantasies of his own primacy and invulnerability—of being *sui generis,* liberated from female origins and the taint of mortality the womb confers.[41]

It is also a heaven of narcissistic phallic textuality: "His idea of paradise was . . . a long row of lovely young boys, in transparent robes of white, . . . singing his poems to his music . . . or otherwise discussing his philosophy, or absorbed in his books." As a figure for male-dominated representational systems that erect themselves above the censored feminine body, Angelshorn can sustain its illusions only so long as "no woman was ever allowed to enter." Yet ironically, "in the very center" of the father's edifice, "most awkwardly for himself and for her," is the ultimate emblem of its disruption: a "little girl" (43). As a figure of female otherness and difference, Calypso is multiply *improper*, failing to reify not only her foster father's properties and *amour propre* but also his appropriations of the right to name and order "reality."

Seraphina's initial response to this anomaly is literally to *make up* (in both senses) *for what is lacking*, to cover over the fact of sexual difference by turning Calypso into a living metaphor, a mirror of man: "He had her dressed up in boy's clothes, . . . much occupied with showing himself to the world as a conjurer . . . capable of transforming that drop of blood of the devil himself, a girl, into that sweet object nearest to the angels, which was a boy" (43).[42] But when he is forced at last to read "the signs" of "his failure," his own impotence to erase the marks of femininity in her ripening body, "with a shiver he turned his eyes away from her forever, and annihilated her" (44).

The critical question of perception that subtends Calypso's relation to her foster father—"What if nobody could or would see you?" (40–41)—suggests the force of her story as a narrative of representation: in a paternal system that encodes "woman" as *lack* or castration, the feminine becomes illegible or invisible, a blank or hole in discourse. Lacking the phallus—that sovereign "angel's horn"—Calypso and all women appear devoid of both significance and signifying power: "In this dark castle the annihilated girl . . . knew that she did not exist, for nobody ever looked at her" (45). To defend the father from engulfment, woman herself must be calypsoed.

Calypso's liberation from the "annihilation" of this phallic specular economy issues from an alternative specularization which discloses the concealed mother at the heart of the masculinist project. Driven by a desire "to be like her acquaintances," to reflect the phallic vision, "Calypso resolved to cut off her long hair, and to chop off her young breasts" (46), thus literalizing the symbolic castration that she already signifies. Hatchet in hand, she seeks the one place in the abbey "where she knew there was a long looking-glass on the wall" (46). What she finds, located "in the very center" of the father's abbey, is the hidden space of the feminine: the long-shut room of "her great-grandmother" ("For, strange to say, the Count had had a grandmother. He had even had a mother"). The hidden room is, of course, a typical Gothic device; but Dinesen puts it to a use that foreshadows Irigaray's analysis of a crucial masculine terror: "the oblivion of incarceration in the shadow and the water of the mother's cave, room, womb, that immemorial home, the blindness shrouding the memory, blocking reminiscence . . . all this the Father vows to do away with by dazzling you with an endless day. . . . *Forgetting you have forgotten* requires a long methodical initiation."[43] Dinesen's puns underline the reduction of woman to "*Outis*" within the paternal domain: "It was a room that was never used; *nobody* would come there" (46; my emphasis). Yet in the very moment that "nobody" dis-covers herself as sacrifice ("She had never seen herself naked in a mirror" [47]), she also recovers herself as the source of new *reflections,* reversing the representational order by which woman is calypsoed: "At that moment she saw in the looking-glass a big figure behind her own. . . . There was nobody there, but on the wall was an enormous painting. . . . In the foreground three young naked nymphs, silvery as white roses . . . young girls of her own age, and of her own figure and face. . . . That it was a scandalous picture she lacked knowledge to see. . . . [W]hat surprised and overwhelmed her was the fact that . . . the whole thing was done in their honor and inspired by their charms" (47–48).[44] Within this "scandalous" re-presentation of woman Calypso learns to read her own difference and to read herself differently—"to create herself" (46) anew. As with Cixous's re-vision of the Medusa, whom the mirror imagery also recalls, Calypso discovers that seen from a woman's perspective, she *means otherwise; kalypso* no longer signifies "nonentity": "Her heart swelled with gratitude and pride, for here they all looked at her and recognized her as their own" (48).

Redressing herself, in both senses, with the "woman's clothes" she finds in the room, she repeatedly scans the mirror, ecstatically reproducing herself in her own image—multiply, orgasmically, reveling in her own body. Seeing herself objectively, she finds herself as (feminine) subject. But unlike the Lacanian construction of the mirror stage, Calypso's jubilant self-recognition leads not to fragmentation, alienation, and acceptance of the law of the father as the price of identity, but to "a great harmony" (48) and a repudiation of that law.[45] Self-consciousness, which for father-haunted men like Kasparson and Maersk constitutes a tragic burden ("who more than the bastard needs to cry out to ask who he is?" [27]), is for woman a potential salvation. For those denied subjectivity, narcissism may become a paradoxical way to liberation, leading not to destruction and destructiveness but to rebirth. Kissing the nymphs like "beloved friends," Calypso leaves the room initially to "cut off [the] head" of her uncle, but that symbolic castration is unnecessary, for seen from her transformed perspective the castrating father, the feared "minister of truth," is already emasculated, impotent even to engender a wish for vengeance: "What did she find? A poor little doll stuffed with sawdust, a caricature of a skull. . . . Had she been afraid of this creature—she, who was the sister of the nymphs . . . ?" (49).

This sense of another kinship enables her to leave the paternal edifice forever, liberating herself from its phallocentric constructions: "They might all have been dead as far as she was concerned. As she lifted the heavy medieval lock of the front door she lifted their weight off her heart." Her movement from the womb/room, the hidden locus of life encrypted in the father's tomblike monument, is restorative in several ways, returning her, like a Persephone, to the mother, and allowing the re-membering of a generative feminine mythos: "She walked over the moors, grave as Ceres. . . . Around the horizon the corn-lightnings were playing in her honor." The moment is also, as Malin's earlier comparison of Calypso to Christ suggested, a feminine version of the New Testament resurrection, as well as another rereading of the Fall. Unlike Eve, whose ejection from the paternal enclosure meant loss of paradise, Calypso's departure promises paradise regained elsewhere, a knowledge beyond the father's law: "In the early morning she came to the house where I was staying. She was wet all through like a tree in the garden. She knew of me, for I am her godmother . . ." (49–50).

Dinesen suggests, then, that "at the very center" (48) of the Gothic construction, as Calypso's story is at the core of Dinesen's own Gothic tale, is a concealed, subversive feminine space, the grandmother's—literally, Great Mother's—womb/room wherein woman blissfully reads, writes, and rights herself, finding in herself, quite literally, what Irigaray terms *ce sexe qui non est pas un*. As the site of a cryptic feminine otherness that undermines the father's prideful erections, the grandmother's room becomes a synecdoche of Dinesen's own peculiar remaking of father-centered narrative traditions in *Seven Gothic Tales:* one recalls that she had planned to place "The Deluge" fourth in the collection, quite literally making the grandmother's room and the godmother's narrative the decentering center(s) of her own book. Ultimately, of course, the two constructs are inseparable: the grandmother's room itself is the purely linguistic product of Malin's "tale," engendered by her "opulent power of imagination" (46), just as that tale is a product of Dinesen's. A fabrication in the strictest sense ("At this point of Malin's narrative, the girl . . . began to listen with a new kind of interest, as if she herself were hearing the tale for the first time"), Malin's narrative is not history, but a figure through which to interpret it: "the story, correct or not, was . . . a symbol" of "what [Calypso] had in reality gone through" (46). The real "mirror" in which Calypso sees herself, then, is the godmother's discourse, that new New Testament through which, as Malin's pun suggests, the daughter is *delivered*—both liberated and reborn (40). Dinesen would later describe the conception of *Seven Gothic Tales* itself in precisely comparable terms. She could not write, she told her brother, "until I had heard my own voice, seen myself in the mirror, as another person to whom one is speaking."[46] As Malin's tale is a "symbol" that gestures toward a larger story of deliverance, so Calypso and Malin are telling "symbols" of their author's own (self)delivery through the "power of imagination of . . . woman" which, like the flood itself, "was enough to sway anybody off his feet" (51).

5

> We are already going at history "backwards." But it is a reversal "within" which the question of the woman still cannot be articulated, so this reversal alone does not suffice. . . . For what is important is to disconcert the staging of representation according to *exclusively* "masculine" parameters, that is, according to a phallocratic order. It is not a matter of toppling that order so as to replace it—that amounts to the same thing in the end—but of disrupting and modifying it, starting from an 'outside' that is exempt, in part, from phallocratic law.
>
> Luce Irigaray, *This Sex Which Is Not One*

Eluding the oppressive assumptions of a patriarchal symbolic order, Nat-og-Dag and Calypso liberate not only themselves, but also the men who have joined them in the free-floating space of the narrative. Dinesen's vision, so far from being simply gynocentric—and thus reifying androcentric hierarchies in reverse—is fluid, all-embracing, challenging the very concepts of centricity and stasis. It is significant that Calypso's story, the structural center of the text, is represented not as some solid historical account of "reality," but explicitly as its re-presentation through "symbol" (46). And the center of *that* center, the grandmother's room wherein "woman" is reread and rewritten, reveals identity not as some totalizing, monolithic presence, but as a series of reflections, each one at once affirming and displacing the others in an infinite resurgence like that of the sea that surrounds the narrative. Just as Malin's "madness" puts the concept of a stable "self" into question, so the "self" Calypso finds in the grandmother's mirror is revealed as the very figure of multiplicity. Even Calypso's name, as a synonym for "deluge," reflects that primal Grand Mother, "the deep" that overflows the Father's dichotomozing, hierarchizing word, just as Nat-og-Dag's name maintains in perpetual interplay the seeming opposites of darkness and light.

That this plural "woman" exceeds exclusive, centralizing impulses is suggested as well in Dinesen's representation of the symbolic "marriages" of the male and female characters in the loft:

> "Come, Jonathan and Calypso," said Miss Malin, "it would be sinful and blasphemous for you two to die unmarried. . . . You are hers,

and she is yours, and the Cardinal and I, who stand you in parents' stead, will give you our blessing. . . . Your marriage must be in every way a more intense affair than the lukewarm unions generally celebrated around us, for you must see her, listen to her, feel her, know her with the energy which you meant to use for jumping into the sea." (53)

What Malin calls a "new marriage rite"—a new *righting* and *writing* of sexual difference—takes place, significantly, "in a clear space in the middle of the circle," with "the sighing of waters all around and beneath" (53), a space where the (re)production of novel meanings gestures towards Dinesen's own scene of creation. As part of a New Testament, this "marriage" reverses and revises the divine marriage in Revelation: the Lamb here is not God the Son but god(the)daughter, the "*agneau pré-salé*" (41), symbolic child of the briny waters her name embodies. It is the "son" Mærsk who receives grace through her. In Dinesen's new Holy Family, where "woman" becomes the sign of potential rebirth in a state outside the law, what might otherwise appear as a revalorization of patri-archal marriage is in fact a further subversion of it. This "new marriage rite" figures not exchange and ownership but interchangeable imagina-tive bliss, generativity, and reciprocal *dépense*. What Malin prophesies as its symbolic consequence is not a reproduction of oneness but the very image of doubleness and difference: the "birth of twins" (52). It was a figure, as we have seen, that Dinesen would repeatedly relate to her own writing.[47]

A comparable reformulation occurs in the symbolic marriage rite through which Malin restores Kasparson to her own version of "legit-imacy," prefiguring Dinesen's "legitimation" of his prototype in *Out of Africa*. In one magnificent gesture, Nat-og-Dag creates a fiction of trans-formation which bypasses both traditional patrilineage and the social codes that support it:

> The actor had risen with her, her *cavalière servante,* and now stood up. She looked at him with radiant eyes.
> "Kasparon, you great actor," she said, "Bastard of Egalité, kiss me."
> "Ah, no, Madame," said Kasparson, "I am ill; there is poison in my mouth."
> Miss Malin laughed. "A fig for that tonight," she said. She looked, indeed, past any sort of poison. She had on her shoulders that death's-head by which druggists label their poison bottles. . . . But looking straight at the man before her, she said slowly and with much grace: "*Fils de St. Louis, montez au ciel!*"

That benediction, reputedly spoken by a priest to Louis XVI just prior to his beheading,[48] becomes here the godmother's claim to imaginative power over both history and fiction: woman's regenerative tale-telling bears the "grace" that washes away the guilt of a broken genealogy and bestows a "sonship" more compelling than any traceable through paternal lines. Anticipating Kofman's reading of woman as "great criminal" and "humorist," Dinesen makes Malin the blessed jester who confers her own (il)legitimacy on the outlaw/bastard/actor.[49] Reinventing him in a way that surpasses even his own spectacular powers of invention, Malin situates him utterly beyond the bounds of father and "*fils*," reconceiving genealogy itself as dependent on the word of the mother, who creates for the orphans and bastards of the world a new story.

As "the death's head by which druggists label their poison bottles" Malin becomes simultaneously the spectral sign of mortality and the medicinal antidote to the "poison" on the "lips" of the father—the remedy that overcomes the taint or contagion inherent in a certain reading of both "bastard" and "woman." Dinesen recalls Plato's play, in *Phaedrus,* on the term *pharmakon,* that "poison" that is also a "remedy."[50] The trope marks another of those ambiguous moments in which Dinesen blurs the boundaries between life and text, for the "poison" that can turn woman into a deadly vessel is literally venereal disease, that contamination spread, like phallocentric discourse, primarily by the operations of masculine desire. Yet Dinesen transmutes even this curse by imagining it differently. As we have seen, she dealt with her own syphilis by symbolically reconceiving it as the price she had paid the devil for the gift of storytelling; as a source of narrative, it could become, like a pearl, "disease turned into loveliness."[51] It is worth recalling that in the *Phaedrus,* as Derrida demonstrates, Plato repeatedly uses *pharmakon* to figure the ineluctable ambiguities, the deconstructions and reconstructions, inherent in *writing.* Thus, though the "Cardinal," as master of disguise and rhetoric, seems, in his final shocking revelation of duplicity, to have the last word, the conclusion suggests that in fact that last word—the *dernier cri,* to invoke Malin's punning jest (38)—is both literally and figuratively *hers.* The story ends not in the *ciel* of *le père,* but in the sea—*la mer*—of *la mère.*

6

> We . . . love fluidity. . . . The birth that is never accomplished, the body never created once and for all, the form never definitively completed, the . . . lips never opened or closed on a truth. . . . Day and night are mingled in our gazes.
>
> Luce Irigaray, "When Our Lips Speak Together"

As "the dawn [is] breaking" and the flood waters overrun "the heavy boards" on which the characters have played out their night of fiction-making, Dinesen creates an analogue of her own narrative in Nat-og-Dag's quotation of *The Thousand and One Nights*—literally the last words in "The Deluge": "'*A ce moment de sa narration Scheherazade vit paraître le matin, et, discrète, se tut.*'" As the pun on the "breaking" of dawn suggests, the passage marks multiple ruptures. Just as the sea dissolves the walls separating inside from outside, so Nat-og-Dag's words dissolve the barriers separating history from fiction, author from narrative. In acting the role of Scheherazade, literally performing the gesture her lines describe (her voice and, presumably, her life end with her quotation), Malin explicitly translates her "self" into her text. In the same moment Isak Dinesen, the originary Scheherazade of the tale, also "falls silent," her voice ceasing with the end of her narrative. Yet these annulments of division suggest not death but rebirth: the silence of Scheherazade, we recall, became a generative matrix, source not only of woman's salvation, but of the father/master's transformation and the engendering of both narratives and children.[52] Dinesen's identification of herself and her character with the author of continually renewable feminine fictions suggests reflexively that out of this moment of dissolution, the tale itself is being born: the rising waters at story's end return us, literally, to its linguistic beginning—"The Deluge"—continually renewing the life of the text. If, like the author herself, the characters "die" into fiction, they also find thereby an ongoing vitality, just as dawn for Scheherazade marked not the predicted end of life, but the beginning of new creations.[53]

Given these complex reverberations and loose ends, "The Deluge" too appears not a firmly finished, closed structure, but a dis-closure of new narrative possibilities. As open and unstable as the rapidly splintering barn, the tale is a disappearing ground whose very existence is marked by *slippage*—of ending into beginning, of one text into another, of "fact" into fiction, author into character, life into story. Just as the flood in Genesis simultaneously effected the destruction of an old world and the rise of a new, so Dinesen's "Deluge" both destroys and creates. Dismantling canonical master-works—patriarchal structures like the barn "floating on the waters" (79)—Dinesen shapes the fragments into the genesis of a new creation, raising another "barn" in the Danish sense of that word: the "child" of the authoring mother whose oeuvre it begins.

6

Reading Contracts

Courtly love is two-faced: adored, deified, assimilated to the idol that accepts homage, she has the rank and honors of the Virgin. Conversely, and the same position, in her powerlessness, she is at the disposition of the other's desire, the object, the prostitute. Under these conditions, what is a woman's desire? What is left of it? What shows?

Hélène Cixous, "Sorties"

Writing to Bess Westenholz in 1926, Karen Blixen reflected ruefully on woman's status as cipher within the gender codes of "the old world order" wherein "'manliness' is a human concept" whereas "'womanliness' . . . signifies those qualities in a woman . . . that [are] pleasing to men, or that they have need of": "somehow [women] did not exist until the men came home." To "illustrate" the difficulties of women who "desire . . . to be human beings with a direct relationship to life in the same way as men," she cites "Milton, when he speaks in '*Paradise Lost*' of the creation of woman: '*He for God, and she for God in him*' [sic]. . . . So it was with men and women in regard to all the glories and possibilities of the world. No work, no talent, no form of productivity could pay woman anything nearly so much as pleasing . . . a man. It is not to be wondered at that they came to devote all their abilities to that." That is, according to the logic of an androcentric symbolic order, all contracts between men and women become variants of prostitution. For Blixen, the objectification this economy forces on women is epitomized by "chivalry, in which one first binds fast the legs of the object of one's homage in order to serve her" (*LA,* 259–63).

Dinesen interrogates this system, and the ties that bind it together, in "The Old Chevalier." Explicating the symbolic contracts it entails, she also addresses the problematic of woman and reading, or—to borrow a phrase from John Berger's classic study of the female nude—of "ways of seeing" woman within phallocentric referential frames.[1] Through the tropes of courtly love that figure the sexual transaction at the core of the narrative, Dinesen relates the act of reading to both a specific historical moment and, more fundamentally, a larger history of social and psychological systems that connect modern bourgeois society, like the medieval social structures that preceded it, to archaic roots. Pivotal to this project, as she indicates through the old chevalier's speculations on "reading Genesis backward" (87–88), are contradictory interpretations of "poor Eve" that simultaneously uncover the ground of the dominant patristic topos of woman as temptress and re-call the name of the mother in its radical sense as the sign of life.[2] If "The Deluge" operates as a "catoptric" rereading of Genesis 1, "The Old Chevalier" presents itself explicitly as a revisionist version of Genesis 2–3. In it, Dinesen narrates the story of woman literally dis-covered as a paradise regained, and of the subsequent rejection and dis(re)membering, within patriarchal consciousness, of what she might signify.

I

> A virgin body has the freshness of secret springs, the morning sheen of an unopened flower. . . . Grotto, temple, sanctuary, secret garden . . . what he alone is to take and to penetrate seems to be in truth created by him. And more, one of the ends sought by all desire is the using up of the desired object, which implies its destruction.
>
> Simone de Beauvoir, *The Second Sex*

On its simplest level, Baron von Brackel's story is a kind of set-piece of *décadence,* a nostalgic remembrance of *temps perdu,* unfolded in response to a philosophical question: "whether one is likely to get any real benefit, any lasting moral satisfaction, out of forsaking an inclination for the sake of principle" (81). The story begins as a narrative reconstruction of his Baudelairean encounter, as a young man in Paris "in the winter of 1874," with "a drunken young girl" (81) who approaches him as he sits despondently in the rain, stunned by the discovery that his mistress has just attempted to poison him. Like a *fleur du mal,* "a fresh bunch of roses in a gutter" (91), the woman is a figure of contradictions: her bedraggled finery and "highly rouged" cheeks mark her as prostitute, while her extraordinary grace, "fresh face," and "grave, childlike expression" bespeak another story, a "sort of mystery" that von Brackel, significantly, never troubles to interpret: "I knew . . . little of what moved her. . . . I . . . took her quite selfishly, without any thought of where she came from or where she would disappear to again, as if she were a gift to me. . . . What she thought of me . . . I can say nothing" (91–92).[3]

Taking her to his own rooms, he begins to "undress her, as I might have undressed a doll," interpreting his activity as the dismantling of one "work of art, the product of centuries of civilization," and the unveiling of another more cryptic one, "a secret which her clothes did their utmost to keep" (93). From the work of his godlike hands there emerges a "masterpiece" (97): "Woman"—"Eve herself, her waist still delicately marked by the stays" which, like the social codes of bourgeois society or the interpretive codes of an androcentric critical tradition, "imprisoned," "dominated and concealed her" (94–97). The name she gives—"Nathalie" (91)—reinforces this vision, suggesting both birth and, in its near-consonance with the Danish *naturlig,* "natural, artless."

In this manifestation, Nathalie appears the antithesis to the other "Eve" in von Brackel's recollections, the mistress whose attempt to murder him had driven him into the streets. Indeed, it is by introducing her plot—in both senses of that term—that he defers his progressive speculations on Nathalie. The first affair had begun as a replay of the rituals of *cortesia:* "My love was both humble and audacious, like that of a page for his lady" (82). As courtly lover he endures repeated humiliation, being reduced, successively, to "a groom failing in his duties," a "hairdresser," and "an absurd little punchinello" overshadowed by the phallic power of "the thought of her husband" (84, 85). But it is not terror that gives that "thought" its force or makes the husband the central motivation in the affair. At the heart of von Brackel's displacing narrative is a further displacement: the story of man's desire for man, which renders woman only a screen or counter: "My feelings for the lovely young woman, whom I adored, were really light of weight compared to my feelings for the young man. If he had been with her when we first met, or if I had known him before I met her, I do not think that I should ever have dreamed of falling in love with his wife" (86).

This rivalrous triangulation prefigures recent analytic paradigms of the homosocial/homosexual desire underlying such seemingly heterosexual structures as marriage and *fin amor.*[4] It is this concealed story of woman's displacement by man that determines all subsequent events in the Baron's narrative. Haunted by the "gigantic shadow" of the husband, von Brackel contemplates ending the affair, "when suddenly . . . she herself produced both the scene and the explanation, such a hurricane as I have never again been out in; and all with exactly the same weapons as I had myself had ready: with the accusation that I thought more of her husband than I did of her. . . . I had no reply, for I knew that she was right. . . ." (85–86). Yet even in confessing this attraction, the chevalier seeks to repress its implications: "I see that I ought not to have started talking about him, even after all these years. . . . He himself has nothing to do with this story" (86). This disingenuous denial generates another, similarly marked by a narrative digression. Acknowledging the truth of the mistress's accusation, the Baron disallows its force, professing amazement at her "competition" with her husband: "She was jealous of him as if he had been . . . her rival, or as if she herself had been a young man who envied him his triumphs. . . . I cannot, of course, know how this had begun between them" (87).

That beginning is unknowable precisely because, as the foundation of the phallocentric symbolic order, it is the unacknowledged, naturalized ground on which the chevalier stands. It is that old "dream of symmetry," as Irigaray puts it, from which woman's subjectivity is excluded like a "blind spot" and within which woman is "set between . . . two, or two half, men, a hinge bending according to their exchanges. . . . Off-stage, off-side, beyond representation, beyond selfhood" caught in a "game for which she will always find herself signed up without having begun to play."[5] Despite the chevalier's professed sympathy with woman's positioning in this game, he reads her resistance to its rules as perverse, unnatural, an instance of sex turned "the wrong way round" (88). As we saw in chapter 5, his subsequent patronizing analysis of "the 'emancipation of woman'" and professed sympathy for "poor Eve" is a masterpiece of ambivalence, its condescension charmingly mixed and masked with sympathy:

> Here were the young women of the highest intelligence, and the most daring and ingenious of them, coming out of the chiaroscuro of a thousand years, blinking at the sun and wild with desire to try their wings. . . . But most women, when they feel free to experiment with life, will go straight to the witches' Sabbath. I myself respect them for it, and do not think that I could ever really love a woman who had not, at some time or other, been up on a broomstick. . . . I have always thought it unfair to woman that she has never been alone in the world. . . . That is a grudge that woman has against the creator: she feels that she is entitled to have that epoch of paradise back for herself. Only, worse luck, when chasing a time that has gone, one is bound to get hold of it . . . the wrong way around. (87–88)

Dinesen implies that within the codes available to him, the Baron can read woman's desire only as a perverse attempt at role reversal, a "wild and mad jealousy of [men's] mustachios" which implies the unmanning of man within a sexual economy that merely replicates the oppositional system it would abolish: "She was desperately fond of me. . . . If she would be Othello, it was I . . . who must take the part of Desdemona. . . . She wished to destroy me so that she should not have to lose me and to see a very dear possession belong to her rival" (89).

Within this frame of reference, his sense of his own security badly shaken by "the abrupt and fatal conviction that she wanted me to die"

(89), the Baron interprets his encounter with Nathalie. No "emancipated woman," but a virginal "Eve" whose "pure faultlessness" and utter submissiveness encourage von Brackel to regard her as a kind of "gift" from the gods, she seems bestowed on him as a healing assurance of his own sovereignty, replacing him within the cultural text which predicates man's mythic status as hero—a chevalier—on his possession of woman: "Reality had met me such a short time ago, in such an ugly shape, that I had no wish to come into contact with it again. Somewhere in me a dark fear was still crouching, and I took refuge in the fantastic like a distressed child in his book of fairy tales" (98). Still fully clothed, he sits down to a champagne dinner with the naked woman, cozily imagining himself as another Adam enjoying his Eve in "what happily married people mean when they talk about the two being one" (99; cf. Gen. 2:24)—a formulation that abolishes her difference by assuming her absolute concurrence with his own "open-hearted" sense of "freedom and security." His later discovery that "she was as innocent as she looked" confirms his reading of her as "mine," his ownership ratified by the signs of her lost virginity (100–101).

Dinesen represents in this encounter the intersection of the symbolic legacy of chivalry and the power dynamics inherent in traditional representations of the female body as the site of masculine desire, signified by the appropriative gaze which that body is constructed to elicit. As Berger notes,

> in the average European oil painting of the [female] nude . . . the spectator . . . is presumed to be a man. Everything is addressed to him. . . . It is for him that the figures have assumed their nudity. But he, by definition, [has] his clothes on. . . . Her body is arranged . . . to appeal to *his* sexuality. . . . The woman's sexual passion needs to be minimized so that the spectator may feel that he has the monopoly of such passion. Women are there to feed an appetite, not to have any of their own. . . . [T]he sexual protagonist is the spectator-owner looking.[6]

Recent feminist film criticism has extended this analysis of male spectatorship as it relates to narrative, demonstrating (to quote Teresa de Lauretis's summary) that "it is men who have . . . defined the object and the modalities of vision, pleasure, and meaning in the basis of perceptual and conceptual schemata provided by patriarchal ideological and social formations." In the trajectory of both the look and the narrative line, "the male is the measure of desire."[7] Dinesen's ironizing representation of the thoughts of the young male artist in "The Cloak" typifies her similar understanding of the economy of the phallocentric gaze: "*What is woman? She does not exist until we create her, and she has no life except through us. She is nothing but body, but she is not body, even, if we do not look at her*" (*LT*, 39).

But Dinesen suggests that in von Brackel's transaction with his female nude, the hierarchic power structure figured through the analogies of man/woman, clothing/nakedness, violation/virginity, owner/property, viewer/viewed, and narrator/story has begun to shift imperceptibly even as it is articulated. The slippage occurs precisely through a feminine repositioning and repossession of language and the look. Like Keats's "Belle Dame," Nathalie sings to her lover "a strange plaintive little song in a language that I did not understand," gazing at him with "wild . . . eyes"—and with a similarly overwhelming result: "All my balance, which I had kept somehow . . . , suddenly left me at the sound of her voice. These words . . . seemed to me more directly meaningful than any I had ever understood. . . . I came slowly down on one knee before her . . ." (101). And like Keats's "knight at arms," Dinesen's chevalier too loses his enchanted lady through the fatal error of believing that he "knows" her in more than the sexual sense, that he has penetrated and possessed her subjectivity and her discourse as he has her body. For at dawn his virgin becomes a whore; in requiring "twenty francs," she reveals as contract what he had taken, in several senses, as a *given,* and thereby divests him of other properties as well: "A great clearness came upon me then, as if all the illusions and arts with which we try to transform our world . . . had been drawn aside, and reality was shown to me, waste as a burnt house" (102). Paradoxically, it is precisely in the moment of acknowledging this Eve as "fallen" that he also *sees* her for the first time: "This was the end of the play . . . the first moment . . . in which I saw her as a human being and not as a gift to me" (102). And it is characteristic of his interpretive stance that to recognize her as reciprocal subject is also to read her as "adversary" (103).

Both recognitions come "too late": automatically, entrapped by the codes he would transcend, he pays her fee out of what he calls "chivalrousness," "as if it were the only natural and reasonable thing to do," unable to imagine any other way to "keep" her "safe within the magic circle of her free and graceful and defiant spirit" (102–3). After her departure, he attempts to collect himself to "get her back" (105), but their roles are now reversed: the nakedness that earlier had confirmed her as his object is now transferred to him, rendering him a powerless, fallen Adam: "I had no clothes on."

2

The idea of death is linked with the urge to possess. If the lover cannot possess the beloved he will sometimes think of killing her; often he would rather kill her than lose her.

Georges Bataille, *Eroticism*

It may be that men always feel that they have "lost something" whenever they speak of woman.

Alice Jardine, *Gynesis*

Judith Thurman has argued that as an impractical, "fragile anachronism" torn like Don Quixote between "aristocratic idealism" and "the materialism that had triumphed over it," Baron von Brackel is Dinesen's "self-parody" and the story a gently mocking "self-appreciation of the author's own predicament in 1931." Certainly, as one whose primary refuge is in stories, the chevalier has obvious affinities with the author who repeatedly represented herself as a female Quixote.[8] Yet in assuming Dinesen's essential agreement with the cultural order von Brackel personifies, following the standard reading of his character as "a noble, even an heroic holdout,"[9] this view obscures the powerful critique of precisely the "idealism"—and ideology—the chevalier represents. For as we have seen, far from simply ratifying the chivalric code the Baron invokes and the androcentric "aristocratic" world view that generated it, the story renders them problematic, enacting their ultimate bankruptcy by showing that under the guise of adoration, they objectify the beloved woman as an eroticized/idealized prize to be won by the lover, a sign within his discourse, a means to his own self-reflections. Ironically, the baron's desire for Nathalie replicates its supposed opposite, the homosexual Seraphina's loathing for Calypso: neither man can "see" woman because his real gaze is on himself.

In drawing attention to the sociocultural context in which the courtly definition of woman is inscribed, implying the inseparability of the poetics and the politics of the female body as "created" by male speculations, Dinesen's text anticipates the observations of Maurice Valency in his classic study of *cortesia:* "The high degree of perfection projected by the lover upon the lady . . . [is] the measure of the lover's personal distinction. In the superlative worth of the lady, the lover finds the surest guarantee of his own pre-eminence, more particularly if his love is returned. The lover's compliments, like all self-flattery, are therefore utterly sincere."[10] "The Old Chevalier" subverts romance and chivalric traditions by revealing their visions of woman as pure projective solipsism, the illusions of a narcissistic male desire.[11] With both his Eves, von Brackel has perceived no more than "the image of a woman in a dim mirror" (82), the figure of his own self-regard. What he has laid bare at last is not woman's truth but his own—and his culture's—sustaining fictions.[12]

The metaphors through which Dinesen represents von Brackel reinforce this point, disclosing the man who creates "woman" as himself the product of particular historical scripts of "manhood." As she would observe in "Daguerreotypes," a major critical intertext for "The Old

Chevalier," "a gentleman's education was an elaborate and costly matter. He was produced through special predetermined . . . and complicated processes. And it is difficult at the present day fully to understand how many of these were intended to give him the proper feeling for women's nobility and the correct attitude towards it. A true gentleman was known primarily by his position on this matter" (*Essays,* 24–25). As the chevalier configures Nathalie, so Dinesen configures him: as a living text, a *character* in several senses, in whom the signs of the "past" "could be traced" (81). Significantly, she compares him not only to Don Quixote but to that prototypical heroic male wanderer, Odysseus, who, as "The Deluge" suggests, founds his own identity on the suppression of woman's. In the multiple echoes with which the text begins—the narrator's comment that the chevalier "had in his day traveled much and known many cities and men" echoes not only Homer but Tennyson's Homeric echoes in "Ulysses"—Dinesen telescopes into a single sentence twenty-seven centuries of masculinist literary tradition, remarking its obsolescence through the name *von Brackel,* the German root of which signifies *waste* or *refuse.*[13]

   In several senses, then, the narrative is an exposé, at once unveiling the female body and uncovering, thereby, the problematics of the masculine drive to own it. Von Brackel believes that he has seen and "known" the naked, natal truth of Nathalie. But though he eats the forbidden fruit of "her body . . . [like] the heaven-aspiring column of a young tree" (97), indeed though he quite literally *authors* her as a figure in his story, the tale shows that the knowledge he gains is not of her at all. Dwelling within a subjectivity that he cannot penetrate, the woman remains inviolate, a hermetic text he does "not understand" (100), utterly beyond the scope of his authorial projects and projections.

   Yet this is, after all, the story of "a young man"—and one reclaimed in its telling by an old man seemingly capable of insight into his own earlier blindness: "As if I had been shown a brilliant caricature of myself or of all young men, I laughed" (105). Moreover, the aged narrator, through the wry, self-ironic exposure of his own youthful folly and the elaborate sympathy he repeatedly professes for "young women," seeks to distance his own perspective clearly from that of the younger self he indulgently recalls: "A young man in love is essentially enraptured by the forces within himself" (82–83). And indeed, the vision of the old man seems far removed from the callow egoism of his earlier self, a living proof of the benign wisdom of age. As Langbaum remarks, "he advances in perception in realizing that he has achieved his perfect night by regarding [Nathalie] only as a symbol and ignoring her humanity."[14] It is surely this sympathetic portrait of the reformed roué—the young chevalier grown older and wiser—that has led most critics to take von Brackel at

his word, to accept him, unproblematically, as a privileged interpreter of
the events he recounts, and to read him as Dinesen's double. Yet the limitations of such a view become apparent upon closer consideration of the
old chevalier as both reader and author of his own "life"—recollection
and autobiographical text—and of woman as its central prop, in every
sense of that term.

The further implications of his fiction unfold with particular vivid-
ness in his ambivalent readings of Nathalie. We have seen that, true to
the medieval context recalled by the tale's title, the chevalier represents
Nathalie as the ultimate paradox, embodying both Eve and the Virgin,
seductress and redemptive, umblemished maiden—those prime polarities
of "woman" firmly installed within the Occidental imagination by medieval texts both patristic and secular.[15] Like contemporary feminist critics,
Dinesen read these ostensibly antithetical categories as interchangeable
terms within an androcentric symbolic economy. As she observes in
"Daguerreotypes," while "the bayadère" or prostitute appears a dialectical
opposite of the virginal "guardian angel," in fact the two are homologous,
"figures" of "the same taboo expressed in different mode" (30). As constructs of the male imagination, moreover, both figures function as mediatory objects—circulating "gifts"—in transactions, whether literal or
literary, operated by masculine desire: "Men of the nineteenth century
viewed their women . . . officially" only "in relationship to man. . . .
Eve was created from Adam's rib; it was for man's sake that woman
existed" (32–33).

Further, "The Old Chevalier" implies that insofar as they serve as
screens for male fantasies, both these representations of woman involve a
symbolic prostitution: Dinesen deftly intertwines the representational
conventions of chivalry, whereby the Baron defines Nathalie and himself, with the conventions engendered around the equally familiar topos
of the "fallen woman," vehicle, in Peter Brooks's phrase, for that "host"
of "touching and victimized creatures who spoke to the reformist social
conscience" throughout the nineteenth century.[16] It is no accident that in
much Victorian iconography, as Nina Auerbach notes, "virgin and fallen
woman unite." Von Brackel's trope of Nathalie as "Eve" is similarly conventional to this genre; the myth of the fall, with its associations of sexuality and death, persistently subtends the plot of prostitution.[17] Through
the Baron's projection of these iconographic conventions onto Nathalie,
Dinesen implies direct affinities between the old chevalier as courtly "author" and those male artists and writers who, while ostensibly inviting sympathy for the lady—whether of the court or of the night—were
also seeking to exploit her as a means to their own enrichment and
aggrandizement.[18]

It is in this double context that Dinesen situates von Brackel's digression on woman as hermetic sign or "mystery" (96), both imprinted and interpreted by masterful man:

> Nothing is mysterious until it symbolizes something. . . . The bread and wine of the church itself has to be baked and bottled, I suppose. The women of those days were more than a collection of individuals. They symbolized, or represented, Woman. I understand that the word itself, in that sense, has gone out of the language. Where we talked of woman . . . you talk of women, and all the difference lies there. . . . The idea of Woman—of *das ewig weibliche* . . . had to us been created in the beginning, and our women made it their mission to represent it worthily, as I suppose the mission of the individual dog must have been to represent the Creator's idea of a dog. . . . (95)[19]

Through the Chevalier's Faustian reading of Nathalie as *das ewig weibliche* (the veiled contempt of his Goethean epithet is conclusively exposed by the canine analogy), Dinesen implies a direct continuity between the condition of prostitution and that of "femininity" as it has been traditionally construed, both being grounded in a woman's service as the endlessly desirable object—the *masterpiece* (97)—of masculine contemplation.[20] If, as Beauvoir asserts, "the figure of the prostitute . . . is one of the most plastic feminine types, giving full scope to the grand play of vices and virtues . . . , capable of summing up thus the vagrant yearnings of men,"[21] so conversely, as Bataille would later write in a commentary reminiscent of Dinesen's analysis in both the letters and "Daguerreotypes," "prostitution is the logical consequence of the feminine attitude," for in both cases "a woman regards herself as an object always trying to attract men's attention."[22]

Paradoxically, the efficacy of this symbolic prostitution to sustain masculine self-esteem depends on its remaining a purely symbolic—that is, *tacit*—contract. The real prostitute's unequivocal invocation of an explicit contract is another story, not only because it implicitly reiterates the commercial structures that govern other phallocentric definitions of sexuality, but because even in the process of deploying her body as object, the prostitute theoretically maintains the position as subject vis-à-vis the man with whom she operates as contractual agent.[23] Her position is ineluctably paradoxical: "Of all woman [prostitutes] are the most submissive to the male, *and yet more able to escape him;* this it is that makes them take on so many varied meanings."[24] The prostitute, in short, eludes all single readings; she epitomizes the woman who will not stay in (her) place. Undeniably, on the one hand, she "sums up all the forms of female slavery at once" and acts as a crucial prop in sustaining a patriarchal society based on the traffic in women.[25] Yet in another sense, as

Dinesen suggests through Malin Nat-og-Dag, it is the prostitute who above all, at least symbolically, is fully self-possessed. "She belongs," as Beauvoir would later remark, "to no man, but yields herself to one and all and lives by such commerce. . . . In the sexual act the male cannot possibly imagine that he owns her."[26]

In a cultural economy in which only males have rights of ownership over female bodies, woman's subjectivity represents a dangerous excess that, by transgressing the bounds of the phallic system, might subvert its claims to dominance. To speak woman's difference from/within masculinist culture, then, is literally to speak, like Nathalie, a foreign tongue—a language that disrupts the constructs by which man situates himself as center. In the old chevalier's early reflections on "the emancipation of woman" and his reading of sexually independent women as "witches" allowing themselves "to be possessed by [no] male but the devil" (88), the patronizing humor with which he seeks to dismiss unappropriable and "inappropriate" women like Lilith suggests his unconscious anxiety about just this point. Phallocentric logic would confine the Other within the economy of the Same: what Dinesen's text insists on, to the contrary, is woman's ineradicable difference and otherness, unamenable to assimilation or appropriation.

The relation of these questions to Karen Blixen's own authorial project is illuminated by Peter Brooks's analysis of the connections between the prostitute's circulation of her body, the circulation of money, and the production of narrative:

> The prostitute . . . stands as the key figure and term of access to [an] eminently storied subworld, realm of power, magic, and danger; she exemplifies the modern narratable. One of Balzac's witty courtesans . . . exactly makes this point as she shows her guests around her sumptuously furnished apartment: "Voilà les comptes des mille et une nuits," she tells them ("Here are the accounts of a thousand and one nights"). The phrase plays on the "*Contes* des mille et une nuits"—The Thousand and One Nights— . . . to suggest that *accounts* in two senses, the narrative and the financial, are interchangeable; that in the life of a prostitute at least, the accounting gives something to recount, money and story flow from the same nights of sexual exchange.[27]

One might argue that the chevalier's need to tell his tale, to turn Nathalie into a figure in his own account, indicates his concern that her ownership of her own body is tantamount to his loss of control not only over her, but over his story—and history. This question of the ownership of discourse is reenacted in the relation of Karen Blixen as woman author (whose self-identification with Scheherazade is multiply apt in this context) to the narrative of male desire the tale recounts. At once represented and doubly displaced by the male pseudonym "Isak Dinesen" and the unlocatable narrative voice that opens the frame story ("My father had a friend, old Baron von Brackel . . ."), she occupies a relation to the authorial voice of the old chevalier not unlike that of Nathalie to his younger self. While upholding the masculine perspective through both the chevalier's first-person narrative and her own male pseudonym, she undermines its authority by suggesting an other way of seeing, an other desire, and an other writing, neither counted on nor comprehended by the phallocentric narrative economy. Undoing the process whereby the old chevalier would enter Nathalie into his account, Dinesen turns him to account in hers. Putting him into circulation, as it were, by retailing his retellings, she subverts the hierarchical oppositional logic whereby man situates himself as sovereign subject-speaker vis-à-vis woman as object.

The depth of the chevalier's anxiety about such reversals is reiterated through his implicit association of Nathalie's dawn request for money with his mistress's attempt to poison him. The two events, though seemingly unrelated, are represented as structurally equivalent: each turns on a gender role-reversal that leaves the baron "sick to death" with "horror and humiliation" (90, 105). Each precipitates a rupture in both his life and its subsequent textualization. But if his shock at the attempted murder is great, it is surpassed by his response to Nathalie's invocation of the commercial basis of their transaction. It is this event which von Brackel seems most anxious to postpone, first in the flesh ("Once before she had sat up and moved as if to leave me, and I had dragged her back") and later in the word—that is, in the peculiar hesitation with which he unfolds his narrative of their encounter.

Let us consider that hesitation. Like the central episode it recounts, the story operates structurally as a progressive unveiling, ostensibly driven by von Brackel's desire, both sexual and rhetorical, to reach the climax (81). Yet what seems most striking is his evident reluctance to tell the tale: he begins it repeatedly, only to swerve away into repeated digressions and postponements, interposing multiple interruptions and delays between himself, his audience, and the "mystery" he proposes to lay bare.[28] A kind of narrative *interruptus,* his tale resembles the "layers of clothes" that "buried" the women of his day, *re*-covering even as it purports to recover the hidden truth of a body and a hidden body of truth. The double entendre in Dinesen's title for the Danish version of the tale reinforces this implication: "*Den gamle vandrende Ridder*"—literally, "The Old Wandering Knight"—underscores the propensity of this knight errant to stray off course.[29]

The Baron's reluctance, as it were, to *approach* Nathalie—what we might, in terms of its narrative consequences, call his will-to-deferral—

becomes inseparable from the will-to-deference associated with the cultural and literary structures the story's title invokes. Both forms of
avoidance—indeed, of averting the gaze—culminate in the final episode
of the tale, a narrative by means of which the old man terminates, simultaneously, Nathalie, his own narration, and the text itself:

> "And did you never see her again?" I asked him. "No," he said, . . .
> but I had a fantasy about her, a *fantaisie macabre,* if you like. "Fifteen
> years later, in 1889, I passed through Paris. . . . One afternoon I
> went to see a friend, a painter . . . , and after we had discussed his
> pictures, and art in general, he said that he would show me the pret-
> tiest thing that he had in his studio. It was a skull. . . . 'It is really,' he
> said, 'the skull of a young woman, but the skull of Antinoüs must
> have looked like that. . . .' I had it in my hand, and as I was looking
> at the broad, low brow, the clear and noble line of the chin, and the
> clean deep sockets of the eyes, it seemed suddenly familiar to me.
> The white polished bone shone in the light of the lamp, so pure. And
> safe. In those few seconds I was taken back to my room . . . on a
> rainy night of fifteen years before." "Did you ask your friend any-
> thing about it?" I said. "No," said the old man, "what would have
> been the use? He would not have known." (106–7)

Von Brackel speaks here, retrospectively, as one who *now knows enough,*
for whom there is no need for further inquiry. His response to the final
question suggests that, unlike his younger self, he has at last stripped
truth to the bone. Like Hamlet, in the figure of the skull he can subject
the story of woman—and the obsessive hold it/she has had over him—to
a final closure, ratified by the very act of narrative that confirms her symbolic demise: "Tell her, let her paint an inch thick, to this favor she must
come."[30] As "pure" sign, its origin and referent forever unknowable, the
skull offers the ideal screen onto which he can project his own interpretation.[31] He reads it as he has read the women in his life, solipsistically, as a
reflection of his own desire. Yet his refusal to know its real origins suggests that he still operates out of anxiety—not only about Nathalie,
whom he here seeks to consign to a "safe" oblivion, but about what she
represents for him. Julia Kristeva's remarks on Baudelaire's "amor mor-
tis" as "a sham" are pertinent to the chevalier as well: "In this perspective
love is not only the reverse side of death but it relies on death. . . . [T]he
loved one is herself stripped of her passion, devitalized, skeletonlike. *She
has thus been made less dangerous.*"[32]

   Like his crude equation of "woman" with "dog," the Baron's narrative
implicitly invites its audience to collude in his project of demystifying—
by dis-mantling—"Woman" through a vicarious participation in her unveiling, her "fall," and her final dissolution. Yet on another level the text
indicates that it is precisely the disassembling—and dissembling—of *das*

ewig weibliche that he most fears. Even in the ostensible finality with which he dispatches her, he remains imperiled by the very figure(s) he seeks, both physically and rhetorically, to command. What more is at stake in Nathalie's dawn revelation that makes him associate it obsessively with dis-ease and death? What further unsettling revelation may, without the discursive veils he deploys against it, dawn on him? Why should the substitution of "purchase" for "gift" create for him such a fatal sentence?

3

> Either . . . woman is woman *because she gives herself,* while the man for his part takes, possesses, indeed takes possession. Or else . . . she is woman because, in giving, she is in fact *giving herself for,* is simulating, and consequently assuring the possessive mastery for her own self. Henceforth all the signs of a sexual opposition are changed. Man and woman change places.
>
> Jacques Derrida, *Spurs/Eperons*

> The question then is how to reconstruct or organize vision from the "impossible" place of female desire, the historical place of the female spectator between the look . . . and the image . . . , represent the play of contradictory percepts and meanings usually elided in representation, and so . . . enact the contradictions of women as social subjects, . . . perform the terms of the specific division of the female subject in language, in imaging, in the social?
>
> Teresa de Lauretis, *Alice Doesn't*

The questions which the conclusion leaves unresolved return us to certain crucial conjunctions operative in the Baron's narrative. In the discourse of (male) desire which, in "The Old Chevalier," *is* the story, Dinesen underlines the entanglements of the discourses of chivalry, prostitution, and virginity within an encompassing rhetoric of eroticism. The ambiguous figure of the prostitute, like the traditional Judeo-Christian bifurcation of woman into temptress and virgin which subtends it, registers in concentrated form the paradoxical conjunction of horror and revulsion with attraction and desire that have repeatedly marked masculine responses to feminine sexuality—that "taboo," as Dinesen called it in "Daguerreotypes," that underwrites the most diverse male representations of woman-as-sign.[33] Within this context, the desirous woman is a figure so gravely threatening to the self-regarding phallocentric order that she must be contained, domesticated, or neutralized, either transformed into an asexual ideal like the Madonna (Dinesen's "guardian angel"), written into patriarchal marriage plots, or cast out as a scapegoat like Eve or the Magdalene.[34] In representing woman as virginal icon, patriarchal authors seek to denature her; in construing her as immanent, quintessential body, the "flesh" over against man's "spirit," they displace onto her the mortality from which man would be liberated. In all cases, they occlude her position as desiring subject.

Just as Eve and the Virgin become, on the symbolic level, interchangeable, so, as Dinesen goes on to argue in "Daguerreotypes," the figures of virgin and prostitute, while marking opposite ends of the androcentric cultural spectrum, also operate homologically as culture's most extreme, paradoxical loci of the "taboo" surrounding eroticism. Beauvoir writes that "the male's hesitation between fear and desire, between the fear of being in the power of uncontrollable forces and the wish to win them over, is strikingly reflected in the myth of Virginity. Now feared by the male, now desired or even demanded, the virgin would seem to represent the most consummate form of the feminine mystery; she is therefore its most disturbing and at the same time its most fascinating aspect."[35] Similarly, though conversely, the prostitute is at once alluring and forbidding, a liminal figure whose body signifies the quintessence of transgression as surely as does the body of the virgin, whose intact "purity" at once forbids and elicits the penetration of its boundaries. "In this way," notes Beauvoir, the prostitute "regains that formidable independence of the luxurious goddess mothers of old, and she incarnates the Femininity that masculine society has not sanctified and that remains charged with harmful powers."[36] As Bataille observes, again in language that recalls "Daguerreotypes," "The sacred or forbidden aspect of sexual activity remained apparent in [the prostitute], for her whole life was dedicated to violating the taboo."[37]

These paradoxes are played out in von Brackel's anxieties about Nathalie. Simultaneously virgin and whore, occupying both polarities on the axis of sexual pleasure and danger, she is the doubly extreme embodiment of forbidden eroticism. The rhetorically revived sexual commerce of von Brackel ("refuse," "trash") with one whose name signifies *birth* symbolically enacts, moreover, that other paradoxical conjunction characteristic of eroticism: the fusion of life with death in the "petit mort" which momentarily shatters the unitary, discrete sense of "self." To give oneself over to eroticism, writes Bataille, is to give oneself over not only to "the effervescence of life" but also to its loss: "The loosing of the sexual urge . . . means a barrier destroyed. . . . [J]ust as the violence of death overturns—irrevocably—the structure of life, so temporarily and partially does sexual violence. . . . Inevitably linked with the moment of climax there is a minor rupture suggestive of death."[38] Dinesen's association of von Brackel with decadence is especially relevant in this context: "In essence, the domain of eroticism is the domain of violence, of violation. . . . The transition from the normal state to that of erotic desire presupposes a partial dissolution of the person as he exists in the realm of discontinuity. Dissolution—this expression corresponds with *dissolute life,* the familiar phrase linked with erotic activity."[39] It is no accident, then, that von Brackel—a kind of corpse of a former age—is first presented to us through the Baudelairean figure of a skeleton "at a *danse macabre*" (81) or that his final figure for Nathalie—another self-projection—is a skull.[40] In an earlier draft of the tale, Dinesen made these conjunctions explicit in von Brackel's summary comment immediately before the concluding narrative: "That is what we come to, then, in life. . . . [I]t may be difficult to say exactly when we are born, and when we die."[41]

Significantly, however, within a phallocentric culture, even this seeming merger of the one with the Other, death with life—this loss of self swallowed up in undifferentiation—does not efface sexual difference. Von Brackel's displacement of his own vulnerability and mortality onto Nathalie, especially as it is associated with her nakedness, anticipates the ideology that can be seen to underlie Bataille's assertions about the operations of eroticism:

> In the process of dissolution the male partner has generally an active role, while the female partner is passive. The passive, female side is essentially the one that is dissolved as a separate entity. . . . Stripping naked is the decisive action. Nakedness offers a contrast to self-possession. . . . Stripping naked is seen in civilization where the act had full significance if not as a simulacrum of the act of killing, at least as an equivalent. . . . [T]he female partner in eroticism was seen as the victim, the male as the sacrificer.[42]

According to this logic, by "sacrificing" Nathalie, the Baron can defend himself momentarily against the threat of his own "nakedness"—just as androcentric analysts of eroticism, via magisterial discourse on the sacrifice of the female "victim," can veil their own complicity in the process they describe.

What happens if the woman fails to participate "properly" in this stereotypically "passive" role? "What if," as Irigaray succinctly puts it, "these 'commodities' refused to go to 'market'?"[43] To the extent that man's sense of himself as sovereign and "safe" (the chevalier's recurrent term) depends on the co-optation and cooperation of woman, her refusal has the implicit effect of a reversal, bringing him face to face with his own "violation" and discontinuity, that ultimate loss of mastery that is the outcome of eroticism taken to its extreme—even "unto death." Von Brackel has already represented this reversal in his relation to his mistress, whose insistent desire he links with uncanny, disorienting "strange powers" and supernatural terror: "I think that I began to be afraid. . . . I had read about her family . . . and learned that there used to be were-wolves among them, and I sometimes thought that I should have been happier to see her really go down on all fours and snarl at me, for then *I should have known where I was*" (84; my emphasis).

By invoking a literal contract, Nathalie, who had seemed to signify his preservation from these uncanny powers, effects a comparable reversal, dissolving the tacit symbolic economy of "femininity" and "masculinity" on which his "security" (99) and sovereignty depend, and thereby dissolving as well the writings and readings of "woman" and "man" that secure the phallocentric order he represents. As prostitute, even in her apparent self-abandon, Nathalie has been enacting "a play" (102): reading her, we, like the Baron, can never know with certainty whether her "gift" of herself was more than part of the script.[44] Arguably, given the outcome of the encounter and Dinesen's presentation of von Brackel as a chronic misreader of women, we may assume that even in her most extreme abandonment, Nathalie never truly *abandons herself,* is never, contrary to von Brackel's reading, truly "violated," either by him or by her own erotic impulses. He, on the other hand, quite clearly loses—not only her, whom in fact he has never really "had," but himself: "I went, in those minutes, through the exact experience, even to the sensation of suffocation, of a person who has been buried alive" (105).

The anguished recognition of both losses, one might argue, motivates the Baron's need to force Nathalie at last to undergo the death she thus resisted, to reduce her to the dissolution and abjection to which he himself, through her, has been subjected. By skeletalizing her, recreating her as skull (as he had earlier recreated his mistress in domesticated topoi as "a very old woman" with "two charming granddaughters" [82]), he achieves in the word what he could not achieve in the flesh, restoring thereby his own fragile mastery and the reassurance that he remains, at last, a unified, transcendent self and, by implication, that the structures of phallic order which that "self" embodies are still intact.

In the chevalier's quest for "some theory and explanation of [his] adventure" (103), Dinesen relates these questions about the politics of the body directly to the larger question of the body politic. For Nathalie, as a "fallen" Eve, represents dissolution and (re)birth in more than the individual sense:

> "This happened only a short time after the fall of the Second Empire . . . and the Commune of Paris. The atmosphere had been filled with catastrophe. A world had fallen. . . . This was also the time of Nihilism in Russia, when the revolutionaries had lost all and were fleeing into exile. I thought of that because of the little song that Nathalie had sung . . . of which I had not understood the words.
> Whatever it was that had happened to her, it must have been a

catastrophe of an extraordinarily violent nature. . . . About all this I thought much, . . . but of course I could not know." (103–5)

As an aristocrat the Baron is ineluctably implicated in the events he imagines to have ruined Nathalie, for it is the social order he represents that the revolutionaries would have overthrown. Thus, in effect, he becomes doubly guilty of her "fall." In the analogy here suggested between the oppression of women and that of disempowered classes, Dinesen at once looks backward to nineteenth century socialist thinkers like Fourier, Marx, and Engels and forward to contemporary socialist feminist analyses of Western social structures.[45] Together with the implications of prostitution as a disastrous degradation brought on by the "ruin" of Nathalie's former life (105), Dinesen also suggests that Nathalie's *ownership of herself* is inseparable from "revolution" in all senses. As Michèle Richman notes, "the symbols men manipulate in order to perpetuate the differential hierarchies which either subordinate or exclude women, children, and the weak, are systematized into codes whose key is their monopoly on power. . . . It has traditionally been argued in favor of [the exchange of women] that it channels the force of sexuality which would otherwise unsettle the fragile foundations of the social order. But . . . the real violence lies on the side of the law which seeks to maintain one segment of society in bondage to the other. . . . [B]y challenging the anachronistic remnants of [this system, women] have at their disposal the most effective weapon to precipitate the demise of the patriarchal order."[46] In the letter with which we began, Karen Blixen anticipated these speculations, seeing the oppression of women as rooted in material "conditions": "Although I do not agree with Karl Marx that all the phenomena of life are caused by the economical situation, I think that it explains many of them" (*LA,* 260). When women begin to interrogate the conditions that denied them access to the goods of society, the entire system is undermined:

> I think that one can see now that those who were . . . filled with horror at the thought of women being made eligible to take the student examination and thought that that would bring about the collapse of the whole existing state of things . . . were right, it did collapse, and took much more with it than they had thought possible; and that is what always happens whenever the very possibility of criticism and radical change in an area previously considered to be raised above it, or immune from it, enters the consciousness. When the idea of it being possible for the French intelligensia to ridicule the king and the monarchy came into being it was followed by the entire French revolution. . . . The same has happened with . . . the ownership of property. . . . I consider then that "feminism" or, if you will, the phenomena that were the basic cause of it, have had far more effect

on and have far more radically divided the old society . . . —that on the whole it should probably be regarded as the most significant movement of the nineteenth century, and that the unheavals it has caused are far from "*done with*" at the present moment. (*LA*, 258–59)

If, as Dinesen implies, the anxiety Nathalie generates in von Brackel fuses personal and political issues, we might speculate that it is this plural terror of dissolution of the masterful, unitary "self," of the dominant social system on which that "self" depends, and of the phallocentric symbolic order sustaining them both that is reflected in the multiple hesitations his narrative enacts and in the *fantaisie macabre* with which it ends. At all these levels, his need to possess Nathalie as eternal rebirth is inseparable from his fear of death, as his allusion to himself as the Orpheus to her Eurydice suggests (105–6).

But even here his *fantaisie* betrays him: for what he presents in the skull is the image of death denatured—"clear . . . clean," and unambiguous, "pure," and thus "safe" (107)—supposedly freed from both the dissolution and the regeneration paradoxically embodied for him in feminine sexuality. As Bataille observes,

> horror at death is linked not only with the annihilation of the individual but also with the decay that sends the dead flesh back into the general ferment of life. . . . [Thus] the moment of greatest anguish is the phase of decomposition; when the bones are bare and white they are not intolerable. . . . In some obscure way the survivors perceive . . . the whitening bones [as] witness to appeasement. The *bones . . . draw the first veil* of decency and solemnity over death and make it bearable. *[They] do not leave the survivors a prey to . . . menace. . . . They put an end to the close connections between decomposition, the source of an abundant surge of life, and death.*[47]

For von Brackel to read Nathalie in the "pure" sign of the skull is to make her "safe" indeed—for himself: to "draw the veil" over his own nakedness, to escape the dangerous "ferment," the surging, fleshly conjunctions of birth and death which she signifies for him, and to effect a final self re(in)statement that will assure his own invulnerability and transcendence—together with that of a symbolic order whose oppressive codes function only by doing "violence" to much of the human race.

4

It is in language—in reading and in writing woman—that femininity at once discloses and discomposes itself, endlessly displacing the fixity of gender identity by the play of difference and division which simultaneously creates and uncreates gender, identity, and meaning.

Mary Jacobus, "Reading Woman (Reading)"

What, then, of the original question to which the chevalier's tale was to provide an answer? Given the ambiguities of his narrative, can we draw any final conclusions? Which, for example, was the "principle," which the "inclination" at stake in his climactic moment with Nathalie? Which (or who) was finally "forsaken"? To whom did the "benefit" accrue? The answers are as elusive as the woman disappearing into the dawn. If anything, we finish "The Old Chevalier" with more questions than when we began.

These states of readerly uncertainty reenact those of the old chevalier. Yet his narrative, as we have seen, attempts to foreclose them. First in experience, then through narration, the Baron seeks to elude and elide the undecidability Nathalie signifies—to fix "woman" (hence "man") even at the price of killing her, (dis)figuring her forever through his skeletalizing discourse. Yet as a sign of the uncanny—that ultimate *fantaisie macabre*—the skull paradoxically undoes his project of mastery even as Nathalie's invocation of a commercial contract undoes his sublime sense of ownership. For as we saw in chapter 1, the uncanny returns the subject finally to the womb, that unsettling site of feminine sexuality and generativity. Hence the skull paradoxically represents a desire that may ultimately be unamenable to the control of man's truth. It is the unwillingness to confront both this uncertainty and all that it signifies, to confront woman's uncodified, undominated sexuality and the mortality from which it is, for him, inseparable, that is revealed both in the obsessiveness with which the chevalier has dwelt on the story he tells and, at the same time, in his peculiar *reluctance to tell it*. The continual deflections, digressions, and deferrals all serve to postpone or interrupt, even as they reenact, that moment of slippage, loss, and unmooring—the discomposing power of *de-composition* in both the physical and the narratological sense—which his reading of woman must inevitably admit.

If "The Old Chevalier" is as much a story about the fate of reading as about the fate of wo/man, it puts in question our own reading practices as well as von Brackel's. Dinesen's repeated association of the Baron's reading with contracts reflexively reminds us of that other contract—between reader and author—implicit in every text. And like recent feminist analysts of the readerly project, Dinesen makes us keenly aware that "reading," like "writing"—whether of the body of the text, the text of the body, or the social text of the body politic—is an engendered activity. Through the tale of the old chevalier, she suggests that "reading as a man" entails stripping, penetrating, and finally murdering one's object—

and that such "reading" leads, paradoxically, to the loss of what one would possess.[48]

Not only as vicarious participant in Nathalie's disrobing and defloration, then, but in the quest to "penetrate" the text, to fix its "truth" through a hermeneutic unveiling like that to which von Brackel subjects Nathalie, the reader risks *becoming* the old chevalier. Insofar as we give ourselves up to interpretation as a form of finalized possession, we too become implicated in the "murder" of woman, in willed blindness to the text of the feminine or the feminine of the text. Yet to read thus finally leads, Dinesen suggests, to the reader's undoing, precisely as it does to the Baron's. For ultimately both "woman" and "text" elude the drive to mastery, slipping away from readerly control as Nathalie slips away from the chevalier, first literally, into the Parisian dawn, then as sign, in the ambiguities and undecidability of the tale through which the chevalier would write her into a final, unified "truth." Thus all readings—including, of course, this one—must finally founder on the upsurge of the text, like the floating barn of "The Deluge," whose dissolution returns us to the mysteries of the fiction that dawns above the ruins.

7

Simian Semiotics

> When men by way of their conventions have got themselves into
> difficulties, let the monkey in.
>
> Isak Dinesen

> Nature and culture abolished, all bodies mingled: animals . . .
> and humans in the same intertwining . . . of this universal jouis-
> sance. . . . The sorceress and the hysteric manifest the festival in
> their bodies . . . , making it possible to see what cannot be rep-
> resented, figures of inversion . . . and in them woman reveals
> the unique power to invert her own body. That makes us women
> want to laugh, a loud and philosophic laughter.
>
> Catherine Clément, "The Guilty One"

I

Midway through "The Old Chevalier" Dinesen introduces a poignant
account of woman's self-referential storytelling:

> She told me, rather sadly to begin with, a story of a very old monkey
> which could do tricks. . . . Its master had died, and now it wanted to
> do its tricks and was always waiting for the catchword, but nobody
> knew it. In the course of this tale she imitated the monkey in the fun-
> niest and most gracefully inspired manner that one can imagine. (99)

This "inspired" feminine mimesis foreshadows both the dominant figure
and the primary interpretive problematic of "The Monkey," which invites us to contemplate the literalization of what Nathalie simulates.
Through the uncanny conflation of woman with monkey on which the
tale turns, Dinesen extends the parables of signification and interpretation elaborated in the first two Gothic tales. Like Nathalie's story,
Dinesen's too recalls a lost or unknown word—not the logos of the paternal "master" but a feminine discourse which, from within the patriarchal symbolic order, can perhaps only be gestured at.[1] "The Monkey"

enacts an alternative vision of psyche, social structures, and language, interrogating the phallocentric epistemologies which construct the "self" and its representations according to an absolutist hierarchical logic that would split human from animal, mind from body, subject from object, self from other, "man" from "woman."

Readers have traditionally regarded "The Monkey" as one of Dinesen's most problematic texts, for it is as stubbornly resistant to critical control as is its eponymous simian protagonist to the dictates of order, reason, and restraint. Attention typically fixes on the hair-raising metamorphosis of monkey and prioress toward which all the tale's energies tend, a transformation that catapults both characters and readers into a narrative space of absolute undecidability which Dinesen (anticipating Todorov's definition) explicitly coded as "fantastic."[2] But the extraordinary conclusion is not the only source of readerly confusion, for Dinesen structures the narrative from its beginning as a series of interpretive disjunctions and conundrums. To read "The Monkey" is to enter a state of hermeneutic anxiety, a vortex of uncertainty that turns the text into a microcosmic version of its own image of the creation:

> The real difference between God and human beings . . . [is] that God cannot stand continuance. . . . And human beings cleave to the existing state of things. All their lives they are striving to hold the moment fast, and are up against a *force majeure*. Their art itself is nothing but the attempt to catch by all means the one particular moment, . . . and make it everlasting. It is all wrong . . . to imagine paradise as a never-changing state of bliss. It will probably, on the contrary, turn out to be, in the true spirit of God, an incessant whirlpool of change. (*SGT*, 121–22)

This passage (which plays obliquely on both Walter Pater's aesthetics and Ruskin's theories of Gothic as "a great system of perpetual change") suggests that "The Monkey" might well be read as a text about the implications of uncertainty and instability in relation to the questions of perception, subjectivity, and signification that pervade *Seven Gothic Tales*.[3]

The tale opens into a space whose very name suggests its ambiguous and anomalous character. "Closter Seven" (a hybrid coinage that crosses lexicons, fusing English *cloister* with Danish *kloster*) is a community of women situated indefinitely somewhere in "northern Europe" at some unspecified moment "between 1818 and 1845." Though the enclave "make[s] use of the name convent, " it is, in fact, "of no religious nature" (109). A permanent retreat for unmarried ladies and widows of noble birth" (109), it typifies that peculiar post-Reformation institution which, after the abolition of nunneries, became one means by which patriarchal societies sought to cope with the perennial problem of the "surplus" single women in their midst. Dinesen prefigures anthropological analyses of the potential social threat embodied in unassimilable persons of "indefinable status," who, as Mary Douglas remarks, "are somehow left out in the patterning of society" and therefore generally are "treated as both vulnerable and dangerous," a source of pollution that must be protectively contained and separated from the rest of the social body.[4] In an androcentric sociopolitical system founded on the institution of marriage, "unmarried ladies and widows," whatever their appearance of staid conventionality, become a potential locus of instability and danger.[5] Ironically, as studies of medieval convents have shown, the very structures designed to circumscribe a potentially threatening anomaly often became instead sites of female power, which may be intensified by its very concentration and isolation.[6] As Karen Blixen noted in an implicit gloss on this dynamic, "Under the disguise we are what we are. . . . With complete loyalty towards our female being . . . we have for thousands of years been abbesses, authoritative leaders of large religious societies, wielding power and influence beyond the country's borders" (*Essays* 81). The tale implies that the most extreme expression of this possibility is the secular convent which, detached from the patristic hierarchies that have traditionally governed even the strongest female religious orders, operates as "a small world of its own" on the margins of the patriarchal order, yet maintains an uncanny influence over "the center of things" (111, 115). If the cloister appears benignly irrelevant, a "safe reclusion" that "moved in an atmosphere of peace and immutability," it is also the "domain" of "dangerous emotions" (111–12). As its figural association with the Pleiades suggests, Closter Seven is a site of female bonding—both *communitas* and communication—outside the domain of masculine desire (133). Here the law of the father yields to a mother, "the Virgin Prioress" around whom both the life of the convent and the narrative of "The Monkey" revolve (109).

Dinesen associates the potential unruliness of this women's world with the animals that dwell within its walls. An antitype to the misogynist male society at Angelshorn, whose ruler deemed "the existence of the brute creation," like the existence of women, to be "an enigma and a tragedy," Closter Seven cherishes a motley menagerie. Its preeminent denizen is the Prioress's "little gray monkey . . . from Zanzibar." A creature neither wholly wild nor fully domesticated, it roams at will both within and without the walls of the convent: feeling "the call of a freer life," it "disappear[s] for a few weeks" into the forest, but returns "of its own accord" (110) to the domestic enclosure. Confounding nature and culture, the monkey, like the closter itself, eludes both easy categorization and rational control. In the absence of her familiar, the Prioress's behavior changes: silent and restless, she becomes "loth to act in the affairs of the house, in which at ordinary times she showed great vigor." The joking reference to the monkey as the Prioress's "*Geheimrat*"—privy councillor—registers not only the intimacy and intricacy of their association but, obliquely, the peculiarly *unheimlich* quality of its covert operations (110).[7]

Into the closter's ambiguous feminine space comes the Prioress's cocky young nephew and godson Boris, fleeing the scandal of the "strange heresy" "*à la grecque*" that has implicated him along with his "regiment and circle of friends" (111–12). His plan to evade the censure of his homophobic society is simple, cynical, and eminently pragmatic: he seeks his godmother's aid in finding a proper wife. It is here that the text begins most insistently to call attention to its own mystifications. Why, given the narrator's stress on the Prioress's penchant for punctuating her discourse with "little Latin phrases" (114), does she speak to Boris repeatedly in French? Why does she fabricate a marriage plot so "absurd" that it shocks even the worldly Boris (117)? Why does she seek to mate her "favorite" nephew (110) with "little Athena Hopballehus"—"a strong young woman of eighteen, six feet high and broad in proportion, with a pair of shoulders which could lift and carry a sack of wheat"? The only child of an aging count with whom, true to her name, she dwells in an "Olympic" relationship of absolute devotion (122), Athena is a woman who not only breaks every traditional code of feminine seductiveness, but could also, Boris imagines, "break" any man as well (129). Does the Prioress suspect that an alliance between Boris and Athena may be incestuous? (The disclosure that the count was once one of Boris's "beautiful mother's adorers" makes his seemingly innocent greeting—"Boris, my child"—appear as an unintentional double entendre.[8]) And what lies behind the disconcerting incestuous joke the Prioress herself makes as her godson departs—"If Athena will not have you . . . I will" (118)? What prompts her hysterical rage at Athena's refusal of Boris? What lies behind the "great supper of seduction" (139) she then arranges—and who is seducing whom? Why does she seek, as she says, "to put [Athena] in a cage" (142)? What motivates the mission of rape on which she sends her reluctant nephew, firming his resolve with an African aphrodisiac? And why, after a mock-epic battle foils his attempt, does she seek to convince Athena that a pregnancy may still ensue? Why, in sum, does the Prioress—initially figured as the epitome of refinement, dignity, good sense, and benignity—increasingly breach every conventional code of logic, probability, decorum, decency, and "womanly modesty," threatening the boundaries of order so thoroughly that she becomes an embodiment of the "catastrophal" (113), a force of excess and transgression that defies the credibility of both characters and readers?

The text makes the answer disarmingly obvious. It lies—in both senses—in the story's title. For it is the monkey's appearance in the spectacularly mystifying Gothic metamorphosis of the tale's conclusion which finally seems to demystify all prior mysteries by revealing that the "Prioress" has, quite literally, *not been herself:* "Where she had been, a monkey was now crouching . . . And where the monkey had been jumping about, rose . . . the true Prioress of Closter Seven" (162). Interpretation, then, is made to hinge on our effort to distinguish between primate and prioress, and thereby to reestablish those clear and distinct ideas traditionally associated with the act of criticism—literally the process of separating one entity from another in order to see each (in the famous Arnoldian phrase) "as it really is." To *apprehend the monkey* would seem tantamount to understanding all the confusions its actions generate—and to gaining a firm hermeneutic grasp of the tale as well. For since, as Dinesen's title indicates, the monkey and its tale are coterminous, to decipher *what the monkey means* is also, presumably, to grasp the significations of the text and of that other designing woman behind the intricacies of its plots. But how do we pin the elusive primate down? Is the split between monkey and mistress really so clear and stable as the narrator would have us believe? Who/what/how does the monkey signify?

2

The ape . . . , since he is rather similar to man, . . . always observes him in order to imitate his actions. He also shares the habits of beasts, but both these aspects of his nature are deficient, so that his behaviour is neither completely human nor completely animal; he is therefore unstable.

Hildegard of Bingen, *Physica*

As regards the individual nature, woman is defective and misbegotten, for the active power in the male seed tends to the production of a perfect likeness according to the masculine sex, while the production of woman comes from defect. . . .

Thomas Aquinas, *Summa Theologiae*

The issue of interpretive uncertainty is inherent in Dinesen's choice of a monkey as the totem beast on which to hang her tale, for with their uncannily human resemblance primates have perennially confounded efforts to establish stable definitions and maintain firm divisions between the human and the animal worlds. A glance at the history of simian iconographies in Europe from the Middle Ages onward (iconographies with which Dinesen, as a student of art history, was familiar[9]) suggests not only the general hermeneutic anxiety provoked by such categorical confusions, but their specific relationship to questions of sexual difference and representation.

From antiquity, as H. W. Janson observes, primates have been regarded as figures "deeply involved in the fundamental questions of man's own nature."[10] Worshiped as a god by the Egyptians, the ape appeared to Christian patristic authors "as an unworthy pretender to human status, a grotesque caricature of man, . . . the prototype of the trickster . . . , linked with the monstrous hybrid beings of myth and fable"—hence as the quintessential *figura diaboli,* a form in which apes and monkeys were associated with the witches' sabbath.[11] By the twelfth century, as increasing numbers of real primates became widely available in western Europe, the diabolic tradition gave way to representations of apes as versions of fallen humanity, a topos in which they were often allied with the figure of woman as Vice or Lust.[12] A variant of this association appears in the widespread exempla and proverbs asserting that spinsters, like (or accompanied by) apes, lead the souls of bachelors to hell—a topos revived by Shakespeare in both *The Taming of the Shrew* (2.1.34) and *Much Ado About Nothing* (2.1.45–50).

These figurations remind us that within dominant Western cultural traditions, the monkey was not alone in being represented as a defective man—*naturae degenerantis homo.* From Aristotle through patristic authors like John Chrysostom, Augustine, and Thomas Aquinas, woman too was construed as man *manqué.* Like the ape, "that most insolent of plagiarists and distorter of a creation made by a good and rational god,"[13] she was repeatedly represented as a flawed and degenerate being who, unconstrained, could also make a monkey out of man.[14] Significantly, as Janson observes, "the Middle Ages associated the ape almost exclusively with female qualities," referring to it "in the feminine gender as *simia,* rarely as *simius.* Its reputation for wiliness, an unstable temper, and sensuality; its connection with the moon . . . , [and] the numerous stories about simian mother love, all helped to fix the female character of the ape in the popular mind." By extension, the ape was also associated with sexuality, especially the "dangerous" forces of feminine seductiveness and desire.[15]

Taken together, these topoi formed a "widely known and influential" symbolic nexus conflating woman, apes, maternity, eroticism, and transgression; hence many medieval and early renaissance depictions of the Fall show Eve in the company of a monkey, often a kind of anticipatory double who eats the forbidden fruit before her.[16] A variant of these motifs appeared in northern European folk tales about woman's creation from the long monkey-like tail with which man, like other animals, supposedly began—a narrative posited on a widespread hierarchical equation: God:man = man:woman = human beings:primates.[17] Dinesen may well have been familiar with Gerard de Nerval's account, in *Un Voyage en Orient*, of the "oriental" version of this legend, wherein woman is created, *faute de mieux*, from a monkey's tail after the monkey had absconded with man's rib; thus woman is "a creature . . . beautiful on the outside but inside full of malice and perversity."[18] The homology of Eve with the monkey finds its polar counterpart in numerous iconographies of that "second Eve," the Madonna, wherein the monkey appears disconcertingly as both antitype and debased double to the infant Christ.[19] This alliance gives new resonance to the Prioress's scandalous comic tale of the Madonna which, framed by the larger narrative of "the great supper of seduction" (139), connects the Virgin—and implicitly "the Virgin Prioress"—with the same transgressive forces of illegitimacy and incest that the monkey embodies and relates them to a female narrative genealogy (143–44).

Inseparable from the ape's widespread connections with concepts of similitude and dissimulation are its links to questions of imitation and signification. "Since the epithet 'ape' had been used to designate spurious pretenders and unworthy imitators by both classical and early Christian writers, the devil, as unworthy imitator par excellence, eventually came to be known as *simia Dei*."[20] Similarly woman—whether figured as misbegotten, incomplete man, as belated creation from man's body, or as pretender to godhood—has been recurrently represented in Occidental discourses as a kind of counterfeit or monstrosity, resistant to both learning and the preservation of her "proper" place in the scale of beings.[21] As a mimetic signifier, simultaneously re-presenting and yet displacing a prior signified in whom the fullness of meaning presumably resides, the transgressive figure of ape/devil/woman becomes analogous not only to the act of troping but to language itself. It is no accident that most medieval philologists, by way of false etymology, linked the principle of similitude with the adjective *simian*.[22] Thus the monkey—and its analogue, woman—appears not merely as a mime, a principle of deviation, mockery, and caprice, but as a figure of figuration, a re-presentation of representation.

This association finds its most direct expression in the playful iconographies in the marginalia of Gothic illuminations, where, as Philippe Verdier notes, "the subversive spirit was given free rein":

> The marginalia of Gothic manuscripts is almost always an eccentric world, at times like an underworld, parasitic on texts and commenting on them obliquely with a devious humor, extending from a

surrealistic imagination to a surreptitious criticism of the 'establishment' in contemporary society and a more or less brazen anticlerical-
ism. . . . [A]s symbolical comments made in a tongue-in-cheek,
bantering way . . . , they are secretly interlaced with the main illustration of the text . . . and they co-exist with the text, but on a distinct
psychic and interpretive level. Semi-abstract and semi-monstrous
patterns, they . . . teem with outcrops of the unconscious."[23]

In the margins of official inscriptions apes and monkeys run rampant,
"imitating or parodying every conceivable human activity from jousting
and hunting to ecclesiastical rites."[24] Comparable subversive figurations
of women also flourish there, engaged in scandalous inversions of ordinary, socially sanctioned sex roles. It is significant, in view of the climactic metamorphosis in "The Monkey," that often in these marginalia "the
animals assume a human appearance" while the human figure "becomes
distorted into the monstrous," suggesting "a secret congeniality" between the two.[25] Such iconographies, Verdier suggests, appear "as the
naive exponents of a woman's freedom movement fighting against the
definition of her condition by the Church or against the rules edicted by
man."[26] But as challenges to the official discourse, working in the margins of the text but ineluctably modifying its central significations, they
might also be read as iconographic figures of woman's countertextual discourse, written from the margins in another sense, and equally "critical
of the establishment": figural counterparts to that mocking feminine
double-talk that Irigaray invokes as a subversive "play with mimesis,"
and Dinesen herself connected with woman's transvestite travesty of the
"masculine . . . paragraphs of the law" which defines her as peripheral
(Essays 83).[27] Like Kristeva's concept of a certain "literature" that fore-
grounds the operations of the semiotic, revealing the instabilities of the
symbolic order whose significations are inseparable from it, these carnivalesque figures are fundamentally revolutionary in the way they "un-
derscore the limits" of the central(izing) "discourse and attest to what it
represses."[28]

European traditions of monkeys and women as subversive signifiers coexist with another set of equally compelling intertexts—sources
Dinesen implicitly evokes with every reference to the monkey's African
origins. As Henry Louis Gates has shown, one of the most widespread
mythic figures in African folk narratives was "the signifying monkey," a
trickster who (in Afro-American interpretations of an African figure) operates outside the bounds, "ever parodying, ever troping, ever embodying the ambiguities of language."[29] Like Zora Neale Hurston, the "first
author of the [Afro-American] tradition to represent signifying itself as a
vehicle of liberation for an oppressed woman, and as a rhetorical strategy

in the narration of fiction," Dinesen found the monkey a peculiarly apt figure for the antihegemonic impulses of feminine subversion.[30]

3

> To play with mimesis is thus, for a woman, to try to recover the place of her exploitation by discourse, without allowing herself to be simply reduced to it. . . . This "style" or "writing" of women . . . resists and explodes every firmly established form, figure, idea or concept.
>
> Luce Irigaray, *This Sex Which Is Not One*

> Women, he thought, when they . . . can let loose their strength, must be the most powerful creatures in the whole world.
>
> Isak Dinesen, "The Monkey"

Like its iconographic predecessors, Dinesen's monkey is an agent of disorder and caprice, a mocking, marginal figure that invades and undermines the dominant symbolic order. Just as monkeys in the margins of illuminated manuscripts disrupted sacred writ with secular wit, producing another kind of illumination that challenged official textuality, so the monkey subverts, through a process of dismemberment which is also a kind of rewriting, the synoptic textual repositories of patriarchy: "It would be found, in the early mornings, on top of the stepladder in the library, pulling out brittle folios a hundred years old, and scattering over the black-and-white marble floor browned leaves dealing with strategy, princely marriage contracts, and witches' trials" (109). These scattered "leaves," metaphorically introducing the wild space of the forest into the ordered world of the library, resemble Dinesen's description of her own embryonic texts—"scattered pages," "blown about . . . down on the floor," "some here and some there"—which, as we have seen, she posed as antithetical to the patriarchal tradition synecdochized by Homeric epic (*OA*, 48). In "The Monkey" a similar fragmentation and dispersal occurs in the multiple appropriations of canonical texts that Dinesen, like her simian protagonist, scatters and redistributes into new patterns. The text implies that though all constructions of meaning are conditioned by the subject's positioning within a web of predetermining discourse, that fabric is nevertheless vulnerable to rifts and rearrangement.[31] In describing Boris's mental discomposure under his godmother's overwhelming influence, Dinesen provides a figure of her own discomposing text, which also "mix[es] up the classics with Scripture and with legends" (159) via a burgeoning intertextual allusiveness (the characters tend to speak and even to *think* in direct quotations) that unsettles the ostensible order of the narrative. But whereas the revisionist readings of the first two Gothic tales focus primarily on Judeo-Christian topoi, "The Monkey" plays most obviously on traditions which, like Boris's sexual preferences, are in several senses *à la grecque* (111).[32]

The phrase, initially a euphemism for Boris's homosexuality, has implications that extend to other forms of phallocentrism as well. One recalls Irigaray's punning argument that patriarchal culture is fundamentally "hom(m)o-sexual" because "the passage into the social [and] the symbolic order . . . is assured by the fact that men [*hommes*] . . . circulate women among themselves," recognizing only masculine desire and reducing woman to the reflection of man.[33] Paradoxically, however, overt male homosexuality as "an 'immediate' practice" as opposed to a "'social' mediation" must be prohibited, not only because it interrupts the symbolic economy operated by the exchange of women, but because its explicit enactments expose the true "foundation of the economic, social, and cultural order," which functions by remaining concealed and naturalized.[34] "The Monkey" elaborates a similar insight, situating male homoeroticism and transvestism within a nexus of other practices and preferences which Judeo-Christian culture has historically sought to suppress, not only through explicit legal or religious interdiction, but by a linguistic censorship that would render them *unspeakable:* incest, the free play of feminine desire, and homoeroticism *between women.* In each case, the repressed returns through the transgression of boundaries presumed to be absolute and "natural."

The implications of all these dislocations unfold in the discussion at Hopballehus about the iconic goddess of love—another god/mother and lady of beasts like the monkey/prioress, and equally duplicitous:

> [Athena] bid him let the Prioress know that she had seen her monkey a few nights ago, on the terrace of Hopballehus, sitting upon the socle of Venus's statue, in the place where a small Cupid, now broken, used to be. . . . The old Count started to speak of the Wendish idols, from whose country his own family originally came, and of which the goddess of love had the face and façade of a beautiful woman, while, if you turned her around, she presented at the back the image of a monkey. . . . But how, asked Athena, did they know, in the case of that goddess of love, which was the front and which the back? (130–31).[35]

Critics have generally read Athena's response as mere naïveté, but one might argue otherwise. Both the goddess, a "symbol . . . of pagan iconoclasts," and Athena are disruptive, improper female figures. Operating iconoclastically like the monkey who scatters textual fragments over the "black-and-white" floor of the library or comically transforms the meaning of the broken statue, Athena "simply" confounds the black-and-white oppositional logic that structures traditional phallogocentric epistemologies. Her question, quite literally *preposterous,* implies the indefinite reversability of "front" and "back," priority and impropriety, suggesting an alternative order within which such hierarchizing terms might be seen as infinitely interchangeable.[36] In this context Dinesen implies that as a metamorphic figure of substitution, displacement, and indeterminacy, the goddess is also, like the monkey, a trope on troping: her "meaning" emerges, quite literally, as the effect of *a turn.*

Whether scattering the leaves of patriarchal discourses, concealing itself among the leaves of the forest, or perched on broken icons amid "layers of fallen leaves," the monkey pervades the leaves of the text at every turn, accumulating energy with each new exfoliation of the narrative. Its image multiplies, replicating itself not only in the Prioress or her iconographic counterpart, the half-simian goddess of love, but in the "patriarch of Hopballehus," figured as an "old-man gorilla" (128, 124), and in Athena as the undomesticated inhabitant of the wilds who first appears as a figurative extension of a storm wind that "had come . . . like an animal of the night" (128–29). Even Boris reflects the monkey's uncanny "caprices" (110) in the most radical—literally *hair-raising*—sense of that term: as he imagines the monkey's eyes watching him from the dark forest depths, his "hair rose a little upon his head" (133).

Yet oddly, for all its "strange powers" and pervasive presence (133), the monkey is never really "present" in the narrative as an object of direct representation until the end; repeatedly referred to, often felt as a haunting, elusive *seer* whose "glinting eyes" rivet and compel from the "shadows" (133), the monkey itself *cannot be seen.* This teasing presence-in-absence rewrites the story's own hermeneutic hide-and-seek with the reader, reinforcing the title's suggestion of identity between the monkey and the text it names.[37] As the drive toward diversion or crisis that unsettles the stability of a preexisting order, the unseen force that generates every major episode, invades every setting, manipulates every major character, and, quite literally, *makes the story happen,* the monkey becomes not only a figure of the tale but a tale of the figural: the principle of narrativity itself. Here Dinesen operates a crucial reversal. Teresa de Lauretis has argued that traditional narrative grammar functions as a linear inscription of masculine desire in which female figures become mere "markers of positions—places and topoi—through which the hero and his story move to their destination and to accomplish meaning": "the female position in narrative is fixed by the mythical mechanism in a certain portion of the plot space, which the hero crosses or crosses to."[38] In the

monkey—both text and figure—Dinesen disrupts this paradigm by dis-
arranging its terms of reference, crossing the oppositions of "male" and
"female" on which it depends, and thus constructing a notion of narrativity as a mobilization of feminine desire which refuses and ruptures
all stable positionings.[39]

4

> Transitivism . . . such that one can pass without fixed identity
> from body to body: from woman to beast, from woman into
> woman. . . . A transition ritual in which civil and symbolic
> identity has disappeared. . . .
>   . . . [B]efore the resolution, the festival of metamorpho-
> sis takes place. . . . The pleasure comes about during the crisis,
> as a substitute for orgasm, mimed in all the forms of dis-
> placement. . . .
>   . . . [Then] she is cured . . . but the celebration is over.
>   Catherine Clément, "Sorceress and Hysteric"

The unsettling forces Dinesen has set in motion reach a climax when the
monkey finally appears:

> At the next moment the glass of the window fell crashing to the
> floor, and the monkey jumped into the room.
>   Instantly . . . as if escaping from the flames of an advancing fire,
> the Prioress . . . ran, threw herself, toward the door. On finding it
> closed, . . . with the most surprising, most wonderful lightness and
> swiftness she heaved herself straight up along the frame, and at the
> next moment was sitting squeezed together upon the sculptured cor-
> nice. . . . But the monkey followed her . . . and was stretching out
> its hand to seize her. . . . [B]ending double, as if ready to drop on all
> fours, madly, as if blinded by fright, she dashed along the wall, but
> still the monkey followed her, and it was quicker than she. It jumped
> upon her, got hold of her lace cap, and tore it from her head. . . .
> There was a few moments' wild and whirling flight. . . . [B]efore
> their eyes, a change, a metamorphosis, was taking place and was
> consummated.
>   . . . Where she had been, the monkey was now. . . . And where
> the monkey had been [was] the true Prioress of Closter Seven. (160–61)

How are we to approach the critical *aporia* this "terrible tornado"
(162) opens up, leaving the observers (and many readers) "too paralyzed
by surprise to speak"? Like the figures it depicts, the scene invites plural
readings. The monkey's manifestation is written in terms of violence and
violation, as a forced breaking and entering, a sexualized encounter that

recalls the earlier rape scene between Boris and Athena, in which "neither knew clearly where his own body ended and that of his adversary began" (153–54). But where that rape failed, this one appears horrifically "consummated"—and more than once. As the first site of penetration, the window marks a liminal, hymeneal margin; transparent and permeable, it is neither "within" nor "without," but the transitional space where these polarities are simultaneously defined and rendered problematic. Rupturing this threshold integument, the monkey also shatters the prioress's body in a grotesque parody of erotic union, its climax a disfiguring instance of the *abject* in the Kristevan sense: the moment when boundaries buckle and opposites merge in a literal *con-fusion* of human and beast, inside and outside, subject and object, ascetic and erotic, self and Other.[40] The sexualized dissolution suggests simultaneously a primal scene and its reproductive consequence—labor and "birth"—literally the splitting of one body into two in what Kristeva has called "the scene of scenes . . . the height of bloodshed and life, scorching moment of hesitation (between inside and outside, ego and other, life and death), horror and beauty, sexuality and the blunt negation of the sexual."[41]

Like the workings of dream, this event enacted in the theater of the body is multiply uncanny: the strange and foreign figure from without couples with the familiar, maternal figure within, revealing thereby their essential interchangeability, the degree to which each inhabits the other—disclosing the Other in the mother.[42] The moment also recalls the catharsis or "abreaction" that releases the hysteric when, in Clément's words, "a foreign body, real or imagined, must leave the body"—a foreign body often imagined as animal and exciting simultaneous horror and fascinated desire in the woman "possessed" by it as well as in the analyst who calls it forth.[43] In the Freudian version of this script the paternal analyst/inquisitor achieves an exorcism precisely through the generation of a certain doubled *story;* the hysteric is "cured" when she can deliver herself of the words that render the "beast" harmless, and the analyst demonstrates mastery over both by capturing them in/as narrative. But this scenario is pointedly disrupted when the "hysteric" refuses to play her designated part.[44] If, as Dianne Hunter argues, "hysteria is feminism lacking a social network in the outer world . . . , a self-repudiating form of feminine discourse in which the body signifies what social conditions make it impossible to state linguistically,"[45] then Dinesen's representation of the prioress/monkey's mutually "self-repudiating" moment may be read in a new light. "The Monkey," like recent feminist analyses, connects "hysteria" with witchcraft, suggests its revolutionary potential as a representation of the transgressive power and consequences of suppressed female creativity, and questions both the possibility and the desirability of the "cure."[46] Split between the roles of authority and transgression, the Prioress becomes both the seemingly "cured" hysteric and the commentator—a double for the author/analyst. Her final words are delivered in learned Latin, which, as Walter Ong has shown, is peculiarly related to the perpetuation of a masculine symbolic order.[47] Literally the last words of the narrative as well, they remark on and appear to close off both the cathartic scene and the text itself. As we shall see, however, the case is not closed so easily.

For the scene of entry is also a scene of writing.[48] Since the prioress "is" the monkey, and "The Monkey" is the text, Dinesen uses its uncanny, subversive operations to gesture toward a discourse specifically associated with woman's *jouissance* that could work at once inside and outside the bounds of normative phallocentric codes, rupturing symbolic claustrations. The relation of monkey to Prioress, especially the dreamlike moment of their fusion and fission, anticipates Kristeva's conception of language as the interplay of the semiotic and the symbolic—a process which, like Dinesen, Kristeva sees as mediated by the "mother's body."[49] More specifically, prefiguring Cixous's conception of *écriture féminine* as a writing of woman's desire, "The Monkey" gestures toward a "language that will wreck partitions . . . and rhetorics, regulations and codes." Like the monkey/prioress or the "admirable hysterics" who subvert the father's solicitations even while appearing to respond to them, such writing has the power to transform the processes of signification: "If woman has always functioned 'within' the discourse of man, a signifier that has always referred back to the opposite signifier which annihilates its specific energy and diminishes or stifles its very different sounds, it is time for her to dislocate this 'within,' to explode it, turn it around, and seize it, . . . to invent for herself a language to get inside of."[50]

In this context, however, the final separation of primate and Prioress would appear to be a movement *out of* the liberating possibilities of that "feminine" language into the apparent unity and coherence of an order where traditional linguistic structures replace and repress the disruptions of the simian/semiotic. At the conclusion of the whirlwind metamorphosis, as "calm again descend[s]" over the room and the text (162), such a distinct division does seem finally reinstated between the monkey and "the true Prioress," epitome of order, priority, and propriety, who is "born" (again) as a coherent subject/text through the reestablishment of divisions: human and animal, self and other, linguistic and nonlinguistic, exalted and debased, "true" and false. This emergence is quite literally signaled by the word of the father: the quotation in Latin, that "proper" paternal language, which the Prioress, as a kind of phallic mother, utters as "moral" and commentary on the wrenching passage we have just witnessed, and with which she, like her author, closes both conflict and text. "*Discite justitiam, et non temnere divos*" (Learn justice, and do not hold the gods in contempt): the line comes from book 6 of the *Aeneid,* that most phallocentric of epics, and represents a warning delivered to Aeneas amidst a sequence of judgments pronounced against parricide, fratricide, adultery, and incest—"crimes . . . unspeakable" precisely to the degree that they undermine the principles that maintain patrilineal culture and discourse.[51]

The schism of monkey from Prioress generates another split as well: "This time Athena's luciferous eyes . . . did not exactly take Boris into possession. She was aware of him as a being ouside of herself; . . . But she was, in this look, laying down another law, a command which was not to be broken: from now, between, on the one side, her and him, who had been present at the happenings of the last minute, and, on the other side, the rest of the world which had not been there, an insurmountable line would be forever drawn" (162–63). If, as commentators generally assume, the recognition and "command" betoken Athena's entry into another version of paternal name and law, marriage with Boris, then the power of the father would indeed appear to be restored, assuring that property—woman and estate—will be transmitted in orderly fashion from one man to another, as the laws of exogamy demand. "If narrative," writes de Lauretis, "is generated by an Oedipal logic, it is because it is situated within a system of exchange instituted by the incest prohibition, where woman functions as both a sign . . . and a value (object) for that exchange. . . . [W]oman properly represents the fulfillment of the narrative promise (made, as we know, to the little boy), and that representation works to support the male status of the mythical subject. The female position, produced as the end result of narrativization, is the figure of narrative closure."[52] Thus, in the conclusion of "The Monkey," as women, goods, and words all seem to fall into their expected places, the restoration of the "proper" symbolic order appears complete. The law and word of the father cast out all that is marginal, anomalous, and threatening, and closure—of both story and interpretation—can occur.[53]

But is the paternal word actually the last? As Kristeva points out, the split between symbolic and semiotic is not absolute and progressive: "*They function synchronically within the signifying process of the subject.*"[54] Though the story seems over when the monkey is ejected, in fact the events of the metamorphosis suggest alternatives at once disturbing and exhilarating. The monkey is, after all, notoriously a *trickster,* as Dinesen indicates in the monkey tale from "The Old Chevalier" with which we began. And the trickster is a "mediator" who "occupies a position halfway between two polar terms . . . , an ambiguous and equivocal character" who blurs the boundaries on which firm identity depends.[55] What trick does Dinesen—whose famous notion that God loves a joke is seldom more divertingly embodied—have up her sleeve in this ending?[56] Is the Prioress's appearance as "herself" not indefinitely susceptible, like the Wendish goddess of love, to another (re)turn, another troping by her double from the tropics?

Consider, for example, the future of Boris and Athena as a consequence of the ambiguous, forbidden "knowledge" the metamorphosis bestows. So far from promising a "legitimate" marriage and hence a "proper" narrative closure, as most critics assume, the moment is explicitly figured as the quintessence of illegitimacy, condensing and culminating all the figures of unrepresentability the text has unfolded. The "insurmountable line . . . drawn" between them and "the rest of the world" implies not reintegration or domesticization but explicitly a positioning under "another law" outside the bounds of dominant culture—a law associated with the "wild" space of the prioress/monkey as godmother and mother goddess. In seeking to establish an incestuous alliance with and between those she calls her "children" (139), to rupture the father-daughter dyad of "Olympic" Hopballehus and the rule of its self-styled "patriarch" ("Grandpapa" in both senses [128]), to incorporate Boris and Athena into her own matriarchal "Trinity" (138), and to make them, as she says, "Ours!" (139), the Prioress has transgressed precisely those rules of exogamy that, *pace* Lévi-Strauss, found patriarchal culture.

She displaces that symbolic economy with a conception of matrifocality and matrilinearity that has affinities with an older theory of culture, rearticulated by Briffault about the time that Dinesen was writing the text. According to this view, exogamy occurs as the outcome of "the expulsion of the males from a cohesive, dominant female group of grandmothers, mothers, daughters, and children, vehicles of the matriarchal psychology and of the mysteries [of] the primordial relation between mother and daughter."[57] Helen Diner notes that Briffault's position "is the exact opposite from Freud's [in *Totem and Taboo*]: not the authority of older men but that of older women enforced exogamy. . . . According to Briffault, motherly love is always instinctively possessive."[58]

This perspective illuminates the focus of "The Monkey" both on female desire and mother/daughter/sister relations and on the problematic triangulated relationship of the Prioress, Boris, and Athena. As feminist theorists have often observed, one of the impulses most rigorously prohibited by phallological imperatives is women's desire for each other.[59] Dinesen implies that what the Prioress ultimately seeks in all her machinations is neither Boris's advantage nor the extension of patriarchal marriage, but access to Athena by whatever means. Toward this end, Boris is reduced to little more than mediating instrument, as much a proxy for the Prioress as the monkey itself; indeed, her desire to make a monkey of her nephew becomes increasingly obvious as the tale unfolds. Boris's role in the "rape" is merely surrogate; as the love potion scene suggests, he literally imbibes his godmother's spirit(s) before the assault. As many ancient myths of origin attributed childbirth to women's impregnation "by contact with numinous animals,"[60] so we might say that the child the Prioress predicts as a consequence of her vicarious union with Athena is the product, or fabrication, of the mother/monkey: "For early man it is just as natural that the numinous progenitor should have animal form as that the great goddess should be endowed with all sorts of animal attributes and appear as an animal."[61]

In this context, the sinister, even brutal quality of the prioress/monkey's manipulations of Athena suggests that given women's positioning within a patriarchal order, feminine homoerotic desire may become warped into a replica of phallic domination and possession: bonding and bondage, as the Prioress's determination to "put [Athena] in a cage" and make her "Ours!" implies, may become horrifically entangled (142, 139).[62] Yet Dinesen also suggests another kind of symbolic affinity between the prioress/monkey and Athena. For all her daughterly devotion to her father, Athena, like the Prioress—and like her author—is "luciferous" (162), a covert revolutionary who wants "to cut off the heads of all the tyrants." She identifies herself with another unruly animal, "*une cavale indomptable et rebelle, / san freins . . . ni rênes, . . . / Une jument sauvage*" (an indomitable, rebellious warhorse, without bit or reins, a wild mare), and believes that only in the overthrow of ancien régimes can one be "*Libre, pour la première fois*" (free for the first time).[63]

The text implies, then, that ultimately the prioress/godmother realizes her desire to possess both a daughter and an explicitly "feminized" son in a reversal of taboos on incest and homosexuality, an overturning of the phallic economy in which men maintain hegemonic power over goods, women, and words.[64] Within a patriarchal framework, her plurality of desire for the alliances and exchanges with/of "unsuitable" partners can only be read as monstrous or "unholy."[65] But Dinesen suggests that if the monkey/prioress is a demonic figure it is precisely because of such a confinement, which denies her both desire and active agency. Her narrative of the entrapment of an African elephant, "which is much bigger and more magnificent than the . . . domesticated Indian beasts," also figures the enclosures culture imposes on women and on feminine discourse: " 'The hearts of animals in cages . . . become grated, as upon a grill, upon the shadow of the bars. Oh, the grated hearts of caged animals!' she exclaimed with terrible energy" (147). Just so "King Solomon, it is known, shut up the most prominent demons of Jewry in bottles, sealed them, and had them sunk to the bottom of the sea. What goings on, down there, of impotent fury! Alike . . . to the dumb struggles within the narrow wooden chests of old women, sealed up by the Solomonic wax of their education" (136–37). Such energies will inevitably find liberation, and when the repressed returns, its terrifying potential is multiplied: "In the end they . . put [the elephant] in chains and [had] a barred house built for him in the menageries. But from that time, on moonlit nights, the whole city . . . began to swarm with the shades of the elephants of Africa, wandering about the place. . . . No people dared any more to be in the town after dark had fallen" (147).

This same multiplicity distinguishes the monkey, whose subversive potential and blithe contempt for confinement is reasserted in the comic aftermath of the metamorphosis: "The monkey crawled into the shade of the back of the room, and for a little while continued its whimpering and twitching. Then, shaking off its misfortunes, it jumped in a light and graceful leap onto a pedestal, which supported the marble head of the philosopher Immanuel Kant, and from there it watched, with its glittering eyes, the behavior of the three people in the room" (162). Here, as elsewhere in Dinesen's Gothic, horror and humor merge in another grotesque coupling. That ambiguous final clause syntactically as well as figuratively fuses the monkey with the philosopher who likewise gazes at the scene—and retrospectively links him, in his turn, with the love goddess on whose statue the monkey, as the god's erotic double, had earlier perched (130). The gesture, in effect, makes a monkey out of Kant—and, implicitly, out of the traditional Western metaphysics and the male philosophical genealogy his bust monumentalizes. Langbaum notes that Kant "conquered for reason the domain of the unconscious," but the passage, like the tale, suggests that our cherished philosophical systems may be as ossified and unseeing as the statue, incapable of conquering "the unconscious," which mocks the most august androcentric reason(ers).[66]

The plural possibilities of the final scene are underscored by the Prioress's name (113). "Cathinka" evokes Dinesen's description in Out of Africa of the mise en abîme effected by matrioshkas, "those Russian wooden dolls . . . which are sold under the name of Katinka," and "which . . . have . . . got another doll inside them, and another inside that"—infinitely reproductive of further self re-presentations (OA, 125). The auditory pun in the title reminds us that the monkey remains the manqué—an untameable principle of transgression, dis-order, and rupture that makes monkeys not only, literally, out of the Prioress as phallic mother or out of the ponderous paternal bust of Kant mockingly mounted in the final scene, but out of every categorical imperative erected by a symbolic order which, as Irigaray has suggested, maintains its own "lofty status" by censoring women's "impulses."[67]

As the dynamic figure of writing, narrativity, and illicit, in-spiring feminine jouissance, what the narrator calls the "mystery" of "secret joy" with which "the Prioress was drunk" (143), the monkey may be momentarily stayed, but the metamorphosis we have witnessed suggests an infinite reversibility between Prioress and primate, between the stasis and apparent coherence of the dominant symbolic order and the disruption, swerve and diversion that mark the beginning of an other discourse, a new story.

But what of the last words of the text? With their monological invocation of the law and their learned Latin, they appear to close off this possibility by constituting a final, unambiguous tribute to paternal authority, subduing the disturbing heteroglossia of the Prioress's earlier discourse, with its unpredictable concatenation of English and French. Even here, however, Dinesen allows for an alternative possibility. For the lines are those not of the Virgilian narrator of *Aeneid,* but of the Sibyl, to whom Dinesen has earlier compared the Prioress (115). As "inspired revealer of things to come," the Sibyl and her oracular utterances are associated with a polylogical womblike space:

> The rock's vast side is hollowed into a cavern
> With a hundred mouths, a hundred open portals,
> Whence voices rush, the answers of the Sibyl.[68]

Linked, like the monkey and its author, with scattered "leaves, the mockery of the rushing wind's disorder," the Sibyl too speaks "riddles, confused with truth." Her mystifying discourse is the product of a struggle between her own voice(s) and the "curb" that would make her "subject to Apollo," the god who, in a passage that parallels Athena's identification with a rebellious, untamed mare, seeks to "tame" the Sibyl's "wild spirit/ Shape . . . her to his control."[69] The Sibyl's struggle with Apollo, rewritten in the monkey/prioress's struggle with the prioress/monkey, is an orgasmic "frenzy":

> The priestess, not yet subject to Apollo,
> Went reeling through the cavern, wild, and storming
> To throw the god, who presses, like a rider,
> With bit and bridle and weight. . . . Apollo rode her,
> Reining her rage, and shaking her, and spurring
> The fierceness of her heart."[70]

While the voice that finally emerges from this struggle seems monologically Apollonian, the text leaves open the possibility that the sibylline "fierceness" is not so easily controlled; her "frenzy dwindle[s]" but does not definitively end. Just as no one can really know front from back of the Wendish goddess, nor recognize unerringly the "true Prioress," so neither we nor Aeneas can be certain which words are "truth," which are "riddles" in the hundred-mouthed sibylline voice that guides the son to the paternal presence. Indeed, the text allows for the possibility that that presence may be as much an "illusion" as the monsters guarding the gates of the underworld to which the Sibyl conducts Aeneas. If, as Dinesen suggested elsewhere, the Sibyl figures woman's subversive creative power (*Essays,* 35), then the very utterance that seems most to proclaim the word of the father may also harbor the signs of its undoing.[71]

This possibility is underscored by the further, more recondite, echoes engendered by the Virgilian text. In Balzac's *Seraphita,* that romance of sexual indeterminancy to which Dinesen alludes in "The Deluge," Pastor Becker seeks to understand the epicene Seraphita's extraordinary powers of divination by reading treatises on witchcraft, especially the *De Praestigiis Daemonum* of John Wier.[72] Rationalizing Seraphita's preternatural abilities by adducing evidence on witches able to speak, miraculously, in many "languages" presumably unknown to them, Becker refers to Wier's claim that women—"especially the old ones"—are peculiarly susceptible to demonic possession because of the weakness, wickedness, inconstancy, and impressionability peculiar to "*le sexe feminin.*" Demonstrating the linguistic multiplicity engendered by demonic possession, Wier takes as a key example the case of the demonically possessed Italian woman who, being asked which was Virgil's finest verse, replied "*Discite justitiam moniti et non temnere Divos.*" In appropriating not only Virgil, but Balzac, Wier, and implicitly the extended discourses on witchcraft within which his text circulated, Dinesen performs a dizzying feat of intertextual prestidigitation, using her own bewitching rewordings of the sibylline text to undo the symbolic order that would destroy both woman and her multivoiced discourse in the name and with the law of the father.

The undecidability inherent in Dinesen's appropriation of Virgil is inseparable from the linguistic transgressions persistently associated with the monkey. To "let the monkey in," as she would advise years later,[73] is to import that enchantment legendarily associated with the Sibyl's leaves and "hundred voices"; to witness, like Athena and Boris, a wonder beyond words; to know what we cannot speak. In the tale's last, contradictory passage Dinesen enacts the oracular, sibylline nature of her own textuality—utterly undecidable, challenging classification, a dynamic play of difference in which all categories, all categorical imperatives, begin to falter. The dreamlike exchange of the metamorphosis, then, couples not just two, but three, four, or more: the monkey, the mother, the text that incorporates them both, and the reader, whose embodying linguistic consciousness both shapes and is shaped by their tale. And the author: "We registered ourselves," Dinesen would write in *Shadows on the Grass,* "among the wild animals" and "laughed at the ambitions" of those who sought to take what was untamed and free and "make [it] respectable" (18). Late in life, in a complex self-reflexive jest, she would laughingly claim the title "Queen of the Northern Monkeys," in effect merging herself, retrospectively, with her own text, and with the godmother, lady of beasts, whose plots it unfolds.[74] In this guise, like Virginia Woolf describing the Manx cat with whom she identifies herself and all other women in *A Room of One's Own,* Dinesen too would pun playfully on the sexual, textual, political and poetic "difference a tail makes" by its presence or absence in phallocentric culture: "No tale can proceed without examining apparently simple questions. And no tail, either."[75] Metaphorically mingling character, text, reader, and author, "The Monkey" playfully performs the procedure its author advocated. "Examining" the "apparently simple questions" of sexual "difference," desire, and narrative, the text suggests that thereby, unseen, hangs the tale of its own engendering.

8

Circulating Sexes, Wandering Words

The woman shall not wear that which pertaineth unto a man,
neither shall a man put on a woman's garment; for all that do so
are abomination unto the Lord thy God.

Deuteronomy 22:5

Different though the sexes are, they intermix. In every human
being a vacillation from one sex to the other takes place, and
often it is only the clothes that keep the male or female likeness. . . . Of the complications and confusions which thus result
everyone has the experience.

Virginia Woolf, Orlando

I

It is not surprising that Dinesen should have chosen "The Roads Round
Pisa" as the opening text of *Seven Gothic Tales,* for beyond its mere
chronological priority (it was one of the only tales virtually completed in
Africa) it operates at many levels as a microcosm of the larger book. Yet
Haas's editorial rearrangement seems again felicitous, for the altered sequence—actually anticipated by Dinesen's own earlier outlines—situates
"Roads" in precisely the same position within *Seven Gothic Tales* as the
tale itself situates Pisa: as the center around which all else revolves.[1] But
the center of this center is literally empty: Pisa itself never appears among
the story's major settings. Indeed, beyond its function as a place name, it
never appears at all except in a brief summary of peripheral events (*SGT,*
212). The most vital narrative possibilities reside, the text suggests, in the
wayward, circuitous spaces outside the bounds.

The transpositions that marked the tale's prepublication history find
analogues in the events of its narrative, which might be read at many levels as a story of alterations and disjunctions—of things cut off from their
"proper" places and of the anxiety such symbolic castrations engender.
Adopting a well-worn fictional convention of dislocation—the male

traveler "on the road" amidst unfamiliar topographies (165, 178)[2]—
Dinesen begins with the figure of linguistic hiatus: an unfinished text.
Unable to complete a letter to his closest friend, Augustus von Schimmelman strolls outside an *osteria* on the way to Pisa one May evening in
1823, reflecting on the causes of his incapacity. Another "melancholy"
young Dane like Jonathan Maersk and his Shakespearean prototype,
Augustus is a recurrent character in Dinesen's writings, reappearing in
both "The Poet" and *Out of Africa,* but even his earliest appearance is re-
duplicative: the narrative begins and ends with his "looking at [him]self
in . . . looking-glasses" (165, 216). Literalizing the metaphoric self-
regard of male characters in other Gothic tales, this "habit" makes Augustus Dinesen's most explicit representation of the phallocentric man
obsessed with his own resemblance (166). His confused philosophical reflections on his writer's block disclose the apprehension that drives that
obsession:

> Have I been . . . really truthful in my letter to him? I would give a
> year of my life to be able to talk to him tonight, and, while talking,
> to watch his face. How difficult it is to know the truth. I wonder if
> it is really possible to be truthful when you are alone. Truth, like
> time, is an idea arising from, and dependent upon, human inter-
> course. . . . The truth about this road is that it leads to Pisa, and the
> truth about Pisa can be found within books written and read by hu-
> man beings. What is the truth about a man on a desert island? And
> I . . . am like a man on a desert island. . . . [M]y friends used to
> laugh at me because I was in the habit of looking at myself in the
> looking-glasses, and had my own rooms decorated with mirrors. . . .
> I looked into the glasses to see what I was like. A glass tells you the
> truth about yourself. (165–66)

In a symbolic order that figures speech as unmediated "truth," writing
becomes an emblem of lack, error, and displacement—a profound threat
to the notion of unified identity. As an author in search of a character,
Augustus is fixed in a kind of infantile mirror stage, terrified lest the
solid-seeming "self" thus present(ed) to itself be but one fiction among
many.[3] Ironically, his prime object of reassurance is also the emblem
of his undoing: "With a shudder of disgust"—a characteristic gesture
to which we shall return—he recalls the "mirror-room of the Panoptikon . . . where you see yourself reflected . . . in a hundred glasses each of
which distorts and perverts your face and figure in a different way. . . .
So your own self . . . [is] reflected within the mind of each of the people
whom you meet . . . into a likeness, a caricature . . . which still lives on
and pretends to be, in some way, the truth about you. Even a flattering
picture is a . . . lie." From the horrors of this speculative *mise en abîme,* he
seeks refuge in the law of the Same—the "love" of the male friend with

whom, in both senses, he *corresponds,* and whose presence, "a true mirror to the soul" (166), might overcome the impotence and alienation the truncated letter represents.[4]

In these figurative homologies of speech, centered presence, and masculinity, it is woman—like writing and the "roads" to which Dinesen analogizes it—who becomes the sign of deviation and discontinuity that dislodges man from the center and fragments his symbolic order, shattering what Irigaray, in a later text on mirroring, calls "the old dream of symmetry" found(ed) in the androcentric speculum.[5] Augustus's reflections on the horror of having *nothing to see* culminate, significantly, with the image of the wife he has fled precisely because he found her lacking. Dinesen suggests that he, like the old chevalier, is a narcissist for whom woman's worth lies in "reflecting" man's desire, "proving to [him] that all is not a dream" (166).[6] Incapable of looking beyond himself, Augustus can only regard as "absurd" his wife's contrary desire to be *seen* in her own right; he dismisses her longing as incomprehensible "jealousy" and "folly" (167).

Yet paradoxically it is woman who shapes and signifies his most persistent yearnings. For Augustus is also a character in search of an author, and the text he seeks is explicitly feminine. Countervailing his aversion to his wife is his nostalgia for the late "maiden aunt" who gave him his dearest possession: a heart-shaped "smelling-bottle" bearing the image of "a pink castle" in a pastoral landscape and the inscription *Amitié sincère.* It is an endlessly generative iconography. In Italy, in her youth, the aunt "had been a guest in that same rose-colored palace, and [her] every dream of romance and adventure . . . attached to it. . . . When he had been a little boy he had shared these fancies of her, and had himself made up tales of the beautiful things to be found in the house and the happy life to be led there. Now that she was . . . dead, nobody would know where it was to be found." While the desire of the living wife puts Augustus to flight, the aunt's desire, safely displaced and distanced by/as graphic figures, literally puts him on the road in another sense, in quest of the "reality" behind the unfinished story of the fetishized bottle: "Perhaps . . . some day I shall come across the bridge under the trees and see the rock and the castle before me" (168). Like woman, the "truth" he seeks is inseparable from the fiction he fears.

These reflections on a woman's story—interruptions to the progress of a masculine text—are themselves "interrupted" by another feminine plot. Augustus's advance along the road is halted by a coach which, careening out of control, runs off the highway and overturns. Its occupant—"a bald old man with a refined face"—effects a comparable disruption of Augustus's interpretive categories, for with the restoration of "his" bewigged bonnet, "the old man" is "transformed into a fine old lady of imposing appearance" (169). As the first in a series of events that expose, through defamiliarization, the instability of the sexual signs by which Augustus reads "reality," this reversal also discomposes the reader, revealing the degree to which we share his conventional perspective. "The Accident" (Dinesen's title for the episode refers not only to the coach but to the woman in the "man") throws Augustus off track in another sense as well, for now both he and his narrative are quite literally carried away by "The Old Lady's Story" (171).

At its simplest level, that story concerns the old woman, Carlotta di Gampocorta (her name an elaborate comic play on woman's notorious "lack"[7]) and her beloved step-granddaughter Rosina, soon to be delivered of a child. Obsessed by a "terror of childbearing" and a covert preference for women, Carlotta has remained virginal, having made continued chastity the condition for her marriage to the widowed nobleman whose young daughter she had adopted as her own. Despite her objections her stepdaughter had married, only to die like her mother in bearing a daughter, whose protection from a potentially fatal heterosexuality Carlotta has subsequently made her life's work.

Here, as in "The Monkey," Dinesen explores the possibility that such possessive maternal desire may reflect and reinforce the very phallic power it seems to contradict, and considers the import of the daughter's refusal to follow the mother's script—refusal, specifically, to mirror the mother.[8] Rewriting her own life, Carlotta betroths Rosina to one of her own former suitors, Prince Potenziani—an aging, vastly wealthy aristocrat who, as she delicately puts it, is "an admirer of our sex" but "incapable of being a lover or a husband," a fact that out of "vanity or weakness" he keeps "secret" by maintaining an entourage of "the most expensive courtesans" (172–73).[9] But Rosina rejects this grotesque match for love of another man, making Carlotta "furious" in the most literal sense: an implacable maternal monster determined to have her way (174). Interpreting her granddaughter's rebellion merely as a sign of the times—a contagion caught from reading women writers (174)—and grieved at Rosina's willingness "to let a man come between" them, she forces her granddaughter to marry against her will. Rosina eludes these maternal machinations by manipulating paternal authority, specifically by raising the question of phallic sufficiency: she seeks a papal annulment "on the ground that [the marriage] had not been consummated" (176). The prince, prostrated by public exposure of his lack (a "scandal" linguistically multiplied by street songs about his wife as "the Virgin of Pisa"), arranges for his young friend Giovanni Gastone—a notorious rake like his better known namesake—to rape Rosina, hoping thus to circumvent the annulment by "proving" his own potency.

But this androcentric plot, like all the others in the tale, is deflected

by unexpected feminine interventions—specifically by that which literally *cannot be (fore)seen* or counted on within a masculine specular economy: feminine desire—another kind of *amitié sincère* between women:

> "Rosina had a friend, Agnese della Gherardesci, whom all her
> life she had loved next to me. Once, . . . they had pricked their fin-
> gers, mixed the blood, and vowed sisterhood. This girl had been
> allowed to grow up wild. . . . She [had] the notion that she looked
> like the Milord Byron, . . . and she used to dress and ride as a man,
> and to write poetry." (174) [10]

Agnese violates traditional gender dichotomies in more than dress, for
she, like "Isak Dinesen," moves readily between "male" and "female"
positions. Thwarted in her attempt to save Rosina from marriage by
effecting a "masculine" rescue (174–75), she disrupts one exchange of
women with another, taking her friend's place in bed so that Rosina may
have a chaste meeting with her lover. But the social order these women
inhabit—which, as Karen Blixen observed, construes woman strictly as
"a sexual being" (*LA,* 263)—exacts a grievously high price for such
feminine free play. The night of the substitution is also the night of the
rape, which deprives Agnese not only of her virginity but also of her poetic voice—a double sacrifice that ironically assures her friend's salvation
(181–82).[11] For Rosina attains her annulment, marries her lover, and conceives the child whose imminent birth has devastated Carlotta. Con-
vinced that both she and Rosina will soon die, Carlotta relents, abandons
her former rigidity, and sends Augustus as emissary of her blessing to her
granddaughter.

These interwoven feminine plots reach a climax in the inn where Augustus stops on his way to complete his mission. In one of those extravagant coincidences by which Dinesen's texts call attention to their own
fictionality, Potenziani, Giovanni, and Agnese—in male disguise—arrive
at the same *osteria.* Believing himself to have been betrayed by Giovanni,
Potenziani provokes a challenge, the terms of which ironically expose the
corrupt gender codes that underwrite a man's "good name" and maintain
him as an upstanding member of the male community. For what is at
stake in this duel—its point of honor, so to speak—is quite literally the
question of whether Giovanni has used his phallic "stiletto" to draw
"blood" from Potenziani's wife (190).

2

Digressions were born of the grossness of heroic minds, unable
to confine themselves to those essential features of things that

were to the purpose at hand, as we see to be naturally the case . . .
with women.

The New Science of Giambattista Vico

Tell all the Truth but tell it slant—
Success in Circuit Lies.

Emily Dickinson

Straight is the line of duty
Curved is the line of beauty.

Isak Dinesen, "The Monkey"

With its plural plots and proliferating discourses, the narrative structure
of the text, like the "Roads" of the title, perpetually circles but never
penetrates a center. Indeed, the question of penetration is in every sense
the pivotal issue of this tale in which the "proper" place of generation—
the body of woman—is always *elsewhere*. While taking to comic extremes Kierkegaard's punning aphorism that "a bride [*en Brud*] and a
breach [*et Brud* = breach, break, rupture] correspond to one another
as female to male,"[12] Dinesen also destabilizes the "correspondences"
posited by its latter two terms. Like Potenziani's unruly bride, "The
Roads Round Pisa" is a text out of bounds, a story of ruptures and revolutions, peripheries and periphrasis. The latter term—denoting "the use
of a negative, passive, or inverted construction in place of a positive, active, or normal construction: a roundabout or indirect way of speaking"—suggests the degree to which locution, like location, is marked by
gender in a tradition that writes negativity, passivity, and inversion as
signs of "femininity" and makes "masculine" synonymous with "positive, active, or normal."[13] The notion of "roundabout or indirect" speech
recalls the definition of woman as a "jest" and diversion in Kierkegaard's
Stages on Life's Way, a crucial masculine pretext for "The Roads Round
Pisa": "To be a woman is something so strange, so mixed, so complex,
that no predicate expresses it, and the many predicates one might use
contradict one another so sharply that only a woman can endure it and,
still worse, enjoy it."[14] As Dinesen implies through Augustus's baffled reflections on his wife, which echo Kierkegaard's dictum, phallocentric
culture constructs an analogy between wayward women, wandering
words, and the meandering "roads" that in this tale are not linear means
to an end(ing) but quite literally figures of *circumlocution.*

In this context it is not surprising that, as Paul de Man observes, the
Western philosophical tradition often treats metaphor with a disparage-
ment similar to that it bestows on women, comparing metaphoric "misuse" of language with the vagaries of "the fair sex": "Like a woman . . .

[metaphor] is a fine thing as long as it is kept in its proper place. Out of place, among the serious affairs of men . . . , it is a disruptive scandal—like the appearance of a real woman in a gentleman's club where it would only be tolerated as a picture, preferably naked, . . . framed and hung on the wall."[15] Similarly, as we have seen, definitions of the "narratable" as a function of "wandering and misinterpretation"[16] recall the traditional image of the unruly woman as the ultimate deviant. Reiterating that topos, Kierkegaard's Constantine remarks condescendingly that woman is "unable to set limits to herself." Unfixed, unstable, perverting the codes of masculine "rationality," she epitomizes excess and monstrosity: "Even Plato and Aristotle take it that woman is an incomplete form, . . . an irrational quantity, which perhaps some time in a better existence might be brought back in male form."[17] His most extreme version of this deviation is the woman who construes herself as a "man"—that is, not as fetishized sexual or aesthetic object, but as active, creative subject, beyond the confinements of gender: "Not satisfied with the aesthetic sphere, she 'goes further,' she would be emancipated—that she is man enough to say. Let that come to pass, the jest will be beyond bounds."[18] In "Roads," as in "The Dreamers," Dinesen both satirizes the rigidly oppositional symbolic order that generates such stereotypical formulations of "man" and "woman" and plays brilliantly on the analogies of femininity, figuration, and narrativity as principles of diversion, ex-centricity, and extravagance: literally, that which wanders outside the bounds. Significantly, Constantine's peroration on woman as the essence of "contradiction" and "nonsense" culminates in a contemptuous portrait of the "brooding authoress" whose texts are like hens' eggs: a man never knows "what [she] is going to lay next."[19] Appropriating and revising these associations, Dinesen celebrates the "deviant," the peripheral, and the circuitous as potential sources of the greatest creativity, suggesting that within a phallocentric order woman becomes the supreme fiction/maker insofar as she simultaneously embodies and engenders the figurative or the narratable. As Karen Blixen would observe in her "Bonfire" lecture, "woman is more of an artist than . . . man," and the greatest male artists "approach the female *modus vivendi*" (77).[20] Throughout the tale, as in its opening episodes, Dinesen truncates male-authored plots with narratives engendered by woman's desire and discourse.

These implications are reinforced in the setting of "The Roads Round Pisa," through which, as through its title, Dinesen evokes the traditional topology that places the city over against whatever is "outside" or marginal to it—the open, unstructured space that perpetually threatens its borders. Tony Tanner has noted that

> the architecture of the city—which includes not only buildings but the related edifices of law, rule, and custom, all of them interre-

lated by language—"architectures" the relationships between the sexes with complete explicitness. . . . Beyond the discourse of the city . . . the bonds of social imperatives and constraints necessarily weaken. . . . The city by definition has limits; whatever falls outside the city ultimately has none. (19)[21]

In "Roads" Dinesen focuses on that "outside" as a locus of possibility—a liminal, contingent, aleatory space where anything can happen. Playing implicitly on the etymological link of "city" with *civilization,* she figures "Pisa" as a complex of values and institutions wherein issues of name, lineage, and legitimacy intersect with figures of the signs, lines, and boundaries that demarcate a patriarchal symbolic order. To travel the roads round Pisa, then, is to traverse, both literally and psychologically, a "feminine" space where randomness, coincidence, and irregularity replace the orderly connections and progressions of masculine *civitas* as of narratological order and authority.

Yet as Tanner adds, by the nineteenth century the simple distinction of inside/outside on which these conceptions are founded was itself eroding: "Whether there is a genuine outside becomes a problem . . . when it comes to seem that the apparent outside is an illusion, a space already socialized in one way or another."[22] Dinesen raises similar questions, but conversely, reminding us that the "outside" also inhabits the "inside," perpetually threatening its seemingly secure centricity. Given the importance of patrilineal marriage as the foundation of *civitas,* and of woman's subordination as the foundation of patrilineal marriage, it is no coincidence that the text's most obvious figure for the perilous "outside" is the destabilization of both gender and marital relations precipitated by disorderly feminine diversions.[23]

Dinesen's choice of Pisa to epitomize "the city" in both its literal and symbolic senses is illuminated by the elaborate connections between the tale's marital thematics and those in her early essay "Modern Marriage." Presented, like "Roads," as a kind of *excursus,* a "wandering" reading of the semiotics of Western culture (*MM,* 64, 72), the text figures the traditional institution of marriage as a "leaning Tower of Pisa" (55), an unstable monument to antiquated social constructs, a "venerable moribundity" and "empty shell" (40) which, though "morally . . . valueless" (52), remains standing by virtue of its vestigial symbolic value. Dinesen's metaphors stress the inseparability of sociocultural and linguistic structures: marriage is not only an edifice whose "walls" threaten to collapse (58) but a "letter" that "killeth" (58, 63), a "word" whose force persists "in name only" (40, 43). That name, however, is not easily abolished, for it is the father's: marriage is the quintessential institution of "patriarchs," erected in the name of "the fatherland and the dynasty" and supported by a paternally conceived divinity: "The God of old times was in every way the God of family, law and order, and thereby marriage" (63).

The ultimate embodiment of this patriarchal force in "Roads" is Prince Potenziani. As the epitome of all the sexually maimed men in Dinesen's canon, he is also, significantly, a personification of phallic power. "Tall and broad, and enormously fat," a great, bloated, over-blown figure, he is comically figured as a kind of walking phallus: his "soft fullness" has "great power behind it"—a "primitive vitality" and "a peculiar grace, as if he had a rhythm all his own." Like the "venerably moribund" culture Dinesen analysed in "Modern Marriage," the aging Potenziani is *made up* in a double sense, his lack and decay concealed beneath "stays" and a cosmetic mask that simulates youthful vigor: "hair . . . dyed jet black," a "face . . . painted and powdered" (*SGT,* 185–86). Potent in name only, he becomes a parody, like Pompilio, of his own appellation. Indeed, we might read him as a prefiguring caricature of the *nom (non) du père* as phallic signifier.[24] It is notable that in the American edition of *Seven Gothic Tales* his name was spelled *Pozentiani,* an orthography that Dinesen altered in the Danish and British editions. The transposition of letters marks an apt slip of the pen, a kind of figura-tive castration, for true to the masquerade thematics of the tale, "Po-zentiani" turns *potency* into a *pose.*

Yet Potenziani is no simple caricature. Like the magisterial phal-locentric literary tradition to which the woman author, like Rosina, is married whether she will or no, he evokes inevitable ambivalence. Re-sembling "the ancient statues of Bacchus," simultaneously godlike and grotesque in his sublime egoism, he possesses a presence and rhetoric so commanding that they overwhelm Augustus and the other men who witness them: "the room became resplendent with his rays" (193). In-deed, like the order he embodies, despite (because of?) his emasculation he continues to operate mythologically in such compelling fashion that even Dinesen's most astute critics have been similarly dazzled by his strange seductiveness. Augustus's bemused reflection that Potenziani "would have made . . . a most powerful and impressive idol" (186) is at once a commentary on the potency of phallocentrism and a striking prophecy of the curious admiration his figure has inspired.[25]

In its sympathetic disposition toward, even adulation of Potenziani, critical tradition remains notably inattentive to the "difference of view" that comes from reading (from) woman's place or placing women's read-ing in this text.[26] In this sense traditional interpretations mirror the re-sponses of Augustus and those other male characters in Dinesen's texts who are so preoccupied with a normative masculine perspective that they cannot see woman as anything but its reflection. Yet Dinesen's repeated reminders that mirrors deceive suggest that we might well look for what the "rays" of the glittering masculine surface obscure: that despite ap-pearances women like Agnese, who remains a covert locus of resistance throughout this scene, may read from another position altogether.[27] The darker side of the "wonderful" old Prince (194) appears explicitly in the dazzling imperturbability with which he authors and authorizes the rape on which his story turns. Yet for all his wealth, legendary power, and ruthlessness, he is incapable of preventing woman's illicit desire, which engenders another story, exposing him as an impotent imitation of a god and giving birth despite him to her own "illegitimate" text, rewriting the scripts of confinement within which he would install her as his prop(erty).

The events surrounding the duel between Potenziani and Giovanni reinforce these implications. In the letter on feminism quoted earlier, Karen Blixen develops an acute critique of all-male shooting parties as "typical demonstration[s] of the old world order":

> The sport, the excitement, the experience, were for the men; for the women they were a kind of mystical rite from which they were ex-cluded—somehow they did not exist until the men came home from the shooting. I have heard Uncle Frederik and Bror say quite seri-ously: 'Gentlemen do not like ladies to be at the butts,'—and that made it absolutely unquestionable that it would be stupid and repre-hensible for the ladies to attempt to take part.[28]

Her remarks are equally applicable to dueling as an exclusively male "rite" and right. In figuring the duel as a kind of text, she adds a third term to this homology, paralleling fighting with writing in an andro-centric narrative tradition predicated on linear progressions and the sense of an ending:

> The dark young Prince . . . looked at the old man. . . .
>   . . . "I think that as a story yours was too long, and even yet it has had no end. Let us make an end tonight." . . .
>   . . . "What an excellent critic you are," [Potenziani] went on, "not only of your own Tuscan songs, but of modern prose as well. That exactly was the fault of my story; that it had no end. A charm-ing thing, an end. Will you come tomorrow at sunrise to the terrace at the back of this house?" (192–93)

The oedipal stakes of this encounter between "the old man" and the "young" (who seeks, at several levels, to "make an end" to the old man by cutting off his "story") remind us that like other masculine contests—including those between the patriarchal literary tradition and the individ-ual talent—the underlying purpose of the duel is to prove "manhood" in every sense of that term. As Ong notes, *contest* is rooted, quite literally, in *testes*. Given Potenziani's spectacular lack in that quarter, Ong's com-ments are especially pertinent to Dinesen's complex parodic treatment of the duel:

> A certain anatomical externality is obvious in the male sexual organs
> of humans and other higher animals, and it is also registered accu-
> rately and indeed exquisitely in certain ways of conceiving of those
> organs. Thus a male has two sexual organs, . . . called 'testes' (Latin,
> *testes,* the plural of *testis,* witness) or "testicles" (*testiculi,* little wit-
> nesses . . .). *Testis* is the word from which 'contest' is derived. . . .
> In line with . . . the etymology of 'contest' (a confrontation of wit-
> nesses), the male finds himself anatomically entered in a contest, on
> trial, having to call witnesses . . . *to give testimony as to what he actually
> is, not a woman, to 'say' that he is a man.*[29]

With incisive irony, Dinesen undercuts these affairs between men by
making a woman their key "witness." Having misread Agnese's male at-
tire as testimony of manhood, Giovanni asks her to act as his second.
Though initially "sanguinary" in her hopes for the death of both men
(196), she ultimately ends the duel in a more subtly killing way: by exposing her *wo*manhood, *testifying* about the night in question, and thus,
paradoxically, confirming the questionable "manhood" of her rapist
while exposing the impotence and precipitating the death of the man
who contracted the rape to prove his own potency.

Potenziani perishes not of a bullet wound, but of a wound to the
heart—another "emasculation"—caused by a double loss: lamenting that
had he not been outwitted, "I should have had her, my lovely child, to
play with still," he dies uttering the name "Carlotta!" Dinesen (who
would later assert, in a rare comment on her own intentions, that he was
"punished according to [his] deserts . . . by death"[30]) writes his demise
as a grotesque, anticlimactic ejaculation: having "stiffen[ed] more and
more into something inanimate," he "fell . . . with a dull thud. . . . At
that moment his pistol, which he was still holding in his hand, went off"
(206–7)—a misfired parting shot in every sense. Given the obvious comedy here, the final baroque representation of the dead Potenziani as a kind
of *alter Christus*—his great bulk dominating "the center of the picture as
much as if he had been slowly ascending to heaven, and they his disciples,
left behind, gazing up toward him"—appears, contrary to a common
critical view, not apotheosis, but parody.

It is through the ambiguous figure of Agnese that Dinesen makes
most explicit the radical implications of the concealed feminine text that
cancels the "great power" of the "old god" (193) of patriarchy. Agnese's
relationship with Rosina is illuminated by another passage from Karen
Blixen's letter on feminist transformations of "the old world order." Anticipating the analyses of contemporary feminist linguists, she deplores
the inadequacy of language to signify woman-as-subject. In an androcentric culture, the woman who assumes the position of "a human being"
rather than merely "a sexual being," who acts as agent rather than object,

can be represented only in displaced, masculinized terms; thus "the young women of today are more . . . '*gentlemen*,'" than "the women of bygone days." When forms of intersubjectivity traditionally defined as exclusively "masculine" occur in "women's relationships with each other" or "between women and men," they alter the traditional discourses of both friendship and "homosexuality": "There is [a] French quotation which runs: "L'amitié uni au désir ressemble tant à l'amour'— in my opinion it not only resembles, it *is* amour. And I think that the morality existing between friends is something higher and more human than that between lovers has usually been,—perhaps just because it cannot be bound. . . ."[31] The *amitié* of Agnese and Rosina enacts this alternative "morality."

While Agnese may appear, *pace* her name, to represent woman as mere sacrificial "Lamb" (190) obsessed by "the recollection of one single hour of [her] life" that she can neither right nor "write" (181–82), in fact she has bypassed victimage and embarked on a quest for a new life. She plans to study astronomy in hopes of discovering a spiraling "road" to an alternative consciousness, an ungendered space beyond the bounds of phallocentric reference, "where there is no time" and where, in a literally revolutionary movement, bodies circulate outside the symbolic economy founded on the traffic in women: "The roads of the planets and stars, their ellipses and circles within the infinite space, must have the power to turn the mind into new ways" (182–83). It is just such a transformed state of mind, language, and society—revolutionary indeed—that Kristeva celebrates in "Women's Time": "a fluid and free subjectivity"—beyond gender, "beyond the horizon, beyond sight, beyond faith itself," "fitted to these times in which the cosmos, atoms, and cells" are "our true contemporaries."[32]

Initially attracted to this extraordinary young "man" through another misreading of sexual signs, Augustus traces in "his" face "a likeness to his friend Karl's as a boy." But Agnese's masculine costume (like her author's), far from signifying simply a would-be identification with men, enunciates a subversive rhetoric of resistance to woman's placement in a masculine economy whose logical consequence is rape: "You do not . . . really think that I am a man? I am not, and . . . am happy not to be. I know, of course, that great work has been achieved by men, but still I think that the world would be a more tranquil place if men did not come in to break up, very often, the things that we cherish" (183). If Augustus is embarrassed by his misreading, Agnese herself remains "quite indifferent to . . . his attitude toward her." Constituting herself as subject, she maintains "the same position" in the figurative as well as the literal sense, transforming thereby his conception of woman's alterity: "He had hardly ever talked to a young woman whose chief interest in the conversation had not been the impression that she herself was making on him, and he reflected that this must be what generally made the converse with women awkward and dull to him. The way in which this young woman seemed to take a friendly and confident interest in him, without apparently giving any thought to what he thought of her, seemed to him new and sweet, as if he suddenly realized that he had all his life been looking for such an attitude in women" (183–84). For the first time, he begins to suspect that the "accent of male and female conversation," like that of "male and female" clothing, might be accidental, dependent not on nature but on "the conventional" scripts engendered by the social order (184). Yet his dawning insight is occluded by the very androcentrism Agnese has led him to interrogate. His reflections on the significance of who wears the pants finally derive not from any awareness of the severe inhibitions imposed and signified by women's conventional clothing but from the same male narcissism that had earlier driven him from his wife: "The company of the girl pleased him in a particular way . . . partly because she was dressed like himself in those long black trousers which seemed to him the normal costume for a human being" (197).

These speculations, like Augustus's earlier reading of the disarrayed Carlotta as an "old man," are paradigmatic of Dinesen's persistent interest in what she called the "meaning" of "fashion" as part of a complex semiotics of gender—a culturally contingent code or "ritual" that functions as "a symbol of the structure and ideology of an epoch" (*Essays,* 55–57, 19; cf. 24–26). In "Roads" as in "Daguerreotypes," she develops a brilliant critique of male and female dress as a social discourse on sexuality whose end is to subjugate woman under the guise of adoration: "The corsets which the ladies of that time wore, . . . were really as much instruments of torture as the bound feet of the old Chinese women, and like them were an accepted symbol of true, fine femininity. . . . No real lady could at any moment from the time she stood up until she went to bed move at all freely" (*Essays,* 56; cf. *SGT,* 93–95). Her analysis here and throughout *Seven Gothic Tales,* as in her own playful cross-dressing in life and in name, anticipates more recent analyses of feminine transvestism as a travesty of phallocentric models and links her to other female modernists who, as Susan Gubar has shown, used cross-dressing as a subversive form of "re-dressing" themselves within a culture that would suppress them through the signs of "femininity."[33]

The motifs of costume, reversal, and remaking find their climactic symbolic expression in the marionette comedy which Augustus and Agnese attend the night before the duel. That drama is not only another play on the interweaving of life and art which the text has been unfolding, but an explicit relation of those imbrications to Dinesen's authorial project. For "the immortal Revenge of Truth" (198), set like "Roads" itself in "an inn" where diverse characters have gathered, is one of her earliest literary productions. Written in 1904, revised and published in Denmark in 1926, the play became a kind of touchstone for her authorship as well as one of her most important theoretical statements about the nature of fiction: "Everybody will remember," remarks the tongue-in-cheek narrator of "Roads," "how the plot is created by a witch pronouncing, upon the house wherein all the characters are collected, a curse . . . that any lie told within it will become truth" (198).[34] Like the dumb show in *Hamlet, The Revenge of Truth* is multiply reflexive. Forming the core of "Roads" just as that tale forms the core of *Seven Gothic Tales,* the marionette comedy synecdochizes the larger fictions that contain it, enacting the conditions of both its own and their engendering through characters who repeatedly comment on their own fictionality.[35] Recalling Augustus's opening speculations (166), we might read the play and the fictions it inhabits as a narratorial "Panoptikon" of mutually mirroring circles and surfaces. Simultaneously reflectors and reflected, they create an infinite regress of mutually reduplicating images—"the fatal space" (to borrow Foucault's felicitous phrase) "in which language speaks of itself."[36]

Dinesen links the characters of the tale to those of the marionette play not only by simile (198, 199, 200, 209) and persistent reflexive analogy but by another meaning inherent in her title, for to be "on the road" is also to be "in transit through a circuit of . . . performances or games," a participant in a mobile theatrics that conjoins "the real" and the role.[37] Agnese's transvestism marks the most explicit representation of sexual ambiguity in the text, but the fluidities of gender played out in her encounter with Augustus operate throughout the tale. Augustus and Potenziani, for example, though both written as "men" and indeed made interchangeable doubles by Augustus's role as Potenziani's "second" in the duel, are also mirror opposites: Augustus a sexually capable man with an aversion to women and latent longings for men, Potenziani a eunuch who suffers from unfulfilled and unfulfillable heterosexual desire. Women alone stir Carlotta's imagination; and the relation between Rosina and Agnese contains a lesbian subtext that can only emerge indirectly, written in the "blood" of symbolic exchanges and substitutions (190).[38]

Dinesen suggests, then, that whether between or within subjects, there is no more a single "sex" than a single text: sexualities are constructed by/within textualities, whether cultural or literary. Like the tale itself, both exist within a shifting, mutable semiotic field, interpretable by reading that is itself the product of a socially constructed and positioned "self." And both sex and text, so far from being absolute, unchanging, and monolithic, are something we circle round, enter and depart, like the characters in the inn, the marionette play, or the larger fiction of *Seven Gothic Tales,* with their continual circulations round Pisa, that site of origin and destination titularly promised but never fully delivered. In using the figure of masquerade to suggest that sexuality, like language, is neither unequivocal nor univocal, neither definite nor definitive, Dinesen prefigures recent demonstrations that "like words, gender identity can be travestied or exchanged; there is no 'proper' referent, male or female, only the masquerade of masculinity and femininity." [39]

Thus, while Augustus seeks a center, symbolized by the single masculine self and certified by the unified specular image in the glass, what he discovers instead is an infinitely fluid, unpredictable world of indeterminate bodies and shifting or problematic genders. It is a world where substitutions and role reversals reveal the truth that fiction has always known, epitomized in the playful "curse" on which the marionette comedy and the text it mimes both turn: that "truth" is inseparable from language, and that language "lies." "Every lie uttered here will become the truth": the words of the witch Amiane suggest that truth is not linear, but (in Dickinson's fine locution) "slant"—the product of the "circuit(ous)"; not the much-traveled path of "the roads of life" (166) but that which comes by the way, as a function of obliquity, diversion and deferral. It is in submitting oneself to this recognition, experiencing the ecstasy—*ex-stasis*—it offers, that one may attain the bliss Augustus has mistakenly sought in an unchanging, unified identity. This elliptical "truth," involving virtually every character in the tale, but especially marked in its female figures, is made most explicit in Amiane, fictive double for that other bewitching woman in this house of fiction, the "Arbiter" (as she wrote in "The Deluge") "of the masquerade." Translating *The Revenge of Truth* into English late in life, Karen Blixen would specify in stage directions that Amiane was to look "as like Isak Dinesen as possible." [40]

The interchangeability of "truth" and "fiction" is underscored in the tale's rhetorical climax, where Dinesen incorporates Dante's *Commedia* into her own text of feminine subversion and transcendence, staging a different sort of duel: the "face to face" confrontation of Giovanni and the woman he has raped. As Potenziani's corpse is carried away, Giovanni speaks to Agnese "in a changed . . . voice," quoting the lines from *Purgatorio* that dramatize the reunion of a prostrate and adoring Dante with a transfigured Beatrice (30.34–39, 31.85–89). The Dantean intertext provides a broader interpretive scope for the thematics of masking and of Agnese's name and role, which imply that she, like Calypso, is a feminized Lamb of God—a surrogate sacrifice whose "blood" has been shed in another's stead (190). For the reunion of Dante and Beatrice, "the great focal point of the Commedia," is also "deliberately set," as Dorothy Sayers notes, as though upon a stage, between . . . masques [designed] for his . . . instruction and to the honour of Beatrice and all she stands for. The persons are still actual existent beings, as all actors are existent beings; but they are actors, and they are presenting a show. . . . [I]n the Masque, Beatrice, Dante's own particular 'God-bearing Image,'— plays the part of the Sacrament. It is at this point that masque and reality become inextricably welded. . . . The form in which the Masque is presented is . . . that of a Corpus Christi procession [wherein] the mystery of the Incarnation will be displayed. . . . In this august and moving moment, Dante brings together all the 'significations' of Beatrice, showing her as the particular type and figure of that whole sacramental principle of which the Host itself is the greater Image.[41]

In Dinesen's text as well, the incarnate, sacrificed word is a feminine *corpus,* but Dante's figures are re-figured; so far from existing as the static medium of a masculine salvation that Giovanni's rhetoric would make her—or the helpless rape victim his memorized "picture" of her perpetuates, the denuded "Daphne" to his commanding Apollo (209)—Agnese regains herself in this confrontation, resisting the text of feminine immobility into which he so magnificently invites her. For despite its daring and beauty, his oblique poetic apology is also, implicitly, another seduction scene. Concluding her own Dantean quotations with Beatrice's warning that "God's vengeance" cannot be evaded by a mere "sop," Agnese deflects Giovanni's rhetoric of remorse and "walk[s] away" into another life, a different story.[42] In this "the most fatal of her missions" (208), it is she, not he, who becomes "The Freed Captive" whom the title of this section names (208): Giovanni, "punished," as Dinesen remarked elsewhere, "according to his deserts . . . with remorse and despair,"[43] simply drops from the text, while Agnese reappears transfigured, "as if a statue had come to life" (210).

Earlier, conversing with Augustus on the differences between men and women, she had remarked that within traditional patriarchal structures "man takes the part of a guest, and woman that of a hostess." To Augustus's Constantinian claim that "a guest wants first of all to be diverted," she has responded simply that "The hostess . . . wants to be thanked" (185). This injunction reappears climactically in the Beatricean passages, a complex play on woman as redemptive sacrament, elevated Host(ess), a feminine Word made flesh and then transformed, via narrative, into word once more. Agnese's claim also obliquely enacts Dinesen's relation to her reader. We have seen that one of her recurrent metaphors for herself was that of "hostess and friend." Here, simultaneously assuming, like Agnese, both "masculine" and "feminine" positions, acting both Dante and Beatrice, she "diverts" the reader-as-guest, offering the body of her own text for consumption as another kind of Host, a blissful feminine *commedia*.

3

> "Which then is the most beautiful: the mother who brings to birth by the force of nature, or the decrepit old woman who brings thee to birth again by her solicitious care? For behold, she has attained the solution of life which is called dissolution, yea she herself is the solution."
>
> Søren Kierkegaard, *Stages on Life's Way*

> The search to perpetuate self-identity stops all contact dead, paralyzes all penetration for fear one may not find oneself always and eternally the same inside.
>
> Luce Irigaray, *Speculum of the Other Woman*

The coda, "The Parting Gift," extends prior reflections on gratitude, bringing to a symbolic climax the discourse on maternity so prominent throughout *Seven Gothic Tales*. Sated with the getting and spending of life in Pisa, which the text distances and dismisses in a single summary paragraph, Augustus accepts an invitation from the Countess to visit her rural villa where, having learned that her presumed "truth" has been un- done and outdone by other women's "lies," she has been reconciled at last with her granddaughter. Arriving amidst a storm, he finds the old woman seated together with mother and infant—"as lovely as any Madonna he had seen in Italy." But this portrait of the Holy Family revises the con- ventions of the genre: "The young father came in and was introduced to the guest; but . . played no greater part in the picture than the youngest Magus of the adoration, the old countess herself having taken the part of Joseph" (215). Self-sufficient and preoccupied, the two hostesses are "di- vided between the child and the storm," which have "brought them into a state of exultation, as if their lives had at this hour reached their zenith" (214). "[S]urprised to realize that the women were all of the opinion that the baby at this stage had reached its very acme of perfection" and baffled by their "exultation," Augustus, who "had never been able to feel any- thing but fear in the presence of very young children," remains excluded from the joy he beholds.

What Dinesen sketches here, on one level, is the restoration of an- other form of *amitié sincère* between women, a mother-daughter love that operates not as domination but as mutuality, a relationship wherein each can be both mother and *other*. This figuration of feminine love intersects with a poetics of maternal bliss, recalling the vertiginous, subversive *jouissance*—"fragile . . . and incommunicable"—that Kristeva explores in "Motherhood according to Giovanni Bellini" as a counterpart of the artist's creative transport: "The speaker reaches this limit . . . only by virtue of a particular, discursive practice called 'art.' A woman also attains it . . . through the strange form of split symbolization (threshold of language and instinctual drive, of the 'symbolic' and the 'semiotic,') of which the act of giving birth consists." Like writing, "the maternal body slips away from the discursive hold" and from the "social programs" within which it would install her.[44] It was surely a similar analogy, among others, that Dinesen implied in affirming, in her "Bonfire" lecture, that woman is more an "artist" than man. If Carlotta's irrational fear of pregnancy—as of the self-annihilating sexual ecstasy that engenders it—also figures a woman's anxiety about authorship, the tale represents the transcendence of those terrors by ending, in effect, with its own beginning: the birth of the (male) child as a peculiarly feminine inscription—one of the few such purely celebratory moments in all of Dinesen.[45] Augustus's rejection of this transfiguring "gift" foreshadows his ultimate failure as both author and reader.

His aversion to the infant—at once a revulsion from the body and its disorderly processes, a metonymic repudiation of woman and all that proceeds from her, and a terror of the destabilizing and potentially appropriative forces her unknowable figure and figurations evoke for him—suggests the threat the newborn child represents to the boundaries of the stable, denatured identity Augustus desires. His mystification at the women's unfathomable pleasure in an uncouth offspring (significantly, one not yet indelibly inscribed by the gender codes of his culture) comically recalls not only medieval patristic warnings against woman-as-body—epitomized in Jerome's diatribe on the "revolting sight" of pregnant women and infants[46]—but also the comparable response of many male authors and critics to the barbaric literary offspring of those whom Hawthorne famously dismissed as a "damned mob of scribbling women." It recalls as well the defensiveness of that other Count Augustus in *Seven Gothic Tales,* the misogynist Platen Hallermund of the "Deluge," who "held the existence of women"—like that of animals—to be "an enigma and a tragedy."[47]

Given the figurative parallels Dinesen draws between women and wild animals throughout *Seven Gothic Tales,*[48] the psychological implications of these diverse masculine aversions are brilliantly illuminated by the brief parable in which Augustus von Schimmelman reappears in *Out of Africa*. Here Dinesen provides an explicit interpretive context for reading masculine fear and loathing within the larger problematic of power, sexual difference, and language constituted by Western discourses of "civilization." Reluctantly fascinated by a hyena in a menagerie in Hamburg, Count Schimmelman hears with "disgust" the proprietor's account of that animal's legendary, prodigious, and ambiguous sexuality: "All Hyenas . . . are hermaphrodites, and in Africa, where they come from, on a full-moon night they will meet and join in a ring of copulation wherein each individual takes the double part of male and female. . . ." Against the challenge this radical duplicity poses to his fundamental ontological categories, Augustus defends himself through the quintessential colonizer's gesture, using language as the instrument of domination, distance, and in-difference:

> "It is a curious thing," said Count Schimmelman, . . . "to realize that so many hundred, indeed thousands of Hyenas should have lived and died, in order that we should, in the end, get this one specimen here, so that people in Hamburg shall be able to know what a Hyena is like, and the naturalists to study . . . them. . . . The wild animals which run in a wild landscape, do not really exist. This one, now, exists, we have got a name for it, we know what it is like. The others might as well not have been."
>
> The showman pushed back his worn fur cap. . . . "They see one another," he said. (301–2)

For a man like Augustus, the possibility of woman's primary relation to woman, or of the "man" in "woman" and vice versa—that is, the possibility of ultimately mutable, fluid "selves" and sexualities—is quite literally incredible. The possibility of another vision, another desire, another narrative, outside the constraints of man-the-namer, is precisely what undoes his Adamic supremacy.

Dinesen's subversive treatment of that supremacy here and throughout "Roads" and *Seven Gothic Tales* resembles similar responses among recent critics to another, more notorious androcentric reflection on the "enigma" of woman: "Throughout history people have knocked their heads against the riddle of the nature of femininity. . . . Nor will you have escaped worrying over this problem—those of you who are men; to those of you who are women this will not apply—you are yourselves the problem." [49] Shoshana Felman's remarks on this Freudian text are equally relevant to Schimmelman's recurrent reflections on woman's strange "folly" (167): "To the extent that women 'are' the question, they cannot *enunciate* the question; they cannot be the speaking *subjects* of the knowledge . . . which the question seeks." But in assuming a position as speaking subject, woman interferes "through female utterance and reading, in . . . male writing"—not by overt rejection but "by disrupting the transparency and misleadingly self-evident universality of its male enunciation."[50]

In the conclusion of "Roads," Dinesen indicates the threat such a female utterance can represent to a man like Augustus. As the rain clears and the Countess takes her guest "to the window to see the view," he becomes "slightly giddy" from the uncanny sense that this landscape is "vaguely familiar":

> "When we first met," she went on, "I told you that I had loved three persons in the course of my life. About two you know. The third and first was a girl of my own age, a friend from a far country, whom I knew for a short time and then lost. But we had promised to remember each other forever, and the memory of her has given me strength many times in the vicissitudes of life. When we parted, with many tears, we gave each other a gift of remembrance. Because this thing is precious to me and a token of real friendship, I want you to take it with you." . . .
>
> Augustus looked at it, and unconsciously his hand went up to his breast. It was a small smelling-bottle in the shape of a heart. On it was painted a landscape with trees, and in the background a white house . . . his own place in Denmark. . . . Underneath . . . were the words *Amitié sincère*. (216)

At the limits of its own representations, the tale folds back upon itself. The figures of the smelling-bottles, mirroring each other in infinite reproductions of feminine *amitié* and reciprocal gift-giving, return us to the beginning, forcing us, like Augustus, to reread the entire story with new eyes—to "see the view" differently. In refocusing our attention on the interpretive problematics with which the tale began, the smelling-bottles, literally signifying a *revival of consciousness,* become symbolic counterparts of *The Revenge of Truth:* microcosmic mirrors of the text that contains them, the "story" Augustus has longed to find "along the roads of life" (166) even as he, like the inn's inhabitants in the marionette play, is already a character inside it. Like the mirror into which he continually gazes, the restored, restorative bottles serve at last as focusing optics by means of which we too can read ourselves reading. But unlike Augustus's mirror, what they reflect is not simply the image of man. For as figures of both Dinesen's text and the "tale" of female *amitié* multiply inscribed within it, the smelling-bottles synecdochize the larger fragmentary "story" of woman, the "Gift" whose contours Augustus, seeing only through his own phallocentric reflections, cannot grasp—even when it literally falls into his hands: "He felt that [telling her about the matching bottle] . . . would have made a tale which she would forever have cherished and repeated. . . . But he was held back by the feeling

that there was, in this decision of fate, something which was meant for
him only—a value, a depth, a resort even, in life which belonged to him
alone, and which he could not share with anybody any more than he
would be able to share his dreams" (216)[51]

For Augustus as male reader, to "share" the significance of what
he has received would be not only to provide a perfect fulfillment to
woman's story—to give Carlotta a "parting gift" equivalent to that she
has bestowed on him—but to participate in its making: to be consciously,
as he has heretofore been unconsciously, "intermixed" (to return to the
epigraph from *Orlando* with which we began) with the tale he has longed
to enter all his life. His earlier thoughts about that longing—"perhaps in
a hundred years people will be reading about me" (158) and "if I have
now at last . . . come into a marionette play, I will not go out of it again"
(199)—become even more resonantly reflexive in this context. Ironically,
his incorporation into a woman's text, so far from effacing the identity he
is so anxious to preserve, is the only way possible to fulfill it, to save his
"character" in both senses of that word by losing himself to a revitalizing
story that would write "man" and "woman" with a new creative reciprocity and fluidity.[52] The "resort" he seeks—literally "refuge, resource,
and escape"—lies in what the bottle signifies, outside the bounds of phallocentric, egocentric reference. As the bottle's picture of "his own place"
suggests, here alone he might assuage his unrequited nostalgia—literally
the desire "to return home" (Gk. *nostos*); yet according to the codes that
shape his consciousness, it is precisely this desire he must resist in order
to "be a man." His reluctance situates him within the same frame of reference as the duelists. As Michelle Rosaldo notes of the peculiarly male
rituals of which the duel is a quintessential instance, "to be a man means
to dissociate [oneself], ritually or in fact, from the home."[53] Once before,
ironically, Augustus's willingness to enter a woman's script had allowed
him to complete his own inscription: before departing on Carlotta's mission, he had finally finished his letter by invoking a passage from *Faust*—
a masculine text that subsequent events have revised beyond his wildest
imagination:

> *A good man, through obscurest aspirations,*
> *Has still the instinct of the one true way.* (178)

Now, instead, he cuts himself off, figuratively emasculates himself, precisely by his avoidance of the unlooked-for home and labyrinthine "way"
emblematized by the smelling-bottle. So grave is his fear of that feminine
text, so obstinate his own need to retain control over both self and story,
that he misses the supreme opportunity of his life: failing to "resort"—
literally re-sort, revise, or reclassify—himself, to undergo the rebirth
such reconceptions would entail, he resorts instead to another kind of

"resort," the same unreconstructed "throng or company" to which he is habituated: "He parted from his old friend . . . with all the expressions of sincere friendship and took the road to Pisa" (216).[54] In seeking to preserve himself, he chooses the way of deathliness, ironically confirming the decay implicit in his own name: *schimmelman* = literally "man of mould."[55]

The possibility that the "truth" Augustus seeks lies forever outside the "one true way" he imagines is reinforced in "The Poet," where he reappears as a middle-aged malcontent: "He had tried a life of pleasure and had been made happy many times. But the road leading from it all into the heart of things he had not found" (380). In "Roads," though literally in possession of the "heart-shaped" emblems of his desire, the embodiments of the "home" toward which his nostalgia turns and yearns, he remains incapable of interpreting their inscriptions. In playing on his parting "expressions of sincere friendship" (216) as mere hollow echoes of the *amitié sincère* the legends evoke, Dinesen suggests that despite his certainty of possessing the "heart" of woman, Augustus in his defensive, egoistic androcentrism has failed utterly to comprehend the riddle or the regeneration her stories offer him. As "the whole landscape" surrounding Carlotta's villa "was veiled to him" by the rain (213), so the terrain of feminine subjectivity, desire, and *amitié* remains concealed from him despite the stunning invitation he has been offered, an uncanny gift, to enter and "share" its territories.

That "parting gift" is offered in his stead to the reader, who also traverses the roads round Pisa. Revising Beatrice's final injunction to Dante to "Take note, and as my speech delivereth / The tale, deliver it again" (*Purgatorio* 33.52–53), Dinesen suggests that it is not in following the "straight" road toward some single final goal, some center where truth is presumed to reside, but in infinite revolutions and transformations, perpetual rewritings and rereadings, that we may reach, paradoxically, the "heart of things." And if that center appears empty, like the smelling-bottles, its emptiness is not nothingness but the potential source of bliss. For the "heart" is also a womblike text, bearer of new stories and perpetually revived awareness for those who can freely read its inscriptions.

9

Ghost Writing

Everything remains to be said on the subject of the Ghost and
the ambiguity of the Return.

—Hélène Cixous, "Fiction and Its Phantoms"

In turning now to three narratives concerned with spectral visions or vis-
itations in relation to the tropes or (Re)turns of fiction, "The Supper at
Elsinore," "The Poet," and "The Caryatids," I want not only to conclude my reflections on *Seven Gothic Tales* but also to suggest how that
text opens outward into Dinesen's later work. Certain connections are
obvious. As the only two fictions set in Denmark, for example, "The
Supper at Elsinore" and "The Poet" prefigure the predominantly Danish
settings of *Winter's Tales* and "New Winter's Tales" (*Last Tales*) and raise
questions about the implications of Dinesen's return, both literally and
literarily, to her native land. "The Supper" also contains elements, as we
shall see, which Dinesen would revive and revise in texts like "Daguerreotypes" and "Babette's Feast," while the issues of mimetic desire and
oedipal triangulation elaborated in "The Poet" anticipate late fictions like
"The Cloak" trilogy.[1] Finally, in examining the connections between the
magisterial male author and the voracious father who would manipulate,
dominate, and ultimately devour his daughters, "The Poet" prefigures as
well the concerns of later narratives like *The Angelic Avengers,* "Tempests" (in *Anecdotes of Destiny*), and "The Immortal Story" (in *Last Tales*).

The case of "The Caryatids" is rather more complicated. Dinesen
had originally planned to include it, together with "Carnival," among
the *Gothic Tales* but subsequently omitted both narratives from the
manuscript, eventually placing "The Caryatids" among her *Last Tales;*
"Carnival" appeared posthumously. Those deletions, and the implicit
open-endedness they introduce into what appears to be a finished text,
set these fictions in a peculiarly haunting and ambiguous relationship to
the rest of Dinesen's oeuvre. If, as Cixous says, "the Ghost erases the
limit which exists between two states," introducing a disquieting "mobility" into what seems fixed and final,[2] then "The Caryatids" and "Carnival" are doubly haunting. For not only does their existence erase the

176

limits of *Seven Gothic Tales,* abolishing quite literally that sense of an ending traditionally associated with closing the covers of a book; but each, like a ghost, would also make a belated return at the outer limits of Dinesen's own writings. I shall return, in my own final chapter, to "Carnival." At the end of this chapter I consider "The Caryatids" and the disclosures its "unfinished" condition effects.

1. "In the power of a power": The Poetics of Possession

One need not be a Chamber—to be Haunted—
Emily Dickinson

"The Supper at Elsinore" is, in several senses, closer to home than any of the other tales in Dinesen's first volume. Elsinore (Helsingør) lies only a few kilometers north of Karen Blixen's own Rungstedlund, itself fictionalized in the narrative through the recollections of Madame Baek, the aged housekeeper with whom the text begins. Like her author, Madame Baek had once been "a little girl in the old inn," and Tanne Dinesen's early adoration of "the great poet Ewald," who had "resided briefly in Rungsted," is simultaneously reenacted and ironized in the encounters the text describes between poet and child. A gaunt, dying outcast, Ewald had only three last wishes, all but one denied: "to get married, since to him life without women seemed unbearably cold and waste; alcohol of some sort . . . ; and, lastly, to be taken to Holy Communion" (234). Yet as Dinesen has Madame Baek recall, so compelling was his presence that even though his "breath sometimes smelled of gin," he could beckon her childish passions with a different sort of high spirits—"tak[ing] her on his knees and warm[ing] his cold hands on her," so that in after years "she imagined the Lord Jesus with his long hair in a queue, and with that rare, wild, broken and arrogant smile of the dying poet" (235). The passage, one of the most pointed of Dinesen's oblique, ironically self-reflective speculations on the father's seductions and the daughter's correspondent fetishizations, becomes a microcosm of the larger text. For "The Supper at Elsinore" is at many levels a tale of death and resurrection, of incarnate words and the forbidden carnal knowledge they displace, and of the haunting "communion" such phenomena engender between men and the women who, seduced into idolizing them, are immobilized by the phantoms of their own erotic fantasies.

Unlike the other tales, the text proceeds with a kind of elegant simplicity, its forward momentum broken only by three flashbacks and two lengthy conversations, the second of which provides the story's title. Indeed, in its insistent evocation of the past and in the chaste, spare quality of its narrative structure, this fiction resembles both the architectural edifice in which it begins and ends—a gray, eighteenth-century house that "echoes" with memories of "old days"—and its aging former occupants, the virginal sisters De Coninck, who, after the mysterious disappearance of their beloved brother, slowly dwindle away, dwelling in the long-dead years when they had reigned as "the belles of Elsinore" (230). In its leisurely, elegiac procession backward through the corridors of memory and its poignant evocation of longing for *temps perdu*, "The Supper" recalls "The Old Chevalier" and "The Dreamers"; yet in a crucial sense it reverses their operative premises, for here it is man who haunts the living, and woman who engenders endless representations of him.

Spectacularly attractive, a dashing privateer whose raids on English ships inspire widespread popular adulation, Morten De Coninck abandons his bride on their wedding day to sail away forever, leaving his two sisters, Fanny and Eliza, bereft and desolate. Subsequently "talked about as a figure out of a fairy tale," he epitomizes the ultimate male literary hero, a type of wandering outcast as ancient as Odysseus and as recent as Byron and his many epigones—including Wilhelm Dinesen and Denys Finch Hatton.[3] Like Lord Jim, that other doomed seaman, Morten too "passes away under a cloud, inscrutable . . . forgotten, unforgiven, and excessively romantic . . . , [leaving] a living woman to celebrate his pitiless wedding with a shadowy ideal . . . a disembodied spirit astray among the passions of this earth."[4] But where Jim is a figure (and figment) of man's imagination, the communal product of Conrad, Marlow, and the other narrators who multiply those masculine authorial voices in reconstructing Jim's story, Morten emerges entirely as the narrative product of woman. Reversing and revising the discourse of courtly love in which woman becomes, to modify Foucault's words, "the unattainable object of the [male] desire of which she is the pure origin,"[5] Dinesen ironically writes Morten as the ever-elusive object of feminine desire and discourse (242), thereby implicitly commenting on her comparable enthrallment with the elusive male figures of her own fantasies.

The sheer fictiveness of his character is suggested through the gap his image opens in the text, like the empty space, "only a faint shadow on the wall," where his portrait had once hung with his sisters' (252). Known by/as absence, Morten paradoxically maintains his power precisely because he *is not there*. To those who remain behind, he is conveyed not by "direct message" but by multiply displaced narratives, "strange rumors that drifted in from the West" (at once geographical locale and place of death), each tale undoing and undone by all the others. It is on these frail fictions that the sisters live as on a starvation diet, consuming their wandering brother as pure story, "manna on which they kept their hearts alive in a desert. They did not serve it to their friends, nor to their parents; but within the distillery of their own rooms they concocted it according to many recipes." Morten's criminality and its consequences —it is rumored "that he had been hanged" (229)—only heighten this attraction. Indeed, as with other legendary adventurers, his greatest power comes with death. It is no accident that his face has a "grave and noble likeness to a skull" (254), or that his name, though a common one in Denmark, also incorporates traces of *le mort*.⁶ Placed altogether outside time as outside the law, forever beyond the reach of desire, he inspires interminable storytelling. The appearance of his ghost in the old house at Elsinore to women who have "read . . . ghost stories all their lives" (254) is the inevitable culmination of these narratives—an explicit revelation of deified word made spectral flesh through a kind of communal female script(ure) whose climactic incarnation transpires at a last supper, the secularized "Holy Communion" toward which the text builds.

But Morten is only the most obvious figure of the dynamic of absence and displacement which the tale presents as the source of (its own) narrative. Fanny and Eliza too are known only by carefully staged self-representations, like "reflections in a mirror," each showing her suitors not a "real woman" but an illusory, elusive "image": "Did she wish that the man would break the glass and . . . turn around toward herself? Oh, that she knew to be out of the question" (220). While this self-fabrication appears to reverse the Medusa effect, "hardening" not the man who gazes, but the woman who conceals herself from his speculations (220), it also serves as a vital protective device. Like Malin Nat-og-Dag or Isak Dinesen, the sisters understand that since the codes of "femininity" fashion woman's subjection, to melt before the seductive masculine gaze is to capitulate to captivity. In this context to refuse matrimony, using the mask of coquetry as both "attraction" and perpetual repulsion, is to remain impregnable in both senses of the term—possibly the only way for women confined within a phallocentric culture to become creators rather than simply procreators:

> Perhaps to them the first condition for anything having real charm was this: that it must not really exist. . . . [T]hey, to whom so very little had happened, [would] talk of their married friends who had husbands, children, and grandchildren with pity and slight contempt, as of poor timid creatures whose lives had been dull and uneventful. . . . [T]hey themselves . . . had chosen the more romantic and adventurous part. . . . They had . . . all possibilities in hand, and had never given them away in order to . . . come down to a limited reality. . . . No one could stop them. (242)

That "adventurous part" finds its most extreme expression in their consuming incestuous desire for their brother, a lifelong passion that reaches its climax in the supper at Elsinore. At one level, of course, this ravenous yearning reifies the gender codes wherein a free-ranging man is exalted through the adoration of an immobilized woman. Karen Blixen wryly recognized the perils of this sort of "possession": "There *must* be something *out of proportion* in the purely personal relationship between people who are in this way 'possessed,' in the power of a power. . . . But on the whole the majority of people have known ecstasy only in these relationships, known what it is to be 'beside themselves.'" Such romantic love—the product of "tangible lies," "displacement," and "transference" —is especially "dangerous and unreliable" because it "has contributed to breaking down the position of women" (*LA,* 322–23). Yet as Dinesen indicates through an implicit play on the other possibilities inherent in "possession," the sisters' romanticized construction of Morten as ungraspable ideal also allows them to perpetuate their independence from the gender codes of their society and their sisterly *inter*dependence: haunted by their brother and their common desire to be both "his" and *him* (255), they also remain self-possessed, "owning" both themselves and Morten as infinitely variable oeuvres they have jointly produced for "each other" (245). If they are consumed by him, they also consume him, nourishing in the process their abilities as storytellers, much as Dinesen had done with Denys Finch Hatton. For if Morten's ghost resembles the narratives he has inspired, a mere trace that signifies an absence, a teasing, tormenting apparition of presence that relentlessly haunts even as it eludes its interpreters, he too has "meaning" only as a sign (re)constructed through the diverse readings and writings of the women whose gaze his ghost solicits. As a small, privileged community of female artists, they make and unmake the man who possesses their collective imaginations. Their sustaining fictions can literally re-call the dead.

Paradoxically, then, while the sisters appear immobile and impotent compared to their virile, charismatic brother, at another level precisely the opposite pertains: this is a world where female authorship supplants male action as the dominant force that shapes "reality," and feminine texts—like feminine desires—may be more potent for the confinement within which they are constrained to operate. Removed, by virtue of Morten's absence, from any danger of literal consummation, the sisters' incestuous passion for "the hanged boy of their own blood" becomes at once a safe way to elude the bonds of wedlock and a radical threat to the order those bonds confirm—a transgression of the fundamental taboo on which androcentric cultures ground themselves. Beneath the elegant narrative decorums of what might seem little more than a quaint tale about "old maids" (257), Dinesen discloses an abyss.

These issues are focused in the sisters' mutual vision of Morten's ghost. In conflating the violation of the incest taboo, the engendering of narrative, and the mutual sharing of food, Dinesen looks forward to contemporary anthropological speculations and (as elsewhere in *Seven Gothic Tales*) backward to Western culture's preeminent myth of origins. Lévi-Strauss observes that "both the exchange of women and the exchange of food are means of securing or of displaying the interlocking of [male] so-cial groups with one another. They are . . . indeed generally thought of as two aspects of the same procedure. They may reinforce each other, both performing the actual function, or one performing it and the other representing it symbolically."[7] Thus the homology between women and food reduplicates that between women and words within androcentric symbolic economies, which function precisely, as Gayle Rubin notes, by prohibiting women from "realiz[ing] the benefits of their own circu-lation."[8] But what of the consequences for masculinist culture if, as Irigaray asks, "*the 'commodities' refused to go to market*," maintaining instead "'another' kind of commerce, among themselves?"[9] Dinesen configures precisely such a possibility. Making women the exchangers, man the ex-changed, she hints at the potentially devastating effects of transgressing the taboo that both represents and insures women's subordination.

Like Genesis 2–3, "The Supper at Elsinore" establishes a symbolic structure that parallels eating, knowing, sexuality, and death with illicit female desire and power. Extending her earlier rereadings of the myth of the Fall, Dinesen reminds us that the human actors who consumed the primal prohibited meal and later had carnal knowledge of each other—another kind of "communion"—are figured not only as husband and wife but as close consanguinous kin, simultaneously "father" and "daugh-ter," "brother" and "sister": "this one at last is bone of my bone, flesh of my flesh."[10] But Dinesen revises both the condemnatory tone and the androcentric focus of the patriarchal interpretive tradition surrounding Genesis 2–3. If, like the "man" in the Hebrew narrative, Morten seems at first the pivotal character around whom all else turns, a closer reading of "The Supper" suggests otherwise: just as "the man" in Genesis 3 silently accepts the forbidden fruit from the hand of woman, becoming the pas-sive object of her operations, so Dinesen writes Morten not, so to speak, as "his own man," but rather as the appendage to his sisters' exchanges, both literal and literary. On yet another level, of course, as the putative object of the women's transgressive longings, Morten is not only a spec-tral Adam but an embodiment of the forbidden fruit itself.

If he is a desirable figure, then, it is ultimately only *as figure* that Dinesen depicts him. Like the forbidden fruit, he exists not as tenor but as a mere vehicle of something other, something literally unspeakable within a masculine discursive economy: the forbidden freedom and power which the sisters, shut within the "Paradise" of bourgeois culture, hun-ger for and the narratives those unsatisfied hungers engender. If woman is the "repressed" of man within phallocentric culture, Dinesen implies that the inverse may be true when woman seeks to construe herself as desiring subject.[11] The apparition of the male outlaw, simultaneously brother and demon lover, is a return of the repressed in the most explicit sense, the uncanny sign and logical conclusion of a life of secret *female* straying outside the bounds. It is no accident that the "hell" to which Morten returns at the stroke of midnight is constructed by his sister's *words* (Fanny's imprecation, "Oh, hell—to hell!" precipitates the ghost's disappearance), or that the sisters are analogized not only to Eve but to Lilith, that more extreme figure of deviant feminine desire, whose power comes directly from her seizure of forbidden language—"the secret word which opens heaven" (240)—literally the name of the Father.[12]

The implications of these conjunctions are made explicit in the first of the two pivotal dinner conversations, a dialogue on woman that interweaves the revisionist biblical hermeneutic and the discourse on witchcraft elaborated throughout *Seven Gothic Tales*. On the night of Madame Baek's visit, the sisters entertain their guests in a manner befitting Malin Nat-og-Dag or Isak Dinesen—"like a pair of prominent spiritual courtesans, . . . leading their admirers into excesses and seducing them into scattering their spiritual wealth and health upon their charms" (236). The conversation turns to flying: "'Oh, if I had . . . wings,' said Miss Fanny, . . . 'by St. Anne, I should fly.'" The Bishop responds patronizingly that men "'mistrust a flying lady'" like Lilith, whom "'neither husband nor angels can master,'" and "'willingly grant [woman] the title of angel . . . and lift her up on our highest pedestal, on the one inevitable condition that she must not dream of, must even have been brought up in absolute ignorance of, the possibility of flight.'" To this phallocratic fantasy Fanny replies with a vision of the free-flying witch: "'We are aware of that, Bishop, and so it is ever the woman whom you gentlemen do not love or worship . . . and who has had to truss up her skirts to sweep the floor, who chuckles at the sight of the emblem of her very thralldom, and anoints her broomstick upon the eve of Walpurgis. . . . In talking about Eve and Paradise, . . . you all still remain a little jealous of the snake'" (240–41). That fable, which recalls Pellegrina's bewitching flights, is itself recalled in the analysis of witchcraft in "Daguerreotypes," the theoretical climax of Dinesen's lifelong musings on "flighty" women.[13] There, in a reflection that retrospectively illuminates the Bishop's remarks, Dinesen suggests that the witch becomes the locus of men's deepest anxieties about "woman" because of the freedom signified by her ability to sit "quite unconstrained astride her broomstick and [take] off" (*Essays,* 33).

We have seen that in her extended discourse on witchcraft, with its celebration of women whose flights, like Lilith's, are also thefts—or repossessions—of both themselves and the words that construct them, Dinesen anticipates contemporary feminist representations of the witch as a subversive, liberatory figure. But what she asks in "The Supper at

Elsinore" finally runs counter to these configurations: what happens when would-be witches suffer from fear of flying? For while longing to soar beyond the confines of their angelic bourgeois existence, both Fanny and Eliza ultimately lack the psychological buoyancy and daring to take off. Despite her brilliant flights of fancy, Fanny ultimately remains grounded, "a great, mad, wing-clipped bird, fluttering in the winter sunset" (250)—a hysteric whose body becomes the rebellious site and sign of repression, her "features," like a text gone mad, marked by "uncanny . . . disfigurement" (238). Eliza, "called . . . 'Ariel,' or 'The Swan of Elsinore,'" appears so "extraordinary" that if "she had indeed unfolded a pair of large white wings, and had soared . . . into the summer air, it would have surprised no one." Yet "in the end she had done nothing": her wings forever unfurled, she appears "quietly, as if intentionally, fading day by day" (243–44). Displacing their own desires onto their brother's spectral image, the sisters become no more than mere shadows, etiolated remnants of the bewitching women who might have been—"elegant spiritual mummies, laid down with myrrh and aromatic herbs" (220).

Their joint conversation with the man of their common dreams enacts their frustration, yearning, and rage:

> "How far away have you been, Morten?" said Eliza, her voice trembling a little. "What multitude of lovely places have you visited, that we have never seen! How I have wished, how I have wished that I were you." . . .
> "Where do you come from, Morten?" Fanny asked him.
> "I come from hell," said Morten. . . .
> Oh, how the heart of Fanny flew upward at his words. She felt it herself, as if she had screamed out, in a shout of deliverance, like a woman in the final moment of childbirth. (255–56)

Yet in the end, Fanny cannot deliver herself from the psychological "hell" of her confinement. Longing for the liberation that Morten's ghost represents, she remains a muted prisoner of her own repressions, which, as Dinesen's puns imply, turn her body into a kind of coffin: "She spoke to him in a hoarse and cracked voice, as if she were heaving it up from the innermost part of her chest. . . . [She] meant to go on speaking, and to lift at last all the deadly weight of her whole life off her, but she felt her chest pressed together . . . and her mouth opened and shut twice without a sound" (268–69).

Ironically, it is the "quiet" Eliza who temporarily transcends frustration to become briefly, through narrative, her brother's mate on the high seas of the imagination. Morten's tale, "like a book of romance and adventure" (259), culminates with the figure of a stolen ship, "La Belle Eliza":

"But what made you decide to become a pirate?" asked Fanny. . . .
"The heart, the heart," said Morten. . . . "I fell in love. . . .
And she was someone else's, so I could not have her without cheating
law and order a little. . . . She was the loveliest, yes, by far the loveliest thing I ever saw. She was like a swan. . . .
. . . I made her a faithful lover. . . . In this way it came to pass
that I was hanged." (259–60)

If "La Belle Eliza" is on one level a classic image of immobilized and
appropriated woman (the ship traditionally personified as female, an inanimate object of high "price" [260] under male control), on another
"she" is the ultimate figure of illegitimacy, flight, and theft: stolen vessel
and outlawed vehicle of piracy, "she" is also the barely displaced sign of
brother-sister incest; in "her" hold the demure "old maid" Eliza is transformed at last into her brother's "chaste, flaming bride" (261), a threat to
the very foundations of patriarchal culture. Far from being mere object,
"La Belle Eliza" also appears animated, like Lilith, by her own demonic
powers (261–62). Indeed, in the sisters' joint construction of Morten's
story as a flight of wish-fulfilling fantasy, "her" control over Morten
increases in direct proportion to his progressive loss of control over
himself.

These contradictions remind us that while the supper at Elsinore is in
one sense a sterile gathering of ghosts, fictions that feed upon fictions, it
is also something potentially different for the women who construct it.
Even in the poignant suggestion of the sisters' ultimate burial within the
symbolic order they would transcend, Dinesen refuses to let the matter—
or the ghosts—rest easily. If, in her ironic rendering of this last supper,
each rereading also constitutes a reinscription of patriarchal deathliness,
and if the sisters De Coninck ultimately miss the very meaning they
themselves have so elaborately constructed, the tale also gestures toward
another resurrection, not of these ghosts and the spectral texts they inhabit, but of the haunting, long-dead author who inhabits *us* as we consume "The Supper at Elsinore."

Like Fanny and Eliza, whose roles as perfect "hostesses" recall that
figure's implications in the *Letters* and the other Gothic tales, Dinesen
concocts for us her guests her own "inspiring" brew (238), an "ex-
otic . . . nectar" like the "rare old rum" that sends its intoxicating fumes
into the "atmosphere," a "mental . . . alchohol which made for warmth
and movement within the . . . veins of [the] guests" (245). It is a transubstantiation in which she becomes both the exalted Host(ess) and the
hierophantic celebrant whose incantatory words effect the miraculous
transformation. One recalls her repeated representations of herself as a
feminine "priest." Writing her texts, she performs that role as a kind of
"conjuring" (237), which offers food for thought and makes spirits rise in

many senses of that phrase. But as the term "conjuring" suggests, the Eucharist to which she invites her readers is figured quite explicitly as a witch's mass, a carnivalesque feminine ritual which she revises and reclaims as the source of her engenderings of narrative: "Real art must always involve some witchcraft" (*LA*, 181). Thus, while "The Supper at Elsinore" is most obviously a story of failed flight, of "all the betrayed and broken hearts of the world, all the sufferings of weak and dumb creatures, all injustice and despair on earth" (249), it nevertheless raises, in depicting that failure, the possibility of a different outcome.

Years later, Dinesen would serve up another version of a climactic supper that elaborates precisely these implications. "Babette's Feast," one of the last texts she would publish before her death, makes explicit what remains covert in "The Supper at Elsinore." As in "The Supper," the setting of the later text is Scandinavia, and its major characters two elderly virgins. But here the haunting presence in the house is a figure not of heroic man, but of revolutionary woman (*AD*, 33). At once "beggar" and "conqueror" (35), benignly maternal and bewitchingly seductive, a festive, unclassifiable figure who makes "righteousness and bliss kiss one another" (59), Babette is also—like Kofman's conception of "the affirmative woman," Kristeva's image of *la mère qui jouit,* or Dinesen's own doubles Malin or Pellegrina—a "great artist" with the "gift of tongues" (64, 61), whose concoctions can transcend and transform the confinements of culture and the misdirections of history. Writing "Babette's Feast" in her old age, at a time when her own body was consumed by incurable illness, Dinesen would enact her artistic transcendence of that carnal confinement, offering her readers a "celestial" feast of words, a "blissful" feminine Eucharist (63) able to redeem those who are failed or thwarted—the Mortens, Fannys and Elizas of the world—through a vision of *dépense* so radical that to partake of it is to move temporarily beyond the phallocentric law into a "blessed" "world" where "anything is possible" (63).[14] Before that consummate festive narrative could be written, however, Dinesen would perform another series of exorcisms—tales that would further enable her own ongoing liberation, through narrative, from the ghosts of masculine power and desire.

2. EXORCISING THE FICTION(S) OF THE FATHER

> Daddy, I have had to kill you.
> —Sylvia Plath, "Daddy"

The last text of *Seven Gothic Tales* opens on a landscape whose shifting topography might be read as a summarizing trope for the book itself:

> In the early years of the eighteenth century, Queen Sophia Mag-
> dalena . . . after a long day's hunting, killed a stag on the bank of a
> tranquil lake in the midst of a forest. She was so much pleased with
> the spot that she resolved to have a palace built there . . . in the
> middle of the lake, with long straight embarkments across the water,
> upon which the royal coaches could drive in all their splendor, re-
> flected, head down, in the clear surface, as had been the stag sur-
> rounded by the Queen's hounds. (357)

"Fifty years later" another woman's illicit *jouissance* makes explicit the latent implications of Artemisian pleasure and disruptive catoptric power
in this site. Queen Carolina Mathilda, married at fifteen to "a debauched
and heartless little king," finds her own bliss in the same wild space that
had enchanted her predecessor. Legendary for "riding to hounds in men's
clothing" (a *riding* that refigures her author's *writing* "in men's clothing"),
she has there an adulterous love affair—a double treason that both challenges the husband's conjugal ownership of his wife's body and threatens
the paternal authority and genealogy on which his reign, both marital
and monarchical, is erected. After the queen is found out and banished,
her lover executed "for pilfering the regalia of the crown," the scandalous
site of feminine desire begins slowly "sinking, of itself, into the lake"
from which it had arisen. Dismantled at last by royal decree, it forms the
foundation for a sign of phallic potency: "a church, . . . erected where
the palace had stood, like a cross upon its grave." Yet despite these attempts to obliterate it, its power persists, for the fragments from its dem-
olition are dispersed "in[to] the houses" of the folk like relics, and the
feminine "blasphemy" it represented is resurrected in/as narrative: "Poets
would . . . sing of the unhappy Queen . . . and see her shadow, flighty
on her flighty steed, galloping past them in the forest" (358–59).

Thus *Seven Gothic Tales* closes, as it had begun, with what Dinesen
in "The Diver" calls the "liquid world"—that perpetually mobile,
"changing" space which may be marginalized by the seemingly stable
domains of "man" but which, like the deluge at Norderney, perpetually
unsettles and threatens those claims to absolute power (*AD,* 18–20). As
the Dinesenean "she fish" remarks, playfully appropriating the imperial
masculine pronouncement as a reflexive comment on her own subversive
texts, "*après nous le déluge*" (*AD,* 20). The parable that opens "The Poet"
suggests that like "the deep" in Genesis 1, that vestige of a vast maternal
body, this free-floating "feminine" force in psyche, culture, and language
is persistently subjected to repression, a process of dismemberment and
burial that would erase its "splendor" from all memory (*SGT,* 358). But
as the text implies through the reliquary traces of the "flighty" queen or
the flights of fancy that recall her, this burial never fully succeeds: the
paternal order remains perpetually imperiled by the uncanny power of

the repressed to rise again in displaced forms, in tantalizing "shadows" and stories. Just as official patriarchal worlds and words are undermined by the sunken site of feminine freeplay which they seek to efface, so, as we have seen, the ostensible patriarchal thematics and linear narrative structures that operate on the surface of Dinesen's fictions are continually disrupted by another text whose presence she will not let us forget—a source of creativity revived, again and again, through storytelling. The final fiction of *Seven Gothic Tales* implies that if the book it concludes appears to be a thoroughly paternal monument, signed and designed, like the church, in the name of the father, its seemingly stable linguistic structure is perpetually threatened with collapse, undermined by the subterranean rifts and currents its walls conceal.

That dynamic is reenacted with violent explicitness in the conclusion of "The Poet," which suggests the full force of the consequences attendant on the return of the repressed, bringing to a horrific culmination the multiple revisions of the biblical myths of origin that unfold throughout *Seven Gothic Tales*. Here Dinesen remakes the scene of the curse in Genesis 3, effecting a stunning series of transformations whereby both the paternal deity and his temporal representative, the man who "rules" over woman through the appropriation of her desire (Gen. 3:16), are conflated with the fallen serpent who had precipitated her transgression and whose "head" her offspring "bruise."

The tale narrates the machinations of Councilor Mathiesen of Hirschholm, "the prominent figure of the town, a citizen of great influence, . . . property and prestige"—and a user and abuser of women (359). His greatest ambition is to be a poet like "the great Geheimerat" Goethe, that exalted "Olympian" ("the superman, he might have thought, if the word had been invented") who has haunted him since the days when he himself had lived in Weimar as in "paradise." As "poet, philosopher, statesman," and "conqueror of women," Goethe epitomizes both patriarchal culture and its synecdoche, the literary tradition, which erases daughters and promises sons "immortality" (360–61). Longing to become "a superman in miniature" but lacking poetic ability, Mathiesen seeks to realize his Nietzschean fantasy by fastening on a surrogate, the young poet Anders Kube, "like a sort of unselfish lover" (364).

That analogy, like the Councilor's adoration of the "great Geheimerat Goethe," underscores what Irigaray calls the "hom(m)osexual" substratum of such alliances.[15] "The Poet" is one of Dinesen's most explicit demonstrations of the mutually inflecting homologies of masculinist literary genealogy and a phallocentric sociosymbolic order wherein male bondings are mediated by female bodies. In this suppressed "hom(m)osexual" economy, the woman Mathiesen selects as screen and conduit in his relation with Anders seems perfectly designed for the role. Fransine

Lerche, both ward and widow of Mathiesen's own "patron," appears an
ideally compliant daughter: "slight" and "demure," "like a doll," and
"ready to do everything that he told her" (367–68). "[S]truck and moved"
upon observing the incipient attraction between her and Anders (by
which he will be "struck" again, more literally, at story's end), the Councilor evolves a "poetic" plan: "a romance called 'Anders and Fransine'"
(370), turning himself into the master-Poet whose plots allow him to incorporate the younger poet's coveted powers. But his designs are disrupted by the woman's own splendid, self-propelling art, which literally
dawns on the Councilor as he spies on her one morning at "La Liberté,"
the aptly named country house she has inherited. Enveloped by a landscape of hyperbolic springtime fertility, the intoxicating expression of a
feminine eroticism ("sweetly dripping rain and mist," "budding groves,"
"the sweet and acid scent of fresh wet leafage," "wet lilac bushes . . . full of
unfolded flowers," and "music" [373–74]), the Councilor, like a voy-
euristic Satan first beholding Eve in the Garden, peers through a window
to see Fransine dance a superb ballet whose blissful choreographies anticipate Benedetta's later "musical" self-discoveries.

This ecstatic creation engenders a major revision of the Councilor's
script. Rejecting his original text, he decides to "procure" this woman
and her potentially subversive art for himself (387), fearful lest she "lift
the young man, whom he had decided for her, off the ground" and
"fly . . . away from his supremacy": "It was a lucky thing that he had
found her out, for he would not lose his poet. Indeed, . . . he should like
to keep them both. . . . A hopeless passion for his benefactor's wife
might make a young poet immortal" (377). In the "paradisial" story of
his own making, then, the "old man" becomes simultaneously the
would-be god who would create both woman and the plots that constrain her, the Satanic figure who would ensnare her, and, in the role of
her husband-to-be, the Adamic namer who would lay double claim to
her through the power of the word. Within this plot woman and her art
seem reduced to mere ciphers whereby the "Poet" may be joined with
"the poet" in an ecstatic enactment of the law of the Same, the climactic
fulfillment of the male "poetic" vocation.

Harold Bloom has declared apocalyptically that the gravest threat to
the continuity of such masculine lines is precisely that which they would
most rigorously repress as the condition of their own perpetuity: "The
first true breach with literary continuity will be brought about in generations to come if the burgeoning religion of Liberated Woman spreads
from its clusters of enthusiasts to dominate the west. Homer will cease to
be the inevitable precursor and the rhetoric of forms of our literature then
may break at last from tradition."[16] "The Poet" anticipates this observation through the figure of Fransine's bliss-full "Liberté," but effects a

major shift of the values Bloom's paradigm implies. Contesting the covertly "hom(m)osexual" economies of patriarchal culture and poetics, Dinesen offers her most explicit representation of their disruption by woman's fabrications. As she has the Councilor reflect of Fransine's "disregard of truth," "this talent of hers" represents "an especially feminine trick, a *code de femme.* . . . Thus did the witches of old make up wax children. . . . In the hands of an amiable witch this pretty white magic might work much good. But if ever a young witch conceives and carries for nine months a child of her own flesh and blood? Ah! it is then that there will be the devil and all to pay" (398–99).

It is just such a bewitching feminine fiction that ultimately undoes the imperial paternal text. The Councilor would make Fransine no more than a means to his own end. That she becomes exactly that in the tale's conclusion is the ironic outcome for which neither he nor the symbolic order within which he operates could ever account. He has read her as pure object of his magisterial manipulations, a sign within a narrative lineage and discourse all his own—a living doll or "sacred puppet" (419). What contravenes that system is to him, quite literally, *unimaginable:* that the sign should get radically *out of line,* the puppet out of hand, with a will and script of its own that prove the undoing of his.

In the darkness before their wedding day, the Councilor discovers Anders and Fransine, "like a young witch under the moon," together in a tryst of her design (411–12). Drunken and desperate, the poet, "face to face" with the Poet, makes the inevitable oedipal move, firing "his gun . . . straight into the body of the old man." With this phallic fusillade—a "retort," in both senses, whose "echoes" make a mockery of the paternal script (412)—the poet/son ruptures not only the Poet/father's body, but also, implicitly, the patriarchal textual *corpus* and hom(m)osexual body politic it represents: "The young man, whom he loved, had meant him to die. The world had thrown him out." Yet in desperate hope "that he might still save himself" and "control his world once more," he "draw[s] himself along, . . . like an old snake which has been run over . . . but still wriggles on . . . , his mouth . . . filled with dust" (413–14). Dinesen conflates Genesis 2–3 with the phallocentric literary tradition and "social order" epitomized in Goethe, whose fetishized "creations," synecdoches of the works of all "the great masters," now assume for the Councilor a cosmic significance, inseparable from both his own designs and those of God the Father: "He was not in Denmark, but in Weimar . . . , the sacred garden itself, . . . the sanctuary. . . . He remembered now: he himself was writing a tragedy . . . , the greatest of his life. . . . There were reminiscences of the Geheimerat's own *Faust* in it. . . . Undoubtedly there would be a social order in the world of fiction as there was everywhere, even in the world of Hirscholm. . . . [S]ud-

denly, . . . the old Councilor understood everything in the world. . . .
He had got inside the magic circle of poetry. He was in the world and
mind of the great Geheimerat" (414–16).

What disturbs this "divine" delusion of grandeur and the "apotheosis" it allows the Councilor is the weeping woman it would discount
(416). Her sobs echo the suffering of all the oppressed women in the
Western cultural tradition, epitomized in the ruined figure of Goethe's
Margaret, whose "mad" songs constitute at once a trenchant analysis and
a devastating condemnation of the Father-Poet's plots:

> My mother, the harlot
> Who put me to death,
> My father, the varlet,
> Who eaten me hath. . . . (416)

Conflating Margaret with Fransine, the Poet experiences one moment of
insight and compassion—"Her sobbing sounded wild and without
hope . . . This was rather cruel of the Geheimrat"—but such pity is
quickly quelled in the name and "in [the] order" of the father—"the plan
of the author, the Geheimrat" (416–17).

It is this overbearing, consuming fatherhood, sublimely self-centered
and utterly unconscious of its own blindness, that Fransine crushes in the
terrible final moments of the narrative. Dinesen writes the Councilor as
both the paternal "ghost" that must be exorcised if woman's voice is to be
heard as any more than a "wild," incoherent, insignificant "cry," and as
the "serpent" whose head is "bruised" by woman's offspring. The great
stone Fransine dislodges in her frenzy figures both the founding walls of
the phallic symbolic order and the monumental pride and obtuseness
which the Councilor, as the representative of that order at its most extreme, has brutally exemplified in his casual objectifications of her. In
this reading his own plots, in every sense, come crashing down upon
him. But the stone also signifies the weight of women's collective creativity, ossified, blocked, and silenced by masculinist traditions, and now become the very weapon with which to strike them down: "Like a maenad,
her hair streaming . . . , she began to tug and tear at one of the big flat
stones of the fence, to get it loose. When she got it out she stood for a
moment, holding it, with all her strength, in both arms, pressed to her
bosom, as if it had been her only child, which the old sorcerer had managed to turn to stone" (419).

The counter-Medusa effect of this final trope recalls the figure with
which this book began, the laughing image of woman seen as for the first
time, not as petrifying monster but as multiple, mobile *other*, elusive and
virtually invisible in the discourses available to the inheritors of Western
culture but imaginable nonetheless.[17] If, in the devastating violence that

ends "The Poet," Dinesen deliberately elicits our horror, it is precisely so that we may contemplate with equal horror that which has provoked Fransine's last desperate gesture: a system that under the rubrics of culture, law, order, and even "art" would suppress and repress—"turn to stone"—this creative mobility in consciousness, culture, and language, discounting and dis(re)membering woman' body, subjectivity, and story, appropriating her "Liberté," in every sense, in the totalizing name of the father. Imagining that monolithic, petrifying figure years later in passages that recall "The Poet," Cixous would call him "the inevitable man-with-rock," whose erections "mangle" woman. It is against this figure that she, like Dinesen, invites women's rebellion, a "smashing" that could release them from the prison wherein phallocentric speculations would confine them: "When the 'repressed' of their culture and their society returns, it's an explosive, *utterly* destructive, staggering return, with a force never yet unleashed and equal to the most forbidding of suppressions."[18]

Significantly, as the great stone crushes the Councilor's head in a perverse fulfillment of the Genesis curse, it is not only his body that perishes but the entire "conception of the world" by which he has operated (420). The condemnation Fransine hurls with the stone becomes Dinesen's implicit indictment of the economies that would obliterate woman's desire and creativity: "'You!' she cried at him, 'You poet!'" That judgment passes into infinity: "from all sides, like an echo in the engulfing darkness, winding and rolling in long caverns, her last word . . . repeated again and again" (420). In this stunning self-reflexive gesture, Dinesen ends *Seven Gothic Tales* with the multiplications of a final furious dismissal, quite literally giving woman the (plural) "last word" in the book.

But that apocalyptic last word is also, paradoxically, another beginning. For in the figure of "the abyss" into which the Councilor falls as he dies, an "engulfing darkness" that from his perspective seems pure chaos, the tale returns us not only to its own inaugural image—the lake and sunken castle that threatens to engulf the monumental paternal structure erected on its "grave"—but also, quite literally, to "The Deluge." And that text, as we have seen, is an alternative genesis that ends, like "The Poet," with the "*dernier cri*" of a woman whose words merge with her author's. But what Dinesen invokes there is not simply a fiction of destruction—the murder of the father and his law—but also a promise of re-creation through the engendering of narrative. In "The Poet," she suggests, like Cixous, that repression disfigures woman, makes her monstrous: trapped "between the Medusa and the abyss," she becomes a furious, uncontrollable avenger filled with destructive force.[19] But as "The Deluge" reveals, it is not this frenzied "maenad" that enchants her author, but her creative counterpart: the laughing woman who, like

Scheherazade, Malin, Pellegrina, or Dinesen herself, overcomes death with storytelling. By returning us, at last, to this beginning, *Seven Gothic Tales* climactically enacts the witch's practice of "reading the Book of Genesis backwards." As Dinesen's own bewitching Genesis, her first "Book" continually performs what it proclaims. Under its spells, *revolutionary* in the literal sense of that term, she returns us to the "liquid world," emblem of all the other upheavals, revolutions, and creations of *Seven Gothic Tales* whereby she would exorcise one version of the father's "Holy Ghost."

And if she appears to do so only to raise up another, to proclaim the story of the mother as an alternative "last word" of her text, merely reversing and hence reifying the hierarchial oppositions that found the patriarchal symbolic order, we do well to read more closely. For in the symbolic coalitions she envisions throughout *Seven Gothic Tales* between the outcasts and "deviants" of culture—bastards, orphans, criminals, actors, tricksters, and women, all players on the margins of the world—she ultimately suggests a dissolution of absolute categories of all sorts, including, finally, even that of the mother—at least within the traditional semiotics through which maternity has been conceived. These dynamic, moving encounters between "heterogeneous elements," whose heterogeneity is not suppressed but multiplied thereby, become her figures for alternative ways of being and seeing.[20] Like Kristeva, Dinesen suggests that such a process undermines narcissistic delusions of supremacy and totalizing truth, opens a new space where creativity may flourish like the characters in the floating barn of "The Deluge," where the subject exists not as finality and closure but in "the free play of impulses."[21] Yet given the near unwritability and unreadability of such a radically *other* text within the confines of the dominant discourse, Dinesen evokes the desiring, delighting mother, *la mère qui jouit,* as a provisional figure of that generative "Liberté" toward which *Seven Gothic Tales* gestures at last.

The echoic, mutually mirroring operations of the tales themselves reiterate this alternative possibility. Reflexively spiraling both into and away from itself, *Seven Gothic Tales* recalls the flight that Dinesen invoked as a metaphor of her own writing, suggesting not a "line," in "one dimension only," nor a two-dimensional "plane," but "the full freedom of three dimensions"—a play of whirling figures without beginning or end (*OA,* 238). In engendering the narratives of her first book, Dinesen illuminated anew the art of *spinning tales.*

That vertiginous art, explicitly associated with the figure of the transgressive, blissful mother, forms the focal subject of "The Caryatids." One of Dinesen's greatest and most problematic fictions, it was, as we have seen, originally planned for publication in her first collection. That she did not, finally, include it in *Seven Gothic Tales;* did not publish the original version at all until near the end of her life;[22] and, finally, did not complete the narrative even then (its subtitle is "An Unfinished Tale") are matters to which we shall now turn.

3. WHIRL WITHOUT END

> How, then, can one return into the cave, . . . the earth? Rediscover the darkness of all that has been left behind? Remember the forgotten mother?
>
> Luce Irigaray, *Speculum of the Other Woman*

> A woman is never far from "mother." . . . There is always within her at least a little of that good mother's milk. She writes in white ink. . . . Everything will be changed once woman gives woman to the other woman.
>
> Hélène Cixous, "The Laugh of the Medusa"

"The Caryatids" begins as a hyperbolically conventional pastoral idyll, set in the French countryside "on a summer afternoon in the forties of the last century." On the banks of "a little river," as in a painterly tableau, "two ladies . . . , like peonies on slender stems," are "bathing three young children," whose clothes are "strewn upon the grass . . . like a flower bed." The central figure of this group, the dark-eyed young mother Childerique, is "holding her naked little son down in the water," while her daughters run "splashing" and "laughing down the river." While the women immerse themselves and their children in the pleasures of the water, the two men in the party, identified ambiguously only as "the husband and the young brother of the dark lady"—neighbors on the adjoining estates of Champmeslé and Haut-Mesnil—"discuss the question of their boundaries, which a change in the course of the river had slightly altered" (*LT,* 107–9). The figure is a telling one, for the text is in every sense a "question of . . . boundaries" and the consequences of their displacement and alteration by forces beyond the control of a patriarchal symbolic economy. The scene radiates conspicuous tranquility, but its "clear" summer weather, "reflected" by the river "as frankly as a mirror" is significantly precarious: across the sunny sky "large . . . clouds" on the horizon "forebode thunder on the morrow."

This same disquiet marks the men's conversation. Their discussion conflates the river's disorderly fluctuations with another figure of deviance, a "gang of gypsies," "poachers" who "gave much trouble" but have always "possessed a position of their own on the estate" by virtue of

their protection by Childerique's late mother the Countess Sophie, former mistress of Haut-Mesnil, and of the fear inspired by their own omi-
nous powers. These powers are rooted in their control of language, a
spell-binding capacity exemplified in the story of the local priest Father
Bernhard, who "disappears" mysteriously after the gypsies turn his own
"Holy Book" against him. One recalls Dinesen's own revisionist use of
Scripture to undermine paternal authority. As wanderers outside the law,
cut off from all known origins, the gypsies embody the very principal of
transgression—literally the crossing of those boundaries that maintain
civilization. It is no accident that they can, without guilt, commit patri-
cide. Unlike those for whom the dead father becomes the very body of
the law, the gypsies, having "buried their father, . . . think no more
about it." Associated with both the natural and the supernatural, they
haunt the margins of the dominant social order, inhabiting a wild, liminal space like that of the forest, where "shades" of both sorts abound
and ordinary hierarchies are undone: "the living are buried" and "the
dead choose to walk about" (110).

Not surprisingly, given women's comparable association with diver-
gence, marginality, and disruption, the most powerful figure of this untamed world is a woman. Like the river, the "graceful" young gypsy
witch Simkie appears to the lord of Champmeslé as an unstable, sinuous
being who defies proper placement: "'If only,' said Philippe, . . . 'we
could get rid of the miller's widow at Masse Bleue. I remember the first
time I saw her . . . in the forest, and . . . tried to stop her and make her
talk with me. It . . . seems to me now . . . that I was holding out my
stick to a smooth little viper that was trying to get round it, indeed she
was hissing at me, maneuvering to the right and the left" (109). Reading
her as a demonic *character,* he figures her also as an unholy text, inscribed
by "the brand, the witch's mark." This radical otherness is the more terrifying because of its threat to Philippe's own security, embodied for him
in both his genealogical heritage and that of his wife Childerique, on
whose "father and all his descendants" Simkie's father "old Udday . . .
once laid a curse" (115).

The scene, then, is constituted as a series of oppositional categories—
civilization/wildness, law/anarchy, security/danger, purity/pollution,
sacred/profane, good/evil. Their epitome is the contrast between the
stable familial relations represented by the idyllic union of Childerique
and Philippe, which has reconciled the formerly alienated estates of
Haut-Mesnil and Champmeslé, and the "unnatural" familial relations
and social disintegration represented by the gypsies. Yet in this world
nothing is as it seems. For at the very heart of the family, Dinesen exposes a scandal, figured by a woman's text. Soon after his marriage
Philippe, exploring the attic of his estate, discovers "a packet of letters,

written by a lady to her lover, by Childerique's mother to his father."
Seeking "some trace of the little boy" he used to be, he finds himself indeed—"his own name" and "sayings" "repeated" in the woman's words.
It is this reinscription of himself as a sign within a feminine discourse that
leads him to the truth of his origins:

> The last of [the letters] was a crumpled bit of paper . . . : "Dear
> Baron de la Verandrye. Just a word. I am sorry for what I said to you
> yesterday. The bearer, the gypsy Udday, has got my message and
> will give it to you correctly, it is too long for me to write, as I am not
> well. Good-bye, good-bye."
> . . . [T]he date . . . was the day of Childerique's birth. (124)

"Struck by a great wave of terror" at the discovery that "Childerique was
his father's child," Philippe burns the letters, planning to conceal their
contents forever from the sister-wife he adores and cannot, despite his
discovery, bear to lose. But like the "verbal message" sent by Sophie
to his father, now forever lost except in the memory of Udday's daughter, the illicit texts remain as a kind of spectral presence, threatening
Philippe's settled world just as the clouds on the horizon threaten the
"fine . . . clear" weather in the opening scene, or the gypsies the social
order of the paternal estates.

Thus, with the stroke of a pen, woman's "word" unmakes the father's world. In this sense "The Caryatids" becomes a haunting synecdoche of the larger text it was to have inhabited, for throughout *Seven
Gothic Tales,* as we have seen, the concealed feminine text uncovers
the instability of the categories on which patriarchal "reality" appears
grounded—revealing law, marriage, patrilineal property, filial identity,
and the name and word of the father to be profoundly inflected by the
very forces they would repudiate: "Thus, he thought, the white house of
Champmeslé was even at this time at once the pride and refuge of her
heart and . . . a house of crime against the law of God, a place of shame.
The three children . . . were both the flowers and the crown of a proud,
old race, and, more terrible than the cubs of the timber wolf, nameless
offspring of dishonor. And he himself . . . was at the same time the head
of the corner of her happiness, and her enemy, the destroyer of all"
(127–28). In "The Caryatids" Dinesen moves beyond the purely symbolic incest represented in texts like "The Monkey" or "The Supper at
Elsinore" to enact a literal violation of the taboo. In demonstrating the
ease with which that transgression occurs she develops her most explicit
representation of the precariousness of an economy founded on the subordination and exogamous exchange of women. Representing itself as
eternal and "natural," this system is continually imperiled by the sup-

pressed feminine Other that can uncover, with "just a word," its provisionality and unnaturalness.[23]

Through the proliferating reflexive imagery of inscriptions, Dinesen also suggests that incest figures the transgressive operations of the narrative itself. As children not only of one father but also of the author who devised both that paternal figure and the masculine mask of her own pseudonym, Philippe and Childerique are "works of the same artist" indeed (125). Significantly, Dinesen has Philippe configure these paradoxes of perverse (pro)creation by recalling the figure in whose name she published her earliest Gothic tales, "Osceola," as a magical double being "who at the very same hour as he was trading horses in the marketplace . . . [was] even as well, in the strong and shaggy shape of a timber wolf, hunting and sleeping in the mountains, . . . trotting upon a trail in the woods or sitting in the snow and howling at the terrified mares and foals" (127–28). Like her later choice of the name Isak, the pseudonym is multiply significant: the historical Osceola (1804–38), famed Seminole war chief, led successful insurrections against the United States government until he was betrayed into captivity. Part Creek, part English, he embodied the same internally divided condition that Dinesen associated with her own literary production. If, as Judith Thurman suggests, Dinesen chose the name in tribute to Wilhelm Dinesen, who "admired Osceola and had himself written under an Indian pseudonym, Boganis,"[24] we should also note the complex counterimplications of the name as the signature of a woman who was not merely the father's unquestioning devotee: as a marginal, subversive, and dangerous figure, Osceola bears less resemblance to "Dinesen's own [male] heroes," who as we have seen are more often than not maimed, castrated, or otherwise symbolically emasculated, than to her many powerful, revolutionary female characters. He is also a sign of her awareness, even at an early age, of the illicit, insurrectionary implications of the daughter's text.

These implications become explicit in "The Caryatids." For just as Childerique's marriage to Philippe is not the innocent alliance it appears, so Childerique herself conceals beneath the domesticated persona of devoted wife and mother qualities that ally her with both the gypsy witch Simkie and her own bewitching mother Sophie, whose name elsewhere in Dinesen's oeuvre bears profoundly subversive connotations.[25] Dead since Childerique's infancy yet still the most compelling figure in her life—"the last word with her" (115)—Sophie was possessed of such a "rich vitality" that "people talked about her as if she were still alive." She had, like her author, "a curious taste" for transvestite "disguise" and "an impulsive heart": "When, on finding a poor tenant's household lamenting a dead mother and a new-born baby, she . . . laid the forlorn child to her full breast" (121)—an offering that recalls Childerique's earlier musings on the illicit bliss of suckling her own children in defiance of social proscription (116). This prohibition, which entangles questions of class, social history, and gender, makes the mother's body the site of danger, a kind of forbidden fruit. Separating mother and child by enjoining their sensuous bond, the taboo prefigures those subsequent oedipal interdictions whereby the boy must separate himself from the mother as the price of entering the symbolic order. But just as she subverts the prohibition on lactation, so Childerique, like her mother, denies the symbolic order that it represents. Reflecting on the "imaginative, defying side of her nature," Philippe sees her as a "Diana" capable of "loosing her fierce hounds on him" and enjoying "the sight of his dismembering." Unlike most women socialized within Western culture, "she had no desire to be desired, and her woman's kingdom of longing, rapture and jealousy seemed to her all too vast" (122).

That "longing" is directed not toward her husband, for whom, as the narrator remarks ironically, "her feelings seemed . . . more those of a sister or comrade than of a woman in love" (128), but toward possibilities outside the bounds of marriage and motherhood—possibilities epitomized in her relationship with the man she believes to be her brother, "the young Lord of Haut-Mesnil," to whom "she showed all the attributes of a passionate and jealous mistress . . . , fondling and petting him, holding his hands and playing with his fingers or running her own fingers through his red locks" (129). So thoroughly has the text naturalized and domesticated the central act of incest between Childerique and her husband, so powerful is the marriage *topos* under which their union is written, that her passion for a man to whom she is not related seems more shocking than her actual marriage to her brother. Indeed, beginning with the verbal ambiguity that makes "husband" and "brother" indistinguishable in the opening scene, their interchangeability persistently disrupts expected boundaries, unsettling our conventions of reading as it unsettles genealogical successions and the psychosocial symbolic order founded on the incest taboo. If, as Michèle Richman argues, "the abolition of the taboo will not inaugurate a reign of sexual anarchy, but . . . overthrow the patriarchal order," then women who challenge "kinship structures based on the incest prohibition have at their disposal the most effective weapon to precipitate [that system's] demise."[26] In "The Caryatids" Dinesen constructs such a challenge both literally, in Childerique's marriage to her brother, and figuratively, in her barely repressed passion for her "brother." It is no accident that Philippe reads the text of the mother's desire as a version of parricide: "As soon as he understood the sense of the letters, [he] got up and locked the door. It was as if he had found his father in here, defenseless and exposed to danger" (124).

Woman's transgressive desire also leads to the powerful final movement of the tale, which draws together the diverse figurative strands connecting Childerique, Sophie, and Simkie with their author. Learning that the "young lord of Haut-Mesnil" intends to marry Simkie and assuming that he is bewitched, Childerique initially seeks to dissuade him by an appeal to filial responsibility, proclaiming as exemplar her own support of the paternal name: "there is not one . . . of the women of Haut-Mesnil, who has disgraced her name, the name of our father. Is it forever . . . the task of the women to hold up the houses, like those stone figures called caryatids?" (132–33). But as in "Sorrow-acre," whose tropes this passage anticipates, the caryatid will become an increasingly destabilizing figure: even as Childerique declares her respectability, she is identified at the level of metaphor with the woman she opposes.[27] Dinesen reminds us that the term caryatid itself originated as a sign of feminine resistance: initially Caryatids were not immobilized female statues but priestesses of Artemis, an affiliation echoed in Philippe's vision of Childerique as Diana.[28] So far from being a petrified upholder of traditional structures, Childerique is "bewitching," a "Circe" (113) or seductive Medusa whose free-floating hair recalls "deities with hair of snakes" and within whose cloak "red fires were smouldering" (130). Her upright attitude conceals the same forbidden affinities for the wild earlier attributed to Simkie:

> [H]is words . . . brought up a swarm of pictures of him and of herself, out on travels in the woods, in those moors or marshes of which he spoke, where they had strayed against . . . orders. . . . They had seen vipers there, and had been looking for wolves. . . . They had been out in search of other things as well, of the dangers and horrors of the world. She had then egged the delicate boy on, indignant of his timidity, and she had triumphed. . . . Their dangers had caused her great delight. . . .
>
> "Ah, indeed," she cried, "you talk like a man! It is the right thing for the lord of Haut-Mesnil to go to the people of the moors . . . to be taught witchcraft . . . [leaving] the women to guard your land. But what about us? Might we not also want to try the taste of poison, to sleep in the woods at night?" She was surprised at her own words; they rushed to her lips on their own. What was she saying? (132)

The repressed that begins its return here through the interstices of rhetoric finds its counterpart in an erotic excess that makes explicit the identification of Childerique and Simkie:

> "Oh, my brother, my dearest love," she said, "I will never let you go. Do you not think that I know more than you, that I can also open up a new world to you? Oh, I can teach you dances too, darkness, magic too." While she spoke she lifted her hand and pressed up his chin.

> The boy turned . . . deadly white under her touch. . . . "No, do not do that," he said, "Simkie has held me, holds me, like that." (135)

This identification culminates in Childerique's journey to Simkie in the forest, a literal transgression of the boundaries between androcentric civilization and the wild and fluid space of eroticism, enchantment, and repressed feminine power: "Childerique paused on the bridge. . . . [T]hese smooth rapid waters rushing away under her feet—were they hers or the miller's widow's—and with whom were they in league?" (138). Her first response to Simkie replicates her husband's—"she felt . . . a deadly nausea at the thought of touching her, as if she had [been] a snake." But soon, moved by the enchanting "air of the room," she is possessed by "a queer fancy":

> She remembered [being] taken, as a child, to see the Queen, . . . and how at her ceremonial she had thought: "Whatever happens, happens because it pleases the Queen." . . . Now, in the presence of the young gypsy the fancy, long forgotten, was recalled. . . . "Why on earth is she like a queen, this slut on her bare feet? Is it really the queens and the gypsies who have all that they want, and only we, the women of the great houses and the estates, who have to work to hold up the world?" The words of the Scripture came back to her: "And we know that all things work together for good to them that love." Her thoughts shied at the name called forth to her. Could it be the same with the Devil as with God? Would he give the equal reward for being loved? "Yes," she thought, "yes, it is so. It is all because Simkie is a witch, this extraordinary content in her. . . . It is the witch's happiness; this is what she sells herself for to the Devil." (139–40)

This "happiness," as Dinesen would proclaim in references to her own bargain with "my angel Lucifer," is woman's power to engender narrative.

The feminine story jointly created by Simkie and Childerique represents the ultimate peril to the father's lines, whether genealogical or linguistic. Like the text itself, the doubled spell they devise challenges not only patrilineage and the proper name that upholds it, but also single meanings, monological interpretation, and certain ends: "Names must never be spoken, that is against the rules of witchcraft. . . . I shall speak for you and you will tell me . . . if it be to your good pleasure. . . . This . . . shall be a charm to turn the heart of your brother, your father's son, entirely away from the woman whom he now loves, and thinks of as his wife. . . , to separate the two forever" (142). Asked for a gift to reciprocate this ambiguous sentence, Childerique wants to reply as a patricentric caryatid—"For honor's sake, for the honor of Haut-Mesnil"—but realizes that "she was really here on her mother's errand, . . . and . . . the

strength and courage of the dead woman were bearing up her own"
(141–42). The text figures Simkie too as maternal, "worn like a woman
with child." And it is a child that she demands, in an implicit threat to
patrilineage and paternal power: "You must bring your little son to help
us make the spell. A male child, who has in him blood common to you,
who will speak the charm, and of him about whom we will speak it.
Blood, Madame, such noble blood is precious in magic" (143).

Finally, to seal their pact, she invites Childerique into the "magic"
room at the heart of the enchanted mill. It is the moment of ultimate
transgression, the climactic crossing from the world and word of the father into a subversive maternalized space: "Childerique stopped on the
threshold for a moment. . . . It was not that she was afraid, . . . but she
felt the fatality of this one step which took her from the daylight of her
life . . . into the play with unknown powers. What made her . . . walk on
was . . . her love of danger. The unknown called to her. She would now
know more of witchcraft" (143).

Inside the "dim," womblike room, "much older than the rest of the
mill" (143), as in the depths of her own unconscious, she confronts at last
what she has sought to repress:

> The room had an atmosphere of its own, made by the presence of the
> water; its breath met you on the threshold. . . .
> At once [it] became alive. Above and below a hundred little
> voices whispered and groaned, the timber creaked and moaned,
> heavy iron sang . . . [and] beyond all the voices rose the roar of the
> wheel and the splashing of water.
> The sweat had sprung out all over the gypsy's face, . . . and she
> had the stiff and empty face of a woman near her confinement. . . .
> "Look down," she said. (144)

Expecting "just water," Childerique experiences instead a total transformation of consciousness and signification: "Then it was as if by a sudden
jerk her own position was changed; she was no longer gazing down, or
there was no longer any up and down in the world. At this, and all at
once, the noise round her changed; it had sense; it spoke" (145). That
"speech" is the sound of the semiotic, a "music" (149) now heard as if for
the first time—what Cixous, describing woman's reawakening to the repressed maternal, would call "the first music of the voice of love" that
"sings from a time before law."[29] The events in the mill room, in reformulating the relation of woman's art to the "maternal," become a microcosm of all the subversive elements in Dinesen's own oeuvre, the murmurs
of a radical, "feminine" language.

Initially such communications are indecipherable: "a great pattern of
glowing red sparks was forming itself. First it was like a wheel, then

settled into a sort of fixity, but what it was she could not tell" (145). Writing lyrically of a comparably disorienting vision of "mother-matter," Irigaray describes a similar "collapse" of "all surfaces and spatial constructions . . . in a conflagration that pushes further and further back the depths of a gulf where now everything is burning": "Fire flares up in the inexhaustible abundance of her underground source and is matched with an opposing but congruent flood that sweeps over the 'I' in an excess of excess. Yet, burning, flowing along in a wild spate of waters, yearning for an even greater abandon, the 'I' is empty still . . . opening wide in rapture of soul."[30] Childerique is similarly "enraptured" by "deep ecstasy about this new world opened to her" (146). Describing that world in metaphors that prefigure Cixous's tropes of the "white ink" of a "feminine" writing as "good mother's milk,"[31] Dinesen brings to a climax the imagery of gestation and lactation that have earlier linked Childerique and her mother. "Transported" by her visions, Childerique enters a "vast" amniotic "space of water," covered by "a thin milky mist." "It was all dim around her, like a big bouquet of foliage, reflected within a thick silver mirror. But she herself—to get this view at all, she must be in the water, the clear surface up to her chin." In the distance, across "the lacteal surface of the water," she recognizes her own home, "the outskirts of the park at Haut-Mesnil." There she sees "a woman in white" meeting her lover. The moment, one of the most dazzling in all of Dinesen's fiction, represents the quintessential embodiment of the *unheimliche* as experienced by a female subject: "A great wave of tenderness and pride exalted her whole being. She knew this lady. . . . It was her mother, the fair and cherished Sophie, younger than herself and bright with beauty and happiness. 'Oh, dear Mother,' she thought, 'apple of my eye, I see you at last'" (146–47).

What she beholds is the scene of her own conception. And in the throes of that uncanny, "ecstatic" vision she becomes one with the mother who conceived her, even as that mother is herself (re)conceived by the daughter's enchanted vision, born of the witch's art. These multiple, reciprocal engenderings reveal a wholly different story from the one in which Childerique had thought herself a character:

> She saw that the two wanted nothing in the world but one another; they clung together, and . . . sank into each other and made one figure only in the half-light. The gestures were all so familiar; it was indeed as if she had seen herself and Philippe in a looking glass. . . .
>
> Had she in real life come upon a pair of lovers like this, she knew that she should have turned her eyes away. Not so here . . . not so with her own mother, in this world of sweet witchcraft. Here everything had a deeper meaning and heart, and the mother and daughter

could well do service to the gods hand-in-hand . . . ; this was as it
should be. (147–48)

Rejoining her mother in a primal "intimacy," she is also joined with the
witch who gave birth to the vision: "The miller's widow was before her,
with drops of sweat in her eyebrows. . . . 'I have shown you true pictures,' [she] said . . . laboriously. 'Yes, yes,' answered Childerique,
wringing her hands as the miller's wife had done before her. 'I shall show
you more tomorrow,' said Simkie. 'Yes, yes, tomorrow,' said Childerique, feeling how long it was before tomorrow, and that the time would
be filled with longing" (148–49).

Through the complex reflexivity of the moment, Dinesen's narrative, like the witch's wheel, turns back upon itself, figuring its author's
own "labor" in the process of bringing the text's "pictures" into being
and the reader's participation in that uncanny act. Just as Childerique's
"position was changed," by Simkie's craft, whose visionary "lacteal"
waters dissolve the ground on which she stands, so too our readerly perspectives, spun in the waves of that whirlpool, are radically altered, unsettled, and dissolved by the "white ink" of a feminine text which, like
the enchanting river, overflows the bounds of traditional phallocentric
textuality and "speaks" the language of the mother "at last." It is no accident that in representing that joyous engendering as a "terrible sweet
drowsiness which . . . lies like honey on [the] tongue and runs . . .
soothingly in all [the] veins" (150), Dinesen uses the same similes that she
would elsewhere employ to describe the effects of dreaming, her most
persistent trope for writing: "People who dream . . . know of a special
kind of happiness which the world of the day holds not, a placid ecstasy
. . . like honey on the tongue"—the "pleasure" and "unearthly bliss" of
"the artist" (OA, 87). As figures for Dinesen's own engendering of narrative, the reciprocal, transformative visions which mark the climax of
"The Caryatids" brilliantly reenact the semiotics of fluid, "maternal"
creation that runs throughout Seven Gothic Tales.

Just as Childerique crosses over into a hitherto forbidden terrain, so a
crossing has occurred in the symbolic structures of the text and the hermeneutic perspectives they elicit: the patriarchal order is revealed as the
site of "horror," while witchcraft, that ultimate "horror" of the patriarchal order, becomes the locus and engenderer of bliss. Where Father
Bernhard, like Freud's male patients encountering the "unheimliche
Heim" of the mother's body, had experienced such uncanny disorienta-
tions as horrific, Childerique experiences them as "deep pleasure," "a
great and sweet, fresh calm" (146–47). These traversals are reinforced by
the shift of narratorial perspective. By the end of the tale the man whose
point of view dominates the first half of the narrative is himself literally

reduced to a *point of (woman's) view:* "Childerique looked toward the horizon and at the figure of her husband, small in the foreground" (151). As the initial consciousness through which we have apprehended the story's events, Philippe elicits our empathy; the reader's "heart," like Childerique's, has "softened to him" as the victim of tragic events beyond his comprehension and has even been led to approve his knowing deception of his wife. Yet Dinesen also shows that even such a sympathetic male character is enmeshed in a symbolic order that maintains itself by suppressing what it construes as the Other. As the man who would crush Simkie like a "viper" and the knowing deceiver who maintains his control over Childerique by burying the scandalous truth of the mother's text, he perpetuates his own position—however benign it may appear—at the cost of woman's freedom, desire, and discourse. Significantly, leaving "the forest path" for "the drive of Champmeslé" after her experience with the vertiginous *jouissance* of witchcraft, Childerique feels "frightened at the sight of her husband" as at a ghost: "It was as if he, the house and garden of Champmeslé and all the life awaiting her there were pale and cold in comparison with the world of witchcraft, as the landscape was pale and cold now compared to the glowing earth and air of an hour ago" (150).

With this last transformation of "vision" (150), the story stops. Dinesen insisted that it must remain, as its subtitle indicates, "an unfinished tale": "It is best that the story ends where it does. Best for the characters and best for us. I did not dare to continue."[32] How are we to read these enigmatic declarations? Behind that question, of course, lies another: how are we to read the text itself? Indeed, as we have seen, at every level the narrative poses the question of reading. Beholding Childerique's attempts to decipher phantasmagoric scenes in which, paradoxically, she is at once an observer and a participant, we also behold our own involvement with the narrative: the "thick silver mirror" of the visionary whirlpool becomes a figure of the text whose bewitching "lines" reflect us to ourselves (147). If what we see there is at first radically disorienting ("there was no longer any up and down in the world"), so too is the abrupt cessation of the narrative, which disturbs us much as the termination of the whirling visions disturbs Childerique. By leaving the tale "unfinished," Dinesen draws attention to the readerly drive for stable closure and completion—for clear "ups" and "downs"—precisely by resisting its satisfaction.

In this context, the entire narrative of Childerique's desire for the world of "sweet witchcraft" and consequent sensual, mystical wanderings in the forest—or of our desire for and wanderings through the text—finds an analogue in Irigaray's description, in "La Mystèrique," of a comparable "nocturnal wandering," the longing it engenders for the "cauldron of identification" with the "matrices" of woman's creativity, and the dis-closures that result: "The walls of her prison are broken, the distinction between inside/outside transgressed. In such ex-stasies, she risks losing herself or at least seeing the assurance of her self-identity-as-same fade away. . . . Moreover, she doesn't know where she is going, and will have to wander randomly and in darkness. And her eye has become accustomed to the obvious 'truths' that actually hide what she is seeking. . . . Though the path she is cutting is a difficult one, she is impatient to set everything else aside and pleads to go on. . . . Expectant expectancy, . . . unbearable sweetness and bitterness, . . . mixed in a jouissance so extreme, . . . so incomprehensible, an illumnation so unbounded that un-knowledge thereby becomes desire."[33]

What are the consequences of these "unbounded," subversive visions, which violate our sense of propriety and proper outcomes much as the witch's "charm" violates social codes and genealogical continuities? Dinesen's refusal to draw conclusions by providing a "proper" ending is illuminated on one level by Childerique's intimation of what is at (the) stake for the woman whose art, within a patriarchal order, can only be perceived as terrifying, illicit, and profoundly threatening: "somewhere at the bottom of it, as if at the bottom of the mill pond, she saw the doom of the witch, the sadness and dreadfulness of her fate" (140). We have seen that Dinesen figured her own writing as a craft of displacement, brought to birth at the price of the artist's own "death." Yet as she has Philippe reflect, "once a woman has turned to witchcraft there is nothing in the world that can turn her off it." If writing was for Dinesen a demonic art of (self)sacrifice, it also held the paradoxical promise of "extraordinary" ecstasy—"the witch's happiness" for which "she sells herself . . . to the Devil" (140). As Irigaray remarks in her own description of "marriage to the unknowable," such an experience "can never be evaded once it has been experienced."[34]

Although Dinesen explicitly offers this "happiness" to her readers, who encounter her bewitching craft each time they enter the "magic" space of the text (141), she also implies that such enchantment comes only, as with Childerique's visions, at a price: the condition that we too abandon ordinary "positions," including desire for "proper" (paternal) ends and conventional conclusions.[35] In her deliberate inconclusiveness, she suggests that there may be no single resolution to the intense moral ambiguities and unimaginable historical consequences set in motion by the revolutions of the witch's wheel. But she also implies the beauty of endless dis-closures; as a model of her own revolutionary narrative art, "The Caryatids," like the fictions of Scheherazade, unfolds a poetics of perpetual promise: "I have shown you true pictures. . . . I shall show you more tomorrow." If, in her plunge into the amniotic waters of witchcraft, Childerique experiences displacement as a kind of death, crossing the barrier that held her in her old life ("The wheel has been turning on your behalf, Madame. . . . The water that turned it . . . will not come back to turn it the other way"), it is also in that immersion, and through the witch's "labor," that she is reborn: Dinesen writes her ecstatic reunion with the mother as a kind of blessed homecoming, the triumph, through narrative, over time and mortality.

Reflecting on "interminable" fictions, Peter Brooks has argued that "the narrative of attempted homecoming" is the story of "the effort to reach an assertion of origin through ending, to find the same in the different, the time before in the time after. . . . Repetition, remembering, reenactment are the ways in which we replay time, so that it may not be lost. We are thus always trying to work back through time to that transcendent home, knowing of course that we cannot. . . . Desire is the wish for the end, for fulfillment, but fulfillment delayed so that we can understand it in relation to origin, and to desire itself. The story of Scheherazade is doubtless the story of stories."[36] In this light, what I have called a poetics of perpetual promise becomes inseparable from a poetics of nostalgia. But might not such a poetics, like the experience of the uncanny, have a different meaning when the author is a woman? For a woman, who literally *embodies* the mother, both writes and *is* the desired "origin." In her persistent identification with her literary "mother" Scheherazade, Dinesen would suggest just that possibility. "A boy's journey," writes Cixous, "is the return to the native land, the *Heimweh* Freud speaks of, the nostalgia that makes a man a being who tends to come back to the point of departure to appropriate it for himself and to die there." But "in woman there is always, more or less, something of 'the mother' repairing and feeding, resisting separation, a force that does not let itself be cut off but that runs codes ragged," allowing the daughter "to inscribe [her] woman's style in language . . . , milk that could go on forever. Found again."[37] The passage reads like an echo of Childerique's ecstatic response to the vision in the "milky mist": "dear mother . . . at last!"

That visionary reclamation offers new ways of thinking about the connections between *Seven Gothic Tales* and *Out of Africa*. Readers have often remarked the apparently radical difference between the two texts, wondering how they could be (to borrow Dinesen's phrase) "works of the same artist." Yet in the epiphanic climax of "The Caryatids"—which, brilliantly recapitulating the poetics of *Seven Gothic Tales*, conflates the engendering of narrative, the desire for "home," and the specter of loss from which both are inseparable—we glimpse the matrix from which Dinesen would create her great memoir.

PART THREE

THE ART
OF SACRIFICE

The will to sacrifice . . . was the disdain of death.

ISAK DINESEN,
"Daguerreotypes"

10

Transporting Topographies: Out of Africa *and the* Poetics of Nostalgia

Nostalgia . . . from Greek *nostos* return home . . . ; akin to OHG
ginesan to survive, Goth *ganisan* to get well, be saved.

Webster's New International Dictionary, 3d edition

Love is a yearning for a country . . . which renders the country
for you a point of destiny. Which country? The one from which
we come, "the place where everyone dwelt once upon a time and
in the beginning." The country from which we come is always
the one to which we are returning. You are on the return road
which passes through the country of children in the maternal
body. You have already passed through here: you recognize the
landscape. You have always been on the return road.

Hélène Cixous, "Fiction and Its Phantoms: A Reading of Freud's
Das Unheimliche (The 'uncanny')"

This country . . . has a kind of charm that not everyone can
understand . . . , one comes to love it in a way I had never
thought one could love other countries besides one's own, one's
childhood country. The fact that most white people here hate it
and have nothing good to say of it brings it in a way still closer to
the hearts of those who feel that they can understand its voice
and that it has spoken to them.

Karen Blixen, *Letters from Africa*

The "yearning" Cixous describes in her revisionist reading of the Freudian text suggests the figurative axis along which we might trace the
transition between *Seven Gothic Tales* and *Out of Africa*. Through the ritual murder that ends "The Poet" Dinesen had temporarily exorcised the
specter of the rapacious, overpowering father. Through the "milky mist"
and "lacteal waters" of "The Caryatids" she had evoked the possibility of
a blissful return to a reimagined maternal generativity. Now she could
shut the door for a time on the haunted house of Gothic fiction. The
ghost, characteristically, would rise again; indeed its persistence surely

accounts in part for her continued interest in writing Gothic narratives.[1] But its hold would appear increasingly attenuated, displaced by the reclamation of feminine creativity represented by the milky whirlpool— "white ink" of the maternal semiotic—in which Childerique ecstatically immerses herself in the powerful, problematic climax of "The Caryatids." The nostalgia that overwhelms Childerique upon seeing her mother for the first time, a moving figure in the witch's waves, is akin to the motive force that engenders *Out of Africa*. "Love is a yearning for a country": Cixous's resonant trope suggests one way to conceive the joyous, uncanny sense of homecoming Dinesen experienced on discovering the place she called "my heart's land," a psychological as well as geographical terrain. It also suggests the import, for her, of losing that place. Yet as "The Caryatids" insists, such losses are not necessarily absolute. We have seen how often, in her letters, Karen Blixen had mythologized Africa as mother. In composing her great memoir Isak Dinesen would recreate that mythos. Like Childerique reliving her own engendering through the power of "sweet witchcraft," in writing *Out of Africa* Dinesen too made a complex return journey "home" through the power of her own bewitching craft, reviving, through the moving figures of language, the matrix of her deepest yearnings. That such a reclamation was inseparable from the alienations of imperialism is one of the ineluctable ambiguities with which any reading of *Out of Africa* must seek to come to terms.

1. TRANSPORTING TOPOLOGIES

"I had a farm in Africa." The famous words, alluring microcosm of the book they begin, are in several senses *transporting*. Like the magical powers of the "Djinn" Dinesen evokes to represent the oneiric experience of flight over the African landscape (*OA*, 239–41), they convey the spellbound Anglo-European reader to that lost paradisial past which forms the still-potent mythic subtext of the book. In so doing, they also rewrite one version of the colonialist dream. Inherent in Dinesen's initial juxtaposition of the European "I" with "Africa" is that system of homologous oppositions whereby the Western psychosocial order has traditionally operated: self/other, same/different, mind/matter, known/unknown, polarities that help sustain the structures and ideologies of imperialism— "settler" versus "native," "civilization" versus "barbarism," "white" versus "black."[2] Yet if, by staging such a confrontation of opposites, Dinesen seems to reconstitute their irreconcilable differences, thereby reinforcing the colonialist mentality, she also prefigures another kind of transport, which the book repeatedly enacts: an unmooring and *carrying across* of the polar terms of the imperial grammar, an intermingling of "I" and "Africa" at the pivotal site marked by the "farm"—which is also the text—that conjoins them. Disclosing the instability of the line that divides them, the internal pluralities and contradictions of the seemingly unitary, stable entities they name, she suggests as well the possibilities of their reciprocity—that "interplay of heterogeneous elements" which she celebrated all her life. It was that same interplay that she repeatedly connected with the engendering of narrative and the operations of the "feminine" in language. Because the oppositional hierarchies that ground Occidental symbolic orders are themselves grounded on the fundamental opposition between "man" and "woman" which Dinesen so persistently interrogated, it is not surprising that tropes of place and displacement in *Out of Africa* are inseparable from questions of sexual difference. As we shall see, the book reveals striking affinities between those whom colonialist discourses have construed as the "Other" of European culture and those historically construed as the Other of man within a broader, more pervasive discourse of sexual domination.[3] The dogma of culture versus nature, "us" versus "them" that structures the logic and ideologies of imperialism also structures the logic and ideologies of gender, which subordinate woman in the name of the father just as colonialist enterprises have sought to subordinate the colonized in the name of civilization—a construct commonly represented as the peculiar property of "the White Man."[4] Both symbolic orders operate within an economy of difference based on a subject/object dichotomy whereby, as Karen Blixen observed, colonized peoples are regarded as inferior, insensate, or subhuman instruments of the colonizers, and women as ciphers who, "merely because they belong to the female sex," do "not exist" outside their relation to men (*LA*, 4–5, 250, 263).[5] And just as questions of gender are inseparable from other global economies of power and commerce, so, Dinesen would repeatedly insist, such economies are themselves inseparable from questions of representation, given the "world of symbols" in and through which we live (*Essays*, 1).

Such a perspective opens new ways of thinking about *Out of Africa*. "In Africa," writes the narrator, "when you pick up a book worth reading . . . your mind runs, transported, upon a fresh deep green track" (*OA*, 90). As this and similar self-reflexive passages imply, *Out of Africa* might be read as a text of transport in many senses. In it Dinesen traverses and intermingles geographies, genders, and genres, as well as the received European categories of "self" and "other," simultaneously disclosing and dissolving the ideology of absolute boundaries just as a vision of landscape from the air, "nine thousand feet up," discloses and, at greater heights, dissolves those geographical "lines" that mark colonial efforts to divide the earth (238)—finite cartographies whose plots would imprint ownership, domination, and static difference onto what is ulti-

mately mutable, multiple, and unconfinable (238). Through a complex
process of dis-figuration, Dinesen both evokes and unsettles imperial
plots, interrogating the "lines" that partition peoples, territories, or subjects, even as she disrupts the symbolic orders that underwrite hierarchical codes of gender in culture and textuality. Given these diverse
problematics, I offer what follows as only a brief, necessarily partial series of speculative meditations. Yet in exploring even a few of these connections, one begins to perceive what a great act of imagination Dinesen
performed in transmuting the raw materials of her years in Kenya into
the complex, luminous text that is *Out of Africa.*

2. REFORMING IMPERIAL WORDS

So sad did it seem that I remembered the saying of the hero in a
book that I had read as a child: "I have conquered them all, but I
am standing amongst graves."

Out of Africa

By contrast to the *Letters from Africa,* with their poignant, emotionally
mercurial account of Karen Blixen's seventeen-year sojourn, *Out of Africa,* published six years after her permanent departure, appears at first
like the receding outlines of the Ngong Hills that mark her "farewell":
"smoothed . . . by the hand of distance" (380,389). In writing the book
she carefully composed herself, in both senses. The authorial voice seems
magnificently controlled, preternaturally restrained as it traces the contours of catastrophe: the ruins of the writer's life, the deaths of her beloved friends, her expulsion from the place she called "my free land, my
endless land"—the "home" where she had longed "to live and die."[6]
Like the topography of the farm whose loss she records, that "landscape
that had not its like in all the world," the book presents itself on the most
obvious level as a clear and timeless *extract*—"Africa distilled up through
six thousand feet, like the strong and refined essence of a continent" (3)—
a lucent elixir concocted from the years of daily, unremitting labor, the
despairing efforts to bring in a coffee crop increasingly inadequate, the
financial attrition, and the relentless struggles with the elements. In this
sense, *Out of Africa* is as much an illusion as the recent motion picture for
which it served as pretext—a film released under the apt rubric "a Mirage
Production." Significantly, *mirage* is precisely the atmospheric effect
Dinesen attributes to the African landscapes (3–4, 312–13). Yet unlike
Sydney Pollack's cinematic romance, which seeks the effect of seamless
transparency, Dinesen's text is a highly reflexive illusion, repeatedly calling attention to its own status as constructed artifact, as to its author's
precariously *constructed* position as colonial "settler."

It is not surprising, given the dazzling lyricism, the fragmented, achronological structure, and the Edenic allusions that figure so prominently throughout the narrative, that traditional readings have stressed its mythopoeic dimensions, focusing almost exclusively on its "timeless" literary effects at the expense of its sociopolitical implications. But such an atemporal vision of *Out of Africa* elides both the text's and the author's problematic relations to history. One of the gravest difficulties confronting a contemporary Anglo-American reader of this book is the conflict between its sheer lyric beauty, the quasi-mythic hold it exercises on Occidental sensibilities, and the disconcerting knowledge of the historical circumstances that formed its conditions of possibility. The interpretive dilemma pivots on a fundamental question: How are we to read a text in which, as Edward Said has astutely remarked of *Kim,* "there is more than one history . . . to be remembered"?[7] In *Out of Africa* as in Kipling's colonial novel, "the imperial experience, while often regarded as exclusively political, . . . also . . . entered into cultural and aesthetic life."[8] In this context Dinesen's recurrent Edenic and maternal tropes might be read as mere vestiges of a colonialist poetics that would plot Africa in Western terms, subsuming its specificity within the ahistorical *topos* of paradise lost or regained.[9] And insofar as Dinesen's making a book out of Africa replicated the colonizing impulse, her effort to recapture through language the land she could not keep might appear as yet another alienation, turning "Africa" into a commodity to be bought and consumed by a Euro-American community which, in the very act of reading, would reenact the imperial gesture of possession.[10]

Yet those explicitly political critiques of Dinesen's relation to colonialism that group her indiscriminately with all other colonialist writers are as problematic as their ahistoricist counterparts, for in condemning *Out of Africa* as nothing more than another imperialist text, they overlook precisely what they accuse Dinesen of overlooking in her treatment of Africans: the possibility of distinctiveness, difference, and specificity.[11] To contest the polarizing rhetoric such critiques often deploy is not to ratify Karen Blixen's participation in the colonialist enterprise or the paternalism—more accurately, maternalism—with which she treated Africans. Nor is it to deny the intricate relation between *Out of Africa* and Western imperialist discourses. The crucial question, however, would seem to be not whether, but in what ways, the text elaborates those connections.

It is difficult, today, to sort out fairly the complexities of Karen Blixen's involvement in a colonialist project that she simultaneously participated in, benefited from, despised, and repeatedly sought to subvert. Certainly, as we saw in chapter 2, she reflects many of the biases common to her era, class, and race. Certainly, too, her African letters and memoirs appear to perpetuate an imperialist mentality through tropes and conventions inherited from centuries of European discourses on Africa. Even her praise of Africans, for example, often echoes the overdetermined topos of the noble "savage" (e.g., 37, 42), which interweaves admiration—"noble found I / ever the Native, / and insipid the Immigrant" (21)—with a kind of condescension that inscribes "the native" not only as highly admirable but sometimes as childlike, capricious, or quaint. Further, such generalizing references to "the native" or "the African" recall that "radical typing" which Said has identified as characterizing colonialist representations of non-Occidental peoples: a "transtemporal, transindividual" categorization of "pre-existing . . . essence" which ignores specificity and difference.[12]

Yet such figurations are far from simple. We recall, for instance, that it was "caprice" and strategically mimed "naïveté" that Dinesen celebrated as elements of the most vital creativity, potent counterforces for dislodging oppressive hegemonic structures. And it was partly from the Africans' "art of mimicry" (19) that she found a model for the heretical duplicities of her own writing. These qualities are epitomized in her appreciative depiction of the Somali women's subversive uses of power to manipulate the system that oppressed them: "witches" whose "ceremonial of primness" and compliant façades concealed "great mightiness" and "risibility," they were adepts at the "fine art" of resistant *mimétisme:* "There was no ignorance in their innocence"; "neither would they rest until they had drunk the heart's blood of their adversary," like "ferocious young she-wolves in seemly sheep's clothing" (177, 79).

Such passages are characteristic of Dinesen's recurrent comparisons of Africans with wild animals—tropes which perhaps more often than any others have been attacked as definitive proof of her "racism." Yet one recalls that she also identified herself and those Europeans she most admired with wild creatures, regarding them as far superior to "tame," self-satisfied, sterile characters like Augustus von Schimmelman or the typical members of the British colonialist establishment.[13] As JanMohamed notes, "in contrast to the colonialist's urge to subdue and reshape the native and the African environment, Dinesen exalts the freedom of the untamed."[14] Further, for all her typifying generalizations about "the African," she also elaborates descriptions of individual Africans—the extended portraits of Kamante Gatura and Farah Aden, for example—which manifest the "ordinary human reality" and the "existential and semantic thickness" that Said finds lacking in most colonialist discourses.[15] Finally, *Out of Africa* suggests that it is precisely the concept of the farm as a project dependent on "capital," part of the "market" process of colonial exploitation (321), that must fail in order for the narrator to enter another order of awareness—a process unfolded in the final chapters.

As this summary suggests, while Dinesen did indeed participate in the colonialist project as both immigrant and author, she also remained remarkably free, given her historical circumstances, of typical imperialistic attitudes. Despite her pleasure in the quasi-feudal role of *dame de manoir,* her relationship with African peoples differed distinctively from that of most other colonists, whose contemptuous rubric for her—"pronative"—marked the rift between them. As JanMohamed observes, in "criticizing in a substantial manner the economic, religious, and ethnocentric motives at the heart of the colonial endeavor," Dinesen constitutes "a major exception to the . . . pattern of conquest and irresponsible exploitation" characteristic of colonialists and colonialist authors.[16]

Consider, for example, the discourse of ownership. While repeatedly speaking of "my farm" Dinesen also reminds us that the land belongs to Africans first, by original and continuing rights: "The white men took over the country. . . . But I bore in mind that not very long ago, at a time that could still be remembered, the Natives of the country had held their land undisputed, and had never heard of the white men and their laws. Within the general insecurity of their existence the land to them was still steadfast. Some of them were carried off by the slave-traders . . . but some of them always remained. Those who were taken away, in their exile and thralldom . . . would long back to the highlands, for that was their own land" (377). Thus, as she wryly notes, "they very likely regarded me as a sort of superior squatter on their estate" (9; cf. 283, 375–78). Her attempt to register, however inadequately, this "regard"— the distinctive, diverse perspectives and cultural specificity of African peoples—is among the most notable features in her representations. Unlike other Africanist writers, who, as Christopher Miller notes, generally denied Africans any connection with a history anterior to the European arrivals,[17] Dinesen stresses the contingency of the colonialist presence: "We white people were wrong when in our intercourse with the people of the ancient continent we forgot or ignored their past or . . . declined to acknowledge that they had ever existed before their meeting with us . . . , and our error of vision . . . caused deep and sad misunderstandings between us and them."[18] In *Out of Africa,* by persistently inviting us not only to see Africans through the narrator's eyes, but to try to imagine seeing Europeans through Africans' eyes, Dinesen attempts to expose that Eurocentric "error of vision," repudiating the power of the all-consuming imperial gaze that would reduce Africans indiscriminately to the status of inert Other or appropriate them as mere signs within an Occidental discourse. This repositioning of the look operates at many turns in *Out of Africa,* suggesting both the perversity of ethnocentrism and the resilient power of the colonized to influence and manipulate the colonizers. "I reconciled myself," remarks the narrator, "to the fact that while I should never quite know or understand them, they knew me through and through" (20).[19] If the "I" here constitutes herself as a subject inseparable from the colonialist system, she also, in ways I shall return to, represents herself as an object constructed by Africans, "turn[ed] . . . into a symbol" in an ironic reversal of her own authority and authorial project (106).

Though extended analysis of Dinesen's complex relation to colonialism is beyond the scope of this study, I want to explore some of her most salient responses to the ambiguities and contradictions inherent in her plural positioning as a European, a colonist, and a woman. I would suggest that by reformulating the question of difference, representing it not merely in terms of hierarchized opposition but as a continual transformational slippage that undermines the Western notion of the single, sovereign, territorializing self, Dinesen also implicitly questions the representational systems that uphold the imperialist project, undermining the language of property and propriety on which it rests. Uncovering "the interplay of heterogeneous elements" in what an Occidental phallocentric ontology would read *in*differently as monolithic, static, and same, she evokes alternative ways of seeing and being that ultimately subvert the politics and poetics of the very systems which, paradoxically, had made *Out of Africa* possible.

3. DECOMPOSING PLOTS: "AFRICA" AND THE SCENE OF SELF-INSCRIPTION

> To undo our own "reality" under the effect of other formulations, other syntaxes; . . . to displace the subject's topology; . . . to descend into the untranslatable, to experience its shock without ever muffling it, until everything Occidental in us totters and the rights of the "father tongue" vacillate—the tongue which comes to us from our fathers and which makes us, in turn, fathers and proprietors of a culture. . . .
>
> —Roland Barthes, *The Empire of Signs*

> "You are I, and I am you."
> *Out of Africa*

The prerequisite of the book's existence is brilliantly telescoped in the double entendre of its title: for Dinesen, to write *Out of Africa* was necessarily also to *be* out of Africa, to have lost already what she would have owned. On its most literal level, the book is the story of the protagonist's effort to *have* "a farm in Africa"—a desire doomed, as the past tense of the opening sentence tells us, from the start. *Out of Africa* narrates the failure of territorialization in every sense. Indeed, recalling Dinesen's description of the European "yearning" to turn "the wildness and irregularity of the country" into "a piece of ground laid out according to rule," a series of "geometrical figures" that would symbolize order, sovereignty, and control (7), one might say that the text is about the *decomposition of her plots,* both literal and literary. The *end*—of both farm and text—is predetermined, she implies, not merely because of the practical considerations of climate, altitude, weather, or financial pressure that brought about the demise of Karen Coffee Company, but because of the ultimately unmasterable nature of Africa and the inadequacy of the representational systems with which Europeans seek to configure it.

This inadequacy is mimetically replicated by the structure(lessness) of the text: discontinuous, fragmentary, and associative rather than linear, geometric, and stable, it, like the world it describes, resists "systematization" (24). Significantly, the only kind of "progress" discoverable in the achronological narrative is an effect of the persistent *breakdown* of those structures that guarantee a European notion of order, political or discursive. The pressures of linear chronology become compelling only as the narrative draws toward its conclusion, where deaths proliferate and the farm gradually slips from the protagonist's grasp, forcing her at last out of Africa. Yet even in the earlier, superficially idyllic sections, that failure—and the history it signifies—is already operative. The reader is initially invited to experience the book as one would the mythic "dreams" whose defiance of temporal logic the narrator describes in the self-reflexive passage at the outset of "A Shooting Accident": "Things happen without any interference from [the dreamer], and altogether outside his control. Great landscapes create themselves, long splendid views, rich and delicate colours, roads, houses, which he has never seen or heard of. . . . All the time the feeling of immense freedom is surrounding him and running through him like air and light, and unearthly bliss" (87). Yet immediately afterward, the "accident" of history ruptures the mythic world of dream in the form of the "shot" that rings out in "the stillness of the night" (89) surrounding these meditations. That shot—fired, tellingly, by an African child who "had acted the part of a white man" by borrowing "his master's gun" (91)—shatters the atemporal, dreamlike idyll of "Africa" even as it shatters the bodies of the Kikuyu children Wamai and Wanyangerri, or as colonialism has shattered the lives of the African peoples: "Death . . . rushed in . . . and left the place in dire devastation" (92).

Langbaum rightly observes that this moment foreshadows the text's conclusion. But prefigurations of that end begin even earlier, most notably in the poignant elegiac passages that conclude "Kamante and Lulu" and anticipate "A Shooting Accident": "During my last years in Africa I

saw less and less of [the bushbuck] Lulu and her family. Within the year
before I went away I do not think that they ever came. Things had
changed, . . . land had been given out to farmers and the forest had been
cleared . . . and houses built. Tractors were heaving up and down where
the glades had been. Many of the new settlers were keen sportsmen and
the rifles sang in the landscape," destroying the "song" of natural generativity associated with Lulu (78–79).[20] Under such murderous pressures,
images of death infect the unspoiled world associated with the bushbuck
and her "forest matriarchy" (78): "the game withdrew to the West. . . . I
do not know how long an antelope lives, probably Lulu has died a long
time ago" (79).

These passages, in turn, are themselves prefigured by still earlier
ones—brief, almost unnoticeable *memento mori* dropped into the narrative like faint contaminating stains, reminding us even in the midst of
its most idyllic moments that the *time before time* it evokes—an idea reinforced by the narrator's imperceptible shift into synchronic present
tense (5)—was always in fact already irrevocably past: "In my day, the
Buffalo, the Eland and the Rhino lived in the Ngong Hills,—the very old
Natives remembered a time when there were Elephants there. . . . But
during my last years in Africa many young Nairobi shop-people ran out
into the hills on Sundays, on their motor-cycles, and shot at anything
they saw, and I believe that the big game will have wandered away from
the hills."[21]

Similar elegiac moments occur throughout the text. Indeed, seen in
overview, as if "from the air," *Out of Africa* describes a relentless trajectory of loss and death, leading to the narrator's ultimate alienation from
the land whereon she had grounded her sense of self: "When I first began
to make terms with fate, and the negotiations about the sale of the farm
were taken up, the attitude of the landscape towards me changed. Till
then I had been part of it, and the drought had been to me like a fever,
and the flowering plain like a new frock. Now, the country disengaged
itself from me" (330). The climactic figure of this shift from dream to
"nightmare" (88, 349) is Denys Finch Hatton's death and burial—that
"grave in the hills" toward which the whole book, like the landscape
around Ngong, imperceptibly but inevitably rises.

The spare, understated summation in the following chapter—"It was
no longer mine" (362)—refers not only to the African farm and all it represents for the narrator, but also to the identity it had founded: "Wherever I walked, the ground fell away under me, and the stars fell from the
sky" (368). Her later description of the Africans' attachment to the land—
one of the book's many explicit indictments of colonialism—is also a self-
referential commentary on her own sense of dispossession: "It is more
than their land that you take away from the people, whose Native land
you take. It is their past as well, their roots and their identity" (375). Just

as the plots that had made up the farm have gradually deteriorated, undone by the powers of the wilderness they were to control, just as the
plots that make up most of the book are little more than meandering,
fragmentary structures, their discontinuities culminating in the random
pastiche of part 4, so the narrator's own plots—the dreams and schemes
that supported her identity—are decomposed: "giv[ing] away" her "possessions one by one" (362, 379), she empties her cherished house, leaving
at last only a hollow space, "like a skull," a place of multiplying "echo"
(364). Dismantling her life in Africa, she likewise dismembers herself—
until, at last, there is "nothing left": "I myself was the lightest thing of
all" (379).

This peculiar relation between the "self" that writes and the elusive
place by which that self is constituted is evoked throughout the book in
representations of farm and farmer as unstable figures *on the edge* in every
sense. A coffee plantation located on "land . . . a little too high for coffee" (7), "twelve miles away" from Nairobi, center of colonialist rule, the
farm occupies an ambiguous, indeterminate space between "civilization"
and "wilderness" (261). As a transitional, mediatory site where "nature"
becomes "culture" and that which is cultivated is perpetually reclaimed
by natural forces, it confounds the boundaries between such seeming
oppositions as "wild" and "tame," "inside" and "outside."[22] Dinesen repeatedly represents it as a locus of uncertainty, its problematic status
underscored by recurrent references to the intractable elements that assault its orderly plots and the wilderness that impinges upon them.

This indeterminacy operates from the outset. In the poetics of landscape that opens the narrative, Dinesen figures "Africa" as a fluid, mobile, and destabilizing space: "The trees had a . . . structure . . . which
was different from the trees of Europe," which "gave to the edge of the
wood a strange appearance, as if the whole . . . were faintly vibrating"
(3), blurring stable, definitive boundaries. The atmospheric effects produce a comparable destabilization and uncanny duplicity: "In the middle
of the day the air was alive over the land, like a flame burning; it scintil-
lated, waved and shone like running water, mirrored and doubled all
objects, and created great Fata Morgana"—those vertiginous optical illusions associated with Morgan le Fay, through whose bewitching craft
Dinesen implicitly figures her own (4). The whole scene is one of continual flux and mobility, of figures that appear and accumulate density
and mass only to "dissolve" and "vanish" like the "clouds . . . travelling
with the wind," or that "change their character many times" like the
Ngong Hills, which, like the narrative that describes them, offer "a
unique view" of Africa (5).

This same elusiveness characterizes the autobiographical subject of
the text. "Here I am, where I ought to be," declares the narratorial voice
in a tellingly reflexive, retrospective gesture (4). But who—and where—

is this "I"? As a European colonist, seeking to claim the "virgin" wilderness, a settler who, as farmer, is "husbandman" to the land, "s/he" (the gender left deliberately ambiguous until well into the narrative) is associated with a tradition that would write selfhood as unitary, stable, autonomous—and male. As feminist critics have often noted, the "I" in traditional androcentric discourses is the signifier of the self-contained, undifferentiated subject, founded on what Domna Stanton calls "the phallic myth of authority."[23] But in *Out of Africa* that peculiarly Westernized "I" is repeatedly rendered uncertain, problematic—perpetually dissolving into the "Africa" to which it is opposed, both syntactically and socioculturally, in the opening sentence of the book. Like the farm situated outside the bounds of urban "civilization," the narrator too is an outsider: neither African nor British, a colonial settler who is regarded by the colonialist establishment as ominously "pro-native," she is also, as a "woman farmer" (371), a contradiction to the typifying image of the colonist as "white man" (91, 377). Like Kamante, with whom she explicitly identifies (31), she too is an "eccentric" and "isolated figure," who represents "a different way" (32) and "precludes classification" (36). As she observes in the poignant passages preceding the description of Finch Hatton's death, "It seemed to me that . . . I myself was somehow on the wrong side, and therefore was regarded with distrust and fear by everybody" (347). As an ex-centric, liminal figure at once inside and outside the colonialist frame of reference, she, like "Africa" or "the Africans" as construed by colonialism, constitutes a site of potential disorder, a profound disruption of those categories of existence which the notion of "an inside" and "an outside" upholds.

Analyzing Derrida's "unmasking and demystification of a host of unconscious or naturalized binary oppositions in contemporary and traditional thought," Fredric Jameson observes that such "metaphysical" dichotomies imply an "ethics":

> The concept of good and evil is a positional one that coincides with categories of Otherness. Evil thus, as Nietzsche taught us, continues to characterize whatever is radically different from me, whatever by virtue of precisely that difference seems to constitute a real and urgent threat to my own existence. So from the earliest times, the stranger . . . , the 'barbarian' who speaks an incomprehensible language and follows 'outlandish' customs, but also the woman . . . or . . . some oppressed class or race . . . [is] feared because [they] are Other, alien, different, strange, unclean, and unfamiliar.[24]

In *Out of Africa* Dinesen (for whom Nietzsche was also a crucial precursor) contests just these sorts of power hierarchies, which she too identified with an ethics of "opposition," "the disease caught from the tradition of dualism."[25] By suggesting the instability and heterogeneity of the categories "I" and "Africa," she also reveals the contingency of the hierarchical categories they initially appear to confirm. Just as the farm exists only as a precarious, progressively deteriorating, marginal enterprise whose plots bear ever-dwindling harvests, so these dominant Occidental plots of sameness and difference also break down as the text unfolds, becoming as unstable as the "faintly vibrating" line dividing woods and plains in a landscape of "doubled" mirage. The text vividly enacts the narrator's paradoxical observation that in Africa the "sense of individuality itself [is] lost in the sense of the possibilities that lie in interaction between those who can be made one by reason of their incongruity" (17). Thus if on one level the initial juxtaposition of "I" with "Africa" appears to be the epitomizing synecdoche of Occidental ideology, on another level it also initiates an interrogation of that ideology. Like the "scintillating," "waving" atmosphere, the ever-changing Ngong Hills, or "the long grass" that "ran and fled like sea-wave" (10), the "Fata Morgana" of Dinesen's fluid prose repeatedly dissolves the Western oppositions by which a certain "self" and its systems are kept in place.

In this perpetually changing world of "laughter," "shine," "play," "music," and "echoes" (12, 16, 19), the author becomes only one among many moving figures, gliding in and out of history, in and out of "dream," sometimes receding, like the Ngong Hills, into "distance" (389), sometimes addressing us with astonishing immediacy. Dizzying shifts of perspective replicate and reinforce this process. Thus, for example, from the predatorial position she occupies during the midnight lion hunt with Denys Finch Hatton, she can be catapulted suddenly into the position of the prey: "When the shot fell, close to me, [it was] as if I had been myself shifted into the place of the lion. . . . 'Move on, move on,' Denys cried to me. . . . [T]he circle of light, which held all the world, and which I commanded, danced a dance. . . . Africa, in a second, grew endlessly big, and Denys and I, standing upon it, infinitely small" (235–36). In similar shifts throughout the narrative, the protagonist's aspiration to occupy the authoritative place of feudal sovereign, dependent on maintaining the consistent perspective of the unitary self, is repeatedly undermined, whether by the ineluctable nature of events which reduce her to "nothing," by the tolerantly amused "contempt" (38) with which Africans like Kamante often regard her ("In a world of fools, I was, I think, to him one of the greater fools"[26]), or by the persistent dismantling of her status as a latter-day Adam for whose "eyes" the world was "created" (15)—the one who sees, names, knows, and therefore owns (238–39). What emerges at last, instead, is the sense of her own utter powerlessness and placelessness:

When I look back . . . it seems to me that the lifeless things were aware of my departure a long time before I was so myself. The hills, the forests, plains and rivers, the wind, all knew that we were to part. . . .

When in the end, the day came on which I was going away, I learned the strange learning that things can happen which we ourselves cannot possibly imagine, either beforehand, or at the time when they are taking place, or afterwards when we look back on them. . . . On such occasions you . . . [become] like a blind person who is being led, who places one foot in front of the other cautiously but unwittingly. Things are happening to you, and you feel them happening, but . . . you have no connection with them, and no key to the cause or meaning of them. The performing wild animals in a circus go through their programme, I believe, in the same way. Those who have been through such events can, in a way, say that they have been through death,—a passage outside the range of imagination, but within the range of experience. (330, 385–86)

This story of desire, dislocation, and loss is told repeatedly, not only in the trajectory of the book as a whole but also in the many parables that serve as its microcosmic reenactments. Consider, as representative example, the narrative of the iguana:

When, as you approach, they swish away, there is a flash of azure, green and purple over the stones, the colour seems to be standing behind them in the air, like a comet's luminous tail. Once I shot an Iguana. I thought that I should be able to make some pretty things from his skin. A strange thing happened then, that I have never afterward forgotten. As I went up to him, where he was lying dead upon his stone, . . . he faded and grew pale, all colour died out of him as in one long sigh, and by the time that I touched him he was grey and dull like a lump of concrete. It was the live impetuous blood pulsating within the animal, which had radiated out all that glow and splendour. Now that the flame was put out, and the soul had flown, the Iguana was as dead as a sandbag. . . . In a foreign country and with foreign species of life one should take measures to find out whether things will be keeping their value when dead. To the settlers of East Africa I give the advice: "For the sake of your own eyes and heart, shoot not the Iguana." (257–58)[27]

Here, as in similar passages throughout the text, *Out of Africa* enacts Dinesen's rueful sense of her own complicity in the doomed desire to hunt and hold the elusive beauty she admired. It is no accident that in the iguana's fate she also figures her own: as she writes later of her imminent departure from Africa, "all colour and life faded out of the world around me" (324). In the text's many parables, as in the larger narrative, the "I" who speaks from the position of the dominating, colonizing European subject also symbolically occupies the place of the Other that seems her object. Both hunter and, like the iguana, sacrificial victim struck down by fate; both European observer and, like the giraffes destined for the Hamburg menagerie, a helpless, hopeless deportee to a place "where no one knows Africa" (299–300); both predator and, like the lions in the torch's "dance," doomed prey, she too must continually "move on, move on," a mobile figure in a "dance" between seeming opposites. Like the shimmering, mirage-laden landscapes of Africa, in whose mutabilities and "irregularity" Dinesen implicitly figures both the "self" and the text that represent them (7, 272), *Out of Africa* constitutes the ever-belated testimony that what it describes cannot be fixed. By demonstrating the ultimate impossibility of possession, the very fact of its protagonist's being transported *out* of Africa, the text compellingly interrogates both the colonialist project of which the farm was a part and the forms of sovereign self-consciousness and imperial authority and authorship associated with that enterprise. Like the dreams and echoes with which it compares itself, the narrative is ultimately both product and producer of radical displacement.

Yet such displacement is not necessarily the source of despair. For *Out of Africa* is a text of transport in another sense as well. As a colonialist narrative that undermines the presumed certainties on which colonialism rests, a rite of "passage" (386) that is also the writing of a passage into a new way of knowing, its operative effect is, in every sense, to *change the subject*. As the narrator remarks of experiencing the "transport" of an earthquake, this destabilization of the grounds of the "self" and its structures initially comes as a terrifying "shock," the presage of annihilation: "When the second shock came, I thought, 'I am going to die, this is how it feels to die.'" But that radical unmooring ultimately becomes an ecstatic liberation: "When the third and last shock of it came, it brought with it such an overwhelming feeling of joy that I do not remember ever in my life to have been more suddenly and thoroughly transported." Comparing herself to Kepler writing on planetary motion ("'I give myself over to my rapture. . . . Nothing I have ever felt before is like this. I tremble, my blood leaps.' . . . Indeed it was exactly the same transport which took hold of me and shook me all through"), Dinesen writes the experience as profound *jouissance,* "colossal pleasure" born of the realization "that something which you have reckoned to be immovable, has got it in it to move on its own" (295).

This imagery of ecstatic dislocation reaches its apogee in the narrator's recollection of flying over Africa, an experience she calls "the most transporting pleasure of my life," a blissful liberation from "the laws of gravitation and time" (238). It is a passage whose tropes, as we have seen, recur throughout her narratives as figures for writing itself:

You have tremendous views as you get up above the African highlands, surprising combinations and changes of light and colouring,
the rainbow on the green sunlit land, the gigantic upright clouds and
big wild black storms, all swing round you in a race and a dance. . . .
The language is short of words for the experience, and will have to
invent new words with time. . . . But it is not the visions but the
activity which makes you happy, and the joy and glory of the flyer is
the flight itself. It is a sad hardship and slavery to people who live in
towns, that in all their movements they know of one dimension only;
they walk along the line as if they were led on a string. The transition
from the line to the plane into the two dimensions . . . is a splendid
liberation of the slaves, like the French Revolution. But in the air you
are taken up into the full freedom of three dimensions; after long
ages of exile and dreams the homesick heart throws itself into the
arms of space. . . . Every time I have gone up in an aeroplane and
looking down have realised that I was free of the ground, I have had
the consciousness of a great new discovery. "I see," I have thought,
"This was the idea. And now I understand everything." (238–39)

In its insistence that possession and dispossession are indivisible, that
the self paradoxically becomes "itself" only when it loses itself, that true
"freedom" means deliverance from linearity, centricity, and control, and
that this liberation is inseparable from a new "language," this passage,
like the thematics of love and loss of which it is the climax, brilliantly
anticipates Kristeva's recent analysis of similar psycholinguistic transports:

The atomized self can only be . . . written as *metaphor*. Conveyance.
Metaphorein. Not a transfer toward an object but "levitation," lifting
the self toward an invisible Other. . . . Metaphor as damaging to
Single meaning, as symptom of its toppling over into infinity, is . . .
the very discourse of love: the place where God topples over into
Satan and *vice versa*.[28]

Dinesen evokes precisely these ineluctable paradoxes and destabilizing
duplicities in the "discourse of love" which is *Out of Africa*—a discourse
predicated, she suggests, on that primal "knowledge that was lost to us
by our first parents; Africa, amongst the continents, will teach it to you:
that God and the Devil are one" (19–20). Such knowledge allows one to
"risk" the self in ways unthinkable within a tradition that depends on the
maintenance of autonomous, unitary subjectivity and absolute control
(19). At every level in *Out of Africa,* as throughout Dinesen's oeuvre, possession and dispossession, self and Other, innocence and guilt, love and
loss—the "divine" and the "diabolic"—are inextricably interwoven.
And as she asserts in the narrative of flying, these forms of interplay are
themselves inseparable from the "words" that express them. To be out of

Africa, then, is to dwell within all the ambiguities of the *written:* the mortal, postlapsarian order of absence, estrangement, and loss which may also be, paradoxically, the beginning of bliss.

4. (Dis)Figuring Africa: The Disintegration of Writing

I had an old wooden screen with painted figures. . . . There in the evenings, when the fire burned clear, the figures would come out, and serve as illustrations to the tales that I told Denys. After I had looked at it for a long time, I folded it up and packed it in a case, wherein the figures might all have a rest for the time being.

Out of Africa

Just as Dinesen imagines her colonial farm, seen "from the air," as a series of cartographic "figures" inscribed on the vast African landscape (7), so *Out of Africa* repeatedly connects its visions of cultural macrostructures—imperialism, race, and gender—to the microstructures of its own textuality, its own linguistic "figures." The text explores thereby the paradox at the heart of representation: that language is at once an instrument of power and the ultimate sign of powerlessness and loss. No more stable than the wavering mirages of memory it would hold fast, its shifting tropes and discontinuous structures constantly carry the narrator away from, even as they gesture toward, that which she desires. The summary of her final departure from Ngong which closes the book might also be read as a retrospective gloss on the futility of the quasi-imperialist effort to recapture Africa in words: "It was not I who was going away . . . but it was the country that was slowly and gravely withdrawing from me, like the sea at ebb-tide" (381). It is no coincidence that at or near the end of each of the book's five sections Dinesen introduces images of untranslatable inscriptions, making writing the representative figure for all the other forms of displacement and transport the text elaborates.[29] Here I want to consider the unfolding of that configuration in part 1 of the text, where Dinesen at once establishes the significance of the trope and prefigures later appearances throughout the book.

The topographical inscriptions—marks, tracks, signs, lines, and "figures"—that pervade the initial descriptions of Africa (1–16) culminate, at the end of chapter 1, in the explicit identification of the "experience" of Africa itself as a function of writing (21), a parallel reinforced at the beginning of chapter 2 by references to the notion of God as a kind of divine author: "When the Africans speak of the personality of God they speak like the Arabian Nights or like the last chapters of the book of Job;

it is . . . the infinite power of the imagination with which they are im-
pressed" (23). These brief figurations are echoed and elaborated in the
narrator's extended description of her own writing, "imagination" becoming her escape from a time of "drought" that simultaneously turns
the farm into a wasteland and imperils the "self" dependent on it: "I was
young, and by instinct of self-preservation, I had to collect my energy
on something, if I were not to be whirled away with the dust of the
farm-roads, or the smoke on the plain. I began in the evenings to write
stories. . . . At first I wrote in the evenings only, but later on I often sat
down to write in the mornings as well, when I ought to have been out on
the farm" (44–45). Thus farming and writing become interchangeable—
a homology underscored by the Kikuyus' view of the interrelatedness of
the two projects: "When I told them I was trying to write a book, they
looked upon it as a last attempt to save the farm" (45).

But this writing is no more secure than the farm for which it substitutes, as Dinesen suggests in subsequent descriptions of Kamante's
veiled "scorn" for her authorial enterprise:

> "Msabu," he said, "do you believe yourself that you can write a
> book?" I answered that I did not know. . . . Kamante now made . . .
> a long pause, and then said, "I do not believe it." . . . [H]e stood
> with the Odyssey itself behind his back, and here he laid it on the
> table. "Look, Msabu," he said, "this is a good book. It hangs to-
> gether from the one end to the other. . . . [I]t does not come to
> pieces. . . . But what you write . . . is some here and some there. . . .
> [I]t blows about, even down on the floor. . . . It will not be a good
> book." (47–48)

The passage, which, as I suggested in chapter 5, situates Dinesen's own
authorial difference from the authoritative patriarchal literary tradition
epitomized by Homer, unfolds an alternative notion of narrative—conceived not in phallic terms as "hard" and "heavy," a monumental construct that "hangs together" in solid and unchanging form, but as a kind
of radical dispersal: "scattered," disorderly leaves and leavings (48), fragmentary and shifting, open to infinite rearrangement. Yet paradoxically, it
is through this fluid, discontinuous series of inscriptions that the narrator
reclaims herself, prefiguring the writing of the very book we read.

The same paradoxical dispersal and reclamation characterize the
reflexive elegiac passages that conclude "Kamante and Lulu." Here "Africa" becomes an uncertain, ever-receding image like the wavering "shadows" that the narrator imagines Lulu remembering as the only remnants
of her days on the farm (79):

> These communications from Africa come to me in a strange, unreal
> way, and are more like shadows or mirages, than like news of reality.

For Kamante cannot write, and he does not know English. When he or my other people take it into their heads to send me their tidings, they go to one of the professional . . . letter writers, who are sitting with their writing desk, paper, a pen and ink, outside the Post Offices, and explain to them what shall be in the letter. The professional writers do not know much English either, . . . but . . . they enrich the letters with a number of flourishes, which makes them difficult to decipher. They have also a habit of writing the letters in three or four different kinds of ink. . . . From all these efforts come the sort of messages that people got from the Oracle at Delphi. There is a depth in the letters . . . , you feel that there is some vital communication which has been heavy on the heart of the sender, . . . But it is wrapped in darkness. The cheap and dirty little sheet of paper that, when it comes to you, has travelled many thousand miles, seems to speak and speak, even to scream at you, but it tells you nothing at all. (79–80)

This process of multiple dislocation is intensified by reiteration: Kamante "puts three or four letters into the same envelope, and has them marked, *1st Letter, 2nd Letter,* and so on. They all contain the same things, repeated over and over." Such mutually displacing repetitions produce not clarification but the breakdown of "communication" (80), promising a plenitude of meaning that amounts to "nothing." As a disjunctive series of palimpsests, the indecipherable traces of a lost presence, these letters become figures of the text that in its turn repeats them, underscoring the futility of the narrator's own project of capturing "Africa" in words.

Yet in the very process of loss and dispersal, a new perspective is engendered:

Kamante writes that he has been out of work for a long time. . . . I was not surprised, for . . . I had educated a Royal Cook and left him in a new Colony. It was with him a case of "Open Sesame." Now the word had been lost, and the stone has closed for good round the mystic treasures that it had in it. Where the great Chef walked in deep thought, full of knowledge, nobody sees anything but a little bandy-legged Kikuyu, a dwarf with a flat, still face. (80–81)

Representing Kamante as a kind of hermetic text like his letters, Dinesen also effects a subtle reversal, for here it is those who experience his material presence who fail to interpret him aright, while those who perceive him specifically *as writing* are able to decipher his secret "word": "What has Kamante got to say . . . ? The lines are crooked and there is no order in the phrases of the letter. But Kamante had in him a greatness of soul of which the people who knew him will still hear the cracked and disordered music" (81). It is this ineffable "greatness" that has the power to overflow the finite "lines" in which it is inscribed, effecting a transformation of the reader's consciousness:

> "Write and tell us if you turn. We think you turn. Because why? We think that you shall never can forget us. Because why? We think that you remembered still all our face and our mother names."
>
> A white man . . . would write: "I never can forget you." The African says: "We do not think of you, that you can ever forget us." (81)

In the tropes of *Out of Africa*—those linguistic "turn[s]" through which Dinesen makes the "[re]turn" to Africa here anticipated—another sort of "turn" occurs as well. So far from sanctioning the Eurocentric perspective—what "a white man . . . would say"—this reversal explicitly denies its hegemonic claim to centrality and dominance. Dinesen suggests that in writing her book, *re-membering* the dispersed fragments and the "mother name," she herself becomes not so much a controlling author(ity) as a written text, an extension and fulfillment of Kamante's complex inscriptions.

In subsequent sections I shall myself "turn" again to the paradoxical representations of writing in *Out of Africa,* but first I wish to take up an issue inseparable from that problematic: the question of reading. It is an issue suggested, most immediately, by the forms of reductive *misreading* Dinesen criticizes in her description of Kamante as a "mystic" text whose "great spirit" is incomprehensible to the narrow optics of the colonial eye, which sees him as nothing but a "bandy-legged . . . dwarf." Recasting Said's use of "orientalism" as a rubric for the constricting mystique projected by colonialist discourses onto whatever imperially constructed Other they would dominate, I would suggest that Dinesen's repeated interrogation and disruption of the Eurocentric perspective, as of the notions of subjectivity and textuality that underwrite it, might be seen as a calculated project of *disorientation*.

5. DISORIENTING READING

> As things began to be systematically organized . . . , my expedition, I believe, was found to be somewhat irregular.
>
> *Out of Africa*

The transgression of literary boundaries—moments when structures are shaken, when language refuses to lie down meekly, or the marginal is brought into sudden focus, or intelligibility itself refused—reveal not only the conditions of possibility with which women's writing exists, but what it would be like to revolu-

tionize them. . . . [A] refusal of mastery, an opting for rupture
and possibility, . . . can in itself make women's writing a challenge to the literary structures it necessarily inhabits.

Mary Jacobus, Reading Woman

Insofar as the reader identifies with the Anglo-European perspective, one
of the crucial projects of *Out of Africa* is to disrupt our ordinary ways
of seeing and reading, a progressive estrangement inseparable from the
text's exploration of its own problematic position in relation to the colonialist, phallocentric frame of reference. Like the "loomings and mirages" of air that "vibrates . . . and creates vast silvery expanses of water
in the dry grass," the miragelike fabrications of the text establish a figural
matrix "very difficult to judge," setting up structures by which "you are
continually deceived" and thereby revealing the inadequacy of ordinary
interpretive perspectives (312–13). This distinctive reading effect is inseparable from the thematics of possession and dispossession the text
elaborates. As with the disorienting process through which the protagonist is forced to regard Africa ("it was not I that was going away, . . .
but . . . the country that was . . . withdrawing from me"), so the reader
comes to regard *Out of Africa*.

The European or American reader who takes up this book is likely to
be struck by the sense of having experienced at once a shaped, coherent,
and fulfilling whole and, simultaneously, a kind of *bricolage*—fragmentary, heterogeneous, almost random. Situated between the discourses of
history and myth, fact and fiction, prose and poetry; partaking gener-
ically of forms as diverse as pastoral elegy, classical tragedy, autobiography, memoir, and travel tale; compounded of narrative, philosophical
speculation, aphorism, parabolic reflection, and song, *Out of Africa* eludes
all single, unitary classifications. But if its internal contradictions and discontinuities are disconcerting (as repeated critical efforts to locate its
organizing principle or generic affiliations suggest[30]), we might look not
to the unassimilable structures of the narrative itself but to our own conventional approaches to what, in several senses, might be called its decided disorder. The text forces a radical transformation of perspective by
repeatedly calling into question not only conceptions of the unitary self
or of "Africa" as a unified, monolithic construct but also conventions of
reading that depend on a traditional notion of the book as a figure of solidity, unity, linearity, and integrity. One recalls, in contrast, the author's
"scattered" pages, "some here and some there," like the "leaves" of dismantled patriarchal texts which the monkey scatters over the "black and
white" squares of the library in *Seven Gothic Tales*. Kamante's concern
that what she writes "will not be a good book" is also prophetic of later
readerly consternation about *Out of Africa*.

In interrogating such conventions, obliquely representing itself as a
wild disarray of fragments, *Out of Africa* establishes a parallel between the
reader's attempts to comprehend its textual disunities and the attempts of
the protagonist to maintain the plots "laid out according to rule" (7)
which she has shaped upon the "the wildness and irregularity" of the African continent. In seeking to tame the "irregularity" of *Out of Africa,* the
Anglo-European reader comes to realize, like the protagonist, "how
keenly the human mind"—at least the imperializing Eurocentric human
mind, shaped by a rationalist epistemological tradition—"yearns for
geometrical figures" (7). The readerly quest for an organizing principle
replicates the colonizing impulse, which would make roads in a wild land
and divide it into farms or suburbs, take free, diverse, and independent
peoples and reduce them to "squatters" and servants. The logical extreme of that impulse is satirized in the absurd arrogance of figures like
Augustus von Schimmelman, who cannot imagine the significance of
wild animals unless they are "seen" and named by the European, translated into nothing more than a reflection of "his own mind":

> "It is a curious thing," said Count Schimmelman . . . "to realize that
> so many hundred and indeed thousands of Hyenas should have lived
> and died, in order that we should, in the end, get this one species
> here, so that people in Hamburg shall be able to know what a Hyena
> is like, and the naturalists to study them. . . . The wild animals . . .
> which run in a wild landscape, do not really exist. This one, now,
> exists, we have got a name for it, and we know what it is like. The
> others might as well not have been." (301–2)

We have seen that in the very process of writing Dinesen suggests
that to *recapture* Africa, to hold it fast in words with a permanence denied
in life, is finally as hopeless a quest as the effort to capture or cage the
wild animals that roam its vast terrain: once shot or trapped they become,
however beautiful, merely remains, traces of what the hunter hunted.
"Hunters," as she wryly observes, "cannot have their own way" (16).[31]
The same is true for the process of reading. Disclosing the futility of her
effort to have "a farm in Africa," Dinesen also insists on the necessary
relinquishment of the desire to control, order, and shape within our own
constructs an Other being that ultimately must elude "regularity" and
"systematization" (24). Like the protagonist in her traversals of Africa,
what the reader learns in traversing Africa-as-text is that those neatly
plotted "geometric figures" for which the narrator initially invites our
admiration are impermanent, fleeting things, the temporary imposition
of shape, certainty, and bounds on that which is properly boundless—an
artificial cultivation of that which forever returns to "wildness," defying

conventional designs. As Karen Blixen observed, "this country is outside the normal bounds of law and order" (*LA,* 290).

If, then, there is a "shape" to be found, framed, or named in *Out of Africa,* we might expect it to be similarly contingent. Here Dinesen's analogies of the narrative to dream or primary myth are illuminating.[32] As in dreams (or in other modernist texts), even its linear, diachronic narratives are subsumed within the discontinuous form of the whole. We can, of course, attain a kind of overview—"Africa seen as from the air"—if we distance ourselves sufficiently from the book's linguistic intricacies. Given a certain remove, we can locate a "plot" (and subplots) much as the protagonist, from the air, sees with sharp clarity the discrete "figures" that make up her plantation. That plot, as we have seen, follows the same line of possession and dispossession that subtends the narrative's varied themes and tropes. Reduced to its starkest form, it is encompassed by the opening sentence of the book.

Similarly, we can discover certain generic affiliations that connect the disparate parts. Following another of Dinesen's figures, we might read *Out of Africa* as a kind of "five-act tragedy" (276), as some Danish critics have done.[33] Dinesen also obliquely suggests its affinity with various musical forms, such as symphonies or fugues (18–21, 276). Yet again, it might be construed as a version of pastoral—in Langbaum's memorable phrase, "the best prose pastoral of our time."[34] In this mode it recalls most explicitly the patterns of pastoral elegy, that quintessential conflation of writing and mourning, complete with the trajectory of grieving which that genre describes and the traditional conventions it developed, from Theocritus and Virgil through Milton's "Lycidas" and Shelley's "Adonais."[35] Dinesen provides ample allusions to support such readings—for example, the narrator's repeated comparison of herself to King Lear in the first instance, or, in the last, the trope of nature's share in the author-speaker's grief, figured climactically by the appearance of the lions on Denys Finch Hatton's grave (360–61). Epitomizing the fusion of Karen Blixen's passion for Africa, her love for Finch Hatton, and her own totemic appellation "Lioness," those splendid beasts come not only out of the Ngong highlands but also directly out of Theocritus's first Idyll, which she and Finch Hatton had read together: "When Daphnis died, the lions of the forest wept."[36]

To say that *Out of Africa* resembles a dream text, then, is not to assert its formlessness but rather to suggest that as with dreams, whatever form we find there may be one that we ourselves belatedly impose. As Dinesen remarks in analogizing dreams and works of art, "If remembered in the daytime they will fade and lose their sense, because they belong to a different plane" (87). Since oneiric figurations exceed or transgress the ordinary structures of logic and traditional genre, to attempt interpretive closure is inevitably to misread: "It is when one begins to lose the consciousness of freedom, and when the idea of necessity enters, . . . that the dream is declining" (88). Thus, even as we track certain generic resemblances that seem to unite the textual fragments into a pattern, we soon discover that all such traces tend to stray off in different, often contradictory, directions, like "the grotesque humorous fantasy" Dinesen describes the Africans deploying when, in the face of the insistent interrogations of European colonists, they sought "to lead us on the wrong track" through the "art of mimicry" (18–19). As with the relation of colonist to African, no sooner has one made certain connections and constructed a reading grounded on them than one realizes how persistently the text escapes those constructions, subverts and even mocks them, putting into question both traditional generic categories and the readerly desire (the product, like the farm, of European "cultivation") to subject the book to the law of genre and orderly structure. One of the most powerful effects the narrative engenders is the tension in the reader (as in the narrator) between the urge to name and know—to find order in or make order out of Africa—and the recognition of how persistently it eludes that control. If our critical efforts reenact the narrator's efforts to make plots out of Africa, text or territory, we discover that the narrative ultimately remains as unmasterable as Africa itself. As with Africans, so with the book-as-Africa: no more than the colonists can we finally "know its real nature" or subject it to hermeneutic mastery (21, 18). In both cases, in the very act of reading we come to understand Dinesen's insistence on the necessary simultaneity of love and loss, on the possibility of "having" only by letting go.

Thus if on one level both the inscription and the reading of *Out of Africa* repeat the colonizing gesture, seeking to capture "Africa" in language, on other levels the text is most powerful precisely in the way it reveals Africa—and itself as "Africa" in words—to be always slipping from the grasp, always existing as/in *excess* of what finite human schemes, both colonial and critical, can contain. "Nature," as Dinesen has Schimmelman remark uncomprehendingly, "is extravagant." In every sense, the text declares that if we would begin to comprehend Africa, we, like the protagonist, must also leave the "roads" constructed by hegemonic European systems (268). As in her flights over Africa, we too must become "free of the ground" of received Eurocentric ontologies and epistemologies (238). Dinesen suggests that the more elevated one's vision, the more liberated one becomes from "laws," the more all conventional plots and "lines" (238)—of land, of the territoriality such shapes signify, or of traditional textuality—evaporate into what, in her letters, she called "the great wide open spaces" that always surround and (temporarily) permit those finite structures.[37] Like her contemporary Virginia Woolf in *A Room of One's Own*, she deplored those "rules" of civilization by which "one was forbidden to walk on the grass," celebrating instead that "writing . . . where no rules are enforced, where everything is permissable" (*LA*, 16, 235).[38]

The very indeterminacy and instability of *Out of Africa*—its refusal and ungrounding of our territorializing efforts to name or tame it—invite us to read ourselves differently as well, seeking not to master but in effect to merge with, submerge ourselves in the narrative as the narrator sought to submerge herself in the life of Africa, to become "like fishes in deep water who for the life of them cannot understand [the] fear of drowning" (19). Just as the protagonist was forced to relinquish her own proprietary relation to the land, so the reader, in relinquishing a single fixed position with regard to *Out of Africa,* also loses the critic's usual secure, proprietary placement as the one who names and claims the text. In a sense, of course, all reading immerses us thus; as we have seen, in "The Diver" Dinesen would use the same figure of immersion and self-abandonment to suggest how we may begin to fathom "poet's tales." But she makes that reading effect even more radical in this, her greatest narrative. Like the "luminous tail" of the iguana, which fades and falls inert when "the live impetuous blood" ceases "pulsating," so the luminous tale that is *Out of Africa* ultimately eludes our best critical marksmanship.

This elusiveness is inseparable from questions of gender. As Dinesen suggests in *Seven Gothic Tales,* the concept of reading as an attempt to lay bare, penetrate, and possess a text is radically inflected by ideologies of sexual difference that encode "man" as desiring agent, "woman" as passive object. In *Out of Africa,* by undermining laws of genre based on such concepts of critical mastery, Dinesen implicitly undermines laws of gender as well. Just as the concept of genre is revealed as a contingent, shifting term, so the essentialist hierarchized opposition "man/woman" which underwrites Western ontologies is represented as problematic rather than self-evident, mutable rather than permanent and universal. Mary Jacobus has observed that "if there is no literal referent to start with, no identity or essence," if "the production of sexual difference can be viewed as textual, like the production of meaning," then "[r]eading woman becomes a form of autobiography or self-constitution that is finally indistinguishable from writing (woman)."[39] This formulation illuminates the relation between Dinesen's simultaneous destabilization of the "self," the text, and the reader, revealing the question of woman as crucial to all the other critical questions her autobiographical narrative raises. By underscoring the inseparability of the politics and poetics of colonialism, writing, and reading from the politics and poetics of gender, Dinesen suggests that the project of changing the subject is particularly crucial when the "subject" is woman.[40]

6. Engendering Africa: Woman and the Wild

The "dark continent" trick has been pulled on her: she has been kept at a distance from herself. . . . She can be incarcerated . . . and tricked into apartheid . . . , but only for a time. One can teach her, as soon as she begins to speak . . . that hers is the dark region: because you are Africa, you are black. Your continent is dark. Dark is dangerous. . . . Don't move, you might fall. Above all, don't go into the forest. . . . *The "Dark Continent" is neither dark nor unexplorable:* It is still unexplored only because we have been made to believe that it was too dark to be explored.

Hélène Cixous, "Sorties"

In "From an Immigrant's Notebook" Dinesen describes "the Concentration Camp for the white women" devised during World War I by colonial authorities who "believed" that in the absence of white male guardians the "ladies" would "be exposed to danger from the Natives" (266). As a synecdoche of female confinement, rationalized in the name of a protective chivalry that reads woman as the property of man, this design is inseparable from the xenophobic ideology of colonialism: the camp concentrates not only "white women" but also white men's anxieties about both gender and race. Perceiving such enclosure(s) as annihilation ("I would die"), the narrator takes flight. Assuming a place explicitly designated as that of "a white man," she leads a safari to deliver "provisions and ammunition" to British and Swedish troops (266). Consequently she becomes, both literally and symbolically, an agent of transport. Her blissful wanderings off the beaten track lead to one of the climactic epiphanies in *Out of Africa,* a fusion of woman and wilderness that reclaims that age-old patriarchal *topos* as a figure for Dinesen's own ecstatic transformation: "The grass was me, and the air, the distant invisible mountains were me, the tired oxen were me. I breathed with the slight night-wind in the thorn trees"—an *inspiration,* quite literally, engendered by the release from confinement within patriarchal structures (272).

This narrative might serve as a figure for the examination of traditional gender structures throughout the text. In representing herself as both "woman farmer" and "master," "husbandman" of the land, Dinesen recalls those letters to Ingeborg Dinesen in which, in a dazzling series of subjective shifts, she wrote herself as both daughter and "husband" to her mother. If, like Adam in the Garden, she must labor to make her plots of maternalized earth bring forth fruit, she also represents herself as maternal, nurturant, and earthy (e.g., 31, 212–27, 371–72), a transgressive androgynous figure as "wild" and "irregular" as the land (7, 16, 272). If she is a kind of sister to Ingrid Lindstrom (208–9), she also becomes "a brother" to Old Knudsen (195). If, as "settler," she reenacts a masculine role, she is also, as an independent woman, an *unsettling* figure in what Elspeth Huxley, echoing a key imperialist trope, called "White Man's Country."[41] By moving freely among diverse subject positions, Dinesen implicitly questions not only those signifying codes that would write "native" and "colonist," "I" and "Africa," as undifferentiated, absolute, and fixed, but also those codes that would sustain the hierarchical division between "man" and "woman."

Yet simultaneously, *Out of Africa* also calls attention to the importance of woman's difference in and from a world still dominated by white men. The multiplicity and "play" (16) with which Dinesen contests dominant gender ideologies recall representations of the feminine in her other narratives. In this context, the "great wide open spaces" of Africa become homologies of the subversive spaces of language wherein woman might write—and right—herself, eluding the symbolic order that would confine her (*LA,* 18, 235). We have seen in earlier chapters the significance of Dinesen's sense of kinship with African women, adepts at the art of illusion and elusiveness, from whom she learned the power of women's strategies for dealing with subordination and oppression. In *Out of Africa* she repeatedly celebrates their strength and dauntlessness in the face of astonishing adversity—a complex spirit of affirmation which she herself seeks to emulate: "They have mixed blood with Fate, and recognize her irony, wherever they meet it, with sympathy, as if it were that of a sister" (34):

> [T]hey were wilder than the men. . . . They had borne a number of children and had seen many of them die; they were afraid of nothing. They carried loads of firewood . . . of three hundred pounds, tottering below them, but unsubdued. . . . And they had a stock of energy in them still; they radiated vitality. This strength, and love of life in them, to me seemed not only highly respectable, but glorious and bewitching. (383–84)

We know that she also discovered in them a model for her own engendering of narrative—the indirection and ironic *mimétisme* which, like the Somali women's subversive storytelling, outwardly conforms to masculinist culture and literary conventions, but communicates, to those who have ears to hear, a different message (178–80). And "the traces" of these women's "many laughters," spreading like "ripples of water," "rising" and breaking like a "clear tide" (*SG*, 102; cf. *OA*, 12, 179)—those "cascades of mirth" that overflowed patriarchal and colonialist confinements (*OA*, 34)—prefigured the laughter that echoes in her pseudonym.

The import of these diverse associations is suggested in the book's final moments, as the narrator, increasingly confronting the pressures of history, also makes increasingly explicit her connection with other female figures: "The people of the farm who grieved most at my departure were I think the old women . . . [with whom] I had always been friends" (383–84). These passages are contextualized by the revisionist treatment of the myth of the Fall that immediately precedes them. It is one of the climactic moments of the book, brilliantly interweaving the figures of farming, writing, and reading within the matrix of sexual difference. Here, Dinesen suggests that what had begun as an Adamic project of possession via nomination ends as a feminine counter-Genesis wherein the act of naming becomes not a mark of ownership and control but a record of dispossession whose very sign is a process of *unwording*:

> Ingrid understood . . . with something of the strength of the elements themselves, what it is really like, when a woman farmer has to give up her farm, and leave it. . . . We walked together from the one thing on the farm to the other, naming them as we passed them, one by one, as if we were taking mental stock of my loss, or . . . collecting material for a book of complaints to be laid before destiny. Ingrid knew well . . . that there is no such book, but all the same the idea of it forms part of the livelihood of women. We went down to the oxen's boma, and sat on the fence, counting the oxen as they came in. Without words I pointed them out to Ingrid. "These oxen," and without words she responded: "yes, these oxen," and recorded them in her book. We went round to the stables to feed the horses with sugar, and when they had finished it, I stretched out my sticky and be-slabbered palms, presenting them to Ingrid and crying, "These horses." Ingrid sighed back laboriously, "Yes, these horses," and noted them down. In my garden . . . she could not reconcile herself to the idea that I must leave. . . . In spite of our old khaki coats and trousers, we were in reality a pair of mythical women. (371–72)

As a text at once palpable and persistently self-deconstructive, the lingering linguistic trace of a world "without words," *Out of Africa* is itself the paradoxical woman's "book" this passage reflexively describes. Like Cixous revising Freud's figure of woman as the "dark continent" of the phallocentric symbolic order, Dinesen suggests that woman's writing, figuratively inscribed in invisible "white ink" or situated in the gaps and margins of patriarchal language, makes her doubly parallel to the figure of Africa as constituted by the imperialist imagination. Both Africa and woman have traditionally figured as the *terra incognita* on which white man could inscribe the signs of his own sovereignty.[42] In *Out of Africa,* as in the later "Blank Page," Dinesen plays on the cartographic conventions whereby European maps traditionally represented the African continent as blank space, source of endless speculations in both senses of the term.[43] She too evokes Africa's—and woman's—ineffable otherness, difference, mystery, and consequent inexhaustible power to engender narrative. But she also reclaims those "blank," "wild" spaces by suggesting the subjectivity and generative power that lies behind or within them.

This process is epitomized in the concluding narrative of "From an Immigrant's Notebook," the tale of a young Danish sailor's *unheimlich* encounter, in "a brothel in Singapore," with "an old Chinese woman" and her parrot, given to her years before by her "high-born English lover": "It could say various sentences in the languages of all the world. . . . But one phrase the old Chinawoman's lover had taught it before he sent it to her, and that she did not understand, neither had any visitor ever been able to tell her what it meant." Asking the boy whether "he could interpret the phrase to her," she makes "the parrot speak its sentence." The boy, seized with uncanny awe of "that terrible beak," recognizes the "classic Greek" of "a verse from Sappho":

"The moon has sunk and the Pleiads,
And midnight is gone,
And the hours are passing, passing,
And I lie alone."

Upon hearing his translation, "the old woman . . . asked him to say it again, and nodded her head" (315–16).

The parable of Sappho's lost "sentence" and dispersed, fragmentary, untranslatable texts—figures for the fragmentations and dispersals of the book that names them, for the losses of the woman author who here implicitly invokes Sappho as literary foremother, and for the unwritten "book of the complaints of women" these allusions prefigure—stunningly reiterates the problematic of love and loss to which Dinesen repeatedly returns.[44] On one level, as the parable implies, the lost connection with the motherland recorded in *Out of Africa* figures a prior lost connection with the mother, every child's first object of desire "once upon a time and in the beginning."[45] The text vividly evokes that irrecoverable wholeness which is remembered, when it is remembered at all, only as uncanny *frisson* or as those vague longings that engender the age-old human dream of a lost or future paradise, of which all other loves are but the shadows. In this context *Out of Africa* surely achieves part of its haunting power by re-presenting that primal separation that constitutes "selfhood" as a condition of insatiable desire, the price of *being in lan-*

guage, which perpetually displaces what it would "translate." It is not surprising, then, that "Africa," like the uncanny "mother" to whom Dinesen repeatedly analogized it, is always the name of something Other: the untranslatable, the unspeakable, the unwritable—a text "without words" (371). As she suggests in the passages on the Somali women's narrations, "God"—that name for irretrievable wholeness and plenitude—*was first Mother,* in both senses of the phrase: "that mighty female deity who had existed in old ages, before the time of the Prophet's God" (180). In Dinesen's remythologization, to go "out of Africa" means also to leave "Her," to undergo a reluctant birth that is also a death(ly) "sentence"—to be propelled into the world of time, alienation and mortality, where language is inseparable from loss.[46]

Yet on another level, as the narratives of the Somali women and of Sappho also suggest, *Out of Africa* provides an alternative vision of language whereby the very act of wording becomes a restoration of life and generativity—"like rain" (277). For Dinesen's narrative offers a return to the lost mother/land via the magic words of that unwritten "book of . . . women" which, presented as a seemingly impossible dream, in fact prefigures the very text that describes it. If Dinesen, anticipating Cixous's revision of Freud, affirmed that "love is a yearning for a country . . . where everyone dwelt 'once upon a time and in the beginning,'" and identified that paradisial "place" with the topography of "the maternal body," that other primal "landscape that has not its like in all the world," she would also, like Cixous, celebrate the possibility of joyous reunion, enabled through a transformative "new" language (238): the maternal "voice" that she associated with Africa and with her own writing of it (*LA,* 60, *OA,* 78).

7. "THE WORLD OF THE WRITTEN WORD": REDEEMING LANGUAGE

All the country was in it, good omens, old covenants, a song.
Out of Africa

The import of such regenerative narration is elaborated in the brilliant story of Jogona Kanyagga with which Dinesen concludes part 2. Made up of the raw stuff of history, the shooting accident with the "master's gun" that left one child dead, another hideously disfigured, and a third in permanent exile, the account becomes one of Dinesen's most complex parables of the paradox of writing—"the world of the written word" (121)—as simultaneously alienating, corrupting, and redemptive.

The death of Jogona's son Wamai and the consequent likelihood of compensatory blood money sparks a dispute over the boy's "legitimate" origins and the forms of remuneration that genealogy might justify. Jogona, out of friendship to the child's father Waweru, had upon his death married Wamai's mother and adopted the fatherless boy, becoming so attached to him that "it appeared that he had . . . forgotten that the child whom he had now lost had not been his own." But "Three old Kikuyu from Nyeri . . . had arrived . . . to plead that Wamai was not the son of Jogona but was their late brother's son, and that therefore the compensation for his death should lawfully fall to them." It is in this disputatious context of word against word, line against line—both genealogically and linguistically—that Jogona asks the narrator "to write down for him the account of his relations to the dead child and his family."

The subsequent creation of this text becomes not only a recapitulation of all those ambiguous self-creations *Out of Africa* records but a reflexive parable of the book's own inscription:

> Jogona's very simple manner was impressive because he felt so strongly about things, and was entirely without self-consciousness. It was evident that he [saw] . . . his present resolution as . . . a great enterprise, which was not without danger; he went to it with awe. I wrote his statement down for him . . . a long report of events more than six years old, and in themselves extremely complicated. Jogona, as he was going through it, continually had to break off his tale . . . to go back in it and reconstruct it. (118)

Like the text that describes it, this narrative is a product of multiple displacements. A complex, laborious "reconstruction" that distances and distorts events even as it seeks to reproduce them, it creates a "maze," "difficult to recollect" and "extremely difficult to follow." As an autobiographical "document" which seeks to found the "self" as a locus of (paternal) truth, it is also, paradoxically, the product of plural fabrications which, by transforming that self into a textual construct, threaten the very stability of what they claim to underwrite. Initially distanced from its source by the inscriptions of memory, the story is further dislocated by being translated from Jogona's native Kikuyu into Swaheli, then by its transition from spoken to written word, a process additionally complicated by the interventions of colonialism: for Kikuyu and Swaheli "had no written language until white people took upon themselves to make one up." This process of plural translation/colonization culminates in the text of *Out of Africa* itself, where Jogona's story appears in English, to be further translated by the reader's interpretation.[47]

On one level, this proliferating inscription might be read as a process of corruption in several senses. One might argue, for example, that in producing the final document for general circulation, Jogona falls from

innocence into "self-consciousness," literally *turning himself to account*—
autobiography as a form of debased currency—in order to profit from
the exchange of blood money generated by Wamai's corpse. To enter into
such commerce is also to become, like the corpse, a kind of dead letter: to
undergo a symbolic death by translating one's "self" into textual *corpus*—
a linguistic construct cut off from its origins like the orphaned child
whose body is the emptied center of the war of words that elicits the account. Significantly, "translation" means not only "a rendering from one
language or representational system into another" but also "a transfer of
property" and "the movement of a body from one place to another."[48] In
this sense, the entry into the "world of the written word"—whether
Jogona's or Isak Dinesen's in *Out of Africa*—would appear no more than a
function of the degradations wrought by the imperialist mentality.

Yet to read thus is to miss the import of Dinesen's tone and metaphoric structure. For she also figures Jogona's text as the locus of rebirth,
a reclaiming of both the orphaned child whom Jogona had loved as his
own son and of the parent who has been severed from that connection. It
is a transformation which occurs, significantly, via a process of feminization: a move from the questions of paternity to the issue of maternity,
from the impositions of law to the engendering of narrative. Telling his
story, Jogona "leaned his face against the wall as the Kikuyu women do
when they are giving birth to their children," a symbolic gestation and
labor that produces a magnificent birth in the process of writing and
reading that recreates his narrative:

> He turned away from me while I was reading, as if to avoid all
> distractions.
> But as I read out his own name, "And he sent for Jogona
> Kanyagga, who was his friend and who lived not far away," he swiftly
> turned his face to me, and gave me a great fierce flaming glance, so
> exuberant with laughter that it changed the old man into a boy, into
> the very symbol of youth.
> Such a glance did Adam give the Lord when He formed him out
> of the dust, and breathed into his nostrils the breath of life, and man
> became a living soul. I had created him and shown him himself:
> Jogona Kanyagga of life everlasting. When I handed him the paper, he
> took it reverently and greedily, folded it up in a corner of his cloak and
> kept his hand upon it. He could not afford to lose it, for his soul was in
> it, and it was proof of his existence. Here was something which Jogona
> Kenyagga had performed, and which would preserve his name for-
> ever: the flesh was made word and dwelt among us full of grace and
> truth. (120–21)

Here orphaned words become the medium by which the self is reborn,
reclaimed, and renamed through a process, both literal and linguistic, of

trans-figuration. And if the author's analogy of herself as God to Jogona's Adam appears merely an arrogant imperialist gesture, we do well to look more closely. For Dinesen suggests that the process of creation works both ways at once. Jogona too is represented as an author. Indeed, in laboring to give birth to his story, for which the narrator is only a kind of midwife, he also provides her with a story to tell, thus bringing about *her* birth as an author and permitting the making of *her* name. In both cases, the creation of his autobiographical narrative prefigures and enables, even as it inhabits, her own. As the text implies, both "Jogona Kanyagga" and "Isak Dinesen" continue to exist only in/as literary constructs. Through their interdependent inscriptions, engendered from disfiguration, orphanage, and death, both authors are both into "life everlasting": "the flesh . . . made word."

As the narrator remarks in reflecting on this event, in Africa "the effect of a piece of news was many times magnified when it was imparted in writing" (123). Like *Out of Africa,* such a text "carried more weight than the ark with the animals in it; it carried a new green world" (122). Thus Jogona's narrative becomes to him, in every sense of Dinesen's punning tautology, "the scriptural word." Regarding it as a "great treasure" with talismanic power, he "made a little leather bag for it, embroidered with beads, and hung it on a strap round his neck," requesting that it be read again to him "from time to time." And "at each reading his face took on the same impress of deep religious triumph":

> The importance of the account was not lessened but augmented with time, as if to Jogona the greatest wonder about it was that it did not change. The past, that had been so difficult to bring to memory, and that had probably seemed to be changing every time it was thought of, had here been caught, conquered, and pinned down before his eyes. It had become History; with it there was now no variableness neither shadow of turning. (124)

While this notion of "History" seems to signify some absolute fixation, casting the written text as an immutable, eternal object, both the tone and the larger context of the passage indicate a more complicated view. As Dinesen would assert in *Shadows on the Grass,* all narrative exists in a state of perpetual flux because "the changes in the world" continually transform the discursive matrices within which it is read. In an ironic self-revision, she underscores that instability by explicitly rewriting the passage above, representing *Out of Africa* itself as a text unmoored by such transitions: "I realized to what extent my own book about Africa *had become history,* as much out of date as a papyrus from a pyramid" (*SG,* 140; my emphasis).

Yet as the Jogona narrative also implies, even in the process of losing

Africa and of making us reenact that loss as the condition of reading the book, Dinesen has caught it as well, not in the sense of achieving some stable, absolute control but in the same ambiguous way that Jogona "caught" both his lost child and himself: through a fragile web of words that reveal "death" as a paradoxical opening to new life, narratives continually revived in the perpetual simultaneity of permanence and change. The passage becomes a paradigm of the book that rewrites it. For *Out of Africa* repeatedly celebrates the act of loving—a child, a land, a people, a lover, a text—not as a form of possession but as an expression of largesse and release, the "liberation" that comes from what Dinesen elsewhere called "the will to sacrifice," "the supreme triumph of Unconditional Surrender" (*Essays,* 55; *SG,* 111). Like her contemporary Marcel Mauss in his groundbreaking study of gift exchange, Dinesen suggests that those who are reckoned richest are those who give most away; paradoxically, being beggared is the surest sign of wealth.[49] Reflecting on this paradox in *Shadows on the Grass,* she would extol "those free forces [that] have set us free as the mountain winds": "Each of their boons to us is a gift, baksheesh, and their highest gift is inspiration" (111). *Out of Africa* enacts that insight, revealing how loss and self-dispersal offer the greatest gain: a radical transformation of subjectivity and what, describing "the grave in the hills," Dinesen called "an infinitely great view" (353).

Her understanding of this "infinite freedom" of imagination (89) is also informed and complicated by a recognition of the telling implications of sexual difference for the one who loves and loses. As she observes in *Out of Africa,* radical *dépense* is particularly familiar to women, adepts in the art of giving and in the festive freedom and "laughter" that can issue therefrom (372, 383–84). The *jouissance* and "new words" that Dinesen associates with her own discovery of such prodigal expenditure prefigure Cixous's lyric celebration of woman, who gives "with open hands" and "takes pleasure in being boundless, outside self, outside same, far from a 'center,' from any capital of her 'dark continent.'"[50] Just so, Dinesen figures her own—and Africa's—"boundlessness" (272). We have seen that if she claims the creator's role, appears to bring "Africa" or "Africans" into being through the power of naming and narration, extends her consciousness outward to encompass them all, so, by naming her in return, "turn[ing her] into a symbol," they call her into being as well: "If I have a song of Africa, . . . does Africa have a song of me?" (79) In such moments of dynamic reciprocity ("Echoes . . . from the one to the other" [21]), she undoes the traditional figure of man-the-namer and plays out a "feminine" mutability and multiplicity: a sex—and a text— that "are not one."

Such rare "gifts" cannot be captured, owned, or exported. Confined, they perish, like the iguana or the caged flamingoes destined for

European display—once free and beautiful, "spreading out . . . like the rays of a setting sun, . . . forming . . . and changing" (239), but reduced by captivity to mere flotsam and detritus (286). Yet if Dinesen asserts that "Africa" cannot be transported, she also shows, as we have seen, how it can transport us. As a moving fabrication (64), a richly figured magical "carpet" (15), her "Africa" is enchanted in the root sense of that word, a "song" that lifts and carries its listeners above the suffering, loss, and death it narrates: "When I have heard this tune again, it has recalled in one single moment all our anguish and despair of the past. It has got the salt taste of tears in it. But at the same time I found in the tune, unexpectedly, surprisingly, a vigour, a curious sweetness" (275).

These implications are reinforced by a culminating narrative which initially seems to undermine them completely. "One week after Denys's death" and shortly before her permanent departure, the narrator, seeking "a sign" that will reveal "the coherence of things" in the face of her devastating losses, witnesses a confrontation between a cock and a chameleon that becomes a symbol, "in miniature format," for her own condition: "The Chameleon stopped up dead at the sign of the cock. He was frightened, but he was at the same time very brave, he planted his feet on the ground, opened his mouth as wide as he possibly could, and, to scare his enemy, in a flash he shot out his club-shaped tongue at the cock. The cock stood for a second as if taken aback, then swiftly . . . struck down his beak like a hammer and plucked out the Chameleon's tongue"—without which "he could not live."

> Very slowly, . . . it came upon me that I had had the most spiritual answer possible to my call. I had even been in a strange manner honoured and distinguished. The powers to which I had cried had stood on my dignity more than I had done myself, and what other answer could they give? . . . Great powers had laughed at me, with an echo from the hills to follow the laughter, they had said among the trumpets, among the cocks and Chameleons, Ha ha! (368–70).

It is that same "laughter," Dinesen suggests, that engenders her narratives. For by acknowledging in-"coherence," figuring her own devastation through the terrible "sign" of the chameleon's lost tongue, she also explicitly links her "song of Africa" to the creations of Philomela, that other tongueless female singer whose wounds issued in an eloquent fabrication—made up, like *Out of Africa,* from fragments: "I have heard the nightingale in the woods of Africa. Not the full song: a few notes only, . . . suddenly stopped and again begun. . . . It was, however, the same melody, the same abundance and sweetness, as were soon to fill the forests of Europe, from Sicily to Elsinore" (283). It is a song revived each time the book is read.

Ultimately, then, for the reader as for the author, *Out of Africa* figures itself as a text of transport in the most profound sense: "a passage outside the range of imagination" (386). If, on one level, it rewrites the colonial script, on another—at its best—it also subverts that text, requires that we give ourselves up, allow ourselves to be lifted and moved, taken outside ourselves, so that we also give up the magisterial project of having and holding just as Dinesen, finally, gave up Africa—gave it up, paradoxically, in order to experience it more freely, in a gesture that gives new meaning to the word "abandon." For only in losing Africa as settled property could she inhabit "Africa" as unsettling text, a "tapestry" like Philomela's, made up of "mysterious" figures which, like the light and shadow of the African forest, "play . . . in many strange ways" (64). Only in going out of Africa could she offer us her own unique and ecstatic entry "into the depths" of what it had taught her (64).

This same paradoxical *ex-stasis* explains the distinctive tone of the text. The authorial voice, as it narrates the break-up of a life, itself refuses to break. Indeed, it is precisely the pressure of great grief contained, the lack of self-indulgent lamentation, that generates much of the book's resonance. In "From an Immigrant's Notebook," Dinesen reflects on how one copes with the loss of all that had seemed to make life worth living. And in her unflinchingly clear-eyed gaze at what Yeats calls "tragedy wrought to the uttermost" she finds a stern consolation, embodied in Jacob's words to the angel after a night of brutal wrestling: "I will not let thee go except thou bless me" (274). That blessing, one recalls, took the form of a new name, symbol of a self reborn:

> The friends of the farm came to the house, and went away again. They were not the kind of people who stay for a long time in the same place. They were not the kind of people either who grow old, they died and never came back. But they had sat contented by the fire, and when the house, closing round them, said: "I will not let you go except you bless me," they laughed and blessed it, and it let them go. . . .
>   My life, I will not let you go except you bless me, but then I will let you go. (275–76)

Despite its ineluctable entanglements in history—indeed, because of them—*Out of Africa* is one of the finest enactments in Western literature of the transcendence and transformation—the festive "laughter"—that may issue from ultimate loss. Benjamin's assertion that "the storyteller has borrowed . . . authority from death" reechoes with profound significance in this context. Those "friends of the farm" of whom Dinesen writes are ultimately her readers, sitting for a moment with a great storyteller, in her own capacious place—the "Africa" that is her book:

We were all of us merged into a unity, so that on another planet we shall recognize one another, and the things cry out to each other, the cuckoo clock and my books to the lean-fleshed cows on the lawn and the sorrowful old Kikuyus: "You also were there. You also were part of the Ngong farm." (275)

The "blessing" of paradise regained that *Out of Africa* finally promises, then, is not the dream of empire, but the bliss of writing and reading. In Dinesen's superb revision of Jacob's wrestling match, the naming that becomes a sign of rebirth is engendered not by the power struggle of agonistic masculine contestants, but by the woman whose only hold on us, or on the past, is a tenuous thread of inscriptions. "I will not let thee go except thou bless me": the vow compresses into a single sentence both her writing of the book and our reading of it. Insofar as *Out of Africa* is "timeless," it is in this sense that it attains that condition.[51] It is the transporting, dreamlike quality of the text as a flight of "words," an aleatory space allowing a contingent, always temporary liberation from the "laws" of temporality (238), that Dinesen evoked by analogizing it to fairy tale—that "once upon a time" that is really "once without a time." Just as Benedetta, discovering in "the rule of the irregular" the lost matrix or chora of a subversive maternal *jouissance,* also discovers her own voice; just as Childerique, overwhelmed by the murmurs of that maternal semiotic in the whirlpool engendered by "sweet witchcraft," is enabled to "see" both herself and her mother "at last"; so Dinesen, in the "wildness and irregularity," the vibrating, waving scintillations, the hypnotic "deep water" of Africa, finds the transfiguring matrix of her own "song." If the state of abandonment to which her narrative invites us is also a promise of return, it is not to a position of power or possession but to that ecstatic imaginative release for which, she suggested, we remain "homesick" all our lives (238)—the maternal body revived as textual *corpus:* "the flesh . . . made word," "the mother name."

"Love is a yearning for a country . . . , 'the place where everyone dwelt once upon a time and in the beginning,' . . . the country of children." Like Cixous rewriting the Freudian text, Dinesen would ultimately re-write her own text through the microcosmic figure of "a child['s] . . . story" (251). It is the iconographically rendered parable wherein the protagonist, after a long night of wandering and painful falls, gazes on the site of his suffering to see that his peregrinations have inscribed the discontinuous figure of a stork, mythic sign of life and generativity (251–53). That narrative also prefigures the reader's quest to find meaning amidst the interpretive pitfalls of Dinesen's text and the devastations it records. It is one of the great achievements of *Out of Africa* to revive in each of us our own particular nostalgia, to reveal to us the commonality of the primal loss that inspires it, and to offer, as para-

doxical consolation, the very words that are inseparable from the wounding. "I will not let thee go except thou bless me." Like the narrator,
with whom, via her book, her readers are transported and momentarily
"merged"—"You also were there. You also were part of the Ngong
farm" (275)—Dinesen suggests that we may "see the stork" only by
learning to let go.   .

Epilogue
Carnival Laughter:
The Theater of the Body

The best of my nature reveals itself in play, and play is sacred.

Karen Blixen, *Modern Marriage*

"To be your own caricature—that is the true carnival!"

Isak Dinesen, "Carnival"

In considering Dinesen's texts as the writing of woman both literally and theoretically, I have attended to their distinctive intricacies, attempting to suggest a way of reading that opens new possibilities for thinking about her engendering of narrative. Here I want to reverse that process, ranging freely across the last two decades of her career to retrieve and replay a series of pivotal scenes, each of which stages "woman" as spectacular icon, simultaneously carnal body and incarnate "word," offered for the consumption of an attentive audience in a moment of blissful prodigality which, like the extravagant insurgencies of carnival, overflows the social and symbolic order that would contain it.[1]

SCENE I

In a rye field on one of the great eighteenth-century Danish manors, a solemn crowd watches a "small figure on a large stage": a "woman struggling with her sickle for her son's life." Her frail body, grotesquely "bent double as if she were walking on her knees," staggers across a vast maternalized landscape, the "bosom" of a "mother" land, its undulating contours artificially "marked" by the "lines" of a paternal order, topographical, architectural, genealogical—a "writing" that proclaims the phallic power of the lord whose name the land is designed to perpetuate, and whose "word" and "law," analogized to the paternal fiat of Genesis and the logos of the Fourth Gospel, have set the conditions of the ex-

247

traordinary "drama" the woman enacts. One of the manor's barns having been burned and a young peasant accused of the crime on the basis of dubious linguistic evidence, the "word" of his enemies against his word, the lord has answered the appeal of the boy's mother by proposing a ritual ordeal: if within a single day she can reap a field that normally would require a man three days to mow, her son will go free; otherwise, he will be taken from her forever, depriving her of her sole means of sustenance. Either choice is tantamount to her destruction.

Out of the untenable, deathly oppositions established by the lord's magisterial order, the woman creates a "triumphant procession" which, so far from reconstituting the name of the father, releases and reenacts the repressed myth of mother origins and sacrifice, recalling that "great female deity" described in *Out of Africa,* "who existed before the time of the Prophet's God." Gathering grain sacred to maternal goddesses in a field like "those of Elysium," she becomes a figure of the life-giving earth whose fruits she harvests "with an ardent, tender craving, like that of a mother who lays a baby to the nipple." Amidst the intense tragic emotions generated by the scene, her "quiet" face is "the only one perfectly calm, peaceful and mild," mirroring the "silent and serene" land she traverses. "Advancing slowly and unevenly," she leads "a divine procession," inscribing another line for the gathered crowd that follows "in her wake," "as if by all means they meant to have part in her work": the "whole throng of onlookers advanced as she advanced, slowly and as if drawn by a string." At last both she and the earth are simultaneously transfigured in a flood of light that obliterates the rigid "lines" of the old lord's world: "With such splendour did the sun emblazon the earth and the air that the landscape was turned into a melting-pot of glorious metals. The meadows and the grasslands became pure gold; the barley field nearby . . . was a live lake of shining silver."

Scene 2

On the eve of the Franco-Prussian war, a woman arrives at a hotel near the German border, where a group of refugees has been detained by advancing Prussian forces. "Flourishing like a rose," she moves among the gathered company like "a lioness . . . among a flock of sheep"—"the central figure in its small world." "Confronted with the danger of the moment," she becomes "heraldic," a "*dame haute et puissante*"—one who "masters the world." The commandant, simultaneously aroused by her "great beauty" and infuriated by her unassailable self-sufficiency, offers to free the refugees if she will come before him to collect their passports, "dressed like the goddess Venus." Curiously unperturbed, she defers the decision to her compatriots: "Ask those who are with me. . . . Their salvation is, to each one of them, more important than mine. Let them decide for themselves if they will buy [freedom] at your price." When the refugees, after an agony of indecision, refuse, the colonel, overwhelmed by these double acts of courage, releases them all. After "a hurried, spare meal of bread and wine" they cross the border, imbued with a profound sense of communal grace. The woman "was still the central figure of their communion, but in a new way, as an object infinitely precious to them. Her pride, her glory was theirs, since they had been ready to die for it."

Visiting Paris years later, a man from this group attends a celebrated cabaret performance, a "show . . . called *Diana's Revenge*," whose "climax" is marked by "the appearance of the goddess Diana herself, with nothing on at all. As she stepped forward bending her golden bow, a noise like a long sigh went through the house. The beauty of her body came as a surprise and ecstasy even to those who had seen her before, . . . *'une chose incroyable.'*" Astonished, the visitor recognizes the "heroine" through whose inspiration the refugees had attained their "salvation."

SCENE 3

A "massive, dark, deadly pale woman"—"haggard and wild-eyed like a hunted animal"—arrives at the cottage of two aging Norwegian spinsters and collapses "on the doorstep in a dead swoon." "Restored . . . to life" by their ministrations, she speechlessly offers an explanatory letter from an old friend of theirs from France, identifying her as "a Petroleuse"—"which word," he explains in an unintentional double entendre, "is used . . . for women who set fire to houses." A Communard who has lost everything in the Paris uprisings, she appeals to the sisters' charity and is accepted, on the strength of an offhand parting remark in the letter, as their unpaid cook.

Twelve years later, a company of celebrants gathers for a birthday dinner in honor of the ladies' father—the founder of the strict, ascetic Lutheran sect they now lead. Having won a fortune in the Paris lottery, the woman has persuaded them to allow her to prepare "a real French dinner." Overawed by the "incalculable nature and range" of her project, for which she imports strange, "undefinable" objects and creatures, "monstrous and terrible to behold," they watch with secret horror as she converts the father's sacred day to her own purposes, transforming the paternal "house" into the site of "a witches' sabbath" and herself into a kind of supernatural figure, "like the bottled demon of fairy tale"— "grown to such dimensions that her mistresses felt small before her."

What her labors produce is a meal beyond imagining, a feast so lavish and inspired that a visiting general—the suave, urbane man who as a youth had loved and left one of the sisters to pursue the worldly rewards of a military career—is "startled" into "silence," "seized by a queer kind of panic," while the stolid, ordinarily "taciturn" parishoners, grown voluble under the effects of the food and wine, receive "the gift of tongues." Transported into an "exalted state of mind," lifted "off the ground, into a higher and purer sphere," all are moved to contemplate what "one might venture to call miracles." The *pièce de résistance, Cailles en Sarcophage,* reminds the general of a triumphal dinner years before at the Café Anglais, "the finest restaurant" in Paris, where the same dish was prepared by the chef, "the greatest culinary genius of the age, and—most surprisingly—a woman!" In her hands "a dinner" became "a kind of love affair," a source of *jouissance* "in which one no longer distinguishes between bodily and spiritual appetite or satiety!" That long-concealed and canceled art is resurrected in the feast they now consume, a secular Eucharist which, emblematized by the "*Sarcophages*" that mark it as her production, revives those long "dead," effecting a regenerating, carnivalizing outpouring of good spirits in every sense, a festive transubstantiation in which "righteousness and bliss . . . kiss one another." Within this enchanted comic space, "anything is possible": the assumed boundaries between body and soul, self and other, past and present are momentarily abolished, and "Time itself" is "merged into eternity." Inspired by the "intoxication" of the woman's "blessed" art and the "infinite . . . grace" of the festival, the celebrants experience a kind of psychological "millenium" that heals old wounds and reconciles deeply entrenched differences with "a heavenly burst of laughter." It is a "miracle" of multiple incarnations—flesh, quite literally, made word in a stream of overflowing benedictions: "'Bless you, bless you, bless you,' like an echo of the harmony of the spheres rang on all sides."

SCENE 4

Dressed all in black, like "a design by Beardsley," a frail, aged woman appears on the stage of a large, crowded auditorium. Her emaciated body is so fragile that she can hardly "stand without support." Her deep-set eyes, glittering "like black diamonds" in the chalk-white face, are redrawn with the added emphasis of kohl. The face is carefully composed, in both senses; she has, both literally and figuratively, *made herself up*. A wry, crooked smile plays about her mouth. Her skin is like deeply lined parchment, a "hundred wrinkles" shaped into "a baroque, beaming mask."

Escorted to a spotlit chair at center stage, she pauses, "and, by way of a salute" to "the overflowing audience," stretches "her fine-boned arm in a gesture . . . as of a hunter beckoning with a riding crop, or as of an actor in the role of Prospero motioning . . . airy creature[s] into existence. . . ." After "catching her breath in . . . weariness," she looks "around the auditorium with . . . a gypsy gaze," and begins to tell stories in a "deep, husky . . . voice"—"the hypnotic voice of . . . Scheherazade." As she speaks, "her face . . . lit like a candle in an old church," the "shock and tension" that have filled the room at the sight of her extreme infirmity give way to rapt attention: "she [holds] her listeners spellbound for two hours," temporarily transforming herself into "the storyteller of all of the market places, beside the campfires, crouched upon the hearths of the world." Later, a witness to the event recalls that "as she concluded, one could hear nothing—not even the rustle of a page," until "the audience rose and burst into deafening applause."

The first of these feminine figures is Anne-Marie in "Sorrow-acre"; the second, Heloïse in "The Heroine"; the third, Babette Hersant in "Babette's Feast." The fourth, of course, is Isak Dinesen, playing "herself" at her celebrated New York appearances in 1959.[2] It is no accident that her own performances should invite comparison with her fictions. In each case the female body becomes the duplicitous corpus whereby woman stages "woman" as a figure of fabrication associated with a tranformative vision of narrative. A feast for the eyes or for the mind, at once consumed and consuming, "she" is both sign and agent of signification, a subject of speculation in every sense: her iconic self-representation, a festive celebration of the redemptive possibilities of feminine art, evokes a surplus that cannot be encompassed by phallocentric structures or hermeneutics.

Thus in "Sorrow-acre" issues of patrilineage, though seemingly primary, are continually disturbed by a countertextual network of references to female origins and generation, just as its apparent "father," Isak Dinesen, is only a public fiction of masculine authority, concealing the fact that this text is after all a mother's child. The narrative indicates that the lines inscribed by Anne-Marie's "procession" mark the beginning of the end of the old lord's regime and the symbolic order it represents.[3] His potency is literally *on the line:* the death of his only son and heir has severed his genealogical continuance and the "earthly immortality" it signifies, threatening "obliteration of his being." His "nominal" heir, his nephew Adam, is an insufficient substitute: holding "the tradition of direct succession" as "sacred dogma," the father needs "a son of his own flesh and blood"; yet he has been unable to sire another child with his young bride. The spectacle of Anne-Marie's body not only provokes heated hermeneutical dispute between father and surrogate son but fuels the oedipal antagonism between them. Adam's incipient attraction to the lord's bride Sophie Magdalena—transgressive "Eve" and forbidden fruit in the lord's "Garden of Eden" (*WT,* 38)—foreshadows the destruction of both the "legitimate" patrilineage and the power it signifies, those "lines" whose contingency and vulnerability the text underscores from the outset by disclosing their dependence on woman's word. The terms of the lord's retributive contract, inspired by the suppliant figure of the "woman amidst the corn ripe to be mowed," make Anne-Marie at once sacrificial victim in a kind of fertility rite by which he seeks to reassert his potency, and scapegoat onto whom he projects the displaced guilt of the crime against his property and authority signified by the barn burning.

But he also construes the woman herself as the literal bearer of the illicit: "she has not got a good name," he contends, because "they tell as a girl she had a child and did away with it." Like the crime of indeterminate derivation, this rumoured transgression threatens the father's priority as origin(ator), as Dinesen implies through translinguistic wordplay linking the two forms of illegitimacy: *barn* in Danish means "child" and *burn* is a homophone of Danish *børn,* "children." In effect, the lord asks the woman to pay not only for her living son, but also for her supposed dead one. Ironically, only by *blotting herself out* can she restore her "good name"—that is, one that subserves the name of the father. Thus the ordeal in the field bears all the marks of a cultural spectacle in which woman's body itself becomes a field for the contention of massive historical and psychological forces, and "the father's figure," "presiding over the scene of the tragedy," becomes "a symbol of the tyranny and oppression of the world" (50). The crucial question—"will the woman fulfill her bargain?" (51)—reverberates with a cultural significance that far exceeds the immediate "scene."

As the figures of inscription that pervade the text suggest, the import of that "bargain" is inseparable from questions of writing. Significantly, in describing her own authorial process Dinesen employed agricultural terms that recall Anne-Marie's labor, figuring her manuscript as a field over which she too "went forward, then went back again in order to go forward a little more."[4] And like the onlookers who follow Anne-Marie "as if by all means they meant to have part in her work," so the readers of the text trace, "as if drawn by a string," the lines she and her author simultaneously produce. Thus "the scene of the drama" (50) is also the scene of the text's inscription, the "stage" (56) whereon Dinesen reflexively enacts the creation of her own "inimitable, dignified exhibition of skilled art"—like Anne-Marie's, a "work which will long be remembered" (67–68). So far from "fulfilling her bargain" with a patriarchal tradition, she uses the very terms of that tradition to resurrect the "forgotten," illicit "story of the woman," undermining the narrative of paternal succession by asserting a female "word" that overflows and dislodges the word of the father in both social and textual genealogies (69). And if that "story" appears to reinscribe woman's subordination to the paternal line, it also enacts her potential victory over it. Though Anne-Marie triumphs only at the price of life itself, "like a sheaf of corn that falls to the ground" (69), the text gestures toward another possibility, for in its lines the duplicitous narrative of female origins and creativity enjoys a "timeless life" like that of the land which engenders and finally names the whole tale—a life that endures, the text suggests, after the surface "lines" of the father have been erased.

The conclusion reasserts this vitality as the narrative doubles back upon itself—its end, paradoxically, also marking its beginning. We enter and leave the text through the all-encompassing story of the land—the "mother of [the] race" (37)—which is recorded microcosmically in the title, adumbrated in the introduction that configures a maternalized earth "marked" by the father's lines, and recapitulated in the final paragraph: "In the place where the woman had died the old lord later on had a stone set up, with a sickle engraved in it. The peasants on the land then named the rye field 'Sorrow Acre.' By this name it was known a long time after the story of the woman and her son had itself been forgotten" (69). Renaming the tale it concludes, the cryptic hieroglyphic stone, which in Dinesen's sources was engraved with the figure of the woman, stands as a symbolic counterpart to the text itself, a monument to feminine labor.[5] Both stone and story, though seemingly erected in the name of the father, in fact commemorate the "forgotten" narrative of woman in circuitous signs that perpetually reinscribe themselves, in a fictive world recreated, a feminine word made flesh, each time their lines are read.

The same sort of transformative script is suggested in the character of Heloïse. Her willing gift of her body as potential sacrifice rescues it from the status of inert object of circulation, shattering the symbolic economy invoked by the commandante's proffered "bargain." Her gesture makes an indelible impression on the young Englishman through whose perspective we view her, compelling a radical rewriting of his former subjectivity and the assumptions that ground it. Having "lived a seclusive life amongst books" sacred to patriarchal tradition—"Biblical . . . , mythological and allegorical figures"—and regarding "the world itself" as a "book," he is also a fledgling author who aspires "to write . . . upon the doctrine of atonement." But in Heloïse he discovers a paradoxical text that surpasses what those others can encompass; she is "like no book in the world," and the script(ure) that she authors ruptures his frame of reference.[6] Through the *act* of offering up her body, whether on the stage of the occupation or in the occupation of the stage, she radically revises the androcentric "doctrine of atonement" via a literalization of "divine" female fleshliness—an alternative feminine version of incarnation. As the stripper who *puts on*—in both senses—chaste modesty, the "Diana" whose nakedness, as a form of costume, is itself a spectacular put-on, she confounds the topos whereby woman's body becomes mere specular object to be penetrated and possessed by the magisterial masculine gaze. Indeed, her self-possession is never more marked than in her moments of greatest self-abandonment, for in *(ex)posing herself,* she also uncovers the impotence of phallic pretensions. Her boldest dramatizations, a series of double reversals in which self-display and self-concealment mirror each other in an endless dialogical oscillation, turn precisely on the element of *reserve,* in its double sense of *restraint* and *excess:* "something left uncomprehended, an unexplored, mysterious area" which phallocentric reflections cannot comprehend. Her mimetic, parodistic play with (self)-referentiality turns woman's body into the very figure of indeterminacy, soliciting and perpetually baffling interpretation.

The reflexive connection of Dinesen's own narrative with this sort of playful, "self"-sacrificial feminine *dépense* is made most explicit in "Babette's Feast." For as Dinesen implies through the *sarcophages* that epitomize Babette's art, it is ultimately the woman's own body that is offered up, in displaced form, through her Eucharistic culinary corpus. After the dinner she is found, "deadly exhausted," "on the chopping block." Having "given away all [she] had" to create her feast, she is emptied out, left again with nothing—in effect consumed by her own artistic production. For the sisters this "self-sacrifice," like the festival it enables, is "beyond comprehension." But Babette answers their condolences with "pity, even scorn": "She rose from the chopping block and stood up before the two sisters. . . . 'Poor?' . . . She smiled as if to herself. 'No, I shall never be poor. . . . A great artist . . . is never poor. We have something . . . of which other people know nothing. . . . Through all the world there goes one long cry from the heart of the artist: Give me leave to do my utmost!'" (*AD,* 67–68).

Those words illuminate the simultaneous self-annihilation and self-creation Dinesen associated with her own engendering of narrative. Though only two of the texts we have touched on are part of *Winter's Tales,* that title might serve as a rubric for all her writings after *Out of Africa.* For *Winter's Tales,* whose publication in 1942 marked the precise beginning of the last two decades of her life, appropriately names the circumstances in which her final narratives were created and gestures toward the waning of their aging author.[7] In the years before her death her body was increasingly ravaged by the pain and debilitation of the syphilis contracted from her husband, which attacked the spinal nerves that control digestion, ultimately causing her to die of starvation. The comic transcendence of her oblique self-reference in "Babette's Feast" appears the more stunning when we recall that she wrote that celebration of transformative consumption at a time when her own body was literally devouring itself. Indeed, her assertion that in writing she died into her art, becoming "a piece of printed matter," was never more poignantly enacted than in these years, as her body gradually withered to skeletal, wraithlike proportions and her writing often had to proceed by dictation while she lay supine to ease the pain that wracked her.[8]

Yet it was typical of Dinesen that she gallantly made the most even of these effects, putting into practice the paradox by which she had lived and written: "By their masks ye shall know them." As the Shakespearean allusion in *Winter's Tales* implies, if that stark collection and the fictions that followed it figure the erasure or repression of woman, they also record her sensational return in/as art through a kind of serious play, a ludic spectacle in which her body, site and sign of feminine generativity, is resurrected from apparent "death" through the medium of her own figuration—fit occasion for the "heavenly burst of laughter" inherent in her pseudonym.[9] As one of her characters observes in a meditation on "woman" in "Carnival," "Your own mask" can "give you . . . that release from self toward which all religions strive"—"mystery, depth, and bliss": "only thus can great works of art be accomplished" (*C,* 67–68). In "The Diver," Dinesen had characterized "poet's tales" as "disease turned into loveliness." In related fashion, she turned her fragile, disease-ridden body into a living work of art, extending the processes that animate her narratives into a wider semiotic space through diverse public performances—elaborate self-stagings which, like her literary pseudonyms and the labyrinthine complexities of her narratives, concealed or put into question the existence of a "real" Karen Blixen even as they flamboyantly proclaimed her presence.[10] Posed as "herself" or crafting herself as sibyl, witch, or clown, literally making a spectacle of herself, Dinesen transformed her dying body into a speaking text, defying mortality by *becoming narrative*—a self-consuming artifact in every sense. Recalling magnetic female figures from her own fictions—Malin Nat-og-Dag, who changes herself from "death's head" to beatific agent of renewal and transcendence in "The Deluge"; Pellegrina Leoni, whose injuries become the source of perpetually renewable fictions; Anne-Marie in her life-giving ritual; Heloïse offering herself as vital element for the "communion" of her compatriots; Lady Flora Gordon, the towering Scotswoman whose exuberant spirits revitalize her fellow sufferers at the sanitorium for syphilitics in "The Cardinal's Third Tale"; the "valkyrie" Ehrengard, whose unbreachable self-possession foils phallic plots of domination, turning the appropriative male gaze back on itself; or Babette simultaneously giving up and reclaiming herself through her Eucharistic feast—their author too presented herself as a gift to be consumed by her audiences in her own festive productions. Merging the body of her fiction with the fiction of her body, she made herself one of the preeminent figures of her own literary corpus: "woman" as both "flesh" and "word." "And the word," as she observed in "Mottoes of my Life," "taken in such earnest is a mighty thing": "*In hoc signo vinces*" (*Essays,* 30).

In her favorite role as "the storyteller who was three thousand years old and had dined with Socrates,"[11] she resembled the "laughing" terracotta figures of old women that Bakhtin saw as the epitome of carnival: her body, like theirs, became the triumphal, uncanny image of "death that gives birth," combining "decaying and deformed flesh with the flesh of new life, conceived but as yet unformed"—what she called, in one of her last fictions, "Immortal Story" (LT).[12] Indeed, in her various playful poses as jester, transvestite, and agent of disruption, of "laughter" and "fearless" feminine "heresy," Dinesen, like the "witty woman" she reflexively acclaimed in "The Deluge," explicitly cast herself as an extravagant embodiment of the "carnival" spirit.

Textualizing woman's body through both writing and self-dramatization, Dinesen's carnivalesque figurations constituted a play with referentiality that made "visible"—to return to Irigaray—"by the effect of playful repetition, what [is] supposed to remain invisible: the cover-up of a possible operation of the feminine in language."[13] Since patriarchal culture makes woman's body a primary site of contestation, the originary property of which, in the name of the father, she herself must be dispossessed, for a woman to (re)claim that body, to mimic "woman" as specular object while simultaneously asserting her position as signifying subject, is to refuse the economy of masculine possession and exchange that would co-opt her and to express, through the very process of feminine masquerade, that "elsewhere" of another meaning, unspeakable within a phallocentric discourse. As Mary Russo astutely remarks, "to put on femininity with a vengeance suggests the power of taking it off."[14] Similarly, to give center stage to that which is commonly marked as *eccentric,* marginal, deviant, and pathological—the old woman's scandalous body as both subject and object of desire—is to play havoc with the androcentric order by opening it to the very forces it would cast out: femininity, illness, and mortality—all treated within traditional Western culture as contaminations that imperil both the phallic body and the phallocratic body politic. In this sense, Dinesen's diverse self-fabrications as story/teller might be read as dis-orderly enactments, in the most literal sense, of a radical *écriture féminine:* a writing of her body which was also a profound commentary on the body of her writing—a double inscription that incorporated the interplay of *theater* and *theory* and recalled the common origins of *carnality, incarnation,* and *carnival.*[15] It was, in every sense, a gesture of recuperation.

In "Carnival"—that early fiction which, with its posthumous publication, became a last word as well—she narrates that interaction as
a process of infinite play with identity, a destabilizing fluidity of sexual rules and roles that writes woman's generativity—the "all-powerful
formula: . . . 'je suis enceinte'"—as the blissful "joke" that subverts paternal preeminence: "Like all women she believed in her heart in the immaculate conception, and did not give the father . . . a thought" (C, 98).
In this mobile, "laughing" space woman changes "the rules of the game"
by posing the "self" as a "dancing" figure of multiplicity and transformation rather than uniformity and stability (88, 100), challenging the
reigning symbolic order with a burst of bawdy puns that declare her desire and voice as "musical" significations outside the strictures of phallocentric Law: "You are mistaken when you think that we love cocks—we
love nightingales. We want a melody . . . that repeats itself, and will go
on. Alas, that you cannot play us" (87). Here, as elsewhere in Dinesen's
texts, the nightingale becomes the image of blissful creativity: "a long
ecstatic festival of song" (*Essays,* 207). Just as Philomela, that quintessential embodiment of woman displaced, dismembered, and mute, filled the
world with the "abundance and sweetness" of her music (*OA,* 283), so
Dinesen, out of radical discontinuity, bodily decay, incalculable loss, and
death, created narratives which, as she wrote in "The Blank Page" of "all
old story-telling women," make "silence . . . speak,"[16] turning *malady*
into *melody* "that repeats itself, and will go on."

It is this ebulliant, paradoxical spirit that informs the final line of
"Carnival," proclaiming the end of final lines: "Everything is infinite,
and foolery as well." That dizzying double entendre (spoken by a woman
disguised, like her author, not only as a man but as a mask—the *commedia
dell'arte* character Arlecchino) might be read as Dinesen's retrospective
carnivalizing commentary on her own engenderings of narrative and its
imitations of, and by, life. Infinite foolery: dissolving the boundaries between youth and age, health and illness, high and low, truth and fiction,
body and text, it recalls the "many laughters" of the name by which we
know her literary corpus. Infinite foolery: out of the place of death, "immortal story."

Notes

Introduction

1. On Dinesen's multiple names see Judith Thurman, *Isak Dinesen: The Life of a Storyteller* (New York: St. Martin's Press, 1982), 5.

2. Beginning with *Out of Africa,* Dinesen published in Scandinavia and England under the name Karen Blixen, retaining "Isak Dinesen" for the texts published in America. On her composition process, see Thurman, *Life,* and Donald Hannah, *"Isak Dinesen" and Karen Blixen: The Mask and the Reality* (New York: Random House, 1971). For the rare exceptions to her usual order of composition, see Liselotte Henriksen, *Karen Blixen: En bibliografi/Isak Dinesen: A Bibliography* (Copenhagen: Gyldendal, 1977). On the differences between the texts of Isak Dinesen and Karen Blixen, see Knud Sørensen, "Studier i Karen Blixens engelsk og danske sprogform," in *Blixeniana* (Copenhagen: 1982), 263–308; Lise Kure-Jensen, "Isak Dinesen in English, Danish, and Translation: Are We Reading the Same Text?" in *Karen Blixen/Isak Dinesen: Tradition, Modernity, and Other Ambiguities: Proceedings of the International Symposium on Karen Blixen/Isak Dinesen* (Minneapolis: University of Minnesota, 1985), 114–19; and Elias Bredsdorff, "Isak Dinesen and Karen Blixen: *Seven Gothic Tales* (1934) and *Syv fantastiske fortællinger* (1935)," in *Facets of European Modernism,* ed. Janet Garton (East Anglia: East Anglia University Press, 1985). In the manuscript drafts, the extent of this linguistic complication is striking. As Hannah notes, "it is impossible to draw a sharp dividing line between the two languages. Most of her unpublished manuscripts and drafts of tales are written in English, others, which seem to be predominantly early work, are written in Danish. The working-notes for the stories are generally written in Danish, sometimes they switch between the two languages—occasionally in mid-sentence" (*Mask,* 68). In the most notable instance of this intertextuality, the manuscript of *Out of Africa,* the English typescript is interlined with a handwritten Danish version of *Den Afrikanske Farm* (*The African Farm*) (KB Archives 129).

3. *Purity and Danger: An Analysis of the Concepts of Pollution and Taboo* (London: Routledge and Kegan Paul, 1966), 152.

4. Dinesen's textual duality has also generated two separate national critical traditions, at least as divergent as her English and Danish texts: the Anglo-American on "Isak Dinesen," the Danish on Karen Blixen. See Poul Houe, "A World of Ambiguities or Ambivalences: Karen Blixen/Isak Dinesen's Art and Life

in Scholarly Perspectives," in *Karen Blixen/Isak Dinesen*, 1-10. On monological discourse and its disruptions, see M. M. Bakhtin, *The Dialogical Imagination*, ed. Michael Holquist, trans. Caryl Emerson and Holquist (Austin: University of Texas Press, 1981).

5. On her reference to *The Angelic Avengers* as her "illegitimate child," see "Isak Dinesen," in *Writers at Work: The Paris Review Interviews*, 4th series, ed. George Plimptom (1976; London: Penguin, 1977), 6-7.

6. On the relation of oral tradition to print culture, see Walter Ong, *Orality and Literacy* (New York: Methuen, 1982). Cf. Walter Benjamin, "The Storyteller," *Illuminations*, trans. Harry Zohn (New York: Schocken, 1969), 87, on storytelling as a cumulative, communal, multivoiced discourse. Dinesen's paradoxical project was to revive this kind of "story" in printed form. See *Essays*, 196.

7. Cf. the Prioress and her simian familiar in "The Monkey" (*SGT*); the interchangeable sisters of "The Invincible Slave Owners" (*WT*); the inseparable heroines of *The Angelic Avengers;* the master and disciple of "The Cloak" (*LT*); Pellegrina and Emanuele of "Echoes" (*LT*); Linnert and Eitel of "A Country Tale" (*LT*); or Pipistrello and Lord Byron of "Second Meeting" (*C*).

8. As we shall see, long before John Barth or Michel Foucault claimed Scheherazade as the quintessential figure of postmodernist writing, Dinesen identified herself and her fiction with Scheherazade's, stressing the import of gender to the generation of potentially interminable, infinitely regressive narrations—for a woman, literally a lifesaving prospect. The culmination of this method would have been her "novel" *Albondocani*. Planned as a series of discrete but intricately interlocking, self-proliferating stories, it remained unfinished at her death in 1962—not surprisingly, given its narratological premises. On the dis-closures of modernist literature, see Frank Kermode, *The Sense of an Ending* (New York: Oxford University Press, 1967); on their specific import for women, see Rachel Blau DuPlessis, *Writing Beyond the Ending: Narrative Strategies of Twentieth-Century Women Writers* (Bloomington: Indiana University Press, 1985). On some of the salient implications of the issues of repetition and literary representation, see J. Hillis Miller, *Fiction and Repetition: Seven English Novels* (Cambridge: Harvard University Press, 1982) and John Irwin, *Doubling and Incest, Repetition and Revenge: A Speculative Reading of Faulkner* (Baltimore: Johns Hopkins University Press, 1975). Dinesen's fascination with repetition situates her within a diverse intellectual tradition that includes Hegel, Marx, and especially Kierkegaard, her countryman, and Nietzsche, whose work was doubly important to her because it was filtered through the influence of the Danish critic Georg Brandes, a friend of both Nietzsche and her father, and her own sometime mentor. The interest in repetition also relates her to her contemporary Freud, subsequent theorists like Lacan, Derrida, and Deleuze, and postmodernist authors like Borges and Barth. This list, of course, elides the question of sexual difference.

9. Thurman, *Life*, 54; Eric O. Johannesson, *The World of Isak Dinesen* (Seattle: University of Washington Press, 1961), v; cf. Hannah, *Mask*, 41, 76, 81-85, 98. For a notable exception to the traditional view, see Aage Henriksen, *De ubændige: Om Ibsen—Blixen—hverdagens virkelighed—det ubevidste* (Copenhagen: Gyldendal, 1984), and "The Empty Space Between Art and the Church," *Scandinavian Studies* 57 (Autumn 1985): 390-99. Even critics who recognize Dinesen's

complexity tend to recuperate it under the sign of unity. Thus Hannah sees the "intricate arabesque of plot-design" as subsumed within "an elaborately completed whole" (*Mask,* 77); Robert Langbaum, her best-known American critic, writes in his seminal *Isak Dinesen's Art: The Gayety of Vision* (1964; Chicago: University of Chicago Press, 1975) that "She gives us within her frame enough intricacy of texture to create an illusion of, perhaps a substitute for, depth" (25); and in *Diana's Revenge—Two Lines in Isak Dinesen's Authorship,* trans. Anne Born (Odense: Odense University Press, 1985), Marianne Juhl and Bo Hakon Jørgensen note "numerous breaks in continuity" as "characteristic features of the Blixen tale" (12) but insist on her obsessive inscription of a single idea: "the predominant role of sensuality and physical consciousness in human life" (243).

10. "On Orthography," *Essays,* 156.

11. *AD,* 71–154.

12. On Dinesen's claim that Pellegrina was her double, see Thorkild Bjørnvig, *The Pact: My Friendship with Isak Dinesen,* trans. Ingvar Schousboe and William Jay Smith (Baton Rouge: Louisiana State University Press, 1983), 46–47; Thurman, *Life,* 262n., 399–400.

13. See Cixous, "Sorties," in Cixous and Catherine Clément, *The Newly Born Woman,* trans. Betsy Wing (Minneapolis: University of Minnesota Press, 1986), esp. 63–70.

14. I use the plural advisedly, for any singular reference to "feminist theory" elides the multiple, heterogenous, and sometimes conflicting voices currently speaking in its name—not to mention those which, while interpreting sexual difference, signifying practices, and sociopolitical gender systems, would disclaim such nomination altogether. Throughout this study I would set the term "feminist" within implicit quotation marks, acknowledging its pluralities, its contradictions, and the forms of misunderstanding it often evokes; acknowledging, too, the inevitable constraints of race, class, and nationality operative in my own particular discourse on "woman."

15. *Towards a Minor Literature,* trans. Dana Polan (Minneapolis: University of Minnesota Press, 1986), 17–26, and Polan's Foreword, xiv. The politics of placement that sustain a view of Dinesen as a minor author, as well as the general perception that she is not precisely locatable within a "European" tradition, are sharply evident not only in her absence from typical English department curricula in America but in the division to which the Modern Language Association, the representative organization of American academic literary criticism, relegates her: "English Literature *Other* than British or American" (my emphasis)—a title that reinscribes both the history of colonialism and the persistent ethnocentrism that is its legacy in the Anglo-American academy. Ironically, that designation situates Dinesen among so-called Third World authors who often, understandably, perceive her merely as a representative of an imperialist social order.

16. Indeed, as Dana Polan notes, their own "deterritorializing" gestures imply a reterritorialization of woman as "a kind of succoring aid to the adventuring male in his quest to go beyond limits"; see *Towards a Minor Literature,* xxvi. Cf. Alice Jardine, *Gynesis: Configurations of Woman and Modernity* (Ithaca: Cornell University Press, 1985), 208–23.

17. In this era that some are calling "postfeminist," my assertion that is-

sues of gender and sexuality are inseparable from the production of meaning in
Dinesen's texts might seem a mere truism, but in Dinesen's case it remains a
major point of critical difference. Critics have long recognized that her narratives
involve reflexive explorations of their own fictionality and of their author's creative project (e.g., Langbaum, *Gayety*, 26). Yet until quite recently most critics
have read her fiction as though her positioning as a woman had little to do with
this reflexivity, assuming that her texts, like her pseudonym, were uniformly androcentric. On feminist challenges to that view, see chap. 1.

18. Like Byron, to whom she ironically compared herself, Dinesen is a
writer whose fascinating life has proportionally overshadowed her work (e.g.,
"Second Meeting," *C*, 338)—a phenomenon recently reinforced by Sydney
Pollack's Academy Award-winning film *Out of Africa* (1985). The relative un-
familiarity of many readers with Dinesen's fiction is partly attributable to her
ambiguous positioning simultaneously inside and outside her adopted literary
language. Never having lived in England or America like her expatriate male
counterparts Conrad and Nabokov, she is excluded from Anglo-American literary canons even though her texts were first published in America and Anglo-
American readers have constituted her largest audience. For these and other
reasons I have begun to suggest, Dinesen's critical fortunes declined somewhat
after her death in 1962, when she was widely recognized as a major contemporary
writer—repeatedly considered, for example, as a leading candidate for the Nobel
Prize in Literature. The current revival of interest in her life and work has been
both epitomized and spurred by the publication of her translated *Essays* and
Letters and Thurman's fine biography, as well as (more problematically) by
Pollack's movie and Gabriel Axel's acclaimed Danish film *Babette's Feast*.

19. On her relation to colonialism, see chapters 2 and 10.

20. Langbaum (*Gayety*, 44) includes *Winter's Tales* as well, but, as he acknowledges, that collection is markedly uneven by comparison with the first two.

21. For Dinesen's own sketch of the trajectory of her career, see "Mottoes
of My Life," *Essays*. Langbaum divides the published English texts into "three
distinct periods": "the first, spectacular period, represented by her first three
books—*Seven Gothic Tales, Out of Africa,* and *Winter's Tales*—in which she appeared as a fully matured artist and made the reputation she has today"; "the long
hiatus of fifteen years during which her only book was the novel, *The Angelic
Avengers*, a thriller . . . published in 1946 under the name Pierre Andrezel"; and
"the third period of recrudescence, remarkable for a writer in her seventies,
which saw . . . two volumes of stories, *Last Tales* in 1957 and *Anecdotes of Destiny*
in 1958, a collection in 1961 of four more African reminiscences, *Shadows on the
Grass*, and the posthumously published story *Ehrengard* in 1963" (*Gayety*, 44–45).
We might add two other phases: Karen Blixen's early Danish publications, collected by Clara Svendsen in *Osceola* (Copenhagen: Gyldendal, 1962); and the
posthumous *Carnival, Letters,* and *Essays*. There are other unpublished or un-
translated manuscripts from Karen Blixen's Danish oeuvre—most importantly,
we need a complete collection of the remaining correspondence and lectures—
but comparatively little that would add significantly to the English corpus.

22. On her rigorous self-revision, see Hannah, *Mask*, 48, 77–81, and Langbaum, *Gayety*, 45.

23. *Isak Dinesen: A Memorial,* ed. Clara Svendsen (New York: Random House, 1965), 10.

24. Throughout this study I use "Karen Blixen" both in references to the authorial signature on the Danish texts and in explicitly biographical commentary on the woman who reinvented herself as "Isak Dinesen."

25. Quoted in Hannah, *Mask,* 12; cf. *Essays,* 196.

26. *Essays,* 1, 142; cf. her similar remarks about photographic images in "Daguerreotypes": appearing to offer direct transcriptions of reality, they are perpetually "changed" by viewers' shifting interpretive perspectives (*Essays,* 19). Cf. *Letters,* 388–89.

27. Thus, for example, I am rather less concerned with addressing the obvious, perhaps inevitable (and I think finally reductive) question—"was Karen Blixen a feminist?"—than with exploring the semiotics of gender in her writing, wherein "woman" and "feminist" become parts of a larger discursive fabric. As I hope to show, the question of whether or not Dinesen might be called "feminist" is misleading not only for an understanding of her complex texts and shifting self-representations, but in terms of the category "feminist" itself, which is neither monolithic nor amenable to stable or absolute definition, embracing at once a widely varying political praxis and a diverse, often contradictory theoretical range. For a capacious overview of the diversity of "feminism," see Catharine R. Stimpson, "Nancy Reagan Wears a Hat: Feminism and Its Cultural Consensus," *Critical Inquiry* 14 (Winter 1988): 223–43.

28. "On Feminism and Womanhood," KB Archives 154, 4.

Chapter One

1. This discourse shifts primarily between those critics who tend to revise and/or remythologize the mother as a figure for feminine creativity (e.g., Sandra Gilbert and Susan Gubar, *The Madwoman in the Attic: The Woman Writer and the Nineteenth-Century Literary Imagination* [New Haven: Yale University Press, 1979]) and those who question this usage as a reinscription of phallocentric codes (e.g., Jane Marcus, "Liberty, Sorority, Misogyny," in *The Representation of Women in Fiction,* ed. Carolyn G. Heilbrun and Margaret R. Higgonet (Baltimore: Johns Hopkins University Press, 1983), 60–97; Jane Gallop, "Reading the Mother Tongue: Psychoanalytic Feminist Criticism," *Critical Inquiry* 13 [Winter 1987]: 314–29). Dinesen, like Julia Kristeva, elaborates both perspectives, often using them to examine each other. Space does not permit a full list of texts in this ongoing dialogue, but see, e.g., Marianne Hirsch, "Review Essay: Mothers and Daughters," *Signs* 7 (Autumn 1981): 200–22; Gubar, "The Birth of the Artist as Heroine: (Re)Production, the *Künstlerroman* Tradition, and the Fiction of Katherine Mansfield," in *The Representation of Women in Fiction,* 19–59; *The (M)Other Tongue: Essays in Feminist Psychoanalytic Literature,* ed. Shirley Nelson Garner, Claire Kahane, and Madelon Sprengnether (Ithaca: Cornell University Press, 1985); Margaret Homans, "Representation, Reproduction, and Women's Place in Language," *Bearing the Word: Language and Female Experience in Nineteenth-Century Women's Writing* (Chicago: University of Chicago Press, 1986), 1–39; Domna Stanton, "Difference on Trial: A Critique of the Maternal Metaphor in

Cixous, Irigaray, and Kristeva," in *The Poetics of Gender,* ed. Nancy Miller (New York: Columbia University Press, 1986), 157–82; Mary Jacobus, "Dora and the Pregnant Madonna," *Reading Woman* (New York: Columbia University Press, 1986).

2. *Desire in Language,* ed. Leon S. Roudiez, trans. Thomas Gora, Alice Jardine, and Roudiez (New York: Columbia University Press, 1980), 237.

3. See "Place Names," *Desire in Language,* 29, on pregnancy as "the ultimate limit of meaning"; and *Powers of Horror: An Essay on Abjection* (1980), trans. Leon S. Roudiez (New York: Columbia University Press, 1982), 155, on labor and birth as disruptions of unifying categories. Crucial here is Kristeva's theory that language itself—hence our self-representations as speaking/writing subjects—is enabled by a perpetual dynamic interplay between those signifying practices she names the "symbolic" (associated with the subject's entry into culture and language under the name and law of the father) and the "semiotic" (associated with the child's experience of kineaesthetic oneness with the body of the mother and prelinguistic sensations). See, e.g., "The Semiotic Chora Ordering the Drives" in *Revolution in Poetic Language* (1974), trans. Roudiez (New York: Columbia University Press, 1984), 23–30, and "Stabat Mater," (orig. "Hérétique de l'amour," 1977), in *Tales of Love,* trans. Roudiez (New York: Columbia University Press, 1987), 234–63.

4. Kenneth Burke, "The First Three Chapters of Genesis," in *The Bible in Its Literary Milieu: Contemporary Essays,* ed. John Maier and Vincent Tollers (Grand Rapids, Michigan: William B. Eerdmans, 1979), 390; Aeschylus, *The Eumenides,* in *Oresteia,* trans. Richmond Lattimore (Chicago: University of Chicago Press, 1953), 158. On the import of gender in this text, which like Genesis 2:4b–3 has become a *locus classicus* for feminist analyses of Western cultural foundations, see Froma Zeitlin, "The Dynamics of Misogyny: Myth and Mythmaking in the Oresteia," in *Women in the Ancient World: The Arethusa Papers* (Albany: SUNY Press, 1984), 159–94.

5. For Dinesen's play on the double entendre of *enceinte* (both "pregnant"— cf. English "confinement"—and "an enclosure or surrounding wall") see *OA,* 262. Cf. Kristeva's similar wordplay in "Motherhood According to Giovanni Bellini," 240.

6. *Moses and Monotheism, The Standard Edition of the Complete Psychological Works of Sigmund Freud,* ed. and trans. James Strachey, 24 vols. (London: Hogarth Press, 1953–74), 13:114. Following J. J. Bachofen's cultural theories in *Das Mutterrecht* (1861), Freud refers to the "revolution in . . . juridical conditions" produced when "the matriarchal social order was succeeded by the patriarchal one" (113), but he celebrates this shift as "a victory of intellectuality over sensuality" (114).

7. "Contingencies of Value," *Critical Inquiry* 10 (September 1983): 17–18.

8. Hesiod, *Theogony,* trans. Apostolos N. Athanassakis (Baltimore: Johns Hopkins University Press, 1983), 35.

9. See E. R. Curtius, *European Literature and the Latin Middle Ages,* trans. Willard R. Trask (New York: Pantheon Books, 1953), 132–33; cf. Terry Castle, "Lab'ring Bards: Birth *Topoi* and English Poetics, 1160–1820," *JEGP* 78 (April 1979): 193–208, on the pervasiveness of "this ancient analogy for [male] literary creation" (194).

10. For analysis of these paradigms, see Teresa de Lauretis, *Alice Doesn't: Feminism, Semiotics, Cinema* (Bloomington: Indiana University Press, 1984), 103−57.

11. *Beginnings: Intention and Method* (New York: Basic Books, 1975), 162.

12. *The Pleasure of the Text*, trans. Richard Miller (New York: Hill and Wang, 1975), 37; cf. Bloom, *The Anxiety of Influence* (New York: Oxford University Press, 1973), and Derrida's association of the mother with language (e.g., *Glas* [Paris: Galilée, 1974]). See also Geoffrey H. Hartman, *Saving the Text: Literature, Derrida, Philosophy* (Baltimore: Johns Hopkins University Press, 1981), 81−90; Eric Sundquist, *Home as Found: Authority and Genealogy in Nineteenth Century American Literature* (Baltimore: Johns Hopkins University Press, 1979). Gilbert and Gubar offer the classic critique of the androcentrism of this discourse (*Madwoman*, 3−104).

13. *The Pleasure of the Text*, 47.

14. On Aristotelian androcentrism see Susan Moller Okin, *Women in Western Political Thought* (Princeton: Princeton University Press, 1981).

15. "The Text, the World, the Critic," in *Textual Strategies: Perspectives in Post-Structuralist Criticism*, ed. Josué V. Harari (Ithaca: Cornell University Press, 1979), 179.

16. "The Case of Maternity: Paradigms of Women as Maternity Cases," *Signs* 4 (Summer 1979): 609.

17. See Raymond Williams, *Problems of Materialism and Culture* (London: NLB, 1980), and Smith, "Contingencies of Value."

18. On the conception of the author as inherently male, see Gilbert and Gubar, *Madwoman*, 3−20.

19. "Existe-t-il une écriture de femme?" (1974), trans. Marilyn A. August, in *New French Feminisms*, ed. Elaine Marks and Isabelle de Courtivron (New York: Schocken, 1981), 162−63. On the pressures compelling women to write as men, see Gilbert and Gubar, *Madwoman*, 65−71. On women and the traditional canon, see Froula, "When Eve Reads Milton: Undoing the Canonical Economy" (*Critical Inquiry* 10 [Dec. 1983]: 321−47); Lillian Robinson, "Treason Our Text: Feminist Challenges to the Literary Canon," *Tulsa Studies in Women's Literature* 2 (1983): 83−98; and Susan Hardy Aiken, "Women and the Question of Canonicity," *College English* 48 (March 1986): 288−301.

20. See Susan Lanser and Evelyn Torton Beck, "[Why] Are There No Great Women Critics? And What Difference Does It Make?" in *The Prism of Sex: Essays in the Sociology of Knowledge*, ed. Beck and Julia A. Sherman (Madison: University of Wisconsin Press, 1979); Elaine Showalter, "Feminist Criticism in the Wilderness," *Critical Inquiry* 8 (Winter 1981): 201; and Edwin Ardener, "Belief and the Problem of Women," in "Belief and the Problem of Women and the 'Problem' Revisited," in *Perceiving Women*, ed. Shirley Ardener (London: Malaby Press, 1975), 1−25.

21. "Feminist Criticism in the Wilderness," 204, and "Literary Criticism," *Signs* 1 (Winter 1975): 435. See also Gilbert and Gubar, *Madwoman*, on women's "palimpsestic" texts, wherein "surface designs conceal or obscure deeper, less accessible (and less socially acceptable) levels of meaning" which they both express and camouflage (73); and Nancy Miller, "Emphasis Added," *PMLA* 96 (1981): 47, and "Arachnologies," in *The Poetics of Gender*, 270−95. On polylogical dis-

course, cf. Bakhtin's notion of heteroglossia (*The Dialogical Imagination* [See in-tro., n. 4]), readumbrated by Kristeva in *Polylogue* (Paris: Seuil, 1977).

22. See, e.g., Langbaum, *Gayety* (intro., n. 9), 5, Hannah, *Mask* (intro., n. 2), 34–35, and Thurman, *Life* (intro., n. 1), 261–62, 331. Recent publica-tions indicate how persistent the androcentric view remains: see, e.g., Anthony Stephens, "Narrative Structure in Karen Blixen's 'The Dreamers,'" in *Festscrift for Ralph Farrell,* ed. Stephens, H. L. Rogers, and Brian Langlan (Bern: Peter Lang, 1977), 121–36, and "The Paradox of the Omnipotent Narrator in the Works of Karen Blixen," *Neophilologus* 62 (April 1978): 297–313; Anders Westenholz, *The Power of Aries,* trans. Lise Kure-Jensen (Baton Rouge: Louisiana State University Press, 1987); David H. Richter, "Covert Plot in Isak Dinesen's 'Sorrow-acre,'" *Journal of Narrative Technique* 15 (Spring 1985): 82–90, and a number of the essays in *Karen Blixen/Isak Dinesen: Tradition, Modernity, and Other Ambiguities* (intro., n. 2), a landmark collection that brings together both Danish and American crit-ics. For early feminist responses to Dinesen see Patricia Spacks, *The Female Imagi-nation* (New York: Knopf, 1972), 384–90, 412–14, and Ellen Moers, *Literary Women* (New York: Doubleday, 1976) 230–31. Susan Gubar's "'The Blank Page' and the Issues of Female Creativity," *Critical Inquiry* 8 (Winter 1981): 243–63, which reads the tale as a major document in the female modernist tradition, has made it a touchstone for American feminist criticism—see, e.g., Froula, "When Eve Reads Milton: Undoing the Canonical Economy," and Gayle Greene and Coppélia Kahn, "Feminist Scholarship and the Social Construction of Woman," *Making a Difference: Feminist Literary Criticism* (London: Methuen, 1985), 1–36. Other diverse feminist readings of Dinesen include Janet Handler Burstein, "Two Locked Caskets: Selfhood and 'Otherness' in the Work of Isak Dinesen," *TSLL* 20 (Winter 1978): 615–32; Robin Lydenberg, "Against the Law of Gravity: Fe-male Adolescence in Isak Dinesen's *Seven Gothic Tales,*" *Modern Fiction Studies* 24 (Winter 1978); Sybil Victoria James, "Caged Birds . . . And Free: Women in the Works of Isak Dinesen," Ph.D. diss., State University of New York at Buffalo, 1978; Florence C. Lewis, "Isak Dinesen and Feminist Criticism," *North American Review* 264 (Spring 1979): 62–72; Gubar, "Blessings in Disguise: Cross-dréssing as Re-dressing for Female Modernists," *Massachusetts Review* 22 (Autumn 1981): 477–508; Susan Hardy Aiken, "Dinesen's 'Sorrow-acre': Tracing the Woman's Line," *Contemporary Literature* 25 (Summer 1984): 156–86, "The Uses of Du-plicity: Isak Dinesen and Questions of Feminist Criticism," *Scandinavian Studies* 57 (Autumn 1985): 400–411, "Isak Dinesen and Photo/Graphic Recollection," *Exposure* 23 (Winter 1985): 29–38, and "Writing (in) Exile: Isak Dinesen and the Poetics of Displacement," in *Women's Writing in Exile,* ed. Mary Lynn Broe and Angela Ingram (Chapel Hill: University of North Carolina Press, 1989); Else Ce-derborg, "Karen Blixen, Her Life and Writings," in *On Modern Marriage,* 17–31; Sara Stambaugh, *The Witch and the Goddess in the Stories of Isak Dinesen: A Feminist Reading* (Ann Arbor: UMI Research Press, 1988); and Judith Rosenberg, "Isak Dinesen and the Stork: Delivering the Female Text," *Tulsa Studies in Women's Literature* 7 (Fall 1988): 297–300. For comparable Danish studies of gender in Karen Blixen's writings see Susanne Fabricius, "Vandrende Riddere og knuste Kvinder," *Kritik,* no. 22 (1972): 67–80; Else Cederborg, "Den camouflerede modstand: Karen Blixens kvindesyn," *Edda,* no. 1 (1979); Marianne Juhl and Bo

Hakon Jørgensen, *Dianas Hævn: To spor i Karen Blixens forfatterskab* (Odense: Odense Universitetsforlag, 1981), trans. as *Diana's Revenge* (see intro., n. 9). See also *Out of Denmark: Isak Dinesen/Karen Blixen, 1885–1985 and Danish Women Writers Today,* ed. Bodil Wamberg (Copenhagen: Danish Cultural Institute, 1985).

23. These women work within an intellectual climate—and often directly within the intellectual traditions—elaborated by forms of post-structuralism associated with Lacan and Derrida. But Irigaray, Cixous, and Kristeva cannot be read simply within the Derridean or Lacanian context: each has elaborated distinctive ways of thinking about the question of "woman." Whatever their diversities, theorists who expose the instabilities of hierarchizing oppositional epistemologies and ontologies are especially useful for understanding a writer like Dinesen, who with equal persistence exposed the operations of such systems.

24. For exemplary discussions of the much-debated differences between "French" and "Anglo-American" feminisms, and the problems and possibilities of attempts to work within/across theoretically different critical perspectives, see Domna Stanton, "Language and Revolution: The Franco-American Disconnection," in *The Future of Difference,* ed. Hester Eisenstein and Alice Jardine (Boston: G. K. Hall, 1980), 73–87; Nancy K. Miller, "The Text's Heroine: A Feminist Critic and Her Fictions," *Diacritics* 12 (Summer 1982): 48–53; Margaret Homans, "Her Very Own Howl: The Ambiguities of Representation in Recent Women's Fiction," *Signs* 9 (Winter 1983): 186–205; Jardine, *Gynesis* (intro., n. 16); Gayatri Spivak, "French Feminisms in an International Frame," in *In Other Worlds* (New York: Methuen, 1987); Elizabeth Meese, *Crossing the Double Cross: The Practice of Feminist Criticism* (Chapel Hill: University of North Carolina Press, 1986); and Toril Moi, *Sexual/Textual Politics* (London: Methuen, 1985).

25. Hannah, *Mask,* 59.

26. Dinesen's use of Portia as a figure of her own ambiguous situation is reinforced not only by Portia's transvestism but by the play's emphasis that English is a foreign tongue to her (*Merchant of Venice* 1.2.70–72). On the link between this linguistic displacement and the "foreignness" of women in patriarchal society, see Phyllis Rackin, "Androgyny, Mimesis, and the Marriage of the Boy Heroine on the English Renaissance Stage," *PMLA* 102 (January 1987): 33.

27. Parmenia Migel, *Titania: The Biography of Isak Dinesen* (New York: Random House, 1967), 239.

28. On the feminine subversions in this text see Aiken, "Dinesen's 'Sorrowacre.'"

29. "Nietzsche, Genealogy, History," *Language Counter-Memory, Practice,* trans. Donald Bouchard (Ithaca: Cornell University Press, 1977), 151.

30. See Natalie Zemon Davis, "Women on Top," in *The Reversible World,* ed. Barbara A. Babcock (Ithaca: Cornell University Press, 1978), 148; Sherry Ortner, "Is Female to Male as Nature Is to Culture?" in *Woman, Culture and Society,* ed. Michelle Zimbalist Rosaldo and Louise Lamphere (Stanford: Stanford University Press), 67–88; and Showalter, "Feminist Criticism in the Wilderness," 192.

31. "Ironie als literarisches Prinzip," in *Ironie und Dichtung,* ed. Albert Schaefer; quoted in Hartman, *Saving the Text,* 167.

32. *Saving the Text,* 167.

33. *This Sex Which Is Not One* (1977), trans. Catherine Porter with Carolyn Burke (Ithaca: Cornell University Press, 1985), 76, 78. See also Miller's application of this text in "Emphasis Added," 38–39.

34. Hannah, *Mask,* 54.

35. See Cixous, "Sorties," *The Newly Born Woman* (intro, n. 13).

36. Showalter, *A Literature of their Own: British Women Writers from Brontë to Lessing* (Princeton: Princeton University Press, 1977), 28.

37. See, e.g., the exchange between Peggy Kamuf ("Replacing Feminist Criticism") and Miller ("The Text's Heroine") in *Diacritics* 12 (Summer 1982): 42–53; and Gayatri Spivak, "Displacement and the Discourse of Woman," in *Displacement: Derrida and After,* ed. Mark Krupnick (Bloomington: Indiana University Press, 1983), 169–95. On transvestism and female authorship, see Gubar, "Blessings in Disguise."

38. Clara Svendsen, *Notater om Karen Blixen* (Copenhagen: Gyldendal, 1974), 91; my translation.

39. On male literary transvestism, see Nancy K. Miller, " 'I's' in Drag: The Sex of Recollection," *The Eighteenth Century: Theory and Interpretation* 22 (Winter 1981): 47–57; and Elaine Showalter, "Critical Cross-Dressing: Male Feminists and the Woman of the Year," *Raritan* (Fall 1983): 130–49.

40. See Karen Blixen's self-description in *Letters,* 279, 406, and self-referential representation of Pellegrina Leoni's final leap into "the abyss" in response to the question "Who are you?" in "The Dreamers" (*SGT,* 327). Cf. also the *horror vacui* Karen Blixen evoked in response to Lindemann's assault on her authorial (pseudo)identity.

41. *The History of Sexuality: Volume 1: An Introduction,* trans. Robert Hurley (1978; New York: Vintage Books, 1980), 62.

42. Quoted in Hannah, *Mask,* p. 50.

43. See *MM,* 67 for Karen Blixen's critique of the use of woman as property in male economies. Dinesen's representation of this marital exchange, based on the structural equivalence of women, property, and words, at once anticipates and undercuts the model of culture developed by Claude Lévi-Strauss, who accounted for the universality of the incest taboo by concluding that men circulate women, like gifts and language, in order to extend their own bonding systems. Lévi-Strauss identifies "the emergence of symbolic thought" with the view that "women, like words, should be . . . exchanged" (*The Elementary Structures of Kinship,* rev. ed., trans. James H. Bell et al [Boston: Beacon Press, 1969], 495–96). Dinesen's suggestion that this masculine power network is neither so stable nor so permanent as it appears anticipates recent feminist critiques of his premise. See Gayle Rubin, "The Traffic in Women: Notes on the 'Political Economy' of Sex," in *Toward an Anthropology of Women,* ed. Rayna R. Reiter (New York: Monthly Review Press, 1975), 157–210; and Michèle Richman, "Eroticism in the Patriarchal Order," *Diacritics* 6 (Spring 1976): 46–53.

44. On the phallus as the privileged signifier marking the subject's entry into the symbolic order dominated by "*le nom du père,*" see Lacan, "The signification of the phallus," in *Ecrits,* trans. Alan Sheridan (New York: Norton, 1977), 281–91. Jane Gallop gives a lucid summary: "The Name-of-the-Father . . . is . . . actually a Lacanian displacement of what Freud bequeathed him/us, the

Oedipal Father, absolute primal Father. Whereas Freud's Oedipal Father might be taken for a real, biological father, Lacan's Name-of-the-Father operates explicitly in the register of language. The Name-of-the-Father: the patronym, patriarchal law, patrilineal identity, language as our inscription into patriarchy." The name and the "no" (prohibition, repression) of the Father is, as Gallop notes, "always an imaginary effect" (*The Daughter's Seduction: Feminism and Psychoanalysis* [Ithaca: Cornell University Press, 1982], 47). Classical representations of the *phallos* often suggest precisely the intersection between biological structure and symbolic meaning implicit in Lacan (although he routinely insists on the phallus as sign rather than anatomical organ, the connections are unavoidable, as Anthony Wilden and others have noted) and parodied by Dinesen. See, for example, K. J. Dover, *Greek Homosexualities* (Cambridge: Harvard University Press, 1978), 128, fig. B370, where two satyrs cavort around a monumental *phallos,* its glans containing a single large eye. On the implications of such figures, see Eva C. Keuls, *The Reign of the Phallus: Sexual Politics in Ancient Athens* (New York: Harper and Row, 1985). Cf. C. F. Jung, *Memories, Dreams, Reflections,* ed. Aniela Jaffé, trans. Richard Winston and Clara Winston (New York: Vintage, 1961), 11–14, on a crucial childhood dream in which Jung saw "a ritual phallus" as a gigantic, enthroned penis, with "a rounded head . . . on the very top of [which] was a single eye" (12).

45. Cf. Cixous, "The Laugh of the Medusa," trans. Keith and Paula Cohen, *Signs* 1 (Summer 1976): 283, on poetry as subversive "feminine" language: "There have been poets who would go to any lengths to slip something by at odds with tradition—men capable of loving love and hence . . . of imagining the woman who would hold out against oppression and constitute herself as a superb, equal, hence 'impossible' subject."

46. I borrow the phrase from Douglas, *Purity and Danger* (see intro., n. 3), which like Dinesen's fiction explores the danger of the "marginal" to that which regards itself as "central." Dinesen's representation of the erotics of reading anticipates Barthes's *Pleasure of the Text,* but with a crucial shift, for in Barthes writer and reader are always "he," even in their most intense discomposures.

47. "Motherhood according to Bellini," 239–40. See also *Revolution in Poetic Language,* 21–106; and "Women's Time," trans. Alice Jardine, *Signs* 7 (Autumn 1981): 16, where Kristeva elaborates on Plato's conception of the cosmic womb space (*chora*) as "nourishing, unnameable, anterior to the one, to God, and, consequently, defying metaphysics." Benedetta's music plays on the etymological kinship of *chora* and *choral.*

48. On the persistent representations of women as subversive forces within the patriarchal state, see Carole Pateman, "The Disorder of Women," *Ethics* 91 (Oct. 1980): 20–34. Cf. Douglas, *Purity and Danger,* 140–58, on women as "pollution" and threat in masculinist tribal societies.

49. The character of Giovanni Ferrar derives most directly from A. E. W. Mason's now-forgotten novel *Musk and Amber;* but there are also other ironically altered intertexts here, notably Balzac's *Sarrasine*—another instance of Dinesen's reflexive representations of her own anomalous situation in a masculine tradition. Her reference to the "seraphic" love affair that ensues suggests a punning reference to another Balzac fiction of unstable gender, *Seraphita.*

50. The castrato is doubly like the woman here: the opera in which he performs, *Achilles in Scyros,* depicts a transvestite Achilles, disguised as a girl, "Pyrrha," by his mother, who seeks thus to protect him from a warrior's death. I am grateful to Else Cederborg for calling my attention to this connection.

51. *The New Science of Giambattista Vico,* trans. Thomas G. Bergin and Max Harold Frisch (Ithaca: Cornell University Press, 1968); Rousseau, *Politics and the Arts,* trans. A. Bloom (Ithaca: Cornell University Press, 1968). For analyses of this topos see Tony Tanner, *Adultery in the Novel: Contract and Transgression* (Baltimore: Johns Hopkins University Press, 1979); and Pateman, "The Disorder of Women."

52. Dinesen's play on Nietzsche's *Die Geburt der Tragödie aus dem Geiste der Musik* (Leipzig: E. W. Fritzsch, 1872) anticipates Derrida's recognition of the continual eruption therein of the discourse of the mother. See *Spurs: Nietzsche's Styles,* trans. Barbara Harlow (Chicago: University of Chicago Press, 1978), esp. 97, on woman "as an affirmative power, a dissimulatress, an artist, a dionysiac." See also Spivak's critique, in "Displacement and the Discourse of Woman," of Derrida's own masculinist assumptions in *Spurs.* On Dionysus's transgression of sexual limitations, see Thomas Rosenmeyer, "Tragedy and Religion: *The Bacchae,*" in *Euripides,* ed. Erich Segal (Englewood Cliffs, N.J.: Prentice-Hall, 1968), 154, and Carolyn Heilbrun, *Toward a Recognition of Androgyny* (1964; New York: W. W. Norton, 1982), x–xi.

53. The topos of male twins has sources in both ancient Near Eastern and Greek mythologies. As Bruno Bettelheim notes, it occurs in thirteenth century B.C. Egyptian papyri (*The Uses of Enchantment: The Meaning and Importance of Fairy Tales* [New York: Vintage, 1977], 91); see also René Girard, *Violence and the Sacred,* trans. Patrick Gregory (Baltimore: Johns Hopkins University Press, 1972), 57; and Heilbrun on the androgynous implications of twins in *Toward a Recognition of Androgyny* (34–45). Dinesen may also have recalled the male twins in George Sand's *La Petite Fadette*—distinguishable only by a mark tatooed into the skin of the elder by the midwife. In an essay that appeared after I had published an earlier draft of this chapter ("The Uses of Duplicity") Naomi Schor analyses the Sand text ("Reading Double: Sand's Difference," in *The Poetics of Gender,* 252–67).

54. *Saving the Text,* 75.

55. Dinesen's representation of the subversiveness of the Madonna anticipates Marina Warner, *Alone of All Her Sex: The Myth and Cult of the Virgin Mary* (1976; New York: Pocket Books, 1978), 34–49, 65–67, 103–17, 147–48, 191, 236–51, and Kristeva's "Stabat Mater" and "Motherhood according to Bellini."

56. *Interfaces of the Word: Studies in the Evolution of Consciousness and Culture* (Ithaca: Cornell University Press, 1977), 23–24.

57. Cf. Barbara Johnson, *The Critical Difference* (Baltimore: Johns Hopkins University Press, 1980): "Difference . . . is not what distinguishes one identity from another. It is not a difference between . . . but a difference within . . . which subverts the idea of identity" (4).

58. Dinesen plays on Baudelaire's fascination with perfume as a condensation, in Kristeva's words, "of an invading as well as an invaded maternal body," "correspondences that . . . become condensed into words and feelings, thus pul-

verizing the identities of all" ("Baudelaire, or Infinity, Perfume, and Punk," *Tales of Love*, 329, 334 ; cf. 318–40). See, e.g., "Le Voyage," "Le Flacon," and "Le Balcon" ("Mère de souvenirs, maitresse des maitresses . . . Ces serments ces parfums, ces baisers infinis"). Dinesen's rereadings of Baudelaire here and elsewhere (e.g., "The Old Chevalier") anticipate Kristeva's.

59. This notion of story also recalls Aristotle's definition of tragedy in the *Poetics* (*Aristotle's Theory of Poetry and Fine Art,* trans. S. H. Butcher [New York: Dover, 1951], 25–29).

60. On Dinesen's subversive uses of Great Goddess mythoi, see my "Dinesen's 'Sorrow-acre,'" and chap. 5.

61. On the relationship of doubleness, duplicity, and diabolism, see Sarah Kofman, "Le double e(s)t le diable," *Quatre Romans analytiques* (Paris: Galilée, 1974).

62. *Gayety,* 55.

63. See E. A. Speiser, *Genesis* (New York: Doubleday, 1964), 10: "Names were regarded not only as labels but also as symbols, magical keys as it were to the nature and essence of the given being or thing." As Bruce Vawter notes, in Scripture "*name-giving* signified control, dominance, taking possession" (*Genesis: A New Reading* [New York: Doubleday, 1977], 43; cf. 74). See Dinesen's similar remarks on the power of naming in *Out of Africa,* 120–24. On the mockery in Sarah's laughter, see Gen. 18:10–12; 21:6.

64. "The Uncanny," *The Standard Edition,* 17:241. Further citations appear in my text. I am indebted to Shoshana Felman's treatment of this essay in "Rereading Femininity," *Yale French Studies* 62 (Dec. 1981): 32–42, and to Cixous, "Fiction and Its Phantoms: A Reading of Freud's *Das Unheimliche* (The 'uncanny')," trans. Robert Denomme, *New Literary History* 7 (Spring 1976): 525–48.

65. "Medusa's Head," *Sexuality and the Psychology of Love,* ed. Philip Rieff (New York: Macmillan, 1963), 212–13. On the applicability of this text to eruptions of political violence, see Neil Hertz, "Medusa's Head: Male Hysteria Under Political Pressure," and Catherine Gallagher, "More About Medusa's Head, I," *Representations* 4 (Fall 1983): 27–54, 55–57.

66. See Irigaray, *This Sex;* Dorothy Dinnerstein, *The Mermaid and the Minotaur: Sexual Arrangements and Human Malaise* (New York: Harper and Row, 1976); Nancy Chodorow, *The Reproduction of Mothering: Psychoanalysis and the Sociology of Gender* (Berkeley and Los Angeles: University of California Press, 1978); de Lauretis, *Alice Doesn't,* 109–57.

67. *Bearing the Word,* 13. Cf. Sarah Kofman, *The Enigma of Woman: Woman in Freud's Writings,* trans. Catherine Porter (Ithaca: Cornell University Press), 203, on the "affirmative woman" who does not believe herself "castrated," and Coppélia Kahn on the "contradiction of using psychoanalytic theory to revise masculinist paradigms": "It is precisely this contradiction that feminists can turn to good account. We are an audience Freud never envisioned; we read in his oedipal scripts of the family drama an irony he did not intend. The irony centers on his grounding of sexual differentiation in the cultural primacy of the phallus, within the context of a family structure which mirrors the psychological organization of patriarchal society. . . . By reading his theory as a mirror of the patriarchal family, feminist critics can deconstruct his account of the creation of gender.

But we can only do this by locating ourselves on the margin of patriarchal dis-course—as daughters of mothers rather than of fathers" ("Excavating 'Those Dim Minoan Regions': Maternal Subtexts in Patriarchal Literature," *Diacritics* 12 [Summer 1982]: 32–41).

68. *LA,* 18. The phrase refers to the African landscape, which Dinesen linked metaphorically with both the maternal body and an alternative discourse, intimated only in the "wild" spaces outside the bounds of the patriarchal sym-bolic order both cultural and linguistic. See chap. 10.

69. Like the description of Benedetta's multiple aesthetic/erotic pleasures, the polyvalence of *capriccio* conjoins the symbolic orders of music, literature, and the visual arts. See Philip P. Fehl, "Farewell to Jokes: The Last Capricci of Giovanni Domenico Tiepolo and the Tradition of Irony in Venetian Painting," *Critical Inquiry* 5 (Summer 1979): 780–82.

70. Hannah, "In Memoriam Karen Blixen: Some Aspects of Her Attitude to Life," *Sewanee Review* 71 (1963): 589; Langbaum, *Gayety,* 26.

71. Cf. Dinesen's remark about her texts: "I love a joke, I love the humor-ous. I often think that what we need now is a great humorist" (*Writers at Work,* 15). Cf. her pervasive use of jester figures and her adoption of the role of the jester in her own self-stagings (Thurman, *Life,* 367–68; Clara Svendsen, *The Life and Destiny of Isak Dinesen,* ed. Frans Lasson [Chicago: University of Chicago Press, 1970], 181).

Chapter Two

1. This critical truism requires reiteration because of the weight the bio-graphical tradition has exerted on prior readings of Dinesen's work; we cannot assume, as critics have often done, that her life offers an unmediated form of ex-tratextual "truth" to which the narratives must be subjected. Even if we grant that biography underwrites fiction, the issues are still hardly self-evident. The question remains, *which* life shall we privilege? Important biographical sources on Dinesen include *LA;* Clara Svendsen, *Notater om Karen Blixen* (chap. 1, n. 38); Thomas Dinesen, *Tanne, Min Søster Karen Blixen* (Copenhagen: Gyldendal, 1974); Bjørnvig, *The Pact* (intro., n. 12); Clara Svendsen, *The Life and Destiny of Isak Dinesen* (chap. 1, n. 71); Migel, *Titania* (chap. 1, n. 27); Errol Trzebinski, *Silence Will Speak: A Study of the Life of Denys Finch Hatton and His Relationship With Karen Blixen* (London: Heinemann, 1977); Thurman, *Isak Dinesen* (intro., n. 1)—now the standard biography; and Anders Westenholz, *The Power of Aries* (chap. 1, n. 22).

2. Dinesen stresses her mother's difference from the Westenholzes, compar-ing Ingeborg to Nora in *A Doll's House* and emphasizing her own sense of iden-tity with her mother. Cf. Ingeborg's similar remarks (*LA,* 428).

3. Huck Finn's exploratory flight is the comic epitome of this male fantasy. Cf. Leslie Fiedler's analysis of the (male) American obsession with this "story of that sacred-heathen love between White man and colored man in a world without women" (*The Return of the Vanishing American* [London: Stein and Day, 1968], 119). On the sexual politics of this mythos, see Annette Kolodny, "Turning the Lens on the Panther Captivity," *Critical Inquiry* 8 (Winter 1981): 345, and *The*

Lay of the Land: Metaphor as Experience and History in American Life and Letters (Chapel Hill: University of North Carolina Press, 1975); Carroll Smith-Rosenberg, *Disorderly Conduct: Visions of Gender in Victorian America* (New York: Oxford University Press, 1985), 92–108. In *Out of Africa* Dinesen anticipates these analyses in her ironic portrait of "Old Knudsen," who narrated his own wandering life as an epic celebrating his "great exploits and achievements" and "had a deep mistrust of woman, and saw her as the enemy of man . . . , out to stop his fun" (56–60, 187–95).

4. For Dinesen's comments on Wilhelm's mythologization, see *LA*, 394–95. Cf. her fictionalized portrait of Wilhelm as Ib Angel in "Copenhagen Season" (*LT*). On the law of the father, see Lacan, *Ecrits* (chap. 1, n. 44), 61–68.

5. Thurman, *Life*, 6–7, 25–26. Thurman acknowledges that "the symmetry is not perfect" (6) and that "it was always 'my mother's family' and not 'my mother' for whom Tanne reserved her deepest resentment" (31), but the preponderance of her argument, by its emphasis on the dichotomy, tends to obscure these subtler provisos.

6. See, e.g., Johannesson, *The World of Isak Dinesen* (intro., n. 9), 92–93, and Hannah, *Mask* (intro., n. 2), 15, 34, 91. Richter's recent remark about "her defense of the ancien régime, her contempt for democratic vistas," and her "elitism" ("Covert Plot" [chap 1, n. 22], 88) typifies this view; cf. Westenholz's unqualified assertion of "her worship of the titled aristocracy" (*Power of Aries*, 67; cf. 68–80). Even Thurman, whose brilliant biography reflects an awareness of gender issues, usually subscribes to these interpretations (e.g., *Life*, 261, 300–301).

7. See Eileen Simpson, *Orphans* (New York: Weidenfeld and Nicholson, 1987).

8. The term "gynocritical" is Showalter's useful coinage to signify "a sustained investigation of literature by women" ("Feminist Criticism in the Wilderness" [see chap. 1, no. 20], 184–85). On the psychosocial formation of gendered subjects, see Chodorow, *The Reproduction of Mothering* and Dinnerstein, *The Mermaid and the Minotaur* (chap. 1, n. 66).

9. "George Sand and the Novel of Female Pastoral," in *Representation of Women in Fiction* (see chap. 1, n. 1), 141.

10. E.g., *LA*, 258–65, 141–42; *MM*, 40–41, 50, 65–69. Cf. "The Deluge at Norderney," as Calypso contemplates a synecdoche of the ancien régime in "mighty coats of armor" in the misogynist bastion of phallic power from which she is an outcast: "they would have been partisans of hers, had they not been all hollow" (*SGT*, 45).

11. In reading the autobiographical elements of "Alkmene" (*WT*), Thurman demonstrates that the eponymous female protagonist, an isolated, misunderstood, illegitimate child, is betrayed by an adored companion whose ambiguous relationship with her combines sibling companionship, sexual allure, and paternal power (30–35). His name, Vilhelm, is a variant of Dinesen's father's. On the relationship between the seductive father and patriarchal cultural structures, see Judith Lewis Herman (with Lisa Hirschman), *Father-Daughter Incest* (Cambridge: Harvard University Press, 1981). On the psychoanalytic implications of this relationship in life and in texts, see Luce Irigaray, *Speculum of the*

Other Woman, trans. Gillian C. Gill (Ithaca: Cornell University Press, 1985), Gallop, *Daughter's Seduction* (chap. 1, n. 44), Diane Sadoff, *Monsters of Affection* (Baltimore: Johns Hopkins University Press, 1982), and Lynda Zwinger, *Daughters, Fathers, and the Novel* (Madison: University of Wisconsin Press, forthcoming). On its literary implications for the authoring daughter, see Sandra Gilbert, "Notes Toward a Literary Daughteronomy," *Critical Inquiry* 11 (Summer, 1985): 355–84, and Christine Froula, "The Daughter's Seduction: Sexual Violence and Literary History," *Signs* 11 (1986): 621–44.

12. *LA,* 315; cf. 163, 258–59, 260–65.

13. *LA,* 204–10, 234–36, 258–65, 305–7, 365–67, 369–74, 390–94. Thurman stresses the complexity and ambivalence of their relationship (*Life,* 58–64).

14. *LA,* 381, 298, 396, 398. In the same letter she celebrates Ingeborg's ability to transfer her constricting environment into a wild space—a "meadow, where 'no one has plowed and no one weeded, but thousands of bees have sipped the honey.'" On Dinesen's association of her own writing with the redemptive figure of woman as a manifestation of goddess religions that antedate Christianity, see Aiken, "Dinesen's Sorrow-acre" and Stambaugh, *The Witch and the Goddess* (chap. 1, n. 22).

15. *LA,* 407; cf. 110–11, 252, 350, and esp. 228–29, on her mother's departure from Ngong: "When I got back to the farm I felt that the sense of loss was almost too hard to bear; but as I turned the corner and the house came in sight a strange thing happened: I felt as if I were coming home to you,—and that is how it has been ever since. . . . Now I can really understand what it means to say that the house where my mother has been is 'forever blessed,' and how true it is. . . . Everything that I have been attached to has taken on a wonderful new value because your eyes have rested on it. . . . Thanks and thanks and thanks again, as long as I live, for coming."

16. On the daughter's (over)involvement with the mother, see Irigaray, "And the One Doesn't Stir without the Other," trans. Hélène Vivienne Wenzel, *Signs* 7 (Autumn 1981): 60–67, and Chodorow, *The Reproduction of Mothering.*

17. See *LA,* 114, 116, 127, 212, 375–76; cf. 269–71, 275–89. These citations (among many others) reveal Dinesen's ambivalence about her relationship to her mother as potentially all-absorbing. Like the speaker in Irigaray's "And the One Doesn't Stir," Dinesen was both drawn into this symbiosis and intensely resistant to it. Cf. Jacobus's analysis of the ambiguous figure of the mother in Wollstonecraft and Irigaray (*Reading Woman* [see chap. 1, n. 1], 276–92).

18. See *LA,* 76, 130, 152, 194–95, 196, 212–13, 274, 289, 300.

19. See *LA,* 300, 319; and 398–400, wherein Blixen elaborates for her mother her own developing thoughts on woman's emancipation.

20. *LA,* 427–28. Cf. similar statements in her later letters to her daughter, quoted in Thurman, *Life,* 275–76.

21. Cf. *LA,* 159, where Blixen celebrates "mobility of the soul," with her later definition of her mother's liberatory "lightness of mind," comparable to Blixen's own (380).

22. For discussions of "The Poet" and "The Caryatids," see chap 9. For "Sorrow-acre," see the epilogue and my "Dinesen's 'Sorrow-acre.'" In "A Country Tale," the subversive word of the peasant mother Lone, which utterly dis-

mantles the world of property, class, and paternal genealogy—maintained in "the name of [the] fathers"—on which Eitel's privilege and security rest, is figuratively associated with "the open landscape" "outside the fence" that demarcates the patriarchal estate, and with the wild space in "the depth of the forest" (*LT*, 191–246).

23. *LA*, 224, 229; cf. 228, 251–52, 267, 298, 310–11. I shall return to the colonialist import of the trope of Africa as maternalized paradise.

24. *Power of Aries*, esp. pp. 81–96. While Westenholz's book is polemical—designed to vindicate his family—it provides a useful corrective to uncritical claims about Dinesen's unmitigated adoration of her father.

25. See Gilbert, "Notes toward a Literary Daughteronomy." Cf. Dinesen's critique of her father's masculinist views of women (*LA*, 263). For the most explicit of her several treatments of the male oedipal paradigm and its peripheralization and objectification of women, see the "Cloak" trilogy ("The Cloak," "Night Walk," and "Of Hidden Thoughts and of Heaven") in *LT*.

26. Quoted in Thurman, *Life*, 338.

27. *LA*, 53. A similar consonance of *mother* and *martyr* occurs in Danish (*moder/martyr*). Feminist analyses of this construct are too numerous to detail, but see, e.g., Simone de Beauvoir, *The Second Sex*, trans. H. M. Parshley (New York: Knopf, 1953), Adrienne Rich, *Of Woman Born: Motherhood as Experience and Institution* (1976; New York: Bantam, 1977), Chodorow, *The Reproduction of Mothering*, Dinnerstein, *The Mermaid and the Minotaur*, and Susan Rubin Suleiman, "Writing and Motherhood," in *The (M)Other Tongue*, (chap. 1, n. 1) 352–77, and "On Maternal Splitting: A Propos of Mary Gordon's *Men and Angels*," *Signs* 14 (Autumn 1988): 25–39.

28. *LA* 315, 321; cf. 378–79, 390, 398–400; and *MM*, where she scathingly criticizes woman's objectification as no more than "an acquisition of tremendously great value for the . . . family" into which she marries (67).

29. *LA*, 261; cf. 328, 346–47, 381–82. Cf. *MM*, 66–67, 70, 81.

30. *LA*, 381–82; cf. 397–400, 403. On her use of Diana as a figure of female independence and rebellion, see Juhl and Jørgensen, *Diana's Revenge* (intro., n. 9).

31. *MM*, 82–84. Cf. Wollstonecraft, "Dedication" to *A Vindication of the Rights of Woman* (1792), ed. Charles W. Hagelman, Jr. (New York: W. W. Norton, 1967), and Mill, *The Subjection of Women*, in *Essays on Sex Equality*, ed. Alice Rossi (Chicago: University of Chicago Press, 1970), 158–61. Dinesen probably read Mill in the Danish translation of Georg Brandes, her sometime mentor and intellectual hero (*LA*, 209; cf. 143–44, 212). See Doris R. Asmundsson, *Georg Brandes: Aristocratic Radical* (New York: New York University Press, 1981), 40.

32. *LA*, 261; cf. 392. Cf. also *MM*, 70. Such remarks cast in ironic light Dinesen's later statement, often cited as proof of her conservativism, that "If I were a man, it would be out of the question for me to fall in love with a woman writer" (*Essays*, 77).

33. Cixous, "Sorties," *Newly Born Woman* (see intro., n. 13), 89–91; cf. Claudine Herrmann, *Les voleuses de langue* (Paris: Editions des femmes, 1976).

34. *Life*, 173; cf. Cederborg, introduction to *MM*, 26–27.

35. See Thurman, *Life*, 61–64. On the late nineteenth-century feminisms to

which Karen Blixen was in part responding, see Elias Bredsdorff, *Den Store Nor-diske Krig om Sexualmoralen: En dokumentarisk fremstilling af saedelighedsdebatten i nordisk litterattur in 1880'erne* (Copenhagen: Gyldendal, 1973); *MM*, esp. 36–71.

36. Juhl and Jørgensen (*Diana's Revenge*, 116–22) and Stambaugh (*The Witch and the Goddess*) also argue that Dinesen should not necessarily be read as antifeminist on the basis of her lectures.

37. For broader definitions of what constitutes the "political" we are espe-cially indebted to Foucault. See also Fredric Jameson, *The Political Unconscious: Narrative as a Socially Symbolic Act* (Ithaca: Cornell University Press, 1981). On the import of reductive notions see Lawrence Scaff, "From Silence to Voice: Re-flections on Feminism in Political Theory," in *Changing Our Minds: Feminist Transformations of Knowledge,* ed. Susan Hardy Aiken, Karen Anderson, Myra Dinnerstein, Judy Lensink, and Patricia MacCorquodale (Albany: State Univer-sity of New York Press, 1988), 1–14.

38. Cf. Kristeva's argument that even liberal feminism, with its just de-mands for equality, and radical feminism, with its celebration of feminine differ-ence, may both support patriarchy by subscribing to its enabling metaphysics of gender difference and unified selfhood—merely reversing its power hierarchies while leaving their oppositional structure in place. Kristeva proposes as more radical a position in which, via linguistic practices which undermine "the very dichotomy man/woman as an opposition between two rival entities," one partici-pates in elaborating "a new theoretical and scientific space where the very notion of identity is challenged" ("Women's Time" [see chap. 1, n. 47], 33–34). Cer-tainly, this position too may be co-opted to deflect a political struggle still neces-sary in a world of persistent inequality and oppression (see Moi, *Sexual/Textual Politics* [chap. 1, n. 24], 12–13, 150–73, and the special issue of *Feminist Studies* 14 [Spring 1988]), but that possibility should not blind us to its genuinely revolu-tionary import. Dinesen's ambiguous relation to various feminisms entails similar contradictions.

39. The significantly named Bror (Swed. "brother") was the identical youn-ger twin of Hans Blixen, whom Karen Dinesen had long loved unrequitedly—another of those intersections of her art and her life: such doubled relations would fascinate Dinesen throughout her career.

40. On this topos, to which I shall return, see Christopher L. Miller, *Blank Darkness: Africanist Discourse in French* (Chicago: University of Chicago Press, 1985), 3–65; "terra incognita" is a common cartographic inscription designating what Europeans called "the dark continent" (6).

41. *African Hunter*, trans. F. H. Lyon (New York: Knopf, 1938), 5.

42. *West with the Night* (1943; San Francisco: North Point Press, 1983), 201.

43. See Ulf Aschan, *The Man Whom Women Loved: The Life of Bror Blixen* (New York: St. Martin's Press, 1987), and Bror's memoirs in *African Hunter.*

44. He had probably contracted the disease from Masai women, themselves infected by earlier European settlers: here was the contagion of colonialism em-bodied in its starkest, most literal manifestation. On the social conditions sub-tending the intercourse of white settlers and African women, see Luise White, "Prostitution, Differentiation, and the World Economy, 1899–1939," in *Connect-ing Spheres, Women in the Western World from 1500 to the Present,* ed. Marilyn Boxer

and Jean H. Quateart (New York: Oxford University Press, 1987), 223–231, and Luise White, "Prostitution, Identity, and Consciousness in Nairobi during World War II," *Signs* 11 (Winter 1986); 255–73; and Janet Bujra, "Women 'Entrepreneurs' of Early Nairobi," *Canadian Journal of African Studies* 9 (1975): 213–34.

45. "Mottoes of My Life," *Essays*, 7.

46. See Dorothy Hammond and Alta Jablow, *The Africa That Never Was* (New York: Twayne, 1970).

47. On the pervasive typology of the colonist as "White *Man*" (my emphasis), see Edward Said, *Orientalism* (New York: Vintage, 1979), 227.

48. *Blank Darkness*, 13, 16.

49. Like women, Africans were represented as anomalous loci of disorder and potential evil. On the parallels drawn between the two groups in Occidental discourses, see Davis, "Women on Top" (chap. 1, n. 30), 148; Elizabeth Janeway, *Powers of the Weak* (New York: Knopf, 1980), 3–5, 7, 235; Pateman, "The Disorder of Women" (chap. 1, n. 48); Showalter, "Feminist Criticism in the Wilderness," 192–93; Jameson, *The Political Unconscious*, 115; Spivak, "Three Women's Texts and a Critique of Imperialism," *Critical Inquiry* 12 (Autumn 1985): 243–62, and part 3 of *In Other Worlds* (chap. 1, n. 24), 179–268; and Londa Schiebinger, "Skeletons in the Closet: The First Illustrations of the Female Skeleton in Eighteenth-Century Anatomy," *Representations* 14 (Spring 1986): 63–71. For Dinesen's sense of this parallel, see *OA*, 18–19.

50. *Manichean Aesthetics: The Politics of Literature in Colonial Africa* (Amherst: University of Massachusetts Press), 57.

51. Thurman, *Life*, 177–78: cf. *OA*, 7–10, 319–32, 374–79; *LA*, 327; and Westenholz, *Power of Aries*, 10–35 for comments on the acreage and economy of the farm.

52. *Manichean Aesthetics*, 52.

53. Ibid., 59–60.

54. *Longing for Darkness*, ed. Peter Beard (New York: Harcourt, Brace, Jovanovich, 1975), n.p.; and Thurman, *Life*, 127.

55. *SG*, 111; *OA*, 384; Thurman, *Life*, 127. Cf. Dinesen's attacks on the notorious hut tax exacted from the Africans by the British authorities: she "was from the beginning appalled to see a proud people so beggared, and she attempted to 'plead the Natives' cause' to each successive governor, to a number of influential settlers who became her friends, and finally to the Prince of Wales" (Thurman, *Life*, 128). On the subversive attention with which "natives" scrutinize "masters," see Frantz Fanon, *The Wretched of the Earth*, trans. Constance Farrington (New York: Grove, 1966).

56. The reference to the Arabian Nights recalls Dinesen's figuration of herself as Scheherazade.

57. *OA*, 179, 34. In explaining her choice of "Isak," Dinesen said that "it was my Kikuyu friends who taught me how to laugh" (Daniel Gilles, "La Pharaonne de Rungstedlund," in *Isak Dinesen: A Memorial* [see intro., n. 23], 181; my translation).

58. Trzebinski, *Silence Will Speak*, 43. See, e.g., Llewelyn Powys's purple description in *Black Laughter* (London: Grant Richards, 1925), 168, and Beryl Markham's recollections in *West with the Night*, 192–93.

59. *Life*, 184-85, 187.

60. "Foreword" to *Essays*, viii-xiii.

61. Published between 1907 and 1925, and collected—with the exception of *Sandhedens hævn* (*The Revenge of Truth*), published in *Tilskueren*, April 1925—by Clara Svendsen in *Osceola* (1962). See also Westenholz, *Power of Aries*, 97-108.

62. For examples of thinly veiled associations of rain with Denys, see *OA*, 274-75, 42-45. Cf. *LA*, 66-67, 71-72, 97-98, 132, 135-36, 359-60.

63. The *Letters* reinforce this fictionalized version of the event (see, e.g., 165, 181, 202, 216, 218-220, 222, 239, 243-251, 256-257, 265, 278-89, 335, 407, 419-21).

64. Dinesen anticipates Foucault's observation that "*The Arabian Nights . . .* had as their motivation, their theme and pretext, this strategy for defeating death. . . . Scheherazade's story is a desperate inversion of murder" ("What is an Author?" in *Language, Counter-Memory, Practice* [see chap. 1, n. 29], 117).

65. Trzebinski, *Silence Will Speak*, 133, 196.

66. His combined honesty and callousness become strikingly evident in his letters, reprinted in Else Brundbjerg's "Kaerlighed og økonomi—*en montage omkring Denys Finch Hattons breve til Karen Blixen*," *Kritik* 66 (1984): 12-47, especially in his response to Karen Blixen's possible pregnancy: he suggests "cancellation."

67. Thurman, *Life*, 184-85.

68. The adjective is Thurman's (*Life*, 153).

69. "When We Dead Awaken: Writing as Re-Vision," in *On Lies, Secrets, and Silence* (New York: Norton, 1979), 38.

70. On this displacement, see Nancy Vickers, "Diana Described: Scattered Woman and Scattered Rhyme," *Critical Inquiry* 8 (Winter 1981): 265-79.

71. On the self-referentiality of this line from "A Country Tale," (*LT*, 214), see Thurman, *Life*, 387. On Dinesen's self-presentations, see, e.g., the portrait of "Isak Dinesen" released in America after her identity became known or the late portraits by Cecil Beaton (*Life and Destiny* [see chap. 1, n. 71], 145, 197, 219).

72. "The Storyteller," *Illuminations* (see intro., n. 6), 94.

Chapter Three

1. "Echoes from the Hills," *SG*, 112-15. The phrase "my heart's land" comes from her poem "Ex Africa" (1925).

2. "Mottoes of My Life," *Essays*, 7. On Dinesen's sense of her own "'exile' with regard to people," and sense of her existential "loneliness" as related to her gender, see 287. On her view of Africa as a place "outside the normal bounds of law and order," see 290.

3. Greek *ēchō*, from *ēchē*, "sound," akin to Latin *vagire*, "to wail or cry," generally "said of a child" (*Webster's New International Dictionary*, 3d ed., s.v. "echo").

4. On the relation of writing to wounding and mourning, see Hartman, *Saving the Text* (chap. 1, n. 12), 118-57, Freud, "Mourning and Melancholia," *The Standard Edition*, 14: 243-58, and Benjamin, "The Storyteller," *Illuminations* (intro., n. 6). For further implications of this configuration for Dinesen, see Aiken, "Isak Dinesen and Photo/Graphic Recollection" (chap. 1, n. 22).

5. See Freud, *The Interpretation of Dreams, The Standard Edition* 4: 308.

6. See John Hollander, *The Figure of Echo: A Mode of Allusion in Milton and After* (Berkeley and Los Angeles: University of California Press, 1981), esp. 64, on the similarity of echo and dream. On the relation of echo and writing, see John Brenkman, "Narcissus in the Text," *Georgia Review* 30 (Summer 1976): 293–327; on the specificity of the contradictory Echo mythoi for woman's writing and difference, see Caren Greenberg, "Reading Reading: Echo's Abduction of Language," in *Women and Language in Literature and Society,* ed. Sally McConnell-Ginet, Ruth Borker, and Nelly Furman (New York: Praeger, 1980), 300–309.

7. "The Deluge at Norderney," 21. Intriguingly, in one of her earliest texts, the poem "Maaneskin" (Moonlight) Karen Blixen associated the figure of Echo explicitly with both laughter and liberation: apostrophizing the free-ranging Artemis, she writes, "Dit Horn har Ekkos Latter vakt" (Your horn roused Echo's laughter) (*Osceola* [see intro., n. 21], 144).

8. Published as the penultimate text of *SGT*. For discussions of Dinesen extensive fictionalization of her "autobiography," see Thurman, *Life,* 133, and Marianne Juhl, "A Comparison Between *Letters from Africa* and *Out of Africa,*" in *Karen Blixen/Isak Dinesen* (see intro., n. 2), 34–39.

9. Fragmentary drafts in Dinesen's African notebooks suggest that this was one of the earliest texts she worked on, though she did not finish it until her return to Denmark; mss. of her tentative tables of contents for *SGT* (KB Archives 121 and 124) show that "The Dreamers" was one of the tales she contemplated putting first in the collection. Hannah, *Mask,* 103–15, notes the persistence of the dream/art analogy in Dinesen's oeuvre. See also Aage Henriksen, *Det Gudommelige Barn og Andre Essays om Karen Blixen* (Copenhagen: Gyldendal, 1965), which takes its title from "The Dreaming Child" (*WT*).

10. The passage rewrites Karen Blixen's description of flying ("like a dream come true") in *LA*: "But now imagine great wide, endless green plains below, . . . and one's own speed high above everything. . . . All the same, . . . it is neither the speed nor what one can see that is the really intoxicating thing about flying, but this: that one is moving in three dimensions . . . ; when you fly you lift up your head and whirl up into space just as easily as when you are on the level. There is actually no longer any up or down. . . . It is the most divine *game* imaginable; you cannot prevent yourself from laughing. . . . And this is actually what I want to write about . . . , that we have to get ourselves up into three dimensions. . . . [T]he capacity of moving in three dimensions is a part of bliss, or . . . transfiguration" (412–13).

11. *This Sex Which Is Not One* (see chap. 1, n. 33), 76.

12. *Reading for the Plot: Design and Intention in Narrative* (New York: Knopf, 1984), 139.

13. E.g., Aristotle's reading of woman as deformed or degenerate man in *The Generation of Animals,* Aquinas's reiteration of this biology to support male domination in *Summa Theologiae,* Rousseau's concept of the "disorder of women," and Freud's notion of female "castration." For an analysis of this pattern, see Pateman, "The Disorder of Women." For the stork parable, see *OA,* 251–53; *LA,* 49, 270, 288–89, 294.

14. See, e.g., Gallop, "Reading the Mother Tongue" (chap. 1, n. 1), 322–26.

15. Stambaugh connects the setting to H. Rider Haggard's *She* ("British

Sources and Isak Dinesen's Conception of the Gothic," in *Karen Blixen/Isak Din-esen*, 58).

16. See Bjørnvig, *The Pact* (intro., n. 12), 46–47, on Dinesen's construction of Pellegrina's story as a version of her own.

17. Cf. the scar of Dionysio/Atanasio in "The Cardinal's First Tale"—another product of a conflagration associated with woman's loss of voice. The association of woman's suppression with a permanent wounding becomes another play on woman's "castration," turned to creative account.

18. "[T]he continent of Europe . . . consists of two parts, . . . separated by a high and steep mountain chain. You cannot cross it except in a few places. . . . Such a place there was near the hotel. . . . I was on my way from the North, where things were cold and dead, to the blue and voluptuous South" (280).

19. To complete the range of "feminine" possibilities under patriarchy, she is also represented as "mother" to one of her lovers (299–300) and as "witch" (309). Cf. Dinesen's analysis of these categories in "Daguerreotypes." The virgin and the whore, as many feminist critics have remarked (e.g., Warner, *Alone of All Her Sex* [see chap. 1, n. 55], 49–67), operate as polarities on the figurative axis epitomizing "woman" in Western culture. Woman as the locus of revolution is a recurrent topos in masculine discourses since antiquity. See Davis, "Women on Top" (chap. 1, n. 30), and Pateman, "The Disorder of Women."

20. Cf. Joan Rivière's analysis of female spectatorship in cinema: through masquerade woman can "manufacture a distance from the image, to generate a problematic within which the image is manipulable, producible, and readable by . . . women," thus eluding the constitution of woman solely via the masculine gaze ("Film and Masquerade: Theorizing the Female Spectator," *Screen* 23 [September/October 1982], 87).

21. *Second Sex* (see chap. 2, n. 27), 170.

22. See "Sorties," *The Newly Born Woman* (intro., n. 13), and Hermann, *Les voleuses de langue* (chap. 2, n. 33), 91.

23. *SG*, 153. As "winged lioness" Pellegrina also resembles the sphinx, forcing each man to answer the question she poses to Forsner at the pass: "Who are you?" (*SGT*, 322). In early manuscripts Dinesen altered Pellegrina's surname from "Rossi" to "Leoni" (KB Archives 123), suggesting the symbolic importance of that figure.

24. Kofman, *The Enigma of Woman*, (see chap. 1, n. 67), 55, 53, 223–25; cf. 50–71. Kofman sees Freud's view of the "narcissistic woman" ("On Narcissism") as comparable to Nietzsche's figure of the "affirmative woman" (e.g., *The Gay Science, Beyond Good and Evil*). Freud's use of *Raubtier* to figure the "narcissistic woman" is peculiarly apt with reference to Pellegrina Leoni, for it literally applies to predatory beasts like the lion, but also suggests, like its English equivalent "raptor," birds of prey like the peregrine falcon.

25. Dinesen's text has obvious affinities with Woolf's famous observation that "women have served all these centuries as looking-glasses possessing the magic and delicious power of reflecting the figure of man at twice its natural size" (*A Room of One's Own* [New York: Harcourt Brace, 1929], 35) and with Irigaray's discussion of the "role of 'femininity'" in Western culture as a "mirror entrusted by the (masculine) 'subject' with the task of reflecting and redoubling himself.

The role of 'femininity' is prescribed moreover by this masculine specula(riza)tion and corresponds only slightly to woman's desire" ("Ce sexe qui n'en est pas un," trans. Claudia Reeder, in *New French Feminisms* [see chap. 1, n. 19], 104). See also *Speculum*.

26. Cf. Marcus's image of Pellegrina as "a python" whose "great coils . . . revolve around" her lovers (*SGT*, 337). The figure obliquely figures the effect of Dinesen's spiraling narratives on her readers.

27. *Newly Born Woman*, 91.

28. Dinesen distinguishes between Lincoln and Pellegrina's other pursuers. Reaching her first, he comes close to understanding her need for imaginative freedom. His willingness to join her in a new sort of play, in both senses, suggests that he may be capable of creating, with her, a different story in which they might participate in genuine mutuality (322–24)—Dinesen's oblique suggestion of a differently engendered world. But the arrival of the other lovers shatters the womblike "house" of fiction in which Pellegrina and Lincoln take refuge (324). Driven by jealousy inspired more by male rivalry than by the woman who is its object, he betrays her: "'Tell them,' I cried. 'Tell them who you are!'" (326). On the rivalries of male mimetic desire, see René Girard, *Deceit, Desire, and the Novel: Self and Other in Literary Structure* (Baltimore: Johns Hopkins University Press, 1965), esp. 1–52.

29. Greek *monasterion*, "hermit's cell," from *monos*, "single."

30. On Don Giovanni and the discourse of seduction, see Kristeva, "Don Juan, or Loving to Be Able to," in *Tales of Love* (chap 1, n. 3), and Shoshana Felman, *The Literary Speech Act: Don Juan with J. L. Austin, or Seduction in Two Languages*, trans. Catherine Porter (Ithaca: Cornell University Press, 1983). In Kristeva's reading of Mozart's opera, Don Giovanni is "an artist with no authenticity other than his ability to change, to live without internality, to put on masks just for fun" (199). As the embodiment of roving *jouissance*, whose "flights . . . show him to be . . . a multiplicity, a polyphony" (193) he is, as Dinesen implies, the masculine counterpart of Pellegrina: another poly-phony, in both senses. Cf. Langbaum, *Gayety* (see intro., n. 9), 99.

31. Kristeva's suggestion that Don Giovanni is ultimately subject to the "primal, inaccessible, prohibited" mother ("Don Juan," 201) illuminates Dinesen's use of the text to expose the feminine power that engenders the male script. In both readings, the seducer becomes the seduced.

32. *This Sex*, 76.

33. See Nina Auerbach, *Romantic Imprisonment: Women and Other Glorified Outcasts* (New York: Columbia University Press, 1987), 274–91. See also Mary Russo, "Female Grotesques: Carnival and Theory," in *Feminist Studies/Critical Studies*, ed. Teresa de Lauretis (Bloomington: Indiana University Press, 1986), 222.

34. Significantly, if Pellegrina is a figure *en abîme*, enacting the ultimate dislocations of language itself, it is also with woman's voice that Dinesen marks transcendence of the abyss: her song "rose and lifted you with her. . . . Had you ever been frightened of anything, . . . she made you feel as safe, above the abyss" (331–32).

35. On the import of this question for feminist criticism, see the Kamuf and

Miller debate (chap. 1, n. 37), and Foucault, "What is an Author?" in *Language, Counter-Memory, Practice* (chap. 1, n. 29).

36. On Dinesen's subversive use of Great Goddess figurations, see especially chaps. 5, 9, and 10; Aiken, "Dinesen's Sorrow-acre"; and Stambaugh, *The Witch and the Goddess* (chap. 1, n. 22).

37. Kristeva describes the "hope" of "avant-garde feminists" that the "demand for difference" not merely reconstitute the old ontological oppositions of man versus woman, but instead channel "into each and every element of the female whole, and, finally, . . . bring out the singularity of each woman, and beyond this her multiplicities, her plural languages, beyond the horizon, beyond sight, beyond faith itself"—a hope "fitted to these times in which the cosmos, atoms, and cells—our true contemporaries—call for the constitution of a fluid and free subjectivity" ("Women's Time" [see chap. 1, n. 47], 33).

Chapter Four

1. Dinesen played with other possible titles (most frequently *Nine Tales,* but also *Nozdref's Cook: Nine Tales* and *Tales by Nozdref's Cook*—after the chef in Gogol's *Dead Souls* who concocted dishes from diverse scraps) before fixing on *Seven Gothic Tales* (KB Archives 121). Of the nine tales most frequently listed in her experimental tables of contents, seven were retained, two omitted: "The Caryatids" (now in *LT*) and "Carnival" (now in *C*). Gothic elements were present from virtually the beginning of Karen Blixen's writing career. Several of her earliest stories, published in Danish journals under the pseudonym "Osceola"—"Eneboerne" (The Hermits, 1907); "Pløjeren" (The Ploughman, 1907); and "Familien de Cats" (The Family de Cats, 1909) drew heavily on the conventions of the genre and strikingly prefigure the concerns of her mature texts. See *Osceola* (intro., n. 21).

2. See Susie I. Tucker, *Protean Shape: A Study in Eighteenth-Century Vocabulary* (London: Athlone Press, 1967), 149–55; and Jerrold Hogle, "Cryptonomy in the Gothic Novel," *Arizona Quarterly* 36 (Winter 1980): 333. This process of linguistic dispersal was magnified in the nineteenth century. I am much indebted to Hogle's groundbreaking work on eighteenth- and nineteenth-century Gothic—including "The Struggle for a Dichotomy: Abjection in Jekyll and His Interpreters," in *Dr. Jekyll and Mr. Hyde After One Hundred Years,* ed. William Veeder and Gordon Hirsch (Chicago: University of Chicago Press, 1988) and "The Ideology of Woman in the Gothic Novel: Power and Submission in *The Mysteries of Udolpho*" (paper delivered at the University of Colorado Conference on the Gothic, 1986). This chapter also owes much to the contemporary rethinking of Gothic fiction exemplified by studies like Tzvetan Todorov, *The Fantastic,* trans. Richard Howard (Cleveland: Case Western Reserve University Press, 1973); Robert Kiely, *The Romantic Novel in England* (Cambridge: Harvard University Press, 1972); Hélène Cixous, "Fiction and Its Phantoms: A Reading of Freud's *Das Unheimliche* (The 'Uncanny')" (see chap. 1, n. 64); Elizabeth MacAndrew, *The Gothic Tradition in Fiction* (New York: Columbia University Press, 1979); Claire Kahane, "Gothic Mirrors and Feminine Identity," *Centennial Review* 24 (Winter 1980): 43–64; Judith Wilt, *Ghosts of the Gothic* (Princeton: Princeton Uni-

versity Press, 1980); Eve Kosofsky Sedgwick, *The Coherence of Gothic Conventions* (New York: Arno, 1980) and "The Character in the Veil: Imagery of the Surface in the Gothic Novel," *PMLA* 96 (March 1981): 255–70; David Punter, *The Literature of Terror: A History of Gothic Fictions from 1765 to the Present Day* (London: Longmans, 1980); Jan B. Gordon, "Narrative Enclosure as Textual Ruin", in *Dickens Studies Annual: Essays on Victorian Fiction,* vol. 11, ed. Michael Timko, Fred Kaplan, and Edward Guiliano (New York: AMS Press, 1983); Ronald Paulson, *Representations of Revolution* (New Haven: Yale University Press, 1983), 215–47; and William Patrick Day, *In the Circles of Fear and Desire* (Chicago: University of Chicago Press, 1985).

3. Horace Walpole claimed in the preface to the first edition of *The Castle of Otranto* that he was merely the translator of the text's Italian original. Ann Radcliffe's *Mysteries of Udolpho,* widely acknowledged as major successor to *The Castle of Otranto,* is set in the Appenines. The term "barbarous" is Sir Henry Wotton's: "I say that such as these [the pointed arches of Gothic architecture] . . . ought to bee exiled from judicious eyes, and left to their first inventors, *the Gothes* . . . , amongst other Reliques of that barbarous Age" (*Elements of Architecture* [1624], quoted in Kenneth Clark, *The Gothic Revival: An Essay on the History of Taste,* 3d ed. [New York: Holt, Rinehart, and Winston, 1962], 14); but it recurs for at least two more centuries as perhaps the single most frequent synonym for "Gothic" (*OED,* s.v. "Gothic" and "Gothicism"). Cf. Ruskin, "The Nature of Gothic," *The Stones of Venice,* vol. 2, in *The Works of John Ruskin,* ed. E. T. Cook and Alexander Wedderburn, 39 vols. (London: George Allen, 1904), 10:185: "Whatever the date of its original usage, it was intended to imply reproach, and express the barbaric character of the nations among whom that architecture arose." John Evelyn's remarks occur in *Account of Architects,* quoted in Clark, 15. The phrase, like many subsequent descriptions, suggests the imprecision typical of the use of the term "Gothic" until at least the late eighteenth century. More recent art historians have refined the term, recognizing the wide variety of quite specific and discrete architectural styles for which the unitary term "gothic" is too crude a designation. The question of which came first, the literary or the architectural Gothic revival, is one that still besets art historians; the phenomena were mutually reinforcing (see Clark, *The Gothic Revival,* 32–33).

4. "The Nature of Gothic," 215.

5. Curtis Cate, "Isak Dinesen," *Atlantic Monthly,* December 1959, 153.

6. Interview in *Politiken,* 1 May 1934; my translation.

7. "Preface to the Second Edition" (1765), *The Castle of Otranto,* rpt. in *Three Gothic Novels,* ed. E. F. Bleiler (New York: Dover, 1966), 22–23.

8. "Nature of Gothic," 239.

9. *Dialogic Imagination* (see intro., n. 4), 55.

10. Ibid., 246.

11. "The Northanger Novels," English Association Pamphlet, no. 68 (London: Oxford, 1927). Sadleir recurs to a perception first articulated by the Marquis de Sade, who noted that what he called "le nouveau roman" was "the inevitable fruit of the revolutionary shocks felt by all of Europe" (quoted in Fiedler, *Love and Death in the American Novel,* rev. ed. [New York: Stein and Day, 1975], 136). See Mario Praz, *The Romantic Agony,* trans. A. Davidson (1930; London: Oxford

University Press, 1970), for discussion of Sade's connection to Gothicism and decadence. This view was contested by Montague Summers in *The Gothic Quest* (London: Fortune Press, 1939), which read Gothic as not a revolutionary but a reactionary genre; but see the recent analyses of Punter, Hogle, Sedgwick, Wilt, Day, and especially Paulson, all of whom confirm Sadleir's—and Dinesen's—interpretation. On Gothic as driven by the desire "épater la bourgeoisie" see Fiedler, *Love and Death,* 134–35.

12. Quoted in Daniel Gilles, "La Pharaonne de Rungstedlund," in *Isak Dinesen: A Memorial* (see intro., n. 23), 179; my translation.

13. Georg Germann, *Gothic Revival in Europe and Britain: Sources, Influences, Ideas,* trans. Gerald Onn (1972; Cambridge: MIT Press, 1973), 9.

14. *Purity and Danger* (see intro., n. 3), 121.

15. See Gordon's Derridean reading of the Gothic as "the first anti-language novel" emphasizing "the temporary, elusive, arbitrary, nature of language" ("Narrative Enclosure," 220–24, 229). On the radical disruptiveness of Gothic, see Fiedler, *Love and Death,* 134–38.

16. "Narrative Enclosure," 230; see also 213, 215, on Gothic as an "orphan" genre, cut off from patrilineal origins. See also Hogle, "Cryptonomy," on gothic as the "bastard" of the eighteenth century's "bastard genres," romance and novel (358). On the problematic status of Gothic romances in literary canons, see Punter, *Literature of Terror,* 15. This embarrassment has also pervaded art historians' response to Gothic revival architecture (see Clark, *The Gothic Revival,* 8). On Gothic revival architecture as a "bastard" form, see Charles L. Eastlake, *History of the Gothic Revival* (London: Longmans, Green, 1872), 54. Dinesen anticipated all these perceptions in "The Deluge at Norderney," especially in Jonathan Mærsk. See chap. 5.

17. "In a literate order whose basis lies in that community of relationships between *signifier* and *signified,* the Gothic suggests the arbitrary nature of the word. . . . The deconstruction of the boundaries between and among mediating texts suggests the ultimately arbitrary nature of textuality, just as the ever-present possibility of incest [in Gothic fictions] threatens to de-construct genealogy. If every parent is a potential lover, then the author(ity) of patriarchy is threatened" (Gordon, "Narrative Enclosure," 218, 233–34).

18. Wilt, *Ghosts of the Gothic,* 10.

19. Linda Bayer-Berenbaum, in *The Gothic Imagination: Expansion in Gothic Art and Literature* (Rutherford, N.J.: Fairleigh Dickinson University Press, 1982), 70, describes the Gothic cathedral as "a building . . . without a center." Cf. Hogle, "Cryptonomy," 340.

20. *Aesthetics: Lectures on Fine Art,* trans. T. M. Knox, 2 vols. (Oxford: Clarendon Press, 1975) 2:685, 635. But Hegel recuperates this disorder by stressing its underlying order: "But this incalculable multiplicity is divided in a simple way, articulated regularly, dispersed symmetrically, both moved and firmly set in the most satisfying eurhythmy, . . . the most secure unity and clearest independence." See Naomi Schor's discussion of this passage in *Reading in Detail* (New York: Methuen, 1987), 28–29.

21. Bayer-Berenbaum, *The Gothic Imagination,* 70.

22. On the breakdown of master-narratives in relation to the decay of tradi-

tional belief systems, see Jean-François Lyotard, *La condition postmoderne* (Paris: Minuit, 1979), 7. As Jardine remarks about this and other texts on the collapse of authority and authorizing discourses, "What is important here is . . . the recognition that delegitimation, experienced as crisis, is the loss of the paternal fiction" (*Gynesis* [see intro., n. 16], 67. Cf. 65–87).

23. Hegel, *Aesthetics*, 2:635. On the nihilistic tendencies of Gothic see, e.g., Day, *Circles of Fear*, and Robert D. Hume, "Exuberant Gloom, Existential Agony, and Heroic Despair: Three Varieties of Negative Romanticism," in *The Gothic Imagination*, ed. G. P. Thompson (Pullman: Washington State University Press, 1974).

24. Bayer-Berenbaum, *The Gothic Imagination*, 65.

25. See *Gynesis*, esp. 24–64. See also Schor, *Reading in Detail*, 3–7.

26. Cf. her interview in the Danish newspaper *Politiken* (1 May 1935): "I expect you know Hoffmann's Tales? It's something like that, and yet not the same."

27. Brooks, *The Melodramatic Imagination* (New Haven: Yale University Press, 1976), 5. On the implications of the Freudian text (from *Moses and Monotheism*) see chap. 1, and Coppélia Kahn, "Excavating 'Those Dim Minoan Regions'" (see chap. 1, n. 67), 32–41. On the Gothic as a text of the repressed maternal, see Kahane, "Gothic Mirrors and Feminine Identity," and Cixous, "Fiction and Its Phantoms."

28. *Love and Death*, 129, 132.

29. On "dread" as the motive force of gothic, see Wilt, *Ghosts of the Gothic*, 5.

30. Thurman, *Life* (see intro., n. 1), 269. Thurman does not associate the prospect that inspired Dinesen's "cheer" with the maternal.

31. *This Sex* (see chap. 1, n. 33), 76.

32. "The Guilty One," in *Newly Born Woman* (see intro., n. 13), 33.

33. *Literary Women* (see chap. 1, n. 22), 108–10. Moers was the earliest to connect Dinesen with what she called "female gothic," but her references to *Seven Gothic Tales* are brief, general, and impressionistic. Following Moers, Punter observes that the "different tone" of Dinesen's Gothic fiction derives from its being "filtered through a pervading and ironic female self-consciousness. . . . [T]he feminism in her writing is not a mere question of attitude or opinion: it is the very fabric out of which her tales are woven, and it is present even when the apparent opinions being expressed are—as they frequently are—deeply and committedly reactionary" (*Literature of Terror*, 379). But he does not elaborate on this insight and even misses its implications, characterizing Dinesen according to the standard critical line as "yearning to reside amid the colour and certainty of an idealised past" and reading *Seven Gothic Tales* simply as quaintly "archaic"—"concerned . . . with the *gentle* and *debilitating* nostalgia which has replaced [terror] as the aristocrat—and the artist—has become increasingly rootless and homeless" (my emphasis). He overlooks the fierce energy of her subversions, the edge and wit with which she interrogates the patriarchal traditions she employs. See also Sybil James, "Gothic Transformations: Isak Dinesen and the Gothic," in Juliann E. Fleenor, ed., *The Female Gothic* (Montreal: Eden, 1983); and Sara Stambaugh, "British Sources and Isak Dinesen's Conception of the Gothic" (chap. 3, n. 15) and *The Witch and the Goddess* (chap. 1, n. 22). On Barnes's Gothic see Jane Marcus "Laughing at Leviticus: Djuna Barnes's Nightwood as Circus

Epic" (Paper delivered at the University of Arizona, 1986). For McCullers's admiration of Dinesen, see Carson McCullers, "Isak Dinesen: In Praise of Radiance," *The Mortgaged Heart* (Boston: Houghton Mifflin, 1940), 269–73.

34. Wilt, *Ghosts of the Gothic*, 11, 12, 50, 65. Cf. Walpole's acknowledgment that *Otranto* was "grounded" on the concept of "the sins of fathers" (*The Castle of Otranto*, preface to the first edition, 18).

35. *Dialogical Imagination*, 246. Cf. Dinesen's similar comments on "patriarchal" traditions (*MM*, 40–53) and on the old order brought to a necessary collapse by feminism (*LA*, 258–265).

36. Punter, *Literature of Terror*, 380, notes the "symbolic" import of Dinesen's "forgetting Walpole's name," but sees it, problematically, merely as an emblem of "the shifting sands of history against which her fiction tries to stand." On Dinesen's repressed anger at her own father, see Westenholz, *Power of Aries* (see chap. 1, n. 22), and chap. 2.

37. On the Satanic mythos, see Praz, *Romantic Agony*. "The gothic novel," notes Fiedler, "was not fully itself until it had discovered and made its center the diabolic bargain" (*Love and Death*, 134).

38. See Gilbert's and Gubar's demonstration that for nineteenth-century women writers "the Gothic/Satanic mode" became a major form of feminine protest against the imprisonment of patriarchal poetics (*Madwoman* [see chap. 1, n. 1], 101).

39. *LA*, 246, 249–50. In "The Fantastic in Karen Blixen's *Osceola* Production," *Scandinavian Studies* 57 (Autumn 1985): 380, Casey Bjerregaard Black also observes that Dinesen used the "fantastic mode" not merely to "entertain" but also "to question, criticize, and put into doubt the moral conventions of her age." The power of these institutions is poignantly revealed in the fact that it was often women like Dinesen's grandmother, who had thoroughly internalized the patriarchal value system, who could become its most rigorous enforcers. See *LA*, 245.

40. As critics from Sadleir on have observed, Gothic fiction tended to become increasingly conservative, even reactionary, as it developed—a highly conventional inscription of the unconventional (see, e.g., Fiedler, *Love and Death*, 138; Summers, *Gothic Quest*, 398–99, 404). The most obvious index of this conservatism is the end of many Gothic texts in a conventional reaffirmation of marriage and "legitimate"—that is, patrilineal—succession, complete with "proper" male inheritance of name and property, including that indispensible mediatory treasure, the wife. However, in "The Ideology of Woman in the Gothic Novel," Hogle argues persuasively that Radcliffe, that preeminent female author of Gothic romance, was pressing toward a much more radical subversion of patriarchal traditions than most critics, even feminist critics, have noticed. And Shelley's *Frankenstein* has been widely read in recent years as a radically subversive text (see, e.g., Gilbert and Gubar, *Madwoman*, 221–47; Johnson, "My Monster/My Self," *Diacritics* 12 [Summer 1982], 2–10).

41. *Witchcraft in the Middle Ages* (Ithaca: Cornell University Press, 1972), 228. Russell notes that the *Malleus* "contributed little original to the witch phenomenon," but its "careful argumentation" and "papal approval . . . fixed the whole system of witch beliefs firmly in the mind of Inquisition and society in general. . . . [I]ts ideas were eagerly borrowed even by Protestants who whole-

heartedly rejected other aspects of Catholicism. Witchcraft continued to develop in the following two centuries, but departure from and additions to the phenomenon as set forth in the *Malleus* were minor" (231).

42. Ibid., 232.

43. See Heinrich Kramer and James Sprenger, *Malleus Maleficarum* (1486), trans. Montague Summers (New York: Dover, 1971). On the ritual scapegoating of woman in "Sorrow-acre," see Aiken, "Dinesen's 'Sorrow-acre'" (chap. 1, n. 22). One of the first commentators to recognize the political implications of the witch trials was Jules Michelet, whose widely-read *La Sorcière* (1862) is among likely pre-texts for Dinesen's reading of witchcraft, together with the work of Jakob Grimm (*Teutonic Mythology,* 1883–88), Hans Christian Andersen, and probably Frazer, Harrison, and Briffault, as well as Margaret Murray (*The Witch-Cult in Western Europe,* 1921), Montague Summers (*A History of Witchcraft and Demonology,* 1926) and Emanuel Linderholm (*De stora haxenprocesserna i Sverige,* 1918). On Dinesen's likely familiarity with Frazer and Harrison, see Stambaugh, *The Witch and the Goddess,* 3, 66, 85. For commentary on the political implications of the witch hunts, see T. R. Forbes, *The Midwife and the Witch* (New Haven: Yale University Press, 1966); Hugh Trevor-Roper, *The European Witch-Craze of the Sixteenth and Seventeenth Centuries and Other Essays* (New York: Harper and Row, 1969); Barbara Ehrenreich and Deirdre English, *For Her Own Good: 150 Years of the Experts' Advice to Women* (Garden City, N.Y.: Doubleday, 1979), 33–68; William Monter, ed., *European Witchcraft* (New York: Wiley, 1969).

44. *Malleus Maleficarum,* 43. See also 42–48, where woman's rhetorical misuse of the "tongue" imperceptibly modulates into the "carnal desires of the body itself." Hence "the word woman is used to mean the lust of the flesh" (43): "a woman is beautiful to look upon, contaminating to the touch, and deadly to keep. . . . For as she is a liar by nature, so in her speech she stings while she delights us. Wherefore her voice is like the song of the Sirens, who with their sweet melody entice the passers-by and kill them . . . by emptying their purses, consuming their strength. . . . When she speaks it is a delight which flavours the sin" (46).

45. For examples of contemporary feminist rereadings of the witch, see Mary Daly, *Gyn/Ecology: The Metaethics of Radical Feminism* (Boston: Beacon, 1978), Ehrenreich and English, *For Her Own Good,* 33–100, and Cixous and Clément, *Newly Born Woman.*

46. *Daughter's Seduction* (see chap. 1, n. 44), 78.

47. Interview in *Politiken,* 1 May 1934.

48. The witch appears as a pivotal maternal figure in the early tale "Pløjeren," *Gads Danske Magasin* (1907), (rpt. *Osceola,* 38–63) and as a subversive creator who makes "lies" into "truth" in the play *Sandhedens Hævn* (The Revenge of Truth). See chap. 8 for discussion of that text. For another analysis of Dinesen's treatment of the witch figure, see Stambaugh, *The Witch and the Goddess,* esp. 35–57.

49. Frederick Schyberg, "Syv Fantastiske Fortællinger," *Berlingske Tidende* (25 September 1935), 11–12. Quoted in Thurman, *Life,* 269. Cf. Gordon: "the ever-present possibility of incest in Gothic texts" as a threat to genealogy and hence to "the authority of patriarchy" ("Narrative Enclosure," 233–34).

50. Interview in *Politiken,* 1 May 1934, my emphasis. Throughout her life, Dinesen cited the Schyberg review as the quintessence of obtuseness.

51. See Jean-Jacques Rousseau, *Politics and the Arts: A Letter to M. D'Alembert on the Theatre,* trans. A. Bloom (Ithaca: Cornell University Press, 1968), 109: "Never has a people perished from an excess of wine: all perish from the disorder of women." For a history of this discourse in Western philosophical traditions, see Pateman, "The Disorder of Women," and Genevieve Lloyd, *The Man of Reason: "Male" and "Female" in Western Philosophy* (Minneapolis: University of Minnesota Press, 1984).

52. On the etymological and anthropological connections of the terms *host, guest* and *enemy (hostis),* and their relationship to the idea of male identity and mastery, see Emile Benveniste, "Hospitality," in *Indo-European Language and Society,* trans. Elizabeth Palmer (Coral Gables, Fla.: University of Miami Press, 1973), 71–83.

53. Significantly, Babette, Dinesen's fictive double, is also regarded as a witch by those for whom she prepares her transformative secular Eucharist, which they initially imagine as a kind of forbidden fruit (*LT,* 44–48).

54. See Ardener, "Belief and the Problem of Women" (chap. 1, n. 20), 3.

55. "Feminist Criticism in the Wilderness" (see chap. 1, n. 20), 200–201.

56. "The Blank Page," *LT,* 104, 100.

57. My emphasis. On the implications of this kind of play, see Johan Huizinga, *Homo ludens: A Study of the Play-element in Culture* (Boston: Beacon Press, 1950). Barbara A. Babcock brilliantly elaborates the outlines of a feminist commentary on play theory in "Specular Play: Reflections and Rever(her)sals" (paper presented in the symposium "Forms of Play in the Early Modern Period," University of Maryland, 1984).

58. *A Philosophical Enquiry into our Ideas of the Sublime and the Beautiful,* ed. James Boulton (Notre Dame: University of Notre Dame Press, 1968). As Punter notes, Burke's text, a crucial influence on the development of Gothic fiction, outlined "an entire new dimension to the relation between literature and fear," that passion "*by which the dictates of reason can be bypassed*" (44–45; my emphasis). There was, as Schor notes, another discourse of sublimity that specifically gendered it as masculine (*Reading in Detail,* 17–22). See also W. J. T. Mitchell, *Iconology: Image, Text, Ideology* (Chicago: University of Chicago Press, 1986), 129.

59. In "The Character of the Veil" Sedgwick criticizes traditional interpretations of Gothic novels for "following the topography of the self derived from Freud" linking "sexuality with depth, repression with surface" (166). She argues convincingly that this model obscures "a second potent range of conventions" connecting sexuality with the "image of the contagious, quasi-linguistic inscription of surfaces" (256). I would argue that, as in the sublime/subliminal etymology, the dynamism of Gothic is a function of the oscillation between—and interchangeability of—"surface" and "depth."

60. *Rabelais and His World,* trans. Helene Iswolsky (1968; Bloomington: Indiana University Press, 1984), 47, 10. Cf. Dinesen, "Carnival," and "Deluge at Norderney," 26. Dinesen's observation that in her dreams/fictions "horror changes hue. Monstrosity and monsters . . . turn to favour" (*SG,* 108) parallels Bakhtin's insistence that "the spirit of carnival liberates the world from all that is

dark and terrifying; it takes away all fears and is therefore completely gay and bright. All that was frightening in ordinary life is turned into amusing or ludicrous monstrosities" (47). Significantly, Bakhtin, like Dinesen, associated the literary version of this carnival spirit not only with Rabelais but with "the best works of Romantic grotesque—most forcefully . . . Hoffmann" (47).

61. Helen Mundy Hudson makes a similar suggestion in "Faces in the Mirror," in *Karen Blixen/Isak Dinesen* (see intro., n. 2), 132.

Chapter Five

1. Dinesen's preferred sequence, maintained in the British and Danish editions, was itself belated: her notes record over a dozen different tables of contents, usually alternating "The Roads Round Pisa" with "The Dreamers" as the first tale (KB Archives 121). The African notebooks contain many fragmentary preliminary sketches for what would become the finished text. Estimates of the number of tales written in Africa vary; Thomas Dinesen said that his sister had completed three stories (*Isak Dinesen: A Memorial* [see intro., n. 23], 10); in "Mottoes of My Life" (26) she claims to have written two; and she told Langbaum near the end of her life that "The Roads Round Pisa" was the only story she recalled completing in Africa (*Gayety* [see intro., n. 9] 43). Surviving manuscripts support Hannah's speculation that several stories were "written in Kenya and then revised, or even entirely rewritten" (*Mask* [see intro., n. 2], 48). Several notebooks lists refer to "The Deluge."

2. On "master narratives" and the erosion of traditional authority systems, see Lyotard, *La Condition postmoderne* (chap. 4, n. 22), 7–8, and Jardine's application of this "crisis in legitimation" to the loss of paternal authority in *Gynesis* (see intro., n. 16), 65–91.

3. Job 38:4–11; cf. 38:16. This figure of the earth as an edifice "based" on a subterranean sea and of creation as a paternal conquest of the maternal "deep" recurs repeatedly in the Hebrew Bible (e.g., Psalms 104:7–9 and 139:9; Proverbs 8:28; Isaiah 51:9–11; Ezekiel 31:4; and Jeremiah 5:22). As the etymology of the Hebrew *tĕhom* suggests, "the deep" controlled by the Lord's *fiat* in Genesis 1 bears linguistic and historical traces of *Tiamat,* great mother goddess of the Mesopotamian myth of origins *Enuma Elish,* a major source of Genesis 1–2:4a. In *Enuma Elish,* itself a belated, patriarchalized product, the goddess, figured as a great sea monster like Dinesen's "gray monster westward," is overthrown by her son/consort Marduk, who makes the earth from her slain body (see Alexander Heidel, *The Babylonian Genesis,* 2d ed. [Chicago: University of Chicago Press, 1951], 98–101); see also E. A. Speiser, *Genesis* (chap. 1, n. 63), 10, and Bruce Vawter, *Genesis* (chap. 1, n. 63), 46, 70. While Dinesen may have been unfamiliar with the etymology of *tĕhom,* she knew the many other Old Testament passages linking "the deep" with a monstrous or illicit female source. Job was one of her favorite texts. The Biblical allusions were reinforced by the Norse mythology in which she was steeped. Martin Ninck summarizes its tropes: "The womb of the primeval mother bears all things. . . . Everything that dwells in the depths . . . is fraught with destiny, and most of all the water that rises up from the depths" (*Wodan und germanischer Schicksalsglaube* [Jena, 1935], 191, 203, quoted in Erich

Neumann, *The Great Mother: An Analysis of the Archetype,* trans. Ralph Manheim, 2d ed. [Princeton: Princeton University Press, 1963], 250–51.)

4. *The Interpretation of Dreams* (1900), *The Standard Edition* (see chap. 1, n. 6), 4:195–97, 5:495. On Freud's admiration for Hamilcar see Kofman, *The Enigma of Woman* (chap. 1, n. 67), 23–24.

5. See, e.g., Johannesson, *World* (see intro., n. 9), 71–75; Langbaum, *Gayety,* 57, 63–70; Hannah, *Mask,* 161; Thomas R. Whissen, *Isak Dinesen's Aesthetics* (Port Washington, N.Y.: Kennikat Press, 1973), 119.

6. On the relation of these structures to patriarchal marriage and the social order it supports, see Tanner, *Adultery in the Novel* (chap. 1, n. 51), 60.

7. "The Guilty One," *Newly Born Woman* (see intro., n. 13), 7.

8. *Adultery,* 3–4.

9. *Beginnings* (see chap. 1, n. 11), 66, my emphasis; see also 83, 93 and esp. 96–100, 141–45.

10. See Homer Obed Brown, "Tom Jones: The 'Bastard' of History," *Boundary 2,* 7 (Winter 1979): 201–33.

11. E.g., "Sorrow-acre," "The Cardinal's First Tale," "Copenhagen Season," 251; and Aiken, "Dinesen's 'Sorrow-acre'" (see chap. 1, n. 22).

12. Dinesen's reverses Freud's evaluation of the materiality of maternity and the hypothetical status of fatherhood (*Moses and Monotheism, The Standard Edition,* 13:114), which Freud valorizes as an advance of the "intellectual forces" over sensual immanence.

13. See Gilbert and Gubar, *Madwoman* (see chap. 1, n. 1), 3–104.

14. In a typical disruption of the boundaries separating "history" from "fiction," Dinesen connects Jonathan with a sea-going lineage, simultaneously suggesting his affinities with the father-haunted Telemachos and playing on the historical prominence of the Maersk shipping company in Denmark.

15. On Mary Magdalene's subversiveness see Warner, *Alone of All Her Sex* (chap. 1, n. 55), 224–35; on Dinesen's play on that subversiveness, see Aiken, "Dinesen's 'Sorrow-acre'."

16. Dinesen rewrites Nietzsche on the death of god: "we have killed him. How shall we comfort ourselves, the murderers of all murderers . . . who will wipe this blood off us? What water is there for us to clean ourselves?" (*The Gay Science,* trans. Walter Kaufman [New York: Vintage, 1974], 181). The famous passage is preceded by a reflection that becomes a major intertext for "The Deluge": "We have left the land. . . . Beside you is the ocean: . . . it does not always roar. . . . But hours will come when you realize that it is infinite. . . . Woe, when you feel homesick for the land. . . . and there is no longer any 'land'" (180–81). On the Duke d'Orleans see Langbaum, *Gayety,* 68.

17. *LA,* 340–41. As Langbaum notes (68), Kasparson's prototype is the notorious Kaspar Hauser, the mysterious German youth variously believed to be the Crown Prince of Baden or an imposter and charlatan. Dinesen may also be playing on Verlaine's version of Hauser ("Pauvre Gaspard"), "who murders his adoptive father and becomes a revolutionary" (Paul Schmidt, "Visions of Violence: Rimbaud and Verlaine," in *Homosexualities in French Literature,* ed. Elaine Marks and George Stamboulian [New York: Cornell University Press, 1979], 232).

18. Or, since *Emmanuel* is itself an appellation for Christ, "the son of the son of God"—a comic redoubling.

19. Cf. "The Cardinal's First Tale," 14; "Copenhagen Season," 251; "Deluge," 73; and Langbaum, *Gayety*, 68.

20. Thurman notes that Malin is "a witty caricature of [Dinesen's] own authorship" (*Life* [see intro., n. 1], 267); Malin's subjects—"jealousy, deceit, seduction, rape, infanticide, and senile cruelty . . . all the perversities of the human world of passion" (*SGT*, 22)—recall the contents of *Seven Gothic Tales*.

21. Benveniste, "Hospitality" (see chap. 4, n. 52), 71–83.

22. On this paradox, see Pateman, "The Disorder of Women" (see chap. 1, n. 48).

23. *Enigma of Woman* (see chap. 1, n. 67), 66, 67, 68.

24. *LA*, 263. Blixen anticipates recent feminist analyses of these and comparable linguistic inequities (e.g., Casey Miller and Kate Swift, *Words and Women: New Language in New Times* [New York: Anchor/Doubleday, 1976]; Dale Spender, *Man Made Language* [London: Routledge and Kegan Paul, 1980]; *Women and Language in Literature and Society* [chap. 3, n. 6]).

25. Langbaum, *Gayety*, 59.

26. *Speculum* (see chap. 2, n. 11), 97.

27. Cf. Kofman's discussion of Freud's discomfort with woman's mobile bisexuality and of the relation of female "frigidity" to the enforced "sacrifice" of women's "sexual interests" within a phallocentric order (*Enigma of Woman*, pt. 2, esp. 206–25).

28. Cf. Bersani, *A Future for Astyanax* (Boston: Little, Brown, 1976), 10; Peter Brooks, "The Idea of a Psychoanalytic Literary Criticism," *Critical Inquiry* 13 (Winter 1987): 334–48, on "the interplay of form and desire" in literature (339).

29. Dinesen's perception of the importance of woman's access to money recalls Woolf's near contemporary speculations in *A Room of One's Own* (see chap. 3, n. 25), 38–41.

30. Cf. Cixous's celebration of woman's lavish *jouissance* as an exalted giving (*dépense*) without reserve (*Newly Born Woman*, 127). See also Michèle Richman's analysis of woman's libidinal excess as a challenge to a phallocentric sexual/cultural/linguistic economy ("Sex and Signs: The Language of French Feminist Criticism," *Language and Style* 13 [Fall 1980]: 62–80).

31. *Satanism and Witchcraft*, trans. A. R. Allison (Secaucus, N.J.: Lyle Stewart Inc., 1939), 88.

32. In equating the deluge of feminine desire with a deluge of discourse viewed as incoherence or insanity, Dinesen's oblique comments on her own transgressive textuality anticipate Kofman's critique of the suppressions of woman's discourse: "It is as if he 'knew' . . . that women were 'great criminals' but nevertheless strove, by bringing about such a reversal as occurs in dreams, to pass them off as hysterics," to permit "speech to women only in order to model it on men's, only in order to condemn their 'demands' to silence" (*Enigma of Woman*, 66–67).

33. On Dinesen's fuller treatment of these issues in "Carnival," see the epilogue. On the relation between carnival and what Malin calls "the world turned upside down," see Bakhtin, *Rabelais* (chap. 4, n. 60); Babcock, ed., *The Revers-*

ible World (chap. 1, n. 30); and Victor Turner, *The Ritual Process: Structure and Anti-Structure* (Chicago: Aldine, 1969).

34. KB Archives 122.

35. *Odyssey,* trans. Albert Cook (New York: Norton, 1967), 1:14–15, 5:1–275.

36. "The Name of Odysseus" (1956), in *The Norton Critical Odyssey,* (New York: W. W. Norton, 1968), 412–13.

37. Ibid., 405.

38. Dinesen's representation of the plight of the little girl forced to erase herself anticipates Irigaray's critique of the phallocentrism of psychoanalytic models founded on the doctrine of woman's "castration." See esp. *Speculum,* 25–98, on the mutilating effects this vision of woman produces, and on the relation of this question to the mirror.

39. As Langbaum notes (*Gayety,* 61), Dinesen models this character on Karl August Georg Max Graf von Platen-Hallermunde (1796–1835), the German Romantic poet satirized by Heine and recalled by Mann in *Death in Venice.*

40. Cf. her comment in *LA,* 264, on phallocentric culture as fundamentally "homosexual" and on male homosexuality as directly related to female subordination. Cf. Campbell, who argues that misogyny and androcentrism were responsible for the homoeroticism of Greek society and the symbolic erasure of women via domestic enclosure (*The Masks of God: Occidental Mythology* [New York: Viking, 1959], 24–26). On male homosexuality as epitomizing phallocentric economy, see Irigaray, *This Sex* (see chap. 1, n. 33), 192–93. On homosexuality and homosociality in Gothic fiction, see Eve K. Sedgwick, *Between Men: English Literature and Male Homosocial Desire* (New York: Columbia University Press, 1985), 21–27, 83–117.

41. Dinesen's manuscript alteration of the castle's initial name, "Angelstein," underlines its phallic signification (KB Archives 122). Her stress on the baron's desire to imagine himself as *sui generis* anticipates Irigaray on "The Unbegotten Begetter," who imagines that "he procreates everything without being himself engendered and *thus puts an end to what has been staked in the game of generation,* . . . turn[s] his back on any beginning that is . . . material and matrical, and that he receives being only from the one who wills himself as origin without beginning. *He who has never dwelled within the mother will always already have seen the light of day*" (*Speculum,* 294–95).

42. As with Seraphina's view of Calypso, the specularization that perceives woman as "mutilated, wounded, humiliated," notes Irigaray, leaves her "overwhelmed by a feeling of inferiority that can never be 'cured.' . . . *whatever works as a super-ego for women apparently has no love of women, particularly of women's sex/organ(s)*" (*Speculum,* 88–89). Seraphina's effort to erase Calypso by dressing her as a boy recalls the efforts of a patriarchal interpretive tradition to assimilate female authors by reading them as if they were men.

43. *Speculum,* 294–96.

44. Although the passage has Nietzchean overtones (e.g., *The Birth of Tragedy,* trans. Walter Kaufman (New York: Vintage, 1967), 62–63), Dinesen characteristically reverses Nietzsche's androcentric focus.

45. For Lacan, the *stade du miroir* is paradoxically negative: the child's initial

"jubilant assumption of *his* specular image . . . in which the *I* is precipitated in a primordial form, before it is objectified in the dialectic of identification with the other, and before language restores to it, in the universal, its function as subject," is inseparable from self-alienation (*Ecrits,* [see chap. 1, n. 44], 2, 4, 5–29; my emphasis). Calypso's self-reclamation prefigures Sophie Magdalena's in "Sorrow-acre"; see Aiken, "Dinesen's 'Sorrow-acre.'"

46. Thomas Dinesen, *My Sister, Isak Dinesen,* trans. Joan Tate (London: Michael Joseph, 1975), 108.

47. The radical possibilities Dinesen seeks to evoke through this transformation of the figure of "marriage" as the conception of a new kind of nonexclusive, nonoppositional discourse anticipate Gallop's observation that "heterosexuality is not simply the meeting of two opposites which keep their opposite identities, but an intermingling of two opposites, a contamination of the opposition, a risking of difference and identity, that risk not being offset by some higher union, the oneness of the homogeneous 'couple'" (*Daughter's Seduction* [see chap. 1, n. 44], 126; cf. 124–27).

48. Langbaum comments astutely on its historical and aesthetic implications (*Gayety,* 70).

49. *Enigma of Woman,* 50–68.

50. In "Plato's Pharmacy," Derrida demonstrates the irresolvable duplicities of the Platonic text (*Dissemination,* trans. Barbara Johnson [Chicago: University of Chicago Press, 1981], 61–171).

51. "The Diver," 12. See Thurman, *Life,* 140, 258, 337, 358.

52. As Arendt notes, "the Thousand and One Nights—whose 'stories [Dinesen] placed above everything else'—were not merely whiled away with telling tales; they produced three male children" ("Foreword" to *Essays,* xiv). Malin's final speech on the uncaging of birds reinforces the liberatory import of her last words (79). As James shows in "Caged Birds . . . and Free" (see chap. 1, n. 55), Dinesen used the caged bird not merely as a traditional emblem of the soul but specifically as a symbol of woman confined within patriarchal symbolic orders.

53. Dinesen later insisted that we cannot know whether the characters live or die: thus the story's ending, like so many of its other apparent "certainties," is ultimately undecidable.

Chapter Six

1. See *Ways of Seeing* (London: Penguin, 1972), 45–82. As the mirror scene in "Deluge" and similar moments in later tales suggest, it was an issue that would engage her throughout her career (e.g., "The Monkey," 121, "Sorrow-acre," 47–48, *E* 156–86). See Aiken, "Dinesen's 'Sorrow-acre'" (chap. 1, n. 22), and Hudson, "Faces in the Mirror," in *Karen Blixen/Isak Dinesen* (intro., n. 2), 130–34.

2. Genesis 3:20: "And the man named his wife Eve (*havvah*) because she was the mother of all the living (*ha'*)."

3. As Dinesen's later allusion to Baudelaire's visions of women suggests (96), the tale repeatedly echoes and subverts the imagery of *Les Fleurs du Mal,*

especially "Le Poison," "A Une Mendiante Rousse," "A Une Passante," "Les Petites Vielles," and "Danse Macabre," from which Dinesen takes her opening depiction of the "*danse macabre*" (81) and the final image of the skull "of a young woman . . . [like that] of Antinoüs" (107).

4. See Irigaray, *This Sex* (see chap. 1, n. 33), 171–72, and Sedgwick's more sympathetic reading of male "homosocial desire" in *Between Men* (see chap. 5, n. 40). Cf. Girard's theory of triangular rivalry as fundamental to narrativity (*Deceit, Desire, and the Novel*).

5. *Speculum*, (see chap. 2, n. 11), 22. Cf. Dinesen's ironic representation of the androcentric reflections of the young male artist in "The Cloak" as he reaffirms his primary attachment to his "master" and symbolic "father": "What is a woman? She does not exist until we create her . . ." (*LT*, 39–40).

6. *Ways of Seeing*, 54–56.

7. Lauretis, *Alice Doesn't* (see chap. 1, n. 10), 67. Lauretis summarizes a prolific field of speculation, initiated by Laura Mulvey's "Visual Pleasure and Narrative Cinema," *Screen* (1975).

8. As Thurman points out, Dinesen called her literary double, Pellegrina Leoni, "Donna Quixote" and referred to her own secretary, Clara Svendsen, as "my Sancho Panza" (*Life* [see intro., n. 1], 261–62).

9. Thurman, *Life*, 261.

10. *In Praise of Love* (London: Macmillan, 1958), 26. For astute reflections on woman's body within a male specular economy, see Susan Rubin Suleiman, "(Re)Writing the Body: The Politics and Poetics of Female Eroticism," in *The Female Body in Western Culture: Contemporary Perspectives,* ed. Suleiman (Cambridge: Harvard University Press, 1986), 7–29, and Irigaray, *Speculum*.

11. Valency notes the subversive possibilities of the courtly love mystique because of a potential role reversal between the lady and her lover, since she was typically a member of a higher social class than he (*In Praise of Love*, 78–79)—a scenario replicated in the chevalier's affair with his first mistress. For other analyses of chivalric misogyny in "The Old Chevalier" see Fabricius, "Vandrende Riddere og knuste Kvinder" (see chap. 1, n. 22), and Juhl and Jørgensen, *Diana's Revenge* (see intro., n. 9), 51–61.

12. Cf. Berger: "To be nude is to be seen naked and yet not recognized for oneself. . . . Nudity is a form of dress" (*Ways of Seeing*, 54). Dinesen's implicit critique of this dynamic parallels both Woolf's classic observation that "women have served . . . as looking-glasses reflecting the figure of man at twice its natural size" (*A Room of One's Own* [see chap. 3, n. 25], 35) and Irigaray's critical reading of Lévi-Strauss's model of culture: "*Commodities, women, are a mirror of value of and for man*" (*This Sex,* 177). On woman as a reflection of male narcissism, see also the analyses of Shoshana Felman, "Rereading Femininity," *Yale French Studies* 62 (1981): 19–44; and Jacobus, "Reading Woman (Reading)," and "Is There a Woman in This Text," in *Reading Woman* (see chap. 1, n. 1).

13. On Dinesen's thorough knowledge of Tennyson, see *LA*, 236.

14. *Gayety* (see intro., n. 9), 79.

15. Warner reviews the oppositions between these two figures of woman (*Alone of All Her Sex* [chap. 1, n. 55], 49–67). See also Frances and Joseph Gies, "Eve and Mary," in *Women in the Middle Ages* (New York: Barnes and Noble, 1978), 37–59.

16. *Reading for the Plot* (see chap. 3, n. 12), 146. On the prevalence and ambiguity of the "fallen woman" in English fiction and iconography, see Nina Auerbach, *Woman and the Demon: The Life of a Victorian Myth* (Cambridge: Harvard University Press, 1982), 150–84. On the historical conditions of nineteenth-century prostitution, see Judith R. Walkowitz, *Prostitution and Victorian Society: Women, Class, and the State* (Cambridge: Cambridge University Press, 1980). Dinesen maintained a lifelong interest in the ambiguous figure of the prostitute. The unfinished story "Cornelia" (KB Archives 147) treats the secret efforts of its eponymous protagonist to reclaim "fallen women" in Copenhagen. While this sort of project, as Auerbach observes, was "one of the few respectable activities available to philanthropically minded Victorian spinsters," it also had "subversive implications" because of the "sisterhood" it established between women victimized at opposite ends of the patriarchal social spectrum.

17. Auerbach, *Woman and the Demon,* 154–60.

18. On the self-aggrandizement of both the courtly lover and the poet who assumed his voice to exalt himself and his art, see Valency, *In Praise of Love,* and Nancy J. Vickers, "Diana Described: Scattered Women and Scattered Rhyme" (see chap. 2, n. 70).

19. This passage, like the one on "the emancipation of women," resembles Dinesen's own analysis, in "Daguerreotypes," of "woman" as sign. Like Dinesen's persona in the essay, the chevalier describes his recollections as "pictures of an age gone by" (97), and there are other parallels (cf., e.g., 95, on the girl's acculturation, and "Daguerreotypes," 29–33). In comparing the texts, however, one needs always to keep in mind the question of who is speaking. "All the difference," as the old chevalier says, "lies there" (95).

20. Dinesen's pun and the critique it implies anticipate recent feminist analyses—e.g., Vickers's "The Mistress in the Masterpiece," in *The Poetics of Gender* (see chap. 1, n. 1), 19–41.

21. *The Second Sex* (see chap. 2, n. 27), 180–82.

22. *Eroticism* (1957), trans. Mary Dalwood (London: John Calder, 1962), 131. Cf. Berger, *Ways of Seeing,* 63: "The prostitute . . . became the quintessential woman of early avant-garde twentieth-century painting."

23. The actual material circumstances of prostitutes are, of course, another story. The question of commercial prostitution is pivotal to the analyses of cultural economies predicated on what Gayle Rubin, echoing Emma Goldman, has called "The Traffic in Women" (see chap. 1, n. 43). In exploring the implications of woman as "gift," Dinesen again anticipates recent feminist critiques of Lévi-Strauss. In asserting that this system operates by keeping the power to exchange exclusively in the hands of men, enforcing women's subordination as the price of culture itself, Lévi-Strauss elides, as Michèle Richman notes, the consequences of this economy for women, as well as woman's perspective on the exchanges in which they are objectified. Since the violence to women on which this phallocentric order is founded is masked by law, to transgress this law is, potentially, to begin its dismantling. Dinesen develops this insight. See Richman, "Eroticism in the Patriarchal Order" (chap. 1, n. 43), 52, and "Sex and Signs" (see chap. 5, n. 30), 62–80.

24. *Second Sex,* 182; my emphasis.

25. Ibid., pp. 523–24: "Marriage is directly correlated to prostitution. . . .

Sewers are necessary to guarantee the wholesomeness of palaces, according to the Fathers of the Church. . . . [A] caste of 'shameless women' allows 'honest women' to be treated with the most chivalrous respect."

26. Ibid., 181.

27. *Reading for the Plot,* 162–63.

28. The chevalier begins his story on page 81, interrupts it immediately with the tale of his former mistress, which he claims "has nothing to do with what I was going to tell," interrupts that story with a third tale, of "her family, whose name ran down for centuries through the history of France" (84), and resumes only to postpone it again with the account of her husband, who "has nothing to do with this story" (85–86), and, again, with the digression on "the emancipation of women" (87–89). Nearly ten pages after beginning, he returns to Nathalie's story, but shortly thereafter, in a gesture emblematic of his entire procedure, he "made a long pause," followed by a Carlylean digression on the semiotics of women's clothes (93–97). Only then, almost two-thirds of the way through the text, does he take up the story he set out to tell. While this chinese-box structure admittedly serves to "caricature" (105) Dinesen's own favorite narrative technique, its purposes and effects here are clearly dramatic, suggesting the chevalier's strong reluctance to get to the point of his commerce with Nathalie.

29. Juhl and Jørgensen note in *Diana's Revenge* that Dinesen's title plays on Oehlenschlager's *Den Vandrende Ridder,* a proto-Gothic Danish text.

30. Act 4 of *Hamlet* is not the only prior masculine text rewritten here. Directly echoing Baudelaire's "Danse Macabre" (and indirectly recalling his "Love and the Skull"), the comparison of the skull to that of "Antinoüs" brings full circle Dinesen's comparison of the old chevalier to Odysseus, and his own sense of Nathalie as "adversary" to be destroyed, since Antinoüs was the first of Penelope's suitors her husband killed. Antinoüs was also the boy beloved by Hadrian, a point that underscores the chevalier's sexual ambivalence. See Juhl and Jørgensen, *Diana's Revenge,* 60, and Stambaugh, *The Witch and the Goddess* (chap. 1, n. 22), 7, for other readings of this allusion.

31. Juhl and Jørgensen offer another reading of von Brackel as unreliable narrator (*Diana's Revenge,* 52–55).

32. *Tales of Love* (see chap. 1, n. 3), 325.

33. See Beauvoir, *The Second Sex,* 118–19, 129–84. Cf. Wolfgang Lederer, *The Fear of Women* (New York: Harcourt Brace, 1968), Freud, *Moses and Monotheism* (see chap. 1, n. 6). The vehemence with which patristic authors disputed Mary's fleshliness (or lack thereof) is especially revealing in this context. See Warner, *Alone of All Her Sex.*

34. On the prostitute as scapegoat, see Beauvoir, *The Second Sex,* 181, 523–41. On the subversiveness of the Madonna, see Warner, *Alone of All Her Sex;* Kristeva, "Stabat Mater" in *Tales of Love* and "Motherhood according to Giovanni Bellini" in *Desire in Language* (chap. 1, n. 2); and Aiken, "Dinesen's 'Sorrow-acre.'"

35. *The Second Sex* 141.

36. Ibid., 181.

37. *Eroticism,* 133. Cf. Beauvoir: "[L]iving on the margin of the hypocritically moral world, . . . the *fille perdue* [is] the invalidator of all the official virtues" (*The Second Sex,* 181).

38. *Eroticism*, 106–7.

39. Ibid., 17.

40. On Baudelaire's obsession with skeletalization and its relation to the "metaphorical games" of language, see Kristeva, *Tales of Love*, 325–27.

41. KB Archives, 124, ms. #1.

42. Bataille, *Eroticism*, 16–18. But see Richman's critique of Bataille's own phallocentrism ("Eroticism in the Patriarchal Order").

43. *This Sex*, 196.

44. Dinesen would have been well aware of Nietzsche's ambivalent remark about woman in *Die fröhliche Wissenschaft* (1887): "sie 'sich geben,' selbst noch, wenn sie—sich geben" ("they 'give themselves' [dissimulate] even when they— give themselves"). See *The Gay Science* (chap. 5, n. 16), 317; Derrida's elaboration in *Spurs/Eperons: Nietzsche's Styles*, trans. Barbara Harlow (Chicago: University of Chicago Press, 1978), 67–71; and Gayatri Spivak's analysis of Derrida's androcentrism, "Displacement and the Discourse of Woman" (see chap. 1, n. 37).

45. See Charles Fourier, *Théorie des Quatre Mouvements, Oeuvres Complètes* (1841), 1:195, and Friedrich Engels, *The Origin of the Family, Private Property, and the State* (1884), both discussed in Juliet Mitchell, *Women: The Longest Revolution* (London: Virago, 1984), 20–24. See also Mitchell's *Woman's Estate* (New York: Random House, 1973), Sheila Rowbotham, Lynne Segal, and Hilary Wainwright, *Beyond the Fragments: Feminism and the Making of Socialism* (1979; Boston: Alyson, 1981); and Michael Ryan, *Marxism and Deconstruction: A Critical Articulation* (Baltimore: Johns Hopkins University Press, 1982).

46. "Eroticism in the Patriarchal Order," 52.

47. "Affinities between Reproduction and Death," in *Eroticism*, 55–56, my emphasis. Cf. Kristeva, *Powers of Horror* (see chap. 1, n. 3).

48. On the difference between "reading as a man" and "reading as a woman" see Judith Fetterley, *The Resisting Reader: A Feminist Approach to American Fiction* (Bloomington: Indiana University Press, 1978); Jacobus, "Reading Woman (Reading)," in *Reading Woman*; Jonathan Culler, *On Deconstruction: Theory and Criticism After Structuralism* (Ithaca: Cornell University Press, 1982), 43–64; Elizabeth Flynn and Patrocinio P. Schweikert, eds., *Gender and Reading: Essays on Readers, Texts, Contexts* (Baltimore: Johns Hopkins University Press, 1986).

Chapter Seven

1. On Dinesen's associations of the monkey with woman's liberation, see *LA*, 306.

2. Responding to the charge that "many people are mystified by the tale," Dinesen said that "The Monkey" was "a fantastic story; it should be interpreted that way" (*Writers at Work* [see intro., n. 5], 18). Cf. Tzvetan Todorov: "In a world which is indeed our world, . . . there occurs an event which cannot be explained by the laws of this same familiar world. The person who experiences the event must opt for one of two possible solutions: either he is a victim of an illusion of the senses, of a product of the imagination—the laws of the world remain what they are; or else the event has taken place . . . but then this reality is controlled by laws unknown to us. . . . The fantastic occupies the duration of this uncertainty" (*The Fantastic* [see chap. 4, n. 2], 25).

3. See Pater, preface and conclusion to *The Renaissance: Studies in Art and Poetry* (1893 text), ed. Donald L. Hill (Berkeley and Los Angeles: University of California Press, 1980), xix–xxv, 186–90; and Ruskin, "The Nature of Gothic" (chap. 4, n. 3), 212.

4. *Purity and Danger* (see intro., n. 3), 95.

5. Rosaldo, "Women, Culture, and Society: A Theoretical Overview," in *Women, Culture and Society,* ed. Rosaldo and Louise Lamphere (Stanford: Stanford University Press, 1974), 38. See also Peggy Kamuf, *Fictions of Feminine Desire* (Lincoln: University of Nebraska Press, 1982), 44–45.

6. See Lina Eckenstein, *Woman under Monasticism* (Cambridge: Cambridge University Press, 1896); Eileen Power, *Medieval English Nunneries* (Cambridge: Cambridge University Press, 1922); Carolyn Walker Bynum, *Jesus as Mother: Studies in the Spirituality of the High Middle Ages* (Berkeley and Los Angeles: University of California Press, 1982), 170–262.

7. See Freud, "The Uncanny," on the paradoxical connections between the *unheimlich* and the *heimlich,* whereby intimacy and eeriness converge.

8. Cf. his comments on "wine-begotten children" (127) and pointed references to Boris as "the son of your mother" (126, 128).

9. See *Writers at Work,* 14.

10. H. W. Janson, *Apes and Ape Lore in the Middle Ages and Renaissance,* (London: Warburg Institute, 1952), 14. See also William C. McDermott, *The Ape* (Baltimore: Johns Hopkins University Press, 1938). Following the practice of these scholars, I use "ape" as a generic term for all simian species.

11. Janson, 14–15; see 13–27.

12. See ibid., 30–31, 46–47, 51.

13. Philippe Verdier here summarizes medieval homiletic exempla ("Women in the Marginalia of Gothic Manuscripts and Related Works," in *The Role of Woman in the Middle Ages,* ed. Rosmarie Thee Morewedge [Albany: State University of New York Press, 1975], 123).

14. For Aristotle's view of apes see McDermott, *The Ape.* On woman as defective or monstrous man, see Aristotle, *Generation of Animals,* trans. A. L. Peck (Cambridge: Harvard University Press, 1943), 103, 133, 410–3, 406; and Lloyd, *The Man of Reason* (chap. 4, n. 51), 2–9. In *Summa Theologiae* Thomas Aquinas, following both Aristotle and a long patristic tradition of repudiating woman's sexualized body, describes woman as "defective and misbegotten" and therefore "naturally subject to man." See *Basic Writings of Saint Thomas Aquinas,* ed. Anton C. Pegis, 2 vols. (New York: Random House, 1945), 1:880. On the vast patristic lore representing woman as dangerous to man, see Katherine M. Rogers, *The Troublesome Helpmeet: A History of Misogyny in Literature* (Seattle: University of Washington Press, 1966), 14–22.

15. *Apes,* 109. Iconographies of the *femme fatale* frequently included monkeys as woman's companions and symbolic doubles (115).

16. See ibid., 124–27; cf. 130–31 on the "widespread" "equivalence of ape and snake as agents of seduction."

17. See ibid., 135.

18. Nerval, *Oeuvres,* ed. Albert Beguin and Jean Ricker, 2 vols. (Paris: Gallimard, 1961), 2:687–88. On the import of this "oriental tale" for woman see Kofman, *The Enigma of Woman* (chap. 1, n. 67), 224–25.

19. E.g., Dürer's engraving "The Madonna with the Monkey" (see Janson, *Apes*, 121, 151), which Dinesen probably knew.

20. Ibid., 19.

21. See, e.g., *Basic Writings of Saint Thomas Aquinas*, 1:880.

22. "As early as c. 600 A.D., and perhaps before, the word *simia* had been explained as a derivative of *similitudo*, probably on the basis of Ennius' *simia quam similis*. . . . , a line so well-known that it almost had the status of a proverb" (Janson, *Apes*, 19-20; cf. 76).

23. Verdier, "Marginalia," 122-23.

24. Janson, *Apes*, 55; see 71, n. 124, and 165-71. Cf. Verdier, "Marginalia," 123.

25. Verdier, "Marginalia," 141.

26. Ibid., 123. Cf. Davis, "Women on Top" (see chap. 1, n. 30), 147-92.

27. Irigaray, *This Sex* (see chap. 1, n. 33), 76. Cf. Clément: "These whimsical illuminations often inscribed in the margins of religious manuscripts, . . . are like a concerted depravity of the Imaginary. Jurgis Baltrusaitis calls it 'the magical antiworld,' the passage from the end of the Gothic to the age of discoveries." Clément associates these marginal figures with the sorceress and the hysteric "outmaneuvering the Symbolic order" (*Newly Born Woman* [see intro., n. 13] 23-24).

28. *Revolution in Poetic Language* (see chap. 1, n. 3), 16-17.

29. "The 'Blackness of Blackness': A Critique of the Sign and the Signifying Monkey," *Critical Inquiry* 9 (June 1983): 687, 686. For another version of the trickster monkey, see "Abou-Mohammed the Lazy and the Enchanted Ape" in *The Thousand and One Nights*.

30. Gates, "The Signifying Monkey," 692. See Hurston, *Mules and Men: Negro Folktales and Voodoo Practices in the South* (1935; New York: Negro University Press, 1970); and Claudia Mitchell-Kernan, "Signifying, Loud-talking, and Marking," in *Rappin and Stylin Out: Communication in Urban Black America* (Urbana: University of Illinois Press, 1972), 315-35. Cf. Dinesen's descriptions, in *OA*, of the Somali women's subversive discursive strategies.

31. See, e.g., 114, 116, 126, 128, 137, 151, 159, 163.

32. For instance, the "Olympic" family romance at Hopballehus, inherent in Athena's name and reiterated in Boris's recollections of Aeschylus's *Eumenides* (151, 159)—which he erroneously "mixes up" with Euripides as well as "with Scripture" in figuring Athena as Samson (159); the implicit comparison of Athena to Antigone, including her appearance out of a whirlwind (128-29), her strong father-fixation, her "fanatical virgin[ity]" (137) and her fierce family loyalties, which put the culture's gender systems into question; the comparison of Athena to Diana (137) and the Sphinx (123), which underscores both her sexual independence and her destructiveness to men (158). Dinesen uses these allusions to examine Greco-Roman confinements of women in the name of civilization.

33. *This Sex*, 170-72.

34. Ibid., 171-72. Such a construction may oversimplify a complex, shifting, context-specific phenomenon (Sedgwick *Between Men* [see chap. 5, n. 40], 19-20), but read as a strategic configuration of tropes—a poetics of culture—Irigaray's text offers an astute insight and intervention into the androcentrism that grounds Lévi-Strauss's influential analysis.

35. On the mother goddess as "our lady of beasts," "queen of the animal world," see Neumann, *The Great Mother* (chap. 5, n. 3), 268–80.

36. Cf. Virginia Woolf on "Love" in *Orlando* (1928; New York: Harcourt Brace, 1956), 117.

37. It also prefigures Irigaray's critique of Freud's "phallomorphic" speculation on woman's sexuality: his (mis)translation of "*nothing* you can see" to "*a nothing to see*" (*Speculum* [see chap. 2, n. 11], 47).

38. *Alice Doesn't* (see chap. 1, n. 10), 109, 139.

39. For a different reading of the monkey as an image of the story and a figure of "the Prioress's id," see Florence Lewis, "Isak Dinesen and Feminist Criticism," *The North American Review* 264 (Spring 1979): 62–65.

40. See Kristeva, *Powers of Horror* (chap. 1, n. 3), 53–79, on that condition of dissolution predicated on the return to the mother's body—the hystera or *chora* whose repression marks the formation of the subject: the monkey's entrance is literally a crossing of the threshold between nature and culture, bestial and human. On the import of liminality as a figure of psychological and cultural transition, see Turner, *The Forest of Symbols: Aspects of Nadmbu Ritual* (Ithaca: Cornell University Press, 1967), and Babcock, "Dancing on the Interstices: Liminality, Reflexivity, and the Spaces in Between," paper presented at the symposium, "The Works of Victor Turner: Past and into the Future," 1984.

41. *Powers of Horror*, 155. The metamorphosis recalls *Dr. Jekyll and Mr. Hyde,* but with a crucial, complicating sexual shift. For a Kristevan reading of Stevenson, see Hogle, "The Struggle for a Dichotomy: Abjection in Jekyll and His Interpreters" (chap. 4, n. 2).

42. On "the theater of the body," see Clément, "Sorceress and Hysteric," *Newly Born Woman,* 10. On the Mother, Otherness, and writing, see, e.g., *The (M)Other Tongue* (chap. 1, n. 1).

43. *Newly Born Woman,* 14. Cf. Freud's *Studies on Hysteria* (1895), *Standard Edition,* vol. 2.

44. E.g. "Dora" in Freud's "Fragment of an Analysis of a Case of Hysteria" (1905), *Standard Edition,* 7:7–112. See Cixous, *Portrait de Dora* (Paris: Editions des femmes, 1976), and *Newly Born Woman,* 99; Charles Bernheimer and Claire Kahane, *In Dora's Case: Freud, Hysteria, Feminism* (New York: Columbia University Press, 1986).

45. "Hysteria, Psychoanalysis, and Feminism: The Case of Anna O.," in *The (M)Other Tongue,* 113–14. As Hunter notes, "The fact that in popular culture the word 'hysterical' is often used in attempts to discredit feminist expression seems to derive from the idea that both hysterics and feminists are 'out of control': neither hysterics nor feminists cooperate dutifully with patriarchal conventions. . . . [T]he attempted discrediting . . . comes from a repressive impulse similar to the defense that creates hysterical symptoms in the first place."

46. See, e.g., Clément, "The Guilty One," *Newly Born Woman,* 3–57. For links between the Prioress and witchcraft, see *SGT,* 109, 149–50.

47. On learned Latin as *patrius sermo,* the quintessential masculinist language of the Western world, see Walter Ong, *Fighting for Life: Contest, Sexuality, and Consciousness* (Ithaca: Cornell University Press, 1981), 36–37, 129–39.

48. I use "writing" here in both the broad Derridean sense and the more restrictive, explicitly textual, sense. Given the parallel between the window rup-

tured by the monkey and the rapelike rupture of the "Prioress's" body, Derrida's play on the hymen as a figure of writing is illuminating. See "The Double Session," in *Dissemination*, trans. Barbara Johnson (Chicago: University of Chicago Press, 1981), 173–286. Derrida treats a text Dinesen probably knew, Mallarmé's *Mimique*, which concerns a highly eroticized scene in *commedia dell' arte*, a form Dinesen herself would repeatedly use as a figure in, and for, her own fiction. Indeed *Mimique* might well serve as a subtitle for "The Monkey."

49. See *Revolution in Poetic Language*, 26–29: "Our discourse—all discourse—moves with and against the *chora*"—that womb-linked "rhythmic space" which "precedes and underlies figuration and thus specularization"—"in the sense that it simultaneously depends upon and refuses it. . . . Drives involve pre-Oedipal semiotic functions and energy discharges that connect and orient the body to the mother. . . . All these various processes and relations, anterior to sign and syntax, [are] previous and necessary to the acquisition of language, but not identical to language. . . . Only in *dream* logic . . . have they attracted attention, and only in certain signifying practices, such as the *text*, do they dominate the signifying process."

50. "Laugh of the Medusa" (see chap. 1, n. 45), 256–57.

51. *The Aeneid of Virgil*, trans. Rolfe Humphries (New York: Scribner's, 1951), 164–65.

52. *Alice Doesn't*, 140.

53. For a psychoanalytic reading of the text as a restoration of the law of the father, see Bill Mishler, "Parents and Children, Brothers and Sisters in Isak Dinesen's 'The Monkey,'" *Scandinavian Studies* 57 (Autumn 1985): 412–51.

54. *Revolution in Poetic Language*, 29.

55. Lévi-Strauss, *Structural Anthropology*, trans. Claire Jacobsen and Brooke Brundfest Schoepf (Garden City, N.Y.: Anchor Books, 1967), 223. See Schor, "Reading Double: Sand's Difference," in *The Poetics of Gender* (chap. 1, n. 1), 248, on this text in reference to "the transatlantic feminist" as a "trickster." See also Gates, "The Signifying Monkey," and Barbara Babcock, "A 'Tolerated Margin of Mess': The Trickster and His Tales Re-considered," *Journal of the Folklore Institute* 11 (March 1975): 147–86.

56. Cf. Dinesen's emphasis, in a discussion of "The Monkey," on her own "comic sense. I love a joke, I love the humorous. The name 'Isak' means laughter" (*Writers at Work*, 15).

57. Neumann, *The Great Mother*, 270, summarizing Briffault, *The Mothers* (1927).

58. Helen Diner, *Mothers and Amazons: The First Feminine History of Culture*, ed. and trans. John Philip Lundin (New York: Julian, 1965), 107, 109.

59. See, e.g., Irigaray, *This Sex*, 170–97, and Adrienne Rich, "Compulsory Heterosexuality and Lesbian Existence," *Signs* 5 (Summer 1980): 631–60.

60. Neumann, *The Great Mother*, 270.

61. Ibid., 272.

62. For divergent views on the implications of dominance and submission in lesbian relationships, see Gayle Rubin, "Thinking Sex: Notes for a Radical Theory of the Politics of Sexuality," in *Pleasure and Danger: Exploring Female Sexuality*, ed. Carole S. Vance (Boston: Routledge and Kegan Paul, 1984), 267–319.

63. These lines from a battle song of the French Revolution conclude a con-

versation between Boris and Athena in which he condescendingly asks whether she is "still a Republican," to which she replies by a passionate celebration of the French Revolution (132), troped via "the Phrygian bonnet"—which, as Neil Hertz has suggested in "Medusa's Head" (see chap. 1, n. 65), has associations with the Medusa and male fear of women—a connection that reinforces the covert affinities the text suggests between women ostensibly opposed on the level of plot. Cf. Dinesen's comments about links between "the French Revolution" and women's overthrow of "the old world order" (*LA*, 258–63).

64. Boris's sexual ambiguity is further elaborated by transvestism: "he had played many ladies' roles in amateur theatricals" (140).

65. Langbaum, *Gayety* (see intro., n. 9), 82–83.

66. Ibid., 88. Dinesen's critique of Kant's logic in *LA*, 313, prefigures Irigaray's (*Speculum*, 203–13). Dinesen's droll fictional treatment of the philosopher may have been inspired by Kant's patronizing treatment of women "advanced in years"—women like herself and the Prioress—in "Of the Difference of the Sublime and of the Beautiful in the Counterrelation of Both Sexes" (from *Observations on the Feeling of the Beautiful and Sublime*, rpt. in *Woman in Western Thought*, ed. Martha Lee Osborne [New York: Random House, 1979], 154–61), a text devoted to maintaining "the charming distinction, which nature intended to make between two human sexes." Like the old chevalier, Kant disdains members of "the fair sex" who engage in "male" pursuits ("laborious study, or painful investigation") as masculinized monstrosities with "perverted taste." His celebration of the old woman who is a model of decorum, "virtue," refinement, "modesty," "discretion," and "a calm benevolence" reads like a prototype of the "true Prioress of Closter Seven"—the very figure Dinesen's "Monkey" dismantles. Kant particularly deplores a woman who expresses sexuality once she enters "old age, an epoch so terrible to all women" (an old woman in love is "disgusting," her desire an attempt to "pervert nature"), and he regards "men [who] adopt effeminacies" and "women [who] affect a masculine air, in order to inspire esteem" as "contrary to the course of nature." Dinesen's text plays havoc with all these assumptions.

67. See *This Sex*, 203–4; 217.

68. *Aeneid*, bk. 6, pp. 143–45. The ape also came to be linked with the Erythraean Sibyl (Janson, *Apes*, 69, n. 105).

69. *Aeneid*, 146. Apollo's strong association with the law and word of the father is most notoriously enacted in *Eumenides*, but Virgil plays on the same associations here, where the "wild" sibyl assumes some of same features of the mother-linked Furies before they are domesticated under the ordering patricentric law at the close of the *Oresteia*.

70. Ibid., 146–47. Dinesen subverts Virgil's text here and elsewhere. Where Aeneas prays to his mother to lead him to the golden bough that will reunite him with his father in Hades—"Help me, O goddess-mother"—Dinesen substitutes the godmother's own machinations to attain, vicariously, her own golden bough— a daughter, Athena.

71. Cf. Gilbert and Gubar's analysis of the Sibyl as a figure of an alternative mythos of female power and generativity in nineteenth-century women's texts (*Madwoman* [see chap. 1, n. 1], 95–99).

72. *Seraphita*, trans. Katherine Prescott Wormeley (Boston: Roberts Brothers, 1889), 156–58.

73. Quoted in Langbaum, *Gayety*, 88.

74. See Migel, *Titania* (chap. 1, n. 27), 193, 197, and *Isak Dinesen: A Memorial* (intro., n. 23), 70.

75. "Isak Dinesen," in *Writers at Work*, 15. Cf. Woolf: "[S]omething seemed lacking, something seemed different" . . . "It is strange what a difference a tail makes" (*Room* [see chap. 3, n. 25], pp. 11, 13). Dinesen's remark occurs at the end of a playful speculation on the connection between monkeys and the problematics of narrative: "INTERVIEWER: Do you like monkeys? ISAK DINESEN: Yes, I love them. . . . Do you think I look like a monkey? INTERVIEWER: Of course. . . . The definition of 'monkey' has not, however, been satisfactorily resolved. This apparently simple question . . . requires careful examination before we may proceed with our story. . . . ISAK DINESEN: (laughs delightedly) But no tale can proceed without examining apparently simple questions. And no tail, either" (*Writers at Work*, 14–15).

Chapter Eight

1. In several tentative tables of contents Dinesen made "Roads" the middle text in the collection (KB Archives 121).

2. On this convention, see Nancy Miller, "Writing (from) the Feminine: George Sand and the Novel of Female Pastoral," in *The Representation of Women in Fiction* (chap. 1, n. 1), 124–25.

3. On the mirror stage, see Lacan, *Ecrits* (chap. 1, n. 44), 1–7.

4. For critiques of the narcissistic masculine fascination with sameness, see Cixous, "The Empire of the Selfsame," *Newly Born Woman* (intro., n. 13), 78–83; Irigaray, *This Sex* (chap. 1, n. 33), 74, 171–72; Johnson, "My Monster/My Self" (chap. 4, n. 40), 10.

5. See *Speculum* (chap. 2, n. 11), 13–129.

6. Cf. Virginia Woolf's observation that women "have served all these centuries as looking glasses . . . reflecting the figure of man at twice its natural size" (*A Room of One's Own* [see chap. 3, n. 25], 35).

7. "Gampo" is Dinesen's phonetic (mis)spelling of Italian *gambo*—"a stem, stalk or shaft"—a phallic root, as it were, whose apparent diminution (*corta, corto* = "short") in female anatomy has contributed to masculine representations, from Aristotle to Freud, of woman's presumably debilitating sexual difference. Dinesen's ungrammatical feminization of the adjective *corto* reinforces this comic wordplay, stressing Carlotta's epicene appearance.

8. On the ambivalent entanglement of mother and daughter, see Irigaray, "And the One Doesn't Stir Without the Other" (chap. 2, n. 16), 60–67; Chodorow, *The Reproduction of Mothering* (chap. 1, n. 66), Johnson, "My Mother/Myself," 2–10; and Jacobus, *Reading woman* (chap. 1, n. 1), 278–92.

9. The American edition of *SGT* spelled the name *Pozentiani*; I use Dinesen's corrected spelling for the British and Danish editions for reasons explained below.

10. Cf. Irigaray: Such love is fundamentally "alien" to a phallic economy,

"For nothing of the special nature of desire *between women* has been unveiled or stated . . . in phallocentric history, in which value is the prerogative of the penis and its equivalents" (*Speculum*, 101). Agnese's function as a double of her pseudonymically transvestite author is suggested by Dinesen's own early use of the pseudonym "Lord Byron."

11. On woman's silencing by traditional legal constructions of rape, see Frances Ferguson, "Rape and the Rise of the Novel," *Representations* 20 (Fall 1987): 88–112. Again Dinesen plays on the Philomela myth, one of her most frequent tropes for the woman writer.

12. Søren Kierkegaard, *Stages on Life's Way*, trans. Walter Lowrie (Princeton: Princeton University Press, 1940), 87.

13. See Beauvoir, *Second Sex* (chap. 2, n. 27), xiii–185.

14. *Stages*, 68. Like "Roads," *Stages* begins with ironic meditations on recollection and reflection (27–36) and proceeds (37–178) as a series of speculations about "the relationship between man and woman" (45). Like the middle portions of "Roads," *Stages* describes a series of spirited dinner dialogues set at evening in a dining room outside a city (here Copenhagen), against the background music of Mozart's *Don Giovanni*, whose "secret, festive seductive strains . . . beguiled Victor [Eremita, one of Kierkegaard's many doubles] by a sense of loss . . . as if Elvira had not been seduced at all but only desired to be" (42–43). Dinesen's references to marionettes, the art of comedy, dueling, cuckoldry, and transvestism, like her allusions to Don Giovanni, also have analogues in *Stages* (53–57, 62, 63, 65–67). But whereas the discourse on woman in Kierkegaard's text is elaborated solely from the masculine point of view, Dinesen dismantles that discourse by inviting us to read (it) from the woman's position. For woman as "jest" and comic contradiction, see Constantine's speech (*Stages*, 61–64). For Dinesen's comment on Kierkegaard's importance for her, see *LA*, 226.

15. Paul de Man, "The Epistemology of Metaphor," *Critical Inquiry* 5 (Autumn 1978): 15–16. See, e.g., Locke, *An Essay Concerning Human Understanding*, ed. John W. Yolton, 2 vols. (London: Dent, 1961), bk. 3, chap. 10, 105–6.

16. Brooks, *Reading for the Plot* (see chap. 3, n. 12), 39.

17. *Stages*, 66–67. Kierkegaard refers to Plato's *Timaeus*, which suggests that men who were imperfect in their former lives are reincarnated as women; and to Aristotle's *Politics*, which describes woman as an "incomplete reflection" of man. In having Constantine cite Plato and Aristotle on "woman [as] an incomplete form" Kierkegaard epitomizes the Western masculinist tradition that has read woman as a kind of monstrosity. For a summary of the philosophical tradition, see Pateman, "Disorder of Women" (chap. 1, n. 48).

18. *Stages* 67. See also 61–66.

19. Ibid., 64–65.

20. Dinesen's own ambivalence about the lack of a female artistic tradition and about the woman writer's problematic position in a phallocentric society appears later in this passage: "Few women have been great artists save in those areas where they do not *create* a work of art but can themselves be said to *become* works of art—that is, as actresses, singers, or dancers"—who "inspire their public in a way a woman painter or woman writer cannot do." Before dismissing such statements as merely reactionary, one must read further, for Dinesen turns the entire

context around in the second half of the essay. What she describes is the bias against women authors and artists within a tradition that identifies writing and painting as exclusively male activities and excludes as "contrary to nature" the work of iconoclastic women like George Sand who enter those arenas (77). Dinesen's seemingly self-deprecating observation that "were I a man, it would be out of the question for me to fall in love with a woman writer" should be read not simply, as Judith Thurman suggests, as proof of Dinesen's ambivalence about her craft, but as a complex, ironic appraisal of the context within which women who would write are situated by the gender codes of androcentric culture. As she says immediately afterward, those who assume her remarks are antifeminist need to analyze them more carefully.

21. *Adultery in the Novel* (see chap. 1, n. 51), 19.

22. Ibid., 23.

23. Tanner summarizes the tradition: "It is marriage that enables men and women to pass naturally from the state of nature to that of culture. . . . [M]arriage is connected to the emergence of man's ability to establish boundaries" assuring patriarchal unity and community. "If marriage is at the center, and the center cannot hold, . . . what then happens to all those other *related* transactions and contracts by which and in which man himself is constituted as man? . . . [B]y extension nothing in society is truly 'bonded'" (*Adultery,* 59, 60, 61, 66).

24. Cf. Lacan, "The Signification of the Phallus," *Ecrits,* 281–91, and *Encore* (Paris: Editions du Seuil, 1975), on "le nom du père," under which repressive sign the subject enters language and culture.

25. See, e.g. Langbaum *Gayety* (intro., n. 9), 6–19; Hannah, *Mask* (intro., n. 2), 133–34; Thurman, *Life* (intro., n. 1), 149.

26. Similarly, commentators generally focus on the agonistic struggles of the male characters throughout "Roads," interpreting the text as a *bildung* of Schimmelman's consciousness or a story of male bonding gone awry through a supposed betrayal that culminates in the duel, commonly read as the fiction's climax. Such androcentric focus is problematized by Dinesen's satire of Augustus's solipsistic self-reflections and consequent misinterpretations. The phrase "difference of view" is Woolf's (*Collected Essays,* vol. 1 [London: Hogarth, 1966], 204). See Jacobus's discussion of its relation to writing and reading woman ("The Difference of View," *Women Writing and Writing About Women* [Totowa, N.J.: Barnes and Noble, 1979], 10–21, and *Reading Woman,* 3–24).

27. On the implications of this difference, see Jacobus, *Reading Woman,* and Flynn and Schweikart, *Gender and Reading* (chap. 6, n. 48).

28. *LA,* 263.

29. *Fighting for Life* (see chap. 7, n. 47), my emphasis. Cf. Rosaldo on male separatist "rituals of authority that define [men] as superior, special, and apart" ("Women, Culture, and Society" 27). On the male literary tradition as oedipal contest, see Bloom, *The Anxiety of Influence* (chap. 1, n. 12).

30. Hannah, *Mask,* 152.

31. *LA,* 262–64. Dinesen speaks here not only of relations between women but also of heterosexual friendship, both being transformed when woman is "a human being"—not merely "a sexual being": "Where the relationship between men and women is concerned, a French author . . . says: To love a modern

woman is homosexuality,—and I think he is right. . . . But I believe it is possible to think that such a 'homosexuality' . . . has been a human ideal that conditions have prevented being realized until now" (*LA*, 264). Dinesen would likely have been familiar with the discourse, evolving in France from the turn of the century through the early 1930s, on "sapphism" as "amitié passionée" between women. See Elaine Marks, "Lesbian Intertextuality," in *Homosexualities in French Literature* (chap. 5, n. 17), 355–62.

32. "Women's Time" (see chap. 1, n. 47), 33.

33. See "Blessings in Disguise: Cross-Dressing as Re-dressing in Female Modernists" (chap. 1, n. 22). See also Gilbert, "Costumes of the Mind: Transvestism in Modern Literature," *Critical Inquiry* 7 (Winter 1980): 391–417; and Shoshana Felman's comments on "the constitutive relationship between sex roles and clothing. If it is clothes . . . alone, i.e., a cultural sign, an institution, which determine our reading of the sexes, which determine masculine and feminine and insure sexual opposition as an orderly, hierarchical polarity; if indeed clothes make the *man*—or the woman—are not sex roles as such, inherently, but travesties . . . of the ambiguous complexity of real sexuality . . . ?" ("Rereading Femininity" [see chap. 1, n. 64], 28).

34. *Sandhedens Hævn, Tilskueren* (May 1926), translated in Hannah, *Mask*, 179–204. The play was performed several times in Denmark between the late 1930s and 1960, when it was republished by Gyldendal (see *Mask*, 116–29). See also Aage Henriksen's *Karen Blixen og Marionetterne* (Copenhagen: Wivel, 1952) the classic study of the marionette comedy in Blixen's work, and its relation to the traditions of the *commedia dell' arte* and to Kleist's "Ueber das Marionettentheater" and Mann's Joseph novels. Thurman notes that the play "was . . . written and rewritten at the moments of Karen Blixen's life that were the most uncertain, formless, and anguished" (*Life*, 205).

35. See, e.g., *The Revenge of Truth*, in Hannah, *Mask*, 181–83, 185–86, 194–95. Commenting on this reflexivity (118–19, 126–29), Hannah notes the similarity between Dinesen's play and Pirandello's *Six Characters in Search of an Author* (138–39).

36. "Language to Infinity," in *Language, Counter-Memory, Practice* (see chap. 1, n. 29). Foucault, like Dinesen, uses Scheherazade's narratives as exemplary of such linguistic replications.

37. *Webster's New International Dictionary*, 3d ed., s.v. "on the road."

38. On "the woman artist" who may "experience herself as bleeding into print" see Gubar, "The Blank Page" (chap. 1, n. 22), 248.

39. Jacobus, *Reading Woman*, 15, elaborating on Felman's "Rereading Femininity."

40. Hannah, *Mask*, 125.

41. "Notes" to *Purgatorio*, trans. Dorothy Sayers (Baltimore: Penguin, 1955), 302–5, 311.

42. The last line of Agnese's Dantean quotation (part of Beatrice's prophesy of the downfall of the Church's enemies) refers "to the ancient Florentine belief that if an assassin could contrive, within nine days after the murder, to eat a sop of bread and wine on the grave of his victim, he would be safe from the vengeance of the family. . . . Beatrice warns the author (or authors) of the crime against the Church that God's vengeance is not so easily evaded" (*Purgatorio*, 315).

43. Hannah, *Mask,* 152.

44. *Desire in Language* (see chap. 1, n. 2), 240–41; see also "Stabat Mater" in *Tales of Love* (chap. 1, n. 3).

45. The other is the birth of the twins in "The Cardinal's First Tale." We need more analysis of the complex implications of Dinesen's own childlessness, miscarriage(s?), and ambivalent feelings about motherhood relative to the maternal thematics that pervades her texts. Most often, her female figures are virgins, sterile would-be mothers, or post-menopausal women who regard their childlessness with varying degrees of elation and regret. Dinesen most often represents women who are mothers in relation not to infants but to adopted and/or adult children, often in a context linking motherhood to "illegitimacy" and death (e.g., "Sorrow-acre," "The Dreaming Child," "Alkemene," "The Caryatids," "A Country Tale"). An analysis of Dinesen's ambivalence about maternity might well begin not only with the several discussions of pregnancy in *LA* (see esp. 274–89), but with an important passage from one of the early typescripts of "The Dreamers," in which the narrator suggests that Pellegrina "sometimes wished for a child of her own": "But this would have interfered with her life on the stage, and she put it off until another day, and that day did never come, because the day of the great disaster came first" (KB Archives 123).

46. Jerome, "Contra Helvidius," *Patrologia Latina,* cited in Katherine Rogers, *The Troublesome Helpmeet* (see chap. 7, n. 14), 14–22. The passage refers explicitly to the question of whether the Virgin ever bore other children and implicitly to the question of the mother's sexual pleasure.

47. The links between Augustus von Schimmelmann and Augustus von Platen Hallermund go beyond their common misogyny. Johannesson notes that Dinesen may have modeled the former Augustus on Thomas Mann's Gustav von Eschenbach, himself modeled on Count August von Platen (1796–1835), the homosexual German Romantic poet on whom Dinesen based the Augustus of "Deluge"; see *The World of Isak Dinesen* (intro., n. 9), 65.

48. For Dinesen's admiration and identification with wild animals see *SG,* 17–20, 56–58.

49. Freud, "Femininity," in *New Introductory Lectures on Psychoanalysis,* trans. James Strachey (New York: W. W. Norton, 1965), 112.

50. "Rereading Femininity," 19–21.

51. Dinesen's imagery implicitly associates Augustus with the misguided Dante (*Purgatorio,* 30.127–35) who, despite Beatrice's efforts to penetrate his "dreams," fails to heed the spiritual "salvation" she offers him, turning aside from the true "way" (*via*) just as Augustus, even as he believes himself in quest of the "one true way" (178), misses the symbolic salvation the bottle signifies. The parallel is heightened by Dante's representation of Beatrice as a mother figure (e.g., 30.79–81).

52. As Mauss remarks, "the obligation attached to a gift . . . is not inert. . . . [T]o receive something is to receive a part of someone's spiritual essence. To keep this thing is dangerous" (*The Gift,* trans. Ian Cunnison [Glencoe, Ill.: Free Press, 1954], 9–10).

53. "Women, Culture and Society," 26.

54. *Webster's New International Dictionary,* 3d ed., s.v. "resort." Dinesen plays on all these diverse meanings, suggesting through the word's contradictory

denotations the internal contradictions Augustus, confronted with a woman's story, experiences.

55. German *schimmel* = "mould, mildew"; cf. *schimmelig,* "mouldy."

Chapter Nine

1. "The Cloak," Night Walk," and "Of Hidden Thoughts and of Heaven" (*LT*).

2. "Fiction and Its Phantoms" (see chap. 1, n. 64), 543, 545.

3. Cf. Dinesen's reinscriptions of her adventurer father (e.g., as Ib Angel in "Copenhagen Season") and her representations of Denys Finch Hatton and Berkeley Cole as atavistic "outcasts" who "did not belong to their century" and lived in quest of an ideal found only in fictions (*OA,* 213–17). But cf. also her representation of her relation to her brother Thomas, in letters that might be read as pretexts for "The Supper": "We will always be close to each other; our thoughts have traversed the same paths . . . and surely will continue to meet in many great countries . . . and on board ship forging grandly ahead. . . . I have a record of 'Wide sails over the North Sea' here . . . and I can never listen to it without . . . [thinking] of you; I feel that we have stood together 'high on the quarterdeck in the morning'" (*LA,* 58; cf. 75–76).

4. Joseph Conrad, *Lord Jim* (1900), chap. 45.

5. Foucault, *The Order of Things: An Archaeology of the Human Sciences* (1970; New York: Vintage, 1973), 210.

6. In *Morten* Dinesen embeds a complex translinguistic pun by combining the Danish definite article *en* (ordinarily attached as a suffix to singular, unmodified nouns) with the French *mort:* death.

7. *The Savage Mind* (Chicago: University of Chicago Press, 1966), 109.

8. "The Traffic in Women" (see chap. 1, n. 43), 174.

9. *This Sex* (see chap. 1, n. 33), 196–97.

10. Gen. 2:23. Taken from man's body, the woman is quite literally his offspring, but as the common "children" of the same paternal creator the two are also, figuratively, siblings.

11. See Miller, "Emphasis Added" (chap. 1, n. 21), for related speculations on women's "repressed" plots.

12. On Lilith narratives in ancient near-Eastern and rabbinic lore, see Raphael Patai, *The Hebrew Goddess* (New York: Avon, 1967), 180–225. According to the best-known version, which Dinesen recapitulates, Adam's first wife Lilith was created, like him, from the earth. A power-struggle ensued between them, enacted as a question of sexual positions and positionings—of who, both literally and symbolically, should be on top. When Adam tried to force her beneath him, she uttered the unspeakable name of God, rose into the air, and flew away to the Red Sea, where she coupled with demons and bore demonic children. Invited back to the garden on the condition of accepting subordination, she refused, but later returned secretly to mate again with Adam on her own terms, remaining a haunting threat to him even after his expulsion from Eden.

13. Cf. also the fantasy of free flight in Karen Blixen's "Vinger" ("Wings"), written before 1909, which prefigures Fanny's longing for escape from the social

order that confines her like one of her own caged birds (217)—"I mit Fængsel synger mit Hjerte / kun om Vinger, kun om Vinger (In my prison my heart sings / Only of wings, only of wings)" (*Osceola*, [see intro., n. 22], 141)—and the discourse on flying and feminism elaborated in her *LA*, especially in those letters written as she worked on early drafts of the Gothic Tales (261–62; 278).

14. Cf. Irigaray, describing woman's creative jouissance as a kind of potlatch: "Nothing has a price in this divine consumation and consumption . . . The soul spends and is spent. . . . In a strictly non-negotiable currency, an expenditure without accountability. . . . The richest person will certainly be the one who most has depleted the stores" (*Speculum* [see chap. 2, n. 11], 194).

15. See *This Sex*, 170–97.

16. *A Map of Misreading* (New York: Oxford University Press, 1975), 33. See Sandra Gilbert and Susan Gubar, *No Man's Land: The Place of the Woman Writer in the Twentieth Century*, vol. 1 (New Haven: Yale University Press, 1988), 131, for a reading of Bloom's analysis. See also *Madwoman* (chap. 1, n. 1), 46–53.

17. See the conclusion of chap. 1 and Cixous, "Laugh of the Medusa" (chap. 1, n. 45).

18. "Laugh of the Medusa," 288–90.

19. Ibid., 289. In *The Angelic Avengers* Dinesen would use this trope to suggest woman's contestation of a vast phallocentric system bent on her destruction. The same figure reappears in *E.* for other readings of "The Poet" as a story of woman's revolt against patriarchal restraints, see Juhl and Jørgensen, *Diana's Revenge* (intro., n. 9) and Stambaugh, *The Witch and the Goddess* (chap. 1, n. 22).

20. KB Archives 154, 4.

21. *LA*, 235. See also Kristeva, *The Revolution in Poetic Language* (chap. 1, n. 3), 203.

22. A translated version ("Karyatiderne. En ufuldendt fantastisk fortælling") appeared in Denmark and Sweden in 1938.

23. Cf. "A Country Tale," *LT*, 191–246, wherein the word of the peasant woman Lone utterly confounds the patrilineal identity of the young lord Eitel. By claiming him as her son—exchanged in the cradle for the true heir of the estate, to whom she was wet nurse—she reduces him to a text forever "cut away" from the "dead father" in whose authorizing "name" he presumes to speak, a "cutting off of roots" that emasculates both son and father, turning them into "shadow, into nothingness," and undoing both the "laws of the [masculine] cosmos" and the official patricentric "story."

24. *Life* (see intro., n. 1), 79–80.

25. See, e.g., "Sorrow-acre" and "The Poet." Sophie is both a common (and royal) Danish name and a reinscription of Sophia, Greek goddess of Wisdom and one of the most persistent embodiments of the resurgence of ancient goddess worship under Christianity. See Aiken, "Dinesen's 'Sorrow-acre'" and Stambaugh, *The Witch and the Goddess*, 22–23, 121n.

26. "Eroticism in the Patriarchal Order" (see chap. 1, n. 43), 52.

27. "Sorrow-acre," 32.

28. OED, s.v. "Caryatid." The phallic appropriation of this subversive female power is suggested by the term's etymological history: "The Greeks . . . destroyed Cárya, a city which had favoured the common enemy, . . . and carried

into captivity the women, whom they compelled to retain their dress . . . in a state of servitude" (R. Chandler, *Travels in Greece,* 1825) (OED). Dinesen in effect reverses and revises this history, dismantling the phallocentric structures that had enslaved the Caryatids.

29. *Newly-Born Woman* (see intro., n. 13), 93. Cf. Kristeva's notion of the "semiotic" as the re-emergence of "the mother's body" in the formation of the subject—a process reenacted in narrative operations that unsettle both the "paternal" figure of the author and the symbolic economies of "kinship and social relations," themselves a kind of narrative grammar (see *Revolution in Poetic Language,* 25–30, 91–104).

30. *Speculum,* 195; cf. 191–202.

31. *Newly-Born Woman,* 193–94.

32. Quoted in Langbaum, *Gayety* (see intro., n. 9), 220.

33. *Speculum,* 192–96.

34. Ibid., 196.

35. Cf. Kristeva's suggestion that the emergence of the semiotic finds its homology in a certain kind of reading wherein one submerges oneself in a text as in "a violent crucible," an experience that "exposes the subject to impossible dangers: relinquishing his identity in rhythm, dissolving the buffer of reality in a mobile discontinuity, leaving the shelter of the family, the state, or religion. The commotion of the practice spares nothing: it destroys all constancy to produce another and then destroys that one as well" (*Revolution,* 104).

36. "Freud's Masterplot," in *Literature and Psychoanalysis: The Question of Reading: Otherwise,* ed. Shoshana Felman (Baltimore: Johns Hopkins University Press, 1977), 298–99.

37. *Newly-Born Woman,* 93.

Chapter Ten

1. See, e.g., "New Gothic Tales" (*LT*) and the quasi-Gothic novel *The Angelic Avengers,* which playfully crosses conventions that recall Ann Radcliffe and the Charlotte Brontë of *Villette* with an ironic narratorial distance reminiscent of *Northanger Abbey.* Following Dinesen's wry designation of the novel as her "illegitimate child," critics have tended to dismiss it, but it deserves serious attention for its groundbreaking reading of female sexual slavery as both logical consequence and hyperbolized synecdoche of a phallocentric order. Connecting the traditions of sentimental bourgeois fiction, the texts of pornography, and the daughter's desire for the father('s), Dinesen anticipates Lynda Zwinger's observation that the "daughter of sentiment" leads ineluctably to pornographic representations of female masochism (*Daughters, Fathers, and the Novel* [see chap. 2, n. 11]). As in "The Poet," the "father" in the novel—whose name, Penhallow, relates him to the patriarchal literary tradition—is destroyed at last by the subversive designs of the (doubled) daughter(s).

2. See Fanon, *The Wretched of the Earth* (chap. 2, n. 55); O. Mannoni, *Prospero and Caliban: The Psychology of Colonization* (New York: Praeger, 1964); Joel Kovel, *White Racism: A Psychohistory* (New York: Random House, 1967); Said, *Orientalism* (chap. 2, n. 47); JanMohamed, *Manichean Aesthetics: The Politics of*

Literature in Colonial Africa (chap. 2, n. 50); Miller, *Blank Darkness: Africanist Discourse in French* (chap. 2, n. 40); and Henry Louis Gates, Jr., ed., "'Race,' Writing and Difference," special issue of *Critical Inquiry* 12 (Autumn 1985).

3. Dinesen's critique anticipates recent speculations on the parallels between women and colonized peoples as construed by patriarchal imperialist cultures. See, e.g., Davis, "Women on Top" (chap. 1, n. 30), 148; Janeway, *Powers of the Weak* (chap. 2, n. 49), 3–5, 235; Showalter, "Feminist Criticism in the Wilderness" (chap. 1, n. 20), 192–93; Jameson, *The Political Unconscious* (chap. 2, n. 37), 115; Spivak, "Three Women's Texts and a Critique of Imperialism" (chap. 2, n. 49), 243–62, and *In Other Worlds* (chap. 1, n. 24), 179–268; Hazel Carby, "'On the Threshold of Woman's Era': Lynching, Empire, and Sexuality in Black Feminist Theory," *Critical Inquiry* 12 (Autumn 1985): 262–77; and "She, The Inappropriate/d Other," ed. Trinh T. Minh-ha, special issue of *Discourse* 8 (Fall-Winter 1986–87).

4. Said, *Orientalism*, 226–27, my emphasis. Said does not note the import of this phrase for women, but rationalizations of white male dominance often explicitly conflated the two groups. See, e.g., T. H. Huxley's insistence that Black physiognomy reflected "a good deal of the feminine . . . character" ("On the Geographical Distribution of the Chief Modification of Man," *Journal of the Ethnological Society*, n.s. 2 [1869–70]: 405). As Douglas A. Lorimer notes, this was one of the widespread tropes of a "scientific" anthropology that underwrote imperialism ("Theoretical Racism in Late Victorian Anthropology," *Victorian Studies* 31 [Spring 1988]: 412–13).

5. Cf. Miller, *Blank Darkness*, 3–65, on the representation of Africa as "otherness," nullity or a blank slate on which Europeans could inscribe their own scripts.

6. "Ex Africa"; *OA*, 352.

7. "Kim, The Pleasures of Imperialism," *Raritan* 7 (Fall 1987): 31.

8. Ibid.

9. See Hammond and Jablow, *The Africa that Never Was* (chap. 2, n. 46); JanMohamed, *Manichean Aesthetics*, 48–52, and "The Economy of Manichean Allegory: The Function of Racial Difference in Colonialist Literature," *Critical Inquiry* 12 (Autumn 1985): 71; Mary Louise Pratt, "Scratches on the Face of the Country; or, What Mr. Barrow Saw in the Land of the Bushmen," in "'Race,' Writing and Difference," 125.

10. On the implications of similar colonizing processes on the part of Euro-American authors, see *Orientalism*; on the European alienation of Africa in particular see *Manichean Aesthetics* and *Blank Darkness*. None of these studies considers at any length the import of gender.

11. E.g., Ngugi wa Thiong'o, *Prison Notes*, African Writers Series (London: Heinemann, 1981): "Baroness Blixen was the separated wife of the big game hunter-cum-settler Baron von Blixen. From him she got no children but incurable syphilis. As if in compensation for unfulfilled desires and longings, the baroness turned Kenya into a vast erotic dreamland in which her several white lovers appeared as young gods and her Kenyan servants as *usable curs* and other animals." Ngugi cites the story of Kitosch (*OA*, 278–82) as definitive proof of Dinesen's "*total acceptance* of the hideous theory" that colonized Africans have "a

fiendish desire for suicide that absolves white murderers. . . . The African is an animal: the settler is exonerated. Not a single word of condemnation for this practice of colonial justice. No evidence of any discomfiture. . . . But I err too in saying the African was considered an animal. In reality they loved the wild game but Africans were worse, more threatening, *instinctless, unlovable, unredeemable sub-animals useful for brute labour*" (34–35, my emphasis). A response to centuries of oppression, such a critique contains many elements of truth; yet it also replicates the very sorts of reductive misreadings it deplores in European writers. Even leaving aside the literalist, decontextualizing construction of the Kitosch passage (which despite its naïveté and Eurocentrism is in fact laden with condemnatory implications) or the erroneous claim that Dinesen depicted Africans as "curs," one might note that while proclaiming a powerful liberationist message to Africans, Ngugi ratifies another form of oppression: androcentrism. Dinesen is identifiable primarily as Bror Blixen's "separated wife"—a construction which, assuming woman's secondary, derivative status, even leads Ngugi to underemphasize her complicity with colonialism (Bror was in fact dependent on the money provided by her family; she, not he, was chief "settler"). Ngugi makes her childlessness a major issue and implies, by rhetorically identifying it with syphilis, that the disease was a deserved consequence of reproductive failure. Finally, in an *ad feminam* that echoes European stereotypes of women writers, he reduces Dinesen's entire authorship to disappointed sexuality and failed maternity: "Karen Blixen, the baroness of blighted bloom turned writer" (37).

12. *Orientalism*, 228–31.

13. See, e.g., *SG*, 18: "We registered ourselves with the wild animals . . . and we laughed at the ambition of the new arrivals . . . to make the continent of Africa respectable." For her satire of European domesticization, see *OA*, 260, 300, 307.

14. *Manichean Aesthetics*, 52.

15. *Orientalism*, 230. In addition to the figures of Kamante and Farah in *OA*, see also *SG*, 3–48.

16. *Manichaen Aesthetics*, 52, 57.

17. *Blank Darkness*, 180–81.

18. *Shadows on the Grass*, 90–91.

19. Cf. *OA*, 19–20, 35–39, 130, 146–53, 258–60. On this reversal, see Jan-Mohamed, "Economy," 83. But JanMohamed overlooks the import of gender in Dinesen's response to colonialism, and ultimately collapses *Out of Africa* back into a monolithic category: the "essence" of "colonialist fiction" (84).

20. The source of that "song," the biblical Song of Songs, is one of the many pastoral texts through which Dinesen revises prior traditions. See n. 35.

21. *OA*, 6; cf. 21, 55. Dinesen used the phrase "time before time" to describe the ethos of myth (*Essays*, 177).

22. As James Kilgo has remarked to me, a similar permeability characterizes the narrator's house, its doors and windows perpetually open to the comings and goings of the inhabitants of Africa (e.g., 45–47, 76–77).

23. "Autogynography: Is the Subject Different?" in *The Female Autograph*, ed. Domna Stanton (Chicago: University of Chicago Press, 1984), 10. See also Sidonie Smith, *A Poetics of Women's Autobiography: Marginality and the Fictions of Self-Representation* (Bloomington: Indiana University Press), 3–45.

24. *The Political Unconscious*, 114–15.

25. Quoted in Thurman, *Life* (see intro., n. 1), 338.

26. *OA*, 35; cf. 18, 20, 33.

27. For other tales stressing the corruption of the attempt to capture, kill, or colonize, see, e.g., "The Oxen," "The Giraffes Go to Hamburg," "Some African Birds," and "Kitosch's Story."

28. *Tales of Love* (see chap. 1, n. 3), 336.

29. See *OA*, 79–81, 118–24, 154, 238, 244, 325–26, 371–72.

30. This effort began with early reviewers, who stressed the book's lack of a clear, chronological narrative line (KB Archives 171). For more recent efforts to characterize its genre, see Langbaum, *Gayety* (intro., n. 9), Hannah, *Mask* (intro., n. 2), and Judith Lee, "The Mask of Form in *Out of Africa*," *Prose Studies* 8:2 (1985): 45–59.

31. This statement appears to contradict Dinesen's celebrations of lion hunting (e.g., *OA*, 227–37; *SG*, 51–57), but like the representations of her love for the land, those of her love for the hunt are charged with complex ambivalence. While figuring the hunt as an eroticized image of desire, "a love affair," wherein "the shot . . . was in reality a declaration of love" (53), she also reminds us that its climax leaves one of its participants dead. And the following lines ambiguate and undermine their antecedents: "When I first came to Africa I could not live without getting a fine specimen of every single kind of African game. In my last ten years out there I did not fire a shot except to get meat. . . . It became for me an unreasonable thing, indeed in itself ugly and vulgar, for the sake of a few hours' enjoyment to put out a life that belonged in the great landscape and had grown up in it" (*SG*, 59). Cf. her wry observation of the masculinist grounding of hunting (*OA*, 182).

32. *OA*, 87; cf. Langbaum, *Gayety*, 132.

33. E.g. Hakon Strangerup, *Nationaltidende* (6 October 1937). See Langbaum, *Gayety*, 120, for a critique of this comparison.

34. *Gayety*, 119. See 119–54 for Langbaum's wide-ranging analysis of *OA*, which he reads as "unified" by "the myth of the fall" (120). Beyond general reference to Dinesen's "idyllic," paradisial vision of nature, he does not elaborate on the text's relation to the pastoral elegiac tradition.

35. Cf. her comparisons of Africa to the "Golden Age" and "Arcadia" (*LA*, 9, 54). For a review and critique of pastoral genre criticism, see Paul Alpers, "What Is Pastoral?" *Critical Inquiry* 9 (Spring 1982): 437–60. Though space does not permit extended analysis of Dinesen's use of the genre, I would suggest that an important source of the text's resonance is Dinesen's brilliant interweaving of Hebraic and Hellenic pastoral modes: to Theocritan and Virgilian traditions she adds a biblical trajectory, moving from Edenic paradise through exile to the promised land of art, from crucifixion to resurrection in/as literature. Woven into this pattern is an elaborate analogy between the Song of Songs and Dinesen's "song" of Africa (78). Crucial to her project is the self-reflexivity inherent in pastoral elegiac traditions—the "digressions" they permit about the writer's "own poetic achievements and aspirations" (James Holly Hanford, "The Pastoral Elegy and Milton's Lycidas," in *Milton's Legacy: The Tradition and the Poem*, ed. C. A. Patrides [Columbia: University of Missouri Press, 1983], 39). Casting the singer/speaker as both shepherd (in Dinesen's case, farmer) and poet, pastoral el-

egy links mourning and writing as joint products of loss. But as Harry Berger notes, it is a strongly masculinist genre ("Orpheus, Pan, and the Poetics of Misogyny: Spenser's Critique of Pastoral Love and Art," *ELH* 50 [Spring 1983]: 27–60). Amalgamating prior pastoral texts, Dinesen revises their androcentric patterns, subverting the masculine perspective by a "feminization" of the speaker that also dislocates conventional pastoral figurations of "masculine" and "feminine."

36. Theocritus, *Idylls,* trans. R. C. Trevelyan (New York, 1925). I am grateful to James Kilgo for suggesting the concept of the totem as a way of conceiving Dinesen's self-figurations as "Lioness."

37. *LA,* 18; cf. 235, and her assertion, in a lecture, that in Africa "at long last one was in a position not to give a damn for all conventions": "here was a new kind of freedom which until then one had only found in dreams." In tropes that echo *Out of Africa* and prefigure the representation of narrative in "The Diver," Dinesen compares this "glorious, intoxicating" experience to the freedom of swimming and flying (Hannah, *Mask,* 29).

38. See *A Room of One's Own* (chap. 3, n. 25), 6.

39. "Reading Woman (Reading)," *Reading Woman* (chap. 1, n. 1), 4.

40. On the relation of woman to "changing the subject" in Occidental discourses, see Nancy Miller, "Changing the Subject," in *Feminist Studies/Critical Studies,* ed. Teresa de Lauretis (Bloomington: Indiana University Press, 1986), 102–20.

41. *White Man's Country: Lord Delamere and the Making of Kenya* (New York: Macmillan, 1935).

42. For the figure of Africa as *terra incognita* in Western discourses, see Miller, *Blank Darkness,* 3–65. For woman as the "blank page" of masculinist fantasy, see Dinesen, "The Blank Page"; and Gubar, "'The Blank Page' and the Issues of Female Creativity" (chap. 1, n. 22). On colonialist alienations as akin to woman's alienation under patriarchy, see Irigaray, *This Sex* (chap. 1, n. 33), 170–91; Cixous, "Laugh of the Medusa" (chap. 1, n. 45), 281–90. See also Spacks's brief but illuminating discussion of Dinesen's "myth of herself" as "archetypal woman" in Africa in *The Female Imagination* (chap. 1, n. 22), 384–89.

43. On these European cartographic traditions see Miller, *Blank Darkness,* 3–23.

44. In "Sapphistries" (*Signs* 10 [Autumn 1984], 43–62), Susan Gubar has discussed Sappho as a "foremother" to female modernist authors. Gubar does not mention Dinesen, but the analysis provides a resonant context for Dinesen's Sappho narrative.

45. Freud, "The Uncanny" (see chap. 1, n. 64), 17:245. Cf. Cixous, "Fiction and Its Phantoms" (see chap. 1, n. 64).

46. Carole Boyce Davies notes that a number of African origin myths also figure the creation of the world as a displacement and destruction of a great mother goddess (Workshop address, The University of Arizona, 1988).

47. And, later, translated into Danish (*Den Afrikanske Farm* [Copenhagen: Gyldendal, 1937], 105–08).

48. *Webster's New International Dictionary,* 3d ed., s.v. "translate."

49. Mauss, *The Gift* (chap. 8, n. 51), 17–45; cf. "Babette's Feast."

50. *Newly Born Woman* (see intro., n. 13), 87, 91, 88. Cf. Irigaray, *Speculum* (chap. 2, n. 11), 194.

51. Again, in exploring the interactive problematics of temporality and narrative engendering, Dinesen anticipates Kristeva's notion of a "time" inseparable from liberatory conceptions of language, attentive to the fluidities of the chora or the "semiotic": "less a chronology than a signifying space" wherein "the very dichotomy man/woman as an opposition between two rival entities may be understood as belonging to metaphysics. What can 'identity,' even 'sexual identity,' mean in a new theoretical . . . space where the very notion of identity is challenged?" ("Women's Time," 34–35). This conception would also undermine the imperial opposition between "native" and "colonist." Yet Kristeva's quasi-utopian anticipation of a time when binary oppositions will be meaningless in a fluid discursive world of difference(s) ultimately risks eliding the effects of both gendered and racialized praxis and the material conditions of culture at a historical moment in which inequities and oppression are still pervasive. I would suggest that it was precisely Dinesen's recognition of these material inequities that led her to *write* so persistently toward the more fluid world Kristeva envisions.

Epilogue

1. I borrow the phrase "the theater of the body" from Clément (*Newly Born Woman* [intro., n. 13], 10), who links carnivalization with the somatic protest of hysterics, witches, and other female outcasts.

2. Quotations drawn from the entries of Nancy Wilson Ross, Leo Lerman, and William Jay Smith in *Isak Dinesen: A Memorial* (intro., n. 23), 40–53; Migel, *Titania* (chap. 1, n. 27), 223–25; and *SG*, 102.

3. See Aiken, "Dinesen's 'Sorrow-acre': Tracing the Woman's Line" (chap. 1, n. 22).

4. Langbaum, *Gayety* (intro., n. 9), 45.

5. Hannah, *Mask* (intro., n. 2), 81–82, reprints "the most important version" of the folk tale on which "Sorrow-acre" is based, from F. Ohrt's *Udvalgte Sønderjydske Folkesagn* (*Selected Folk-Tales from South Jutland*, 1919). It concludes: "On her grave, a stone has been laid, on which she is still shown. To this day it is known as Sorrow Acre." Dinesen has the lord omit the woman (his stone bears only the image of "a sickle"), suggesting the extent to which the symbolic order of the father attempts to erase female figurations. Ironically, the lord becomes the ultimate victim of her sickle's emasculating power.

6. Similarly, the text itself implicitly performs a revisionist critique of Maupassant's "Boule-de-suif," in which the "heroine" is a prostitute who gives herself to the German officer and is subsequently rejected by those she aided, and of the Heloise-Abelard legend.

7. Completed during the occupation, it also reflects the deadly chill which spread throughout Europe with the Nazi invasions. See Thurman, *Life* (intro., n. 1), 293–305. "The Heroine" explicitly relates oppressive psychosexual structures to the structures of war. Cf. Woolf, *Three Guineas* (London: Hogarth, 1938), and Klaus Theweleit, *Male Fantasies*, vol. 1, *Women, Floods, Bodies, History*, trans. Stephen Conway (Minneapolis: University of Minnesota Press, 1987).

8. Thurman, *Life*, 314–17, 384–88.

9. See *The Winter's Tale* 5.3. In Shakespeare, however, Hermione's restorative miming of "herself" as statute, and the regenerations that artifice en-

genders, are recuperated at the end of the play, both mother and daughter being reabsorbed into the patriarchal family. Dinesen's revisionist response to Shakespeare invites comparison with Woolf's in *To the Lighthouse,* which, as Maria di Battista shows, revives the Demeter-Persephone myth inherent in *The Winter's Tale,* elaborating the story of the suppressed mother and the lost daughter reborn and reunited through woman's art (*Virginia Woolf's Major Novels: The Fables of Anon* [New Haven: Yale University Press, 1980], 64–110).

10. See Thurman, *Life,* 348–50; Svendsen, *The Life and Destiny of Isak Dinesen* (chap. 1, n. 71), 181, 197.

11. *Essays,* 18; Thurman, *Life,* 331.

12. *Rabelais* (chap. 4, n. 60), 25.

13. *This Sex* (chap. 1, n. 33), 76.

14. "Female Grotesques: Carnival and Theory" (see chap. 3, n. 33), 224.

15. On *écriture féminine* as a contestational form of theorizing woman's place in phallogocentric culture, see Cixous, "Sorties." See Suleiman, *The Female Body in Western Culture,* on "the contemporary attempt, by women, to rewrite and rethink the female body" (8). On the subversive dynamics of female performances see Auerbach, *Romantic Imprisonment* (see chap. 3, n. 33), and Russo, "Female Grotesques."

16. "The Blank Page," *LT,* 100.

Index